THE CONTRADICTORY COLLEGE

SUNY Series
FRONTIERS IN EDUCATION
Philip G. Altbach, Editor

The Frontiers in Education Series draws upon a range of disciplines and approaches in the analysis of contemporary educational issues and concerns. Books in the series help to reinterpret established fields of scholarship in education by encouraging the latest synthesis and research. A special focus highlights educational policy issues from a multidisciplinary perspective. The series is published in cooperation with the Graduate School of Education, State University of New York at Buffalo.

Teacher Education Policy: Narratives, Stories, and Cases
—Hendrik D. Gideonse (ed.)

Beyond Silenced Voices: Class, Race, and Gender
in United States Schools
—Lois Weis and Michelle Fine (eds.)

Troubled Times for American Higher Education:
The 1990s and Beyond
—Clark Kerr

Higher Education Cannot Escape History: Issues for the
Twenty-First Century
—Clark Kerr

The Cold War and Academic Governance: The Lattimore Case
at Johns Hopkins
—Lionel S. Lewis

Multiculturalism and Education: Diversity and Its Impact on Schools
and Society
—Thomas J. LaBelle and Christopher R. Ward

The Contradictory College: The Conflicting Origins, Impacts, and
Futures of the Community College
—Kevin J. Dougherty

THE CONTRADICTORY COLLEGE

The Conflicting Origins, Impacts, and Futures of the Community College

Kevin J. Dougherty

STATE UNIVERSITY OF NEW YORK PRESS

Published by
State University of New York Press, Albany

© 1994   State University of New York

Production by Ruth Fisher
Marketing by Fran Keneston

For information, address the State University of New York Press,
State University Plaza, Albany, NY 12246

Library of Congress Cataloging-in-Publication Data

Dougherty, Kevin James.
   The contradictory college :   the conflict origins, impacts, and
futures of the community college / Kevin J. Dougherty.
       p.   cm. — (SUNY series, frontiers in education)
   Includes bibliographical references and index.
   ISBN 0-7914-1955-X. — ISBN 0-7914-1956-8 (pbk.)
   1. Community colleges—United States.   2. Education, Higher—
United States—Aims and objectives.   3. Higher education and state—
United States.   I. Title.   II. Series.
LB2328.15.U6D68   1994
378'.052'0973—dc20   93-30837
                                                                    CIP

10   9   8   7   6   5   4   3

To Beth Stevens and Jerry Surasky,
without whose support
this book probably would not have been written

Contents

Acknowledgments

Many people have played an important role in this book's genesis. Two people saw me through all of that passage. Above all, my wife Beth Stevens provided love and encouragement, excellent intellectual advice, and generous understanding. Jerry Surasky was a good friend, providing wise counsel and warm support over many years.

Present at the beginning were several friends who provided me with much intellectual stimulation, cogent criticism, and good friendship as I was framing this research and carrying out its early stages: Jerome Karabel, Steven Brint, David Karen, Katherine McClelland, David Swartz, Paul DiMaggio, Lauri Perman, and David Riesman. Jerry Karabel played a particularly important role, because he launched much of the debate on the social role of the community college and provided its first compelling arguments. In addition, I received useful advice from my dissertation committee of Lee Rainwater, Donald Warwick, and Gosta Esping-Anderson.

After the dissertation, my research on the community college expanded beyond examining its origins to also analyzing its impact on students and how one might go about mitigating the negative elements of that impact. Moreover, I deepened my study of the origins of the community college by expanding the number of states covered and clarifying the social and political theory informing my analysis. Many people gave me good advice in this period: David Lavin, Fred Pincus, David Labaree, L. Steven Zwerling, Arthur M. Cohen, Florence Brawer, Caroline H. Persell, Floyd Hammack, David Crook, Beverly Burris, Henry Etzkowitz, Richard C. Richardson, Jr., Daniel Levy, Frances Rust, Robert Lawrence, and several editors and referees at the *American Journal of Education, Sociological Forum,* the *Journal of Higher Education,* and the *Harvard Educational Review.*

Finally, as this book came together, it happily received the strong support of Philip Altbach, Lois Patton, Ruth Fisher, Fran Keneston, Nancy Ellegate, and other editors at the State University of New York

Press. In addition, Susan Semel, Alan Sadovnik, David Labaree, Michael Apple, and Larry and Sophie Stevens played important roles in midwifing its birth.

I wish to thank all the people, some 150 in number, who consented to being interviewed for this study. In addition, I appreciate the help of the staff of the state libraries in Illinois, Washington, New York, and California and the university libraries at Harvard University and New York University for their help in securing documents. Stephanie D'Angelico, Marco Brown, Michael Oppelt, and Angela Potenza provided important research assistance. Finally, I thank those responsible for the grants I received from the National Institute of Education (1980–1981) (G-80-0136), the graduate student research fund of the Harvard University Department of Sociology (1981–1982), and the faculty research fund of Manhattanville College (1985).

Chapters 3 and 4 of this book are based on research that was first published in the following: "Community Colleges and Baccalaureate Attainment," *Journal of Higher Education,* Vol. 63, No. 2 (March-April 1992): 188–214. Copyright © 1992 by The Ohio State University. All rights reserved; and "The Effects of Community Colleges: Aid or Hindrance to Socioeconomic Attainment?" *Sociology of Education* 60 (April 1987): 86–103. Copyright © 1987 by the American Sociological Association. All rights reserved.

Chapters 5 through 9 are based on research that first appeared in "The Politics of Community College Expansion," *American Journal of Education* 96 (May 1988): 351–393. Copyright © 1988 by The University of Chicago. All rights reserved.

Chapters 10 through 14 are based on research that was first published in "Educational Policy-Making and the Relative Autonomy of the State: The Case of Occupational Education in the Community College," *Sociological Forum* 3 (Summer 1988): 400–432. Copyright © 1988 by Plenum Publishing Corporation. All rights reserved.

Chapter 15 is a revised version of "The Community College at the Crossroads: The Need for Structural Reform," *Harvard Educational Review* 61:3, pp. 311–336. Copyright © 1991 by the President and Fellows of Harvard College. All rights reserved.

Part of Chapter 16 first appeared in "Analyzing the Development of Education in America," *Studies in American Political Development* 6 (Fall 1992): 445–462. Copyright © by Cambridge University Press. All rights reserved.

Section I
Introduction

CHAPTER 1

The Community College's Importance
and Controversiality

Community colleges have not received the attention they deserve. These public two-year colleges play a crucial role in American higher education and, indeed, American life. Yet both scholars and laypeople often know very little about them, believing they are only a peripheral part of the collegiate system, a catch basin for those few students unable or unwilling to enter "regular" colleges. But this ignorance is badly mistaken. Because of their great number, openness to nontraditional students, and key role in vocational training, community colleges occupy a central place in higher education and are vitally relevant to many areas of social life.

Public two-year colleges account for over one-quarter of all higher educational institutions in the United States, numbering 968 in 1989. In that year, these colleges enrolled 4.8 million students, 35.8% of all college students, and 44.3% of all college freshmen (U.S. National Center for Education Statistics, 1991a: Tables 162, 169, 226, pp. 168, 176, 232).[1] Given their centrality to higher education, community colleges have come to dominate plans for extending college opportunity in a systematic and cost-efficient way.

Beyond their number, community colleges are distinctive for their "open door" admissions policy. Community colleges usually require only that entrants have a high school diploma or be 18 years of age. As a result, community college students are more heavily working class, minority, female, and older than are four-year college students (Adelman, 1992; Cohen and Brawer, 1989; Grubb, 1991). For example, 22% of community college students are minority (black, Hispanic, Asian, and Native American) (versus 18% of four-year students), 57% are female (versus 53%), 10% have family incomes below $15,000 (versus 6%), and 37% are over 30 (versus 25%) (U.S. Bureau of the Census, 1993: 61; U.S. National Center for Education Statistics, 1992a: 170, 176, 203). These differences are anatomized in Table 1–1.

Given its appeal to "nontraditional" students, efforts to increase equality of educational opportunity often put the community college at

3

TABLE 1–1

Differences In Student Composition Between Public Two-Year Colleges
and Four-Year Colleges

	Public two-year colleges	Four-year colleges	All higher education
Proportion of Each Institution			
1. Dependent students 18–24 with family incomes (1991)			
Below $15,000	10.1%	6.2%	7.2%
$25,000–$34,999	16.2%	12.0%	13.2%
Over $75,000	11.1%	22.6%	19.4%
2. Minority students (black, Hispanic, Asian, Native American) (1990)	22.0%	17.7%	19.8%
3. Female students (1990)	57.4%	52.7%	54.5%
4. Students age 30 and older (1987)	36.5%	24.6%	27.0%
5. Students with high school grade point averages C+ and below (1992)	24.7%	14.2%	17.0%

Sources:
1: U.S. Bureau of the Census (1993).
2–4: U.S. National Center for Education Statistics (1992a: 170, 176, 203).
5: Cooperative Institutional Research Program (1992:13).

their center. The highly influential Carnegie Commission for Higher Education (1968–1973) made the community college the centerpiece of its call for universal access to higher education:

> The Commission believes that access to higher education should be expanded so that there will be an opportunity within the total system of higher education in each state for each high school graduate. . . . The Commission recommends that all states enact legislation providing admission to public community colleges of all applicants who are high school graduates or are persons over 18 years of age who are capable of benefiting from continuing education. (Carnegie Commission on Higher Education, 1970: 15)

And in recent years, the Ford Foundation has devoted quite sizable resources to increasing the number of minority college graduates (Donovan, Schaier-Peleg, and Forer, 1987: 1–3). A key component of this program has been an effort to improve transfer programs in community colleges, since they play a particularly important part in the baccalaureate attainment process for nonwhite students (Pincus and Archer, 1989; Richardson and Bender, 1987).

Finally, the community college is noteworthy for its commitment to occupational education. Depending on the estimate, 40 to 60% of all community college students are enrolled in occupational-education programs, and these students make up over half of all students in all forms of postsecondary vocational training (Cohen and Brawer, 1989: 209; Grubb, 1991: 203, n7; idem, 1992b; Palmer, 1990a: 22).[2] In fact, community college vocational students make up a large bulk of our nation's graduates in such diverse and important occupations as nursing, computer operations, and auto repair. As a result, any substantial policy regarding vocational education, employment training, or laborpower development invariably addresses the role of the community college. Furthermore, community college vocational education programs are of importance to any effort to equalize life chances. A disproportionate number of occupational-education enrollees are nonwhite and working class in background. In Illinois, for example, nonwhites made up 49% of occupational-education students in fall 1986, but only 14% of nonoccupational students (Illinois Community College Board, 1986c: 9–10).

The Debate Over the Community College

Now in its "fifth generation" since its inception around the turn of the century, the community college is beset by controversy over its impact, origins, and future. Should it continue as a comprehensive institution, offering vocational training, adult education, and university preparation, or should it shed one or the other of these dimensions? If it should narrow its role, which function should become central (Breneman and Nelson, 1981; Clowes and Levin, 1989; Cohen and Brawer, 1987; Cross, 1985; Gleazer, 1980; Kerr, 1980; Richardson and Bender, 1987)?

A major spark for this debate has been the sharp decline in the community college's role in baccalaureate preparation over the last 20 years. The number of community college transfers to four-year colleges has dropped sharply in both absolute and relative numbers. With regard to relative numbers, Grubb estimates that nationally the proportion of recent community college entrants transferring to four-year colleges within four years dropped from 28.7% of those entering community college in 1972 to 20.2% among those entering in 1980 (Grubb, 1991: 201–202). Meanwhile, the absolute numbers of transfer students dropped from the 1970s through the mid-1980s. In California, the community college transfers to the University of California and California State University systems plummeted from a peak of 43,539 in 1975 to 32,622 in 1986 and then rebounded slightly to 35,327 in 1988 (California Postsecondary Education Commission, 1986: 4). On the East Coast, in New York State, the number of students transferring from the community colleges of the State University of New York system to the senior colleges dropped from 7,606 in fall 1975 to a low of 5,753 in 1980 and then slowly rebounded to 6,972 in 1988 (State University of New York, 1976, 1989). And in Florida, the number of community college students transferring into the state university system dropped from 9,298 in fall 1981 to 7,983 in fall 1987 (Florida State University System, 1983: 37; idem, 1989: 20).

The debate over the future of the community college is rooted in a long-standing and still active debate over its impact and its origins. Those who would continue or even intensify its current emphasis on nonbaccalaureate education view its impact and its origins in very favorable terms. For them, the community college is the most effective democratizing agent in higher education. It has opened college opportunities to those who would otherwise be unable to attend, either because of poverty, poor high school records, or vocational interests. This commendably egalitarian impact stems from the community college's virtuously democratic origins. It is the product of "a grass roots, organized-at-home coalition" uniting would-be college students, their parents, business and labor, and political officials responsive to their constituents' interests (Gleazer, 1968, 1980).

But those who insist on the community college's collegiate character, especially those who would transform it into a four-year college, are much less approving of its impact and origins. To these critics, the community college today is a college only in name, for it is really "part of an educational tracking system that reproduces social inequality." Although it may let in otherwise excluded students, the community college fails to deliver the educational and occupational opportunity it promises. And its false promises are reflective of dubious origins, for it was spawned by "the more privileged sectors of society," especially the leaders of private industry (Pincus, 1983: 4).

Despite the vigor, and occasional vitriol, of the debate between the community college's defenders and its critics, surprisingly little territory has changed hands between them. Too often the issues in contention have not been clear, so that the contestants have never really joined battle but have simply shot in each other's general direction. For example, the critics and defenders have expended much ink on the question of whether the community college aids or hinders the educational and economic success of its students. The critics, arguing that three-quarters of the community college's students wish to get a B.A., note that less than a fifth succeed. The defenders, believing they are repulsing this charge head-on, counter with the argument that the community college allows more students to enter higher education than any other institution. The problem with both claims is that they actually lie at an oblique angle to each other: both, or neither, may be right. The community college could be very good at allowing students access to higher education and yet be poor at helping them achieve a baccalaureate degree. But, even when the critics and defenders have directly joined battle, they often have shot at each other with evidence of lower caliber than claimed. All too frequently, one or another claim has been advanced on the basis of anecdotes, unrepresentative cases, and poorly controlled studies.

The Aims of This Book

The purpose of this book is to resolve the debate between the critics and defenders of the community college on three key issues. The first is, What is the impact of the community college, not only on students but also on business and the elite universities? Does the community college benefit all three, as its defenders claim, or does it benefit the last two at the expense of students, as its critics charge? For both critics and defenders, this issue of impact has been tightly enmeshed with the question of the origins of the community college: Why and how did the community college develop? Was it the product of a grass roots movement centered around students and their parents or of an elite venture managed by business? Those claiming elite origins argue that the prize being sought was a community college that would be highly oriented to vocational education. This raises the third issue: Why did the community college differentiate its originally academic program to become so strongly vocational? Was it in service of both students and the economy, or was it of business alone?

This book does not simply arbitrate among the competing claims made by the defenders and critics of the community college. The debaters have posed these claims in zero-sum terms, as if only one side can be correct. But the community college is too complex and contradictory an institution to be so easily captured. It presents its observers with a Janus face. On some questions, its defenders and critics are both correct. On others they are both incorrect. And on all questions, they are incomplete. What is needed is a perspective on the community college that puts its contradictory nature at the very center. In this book I offer such a perspective, which I term the "relative autonomy of the state" explanation. This perspective holds that the community college has been shaped by a wide variety of groups, including not just private interest groups such as business and students, but also government officials, ranging from presidents to local educators. In fact, pursuing values and interests their own, these government officials have put their own unique stamp on the community college.[3]

As a consequence of its diverse origins, the community college is a hybrid institution, combining many different and often contradictory purposes. It is a doorway to educational opportunity, a vendor of vocational training, a protector of university selectivity, and a defender of state higher education budgets (by providing an alternative to expanding the costly four-year colleges). Such eclecticism can breed synergy. But in the community college's case it has sown contradiction. The institution's desire to provide baccalaureate aspirants with educational opportunity has been undercut by its other purposes of providing vocational training and saving state governments money. The community college's concern with vocational education has led it to stint on transfer education, as it has shifted funds and attention to developing vocational programs. And its purpose of saving the state money by being a two-year commuter institution has meant that it has renounced such important means of promoting student retention and baccalaureate success as providing a campus residential life and upper-division programs.

The findings in this book have an import that goes beyond simply settling what may seem a parochial debate over the community college's origins, impact, and future. First, they indicate the need for major changes in our educational policy. Postwar American higher education policy has been premised on the belief that the community college's defenders are correct that it has a profoundly democratizing impact. But if, as I will show, the community college's antidemocratizing effects are as powerful as its democratizing ones, we must fundamentally rethink its structure and its role in higher education. At the very least, we need to thoroughly reshape how community colleges operate. But we also must seriously consider transforming them into profoundly different institutions, perhaps going so far as to convert them into branches of the state universities or even into four-year colleges.

Second, my findings on the causes of the community college's origins and vocationalization suggest new directions for scholarship on educational change, politics of education, and political sociology. The fields of educational change and educational politics have been divided into camps very similar to those of the critics and defenders of the community college. Hence, these fields should benefit as well from the introduction of the state relative autonomy perspective developed here. Meanwhile, the field of political sociology would benefit from my findings in a different way. The state relative autonomy perspective is not new to political sociology; in fact, it originated there. But in applying state relative autonomy theory outside its original home domain of the actions of the national state in the areas of foreign and economic policy, I have had to modify its terms. And these modifications suggest important ways in which the original formulation of the state relative autonomy theory should be transformed in order to broaden its scope and power.

The Content of the Chapters

Chapter 2 sets the stage for the subsequent chapters by deepening our understanding of the debate over the community college. The chapter begins by elaborating the competing claims of the community college's defenders and critics, showing that their positions have very strong affinities to three well-known theoretical schools in sociology and political science: "pluralist functionalism" in the case of the community college's defenders; and "instrumentalist Marxism" and "institutional" theory in the case of the critics. With these positions anatomized, Chapter 2 lays out the competing "state relative autonomy" perspective that I have developed in order to avoid the weaknesses of functionalism, instrumentalism, and institutionalism.

The next 12 chapters, making up Sections II through IV of the book, are organized around each of the main issues in contention between the critics and defenders of the community college. Chapter 3 addresses the issue that first sparked the debate over the community college: the question of its impact on students, business and the economy, and the elite state universities. The focus is on the highly contentious question of whether the institution aids or hinders its students' educational and economic success, but the chapter also carefully analyzes two other claims on which the debaters are in covert agreement: that community colleges are highly responsive to the labor market's demand for "middle-level" workers, and that they allow elite state universities to remain selective in their admissions by diverting away less able students. In all cases, the chapter evaluates these claims by critically synthesizing and theoretically elaborating a wide variety of quite scattered and often ignored empirical studies on these questions.

Chapter 3 concludes that the critics and defenders of the community college each capture a different and partial truth about the community college's impact. Both camps are correct that the community college has helped elite universities maintain selective admissions. Furthermore, as the critics claim, the community college is inferior to the four-year college in aiding the educational and economic success of its students. Community college entrants get fewer bachelor's degrees and fewer years of education and less prestigious and well-paying job than *comparable* students entering four-year colleges. On the other hand, the defenders appear to be correct that the community college allows more students to enter college than does the four-year college. Moreover, community colleges are marginally superior to postsecondary vocational schools, both public and private, in getting their students more education and better paying and more secure jobs. Finally, both the critics and the defenders overestimate how well the community college meets the labor market's demands. Not infrequently, community colleges produce both more and less vocational graduates than the labor market demands.

Chapter 4 offers an extended analysis of the features of the community college that hinder its students' pursuit of a baccalaureate degree. In particular, this chapter develops a theory of the *institutional* factors that cause community college students, in comparison to similar four-year college students, to less often persist during the first two years of college, less often move on to the sophomore and junior years at four-year colleges, and less often survive through the senior year at four-year colleges. To explain how community colleges contribute to their students' higher dropout rate, the chapter focuses on community colleges' relative inability to socially and academically integrate their students through such devices as offering campus residence and integrating students into the social and academic life of the college. The chapter also examines why community college students have a low rate of transfer to four-year colleges, pointing to such institutional factors as lack of financial aid, community colleges' weak encouragement of transfer (in good part because of their strong emphasis on occupational education), and four-year colleges' weak interest in students coming out of community colleges. And to explain why community college transfers more often succumb in the junior and senior years than do four-year college natives, the chapter analyzes the impact of credit loss in transfer, difficulty in securing financial aid, poorer preparation for the academic demands of upper-division courses, and inadequate efforts by universities to socially integrate community college transfers.

Because the community college's impacts have been taken as indicative of its founders' intentions, its critics and defenders have moved from debating its effects to disputing its origins. This dispute is the subject of Chapters 5 through 9 in Section III. The critics and defenders have clashed over what social groups, motives, and forces have led community colleges to proliferate nationwide since their first appearance in 1901. To settle this debate, Section III examines the actors and motives behind efforts at the national, state, and local levels to promote the founding and expansion of community colleges. Five states are examined in close detail: four that developed large community college systems (New York, Illinois, California, and Washington) and one that did not (Indiana). This approach greatly advances the study of the community college's origins by acknowledging the federal nature of our governmental system and therefore the great vertical and horizontal variation of the U.S. educational system. Unlike other historical analyses of the community college, this chapter does not try to simplify the research task either by staying only at one level of government or by examining all three levels but referring to only one state. Rather, it examines all three levels in five states in different parts of the country.

The chapters making up Section III find evidence at considerable variance with the arguments of the functionalist, instrumentalist Marxist, and institutionalist theories. Most explanations of the rise of the community college make either students or business the heroes of this epic. However, although these actors sometimes have played important roles, Chapters 5 through 9 show that the main initiative has lain with government officials. They strongly promoted the community college even when business and students were not demanding this. The institutional theory of Brint and Karabel (1989) and Labaree (1990) has explored part of this governmental role, highlighting how state universities have strongly supported the community college as a means to protect the selectivity of university admissions and the scarceness of university degrees. But as the chapters in section III demonstrate, several other governmental officials, ranging from local school superintendents to state governors and federal officials, played just as pivotal roles in founding community colleges. Moreover, the motives that drove their actions were far more varied than institutional theory acknowledges. They also included, for example, local school superintendents' desire to expand educational opportunity and make a name for themselves as educational innovators and state governors' wish to keep state higher education budgets down by channeling students away from high-cost state universities. As Chapters 5 through 9 show, these values and self-interests not only spurred government officials to act on their own but also allowed business and students to exercise a passive, hidden, but yet very powerful influence over government policymaking. The value government officials put on equality of opportunity, for example, led them to benefit students by expanding college access through the community college, even if students were unaware of what was at stake and failed to participate politically. Furthermore, self-interest also led government officials to act in conformity with the interests of business and students even if the latter were silent. For example, elected officials' interest in economic growth, because it enhances their electability, has led them to provide business with favors such as publicly subsidized employee training through the community college. In short, government officials have exercised a forceful, autonomous role in the development of the community college, but this autonomy has been *relative,* that is, conditioned by the structural and ideological power of business and, less so, students.

After the establishment of the community college, the most notable entry in its institutional biography has been its shift toward a strongly vocational orientation. Chapters 10 through 14 in Section IV address the causes of this vocationalization by analyzing occupational education policymaking at the national level and at the state and local levels in four states (California, Washington, Illinois, and New York). Section IV moves beyond the conventional wisdom proffered by functionalist and instrumentalist theory by showing that, although students and business did participate in the process of vocationalization, the central figures again were government officials. But these officials included not just the community college and university officials highlighted by the institutional theory of Brint and Karabel (1989) but also state governors and chief state school officers and federal executive and legislative officials. In the vocationalization of community colleges, as in their founding, government officials enjoyed considerable relative autonomy. They shaped the community college curriculum in ways that benefited not just business but also themselves.

Chapters 15 and 16 of Section V sum up the findings of the preceding chapters and draw their implications for scholarship and public policy. Chapter 15 addresses the issue of what direction the community college should take in the future. The community college's obstructive effect on baccalaureate attainment calls into question its dedication by the federal and state governments as the central portal for access to higher education. But if there is a clear need for reform, it is less evident whose prescriptions should be followed: those of the community college's defenders, who want incremental changes in how the community college operates, or those of the critics, who sometimes have called for a revolutionary transformation of the community college's very structure? Chapter 15 examines both these nonstructural and structural reform programs in detail, holding their arguments against the light of research. It concludes that we need to combine both kinds of reforms, seeing them as the short-term and long-term components, respectively, of a comprehensive strategy of transforming the community college.

Chapter 16 concludes the book by taking up the theoretical implications of the findings on the politics of community college expansion and vocationalization in Chapters 5 through 14. Noting that the study of educational change exhibits theoretical divisions quite similar to those characterizing scholarship on the community college, Chapter 16 shows how this field would benefit from an injection of the "state relative autonomy" perspective developed in this book. The chapter then moves to showing how this perspective would also enrich the field of politics of education. This field has acknowledged that educators often act with considerable autonomy in educational policymaking. But it has failed to examine how that autonomy is rooted in their values and self-interests and to extend that insight to other governmental officials. Although deeply influenced by political sociology and the theory of the state, the state relative autonomy argument also has criticisms to make of its parents. To be sure, the findings in Sections III and IV confirm the thesis in political sociology that government officials exercise great autonomy in policymaking. At the same time, this study also shows that political sociologists have too narrowly conceptualized who these "state managers" are and what self-interests animate them. Political sociologists have focused on national officials and their interests and paid too little attention to subnational officials, who have distinct interests of their own. Hence, the chapter closes by sketching this needed extension and correction of state manager theory in political sociology.

CHAPTER 2

The Debate Deepened

Chapter 1 has given us a taste, but not yet the full substance, of the competing positions of the community college's critics and advocates. We have not yet captured the precise ways their claims diverge and converge, how one might go about settling this debate, and what alternatives there are to both positions.

Though they have skirmished on numerous issues, the advocates and the critics of the community college have principally joined battle along three lines. The earliest battle was waged over the effects of the community college: Is it an avenue of opportunity for its many working-class, minority, and female students, or is it a blind alley blocking off equality? From this debate over impact, the battle transmuted itself into one over origins. The critics moved from their claim that the community college reproduces inequality to arguing that this effect has been deliberate: the community college owes its origins to the self-interested actions of the capitalist class and the elite state universities. The community college's advocates have countered that the community college actually sprang from the demands of a grass roots coalition centered around students and their parents. The battle then ended on the subject of the forces behind the rapid growth of occupational education in the last 30 years. Was this vocationalization principally driven by the demand of business for publicly subsidized employee training, by the need of students for job training, or by the desire of entrepreneurial community college presidents to establish a lucrative market for their institutions?

This chapter lays out the arguments of the critics and advocates of the community college on the three key questions: What is its impact? To what does it owe its origins? and Why was it rapidly vocationalized? My aim is to isolate the key contentions and to capture their rhyme and reason. But I am not bound solely by the debaters' words and self-understandings. Social commentators often are unaware, mistaken, or even deceptive about the full implications of their arguments and their resonances with other discourses. But as judges of this debate, we must be aware of these larger reverberations, for they allow us to more fully appreciate both the combatants' contributions to scholarship and their errors of commission and omission. Hence, besides isolating the main claims of the critics and advocates, this chapter also uncovers the strong lines of affinity, if not provenance, connecting those claims to three well-known theoretical schools in sociology and political science: "pluralist functionalism" in the case of the advocates; and "instrumentalist Marxism" and "institutional" theory in the case of the critics. An awareness of these theoretical antecedents allows us to better spot the weaknesses of the three positions because we can draw from the general commentary on their theoretical parents. In addition, we can more easily export the findings derived from a local critique of arguments concerning the community college to other areas of scholarship where similar arguments have arisen: for example, the fields of educational change and educational politics.

In addition to describing in detail the positions taken by the community college's critics and advocates, this chapter also advances an alternative. Although the critics and advocates explain a goodly portion of the impact, origins, and vocationalization of the community college, they also miss crucial facets of these phenomena. Most basically, they treat the community college as a moral unity: it either has beneficent effects and pure origins or malignant consequences and a bastard birth. But the community college is a much more contradictory institution than they acknowledge. It has both good and bad effects and was conceived for both publicly motivated and self-interested reasons. Hence, to remedy the explanatory deficiencies of both the functionalist advocates and the instrumentalist and institutionalist critics, I counter with an alternative, the "state relative autonomy" argument, that subsumes and transcends their arguments.

The Debate Over the Effects of the Community College

The first shot in the debate between the critics and the advocates of the community college was fired over the issue of its impact on students. Is the community college a broad avenue of opportunity or a cul-de-sac protecting class privilege? But underneath the fury of this clash, the debaters implicitly agree that the community college has effectively met business's demands for trained workers and elite state universities' desire for a means to turn away less attractive students. Let us review in turn the claims of the various schools of commentary on this question, ending with an analysis of the deficiencies of this debate.

The advocates of the community college, although aware of each other, probably do not see themselves as a theoretical school. Yet they constitute a school because their key arguments about the community college's establishment, vocationalization, and impact are quite similar. And they are a theoretical school because their common arguments are not a loose assemblage of claims but a set of tenets that are logically organized and closely resemble functionalist theory in the social sciences.

These advocates describe the community college as serving several central needs of society: providing college opportunity, training middle-level workers, and preserving the academic excellence of our universities. Leland Medsker, a leading community college researcher and commentator, speaks to the first function:

> The two-year college . . . is perhaps the most effective democratizing agent in higher education. It decentralizes post-high school opportunities by placing them within reach of a large number of students. It makes higher education available at a low cost to the student and at moderate cost to society. (Medsker, 1960: 4)

Community colleges, these advocates claim, democratize college access by being plentiful, nearby, and inexpensive, by offering vocational education and adult education in addition to more traditional college offerings, and by adhering to an "open door" admissions policy that imposes few entry requirements. As a result, community colleges attract many students who are not capable of or interested in attending more traditional colleges because they have poor academic records, have strongly vocational interests, or are beyond traditional college age. Meanwhile, traditional college students who happen to attend the community college have the option to take university parallel courses and eventually transfer to a four-year college (Cohen and Brawer, 1989: 17; Medsker, 1960: 4, 17; Monroe, 1972: 25–32).

Besides democratizing college access, the advocates argue, the vocational emphasis of the community college also serves the needs of the economy by training "middle-level" workers (Cohen and Brawer, 1989: 17–18; Medsker, 1960:4; Monroe, 1972: 33). As Charles Monroe puts it,

> The community college is becoming the educational agency which trains persons for entry into an ever widening number of skilled jobs. . . . In addition, the community college must retrain employees for new jobs as old jobs become obsolescent. . . . One point on which friends and critics of the community college

agree is that the need for occupational training will increase greatly in the years ahead. (Monroe, 1972: 33)

Finally, say the advocates, the community college has helped our leading state universities preserve their academic excellence. By drawing off younger and less able students, it has allowed the universities to concentrate their resources on juniors and seniors and more able students (Clark, 1960: 159–160; Gleazer, 1968: 51; Monroe, 1972: 37–40). Edmund Gleazer, Jr., for many years the executive director of the American Association of Community Colleges,[2] noted this "safety valve" role:

> A concomitant to nonselective admissions practices in the community college is greater selectivity by the university. . . . A university can be highly selective, and there are substantial arguments why it should be, if the total state program, through the community college, offers students who cannot qualify initially for the university the opportunity to continue their work. (Gleazer, 1968: 51)

The proponents of the community college betray little awareness of how their arguments resemble, and often draw on, functionalist theory.[3] Yet their claims—that the community college serves society by providing social mobility, job training, and protection for high-quality universities—closely resembles functionalist theory in sociology. This theory typically focuses on the social "functions" of institutions, that is, how they serve fundamental needs of society as a whole. In the case of the schools, functionalists stress that the educational system inculcates the fundamental values and norms of society, prepares and certifies people for jobs, allows for social mobility, and creates new knowledge (Clark, 1962; Dreeben, 1967; Goslin, 1965; Parsons, 1959; Trow, 1961).

The Instrumentalist Marxist Critics[4]

The critics have stated a set of claims about the community college's origins and impact that forcefully contradict the advocates' positive evaluation of the institution. They argue that the community college upholds only in word, and vitiates in practice, the ideal of equality of opportunity. In their view, the community college's real social role is to reproduce the class inequalities of capitalist society (Bowles and Gintis, 1976: 208, 211–212; Karabel, 1972: 523–526, 543, 547, 552; Nasaw, 1979: 219–222, 228–229, 235; Pincus, 1974: 18; Zwerling, 1976: xix, 61). The community college does this in three ways.

First, it provides business at public expense with trained workers who will smoothly fit into the capitalist enterprise. They have the needed skills and a willingness to accept the authoritarian work relations that capitalism demands. Fred Pincus, for many years a leading critic of the community college, states:

> [C]ommunity college critics . . . argue that community colleges are part of an educational system that reproduces social inequality. . . . The leaders of private industry get workers who are trained at public expense. The more privileged sectors of society are less likely to be challenged since the aspirations of working class and minority students are lowered ("cooled out") by community colleges. (Pincus, 1983: 4)

Furthermore, the community college maintains class inequality over the generations by ensuring that working-class children inherit their parents' social class position. In *Second Best,* L. Steven Zwerling holds that

> not only is maintaining the social hierarchy a primary function of the community college, but the community college is also remarkably effective at the job. It takes students whose parents are characterized primarily by low income and educational achievement and slots them into the lower ranks of the industrial and commercial hierarchy. The community college is in fact a social defense mechanism that resists changes in the social structure. (Zwerling, 1976: xix)

Finally, in tracking by social class, the community college protects selective admissions at the higher education institutions most often patronized by members of the capitalist class: namely, four-year colleges and, most particularly, the elite universities. Educational historian David Nasaw notes the community college's diversionary role:

> For the higher education system to function properly, two-year students must somehow be diverted from the four-year schools. The scarcity of the bachelor's degree must be protected. . . . This diversionary role of the two-year college is, again, not accidental, but an intended, intrinsic function of these schools within state systems. (Nasaw, 1979: 228–229)

To document this third effect, the critics argue that three-fourths of community college entrants wish to attain at least a bachelor's degree, but very few succeed. Instead, most entrants, particularly those from working-class and minority backgrounds, either drop out or are "cooled out" by being shunted into occupational-education programs with little economic payoff (Karabel, 1972: 531–536; Nasaw, 1979: 225–228; Pincus, 1980: 349–354).

If the advocates of the community college are largely unaware of their theoretical pedigree, the critics are much more aware. Several of them explicitly draw on Marxism and label themselves Marxists.[5] They accept the general Marxist tenet that our society is divided into separate and antagonistic social classes under the domination of the capitalist class (the corporate business elite). Moreover, they see the major institutions of society as bent to the task of holding together that conflict-ridden society and facilitating the pursuit of profit by the capitalist class. What makes this school "instrumentalist" as well will be discussed under its views of the origins of the community college.

The Institutionalist Critics

In their recent book, Steven Brint and Jerome Karabel (1989) largely repeat the terms of the instrumentalist analysis of the impact of the community college, albeit with a softer edge.[6] They argue that community colleges function to finesse the contradictions between conflicting values in American society:

> Like the American high school, the community college over the course of its history has attempted to perform a number of conflicting tasks: to extend opportunity and to serve as an agent of educational and social selection, to promote social equality and to increase economic efficiency, to provide students with a common cultural heritage and to sort them into a specialized curriculum, to respond to the demands of subordinate groups for equal education and to answer the pressures of employers and state planners for differentiated education, and to provide a general education for citizens in a democratic society and technical training for workers in an advanced industrial economy. (Brint and Karabel, 1989: 9–10)

Community colleges, in short, are agencies for the "management of ambition," reconciling students' high demand for, and society's limited supply of, college-level positions (Brint and Karabel, 1989: 7–10, 213).

More particularly, community colleges attract students who might otherwise enter state universities, thus allowing those institutions to remain selective and avoid overproducing college graduates. In fact, community colleges further reduce the danger of having too many over-educated students by channeling students into vocational programs and away from baccalaureate studies (Brint and Karabel, 1989: 10, 90–91, 213, 226).

For students, this "diversion effect" results in lower educational attainment. Especially because many of them are pulled into vocational programs, they end up with lower educational and economic attainment than if they had entered four-year colleges. They receive fewer baccalaureate degrees, and they enter less prestigious and remunerative jobs. As a result, community colleges have become "the bottom track of the system of higher education's increasingly segmented structure of internal stratification" (Brint and Karabel, 1989: 121–124, 206, 226).

A New Perspective: The Relative Autonomy of the State

At this point, we can see that the debate between the critics and advocates over the effects of the community college primarily centers on its impact on students. The functionalist advocates see the community college as democratizing access to higher education, while the instrumentalist and institutionalist critics portray it as hampering attainment of the baccalaureate. Otherwise, all three parties agree about the community college's impact on the labor market and higher education: it produces the trained employees desired by business, and it allows state universities to be more selective in their admissions.

As I will show in Chapter 3, however, the critics and defenders only capture part of the truth. The instrumentalist Marxist and institutionalist critics are correct that the community college is inferior to the four-year college in helping baccalaureate aspirants succeed. Drawing on much more thorough and sophisticated data than they use, Chapter 3 demonstrates that community college entrants do get fewer bachelor's degrees and poorer jobs than *comparable* students entering four-year colleges. On the other hand, it also shows that the functionalist defenders appear to be correct that community colleges have a democratizing role: they allow more students to enter college than do four-year colleges, and they are more beneficial for students aspiring to less than a baccalaureate degree. Moreover, both camps are correct that the community college has helped elite universities maintain selective admissions.

However, even when merged, the perspectives of the advocates and critics of the community college fail to capture important parts of the community college's social role. The critics of the community college have failed to convincingly explain why the community college hampers baccalaureate aspirants. Hence, I devote Chapter 4 to charting the reefs on which the ambitions of so many students are wrecked.

In addition, both the critics and the defenders misperceive the community college's real role in occupational preparation. They greatly overestimate its responsiveness to the labor market's demands. Chapter 3 demonstrates that, far from being the obedient servant of either students or business, the community college often produces both more and fewer vocational graduates than the labor market requires and can even absorb. A major reason for the community college's clumsy dancing to the rhythms of the labor market is that its dance masters have not just been students and business but also a wide variety of government officials pursuing interests of their own. As I will show, this relative autonomy of the state becomes crucial to explaining why the community college arose and became so thoroughly vocationalized. Because of its diverse, hybrid origins, the community college is a quite contradictory, even incoherent, institution.

The Debate Over Why Community Colleges Were Established

Like many scholars and laypeople, the advocates and critics of the community college believe in moral symmetry. If an institution is good or bad in its effects, then it must be similarly good or bad in its origins. In the case of the advocates, since they view the community college as democratizing in its impact, they move easily to arguing that it is democratic in its origins. The critics, meanwhile, moved by the inegalitarian consequences of the community college, portray it as the product of a much seamier conception.

The Functionalist Advocates

The defenders of the community college paint it as the product of a broad-based coalition of forces with students and parents at their center. According to Charles Monroe, formerly head of one of the Chicago community colleges, the community college rose with

> the burgeoning number of high school graduates clamoring for a college education, the growing demands of business and industry for technically trained employees, the existence of local communities which had both sufficient taxable wealth and population willing to support a community college, and most important a body of parents and citizens who aspired to have their children enjoy the fulfillment of a dream for a college education. . . . (Monroe, 1972: 13)

As the quotation from Monroe indicates, the advocates emphasize the role of students and parents demanding college opportunity (Cohen and Brawer, 1989: 5; Medsker, 1960: 18; Monroe, 1972: 13). But they also note the involvement of various other private and public actors.

Business supported community college both out of a commitment to equality of educational opportunity and a desire for trained employees

(Eells, 1931: 133, 196; Monroe, 1972: 13, 85). Monroe notes that "the need for trained employees in the middle-level occupations is a primary reason why business and industry leaders have come to support the public community colleges" (Monroe, 1972: 85).

In addition, the advocates note, the state universities supported the development of community colleges. They were committed to the goal of equality of educational opportunity, but they also feared being swamped by students and wanted to emulate the German model of universities devoted to research and graduate training (Bogue, 1950: 81; Cohen and Brawer, 1989: 5–8, 14; Eells, 1931: 45–52; Medsker, 1960: 10–11; Monroe, 1972: 7–12, 37–40). The proponents of the community college note that this attraction to the German model was especially strong in the pre–World War I period. As early as the 1860s, the leaders of Stanford University and the Universities of California, Chicago, Illinois, Michigan, and Minnesota called for universities to concentrate on upper-division and graduate education, accepting only the best students who were able and willing to continue with their education after the lower-division "junior college."

It is important to realize that those defending the community college do not see the desire of universities to narrow their doors or of business to secure employee training as inimical to the needs of society or of students. Instead, they view greater selectivity as preserving the university as a "citadel of learning" and employee training for business as meeting the needs of students as well as business.

While highlighting the role of the state universities, the functionalist advocates also make scattered reference to a number of other public actors: local educators, state school superintendents and state higher education boards, and federal officials. In each case the dominant motive cited was a desire to expand equality of opportunity (Bogue, 1950: 88, 92–93; Eells, 1931: 56–57, 91–93, 96–98, 106–107; Fretwell, 1954: 73, 90–92, 113–124; Fields, 1962: 26–29, 63; Gleazer, 1968: 15; Medsker, 1960: 237, 252, 256, 262, 269, 282; Medsker and Tillery, 1971: 15, 20; Monroe, 1972: 10–15, 353, 357).

In their view of policy as the product of the participation of a multiplicity of groups, none of which is dominant, the advocates of the community college are advancing what is essentially a pluralist theory of politics.[7] Pluralism views policymaking as a process of incremental adjustments between a host of self-seeking interest groups and individuals who try to maximize their interests within rules of political competition that enjoin drastic or coercive action. They see the political system, like a perfectly competitive market, as almost invariably addressing the fundamental interests of society, at least in the long run, because it is open to the participation of virtually any interest group and individual. As a result, pluralists reject any argument that power is concentrated in the hands of a single group, such as business, which dominates across several important domains of political action. Instead, they talk of "dispersed, noncumulative inequalities" (Dahl, 1961). (For more on pluralism, see Polsby, 1981, and Alford and Friedland, 1985.)

The Marxist Instrumentalist Critics

Whereas the functionalist advocates focus on democratic demands, the Marxist instrumentalist critics stress capitalist commands. These critics agree that community college expansion has been fueled in part by a widespread desire to increase higher education opportunity. But they add that this desire eventuated in the expansion of community colleges in particular because the capitalist class believed that these kinds of colleges would better meet its interests in securing occupational education and protecting selective university admissions (Bowles and Gintis, 1976: 208; Karabel, 1972: 552; Nasaw, 1979: 215–225, 233; Zwerling, 1976: 63–73). Clearly, the Marxist instrumentalists are not alone in arguing that the community colleges were championed as a means to enhance university selectivity, for the functionalist advocates make the same claim. Where they differ is that the instrumentalist school portrays this desire as stemming from an elite interest in preserving class differences in educational attainment rather than a wish to serve the public interest (Bowles and Gintis, 1976: 208; Karabel, 1972: 524, 547; idem, 1974: 14; Nasaw, 1979: 205, 208–213, 228–229; Zwerling, 1976: 63–73). Jerome Karabel, the first major critic of the community college, argued in a much quoted statement:

> The system of higher education, forced to respond to pressure for access arising from mobility aspirations endemic in an affluent society . . . , has let people in and has then proceeded to track them into community colleges and, more particularly, into occupational programs. . . . This push toward vocational training in the community college has been sponsored by a national educational planning elite whose social composition, outlook, and policy proposals are reflective of the interests of the more privileged strata of our society. (Karabel, 1972: 552)

Samuel Bowles and Herbert Gintis echo this description:

> [T]he booming community college movement has created a class stratification within higher education parallel to the hierarchical relationships of production in

the modern corporation. An expansion of the number of students in higher education has thus been facilitated without undermining the elite status and function of the established institutions. (Bowles and Gintis, 1976: 208)

Especially in the case of the explicitly Marxist members of the critical school, the political theory that underlies their view of the politics of community college expansion is one that we can call "instrumentalist" Marxism. Although Marxists generally agree that the needs of the capitalist class profoundly shape all institutions in society, they differ on how this comes about. For instrumentalist Marxists, the key equilibrating mechanism is the self-conscious political action of the capitalist class (the owners and top executives of corporations). It captures control of the state—of which the school system is a part—through such means as placing its representatives in office, and it then uses the state as an instrument to realize its interests.[8] This notion of the self-conscious intervention of the capitalist class is very much evident in the work of Bowles and Gintis, Karabel, and Pincus (Bowles and Gintis, 1976: 205–208; Karabel, 1972: 543–547; Pincus, 1974: 33). It is evident in statements such as "the mobilization of the professional and capitalist elites for structural change in higher education" (Bowles and Gintis, 1976: 205).

The Institutionalist Critics

Brint and Karabel (1989) and Labaree (1990) reject the argument that either student or business demand fundamentally explains the development of the community college. They correctly note that community colleges proliferated even when students and business were silent.

Instead of business and student demand, these critics stress the impact of the internal dynamics of the institution of higher education (Brint and Karabel, 1989: 15–17, 214–220; Labaree, 1990: 223–227). It is this focus on institutional dynamics that leads Brint and Karabel to label their approach "institutional." And because Labaree is so much in agreement with them, I have extended this appellation to his approach as well.

Drawing on organizational theory, the institutionalists conceive of higher education as an "organizational field" composed of competing colleges and dominated by the universities and business. Lacking the securely institutionalized position of the European universities, American higher educational institutions compete for prestige and resources. Within this Darwinian universe, universities are at the top of the food chain, securing the best students, the most revenues, and the greatest prestige. Their central concern has been to protect their academic and social exclusivity in the face of the constant clamor for admissions by underprivileged students pursuing social mobility. In order to avoid having to throw their doors open to the teeming masses of academic immigrants, the universities have supported the expansion of an alternative, namely, the community college (Brint and Karabel, 1989: 26–27, 35, 208; Labaree, 1990: 223–224).

> The pattern of expansion in American higher education has always been to create a new form of college to deal with each new wave of college enrollments. . . . The colleges from the first two waves [the private colleges and universities and the elite state universities] used their superior influence to protect themselves from the growing number of students pursuing post-secondary education by introducing new institutions at each spurt in enrollments. . . . The exchange value of a college's credentials is a function of their relative scarcity in the credentials market. . . . Creating new forms of higher education instead of expanding old ones was a way to meet the political demand for access while protecting the market position of existing colleges. (Labaree, 1990: 223–224)

Hence, the institutionalists note the vigorous role of university officials such as Alexis Lange of the University of California and David Starr Jordan of Stanford University in securing the passage of the pioneering community college enabling act in California in 1907 (Brint and Karabel, 1989: 26–27).

Brint and Karabel (1989) go beyond Labaree in stressing the role not only of the state universities but also of the American Association of Community Colleges (AACC). They argue that, beginning in the 1920s, the AACC began developing the idea of the community college as a primarily vocational institution. This idea proved in time to be very popular with the state universities and state and federal policymakers and thus played a major role in the rapid growth of the community college (Brint and Karabel, 1989: 34–46, 54–66, 77–78, 96–100, 107–108, 124–126, 208–210). (For more on this, see the discussion below on the origins of vocationalization.)

While focusing on the state universities and the AACC, the institutionalists also note the role of such other actors as business leaders, state government officials, and federal officials (Brint and Karabel, 1989: 29, 54, 68–72, 97, 145, 147, 213, 216–218). However, with the possible exception of business, these actors are not given anything near the central role of the state universities and the American Association of Community Colleges.

The State Relative Autonomy Perspective

The preceding perspectives have offered a host of candidates for the role of principal promoter of the community college. Functionalists say it has been students and their parents. Instrumentalist Marxists give us business. And institutionalists point to the state universities.

I find that there is some truth to all these accounts, but they also all fail to mention many key protagonists. Drawing on case studies of five states reported in Section III, I find that the existing accounts largely ignore an absolutely key set of actors in the community college epic: government officials. Local school superintendents and high school principals were the central instigators of local drives to found community colleges. In fact, they often were the ones who prompted what business and student participation there was to be found. At the state level, state governors, legislators, and chief state school officers—along with the state university officials highlighted by institutional theory—were the prime movers in securing state aid for community colleges. And at the national level, the president and Congress strongly supported the enactment of federal aid for community colleges.

Not only did government officials strongly champion the community college even in the absence of strong private demand, but to a great extent they did this on the basis of values and interests of their own. The institutionalists have identified one of these self-interests: the desire of state universities to use community colleges to protect the selectivity of their admissions and the scarcity of their credentials. But the self-interestedness of government officials in the community college went well beyond this point. Local educators founded community colleges in good part because this brought them professional prestige and gave them access to college-level jobs. By establishing a community college, local principals or superintendents could attract the acclaim of their peers and of the professional elite at the universities. Moreover, founding a community college gave local educators a chance to become college administrators and teachers because the initial staff members were usually first recruited from the sponsoring high schools or districts. State governors, furthermore, promoted community colleges in order to enhance their reelection chances. For example, by dispensing with the need to build and operate costly dormitories, community colleges promised to help governors keep down the state higher education budget, thus lessening the need to engage in such politically costly actions as raising taxes or cutting other government programs.

The self-interested initiative that government officials have exercised does not mean that private interest groups have not powerfully shaped the development of the community colleges. As the relative autonomy of the state perspective recognizes, government officials are only *relatively* autonomous. The instrumentalist Marxists are correct that business has exerted great influence. But they make the grievous mistake of believing that this influence has rested primarily on business's self-conscious intervention in policymaking. Instead, it has been based as much on the simple fact that government officials have also been *constrained* by business's command over society's resources.

Power based on *constraint* operates when government officials enact policies that benefit a private interest group not because of that group's self-conscious political participation but because government officials believe either that such action is just or that it is necessary to get that interest group to act in ways that will benefit government officials.[9] I call these two forms of constraint "ideology" and "resource dependence." (The theoretical antecedents of my concept of constraint are discussed in the appendix to this chapter.)

"Resource dependence" or "inducement" arises when government officials act in ways that benefit an interest group, even if it does not demand that action, because they believe that to realize goals of their own they need to draw on or mobilize resources that the interest group monopolizes.[10] In order to secure that access, government officials offer inducements to the interest group in question. In short, constraint through resource dependence arises from the intersection between an interest group's monopolization of a resource (such as capital for economic growth) and government officials' need for that resource in order to realize their self-interests. The development of the community colleges provides a very nice example. State governors are very interested in economic growth for it brings all the things that gladden voters' hearts and make them look kindly on incumbent elected officials: higher wages, increased employment, and more tax revenues to fund programs without requiring higher taxes. But business controls the capital investment decisions that drive economic growth. One way governors have tried to pry that capital loose has been to offer business an attractive carrot: publicly subsidized employment training through the community colleges. The result is that business's need for employee training has been met not just through its political mobilization but through its power of constraint over government officials, founded on the latter's dependence on business-controlled resources.

Ideological constraint, meanwhile, arises when government officials hold beliefs—about what is desirable either for themselves or another group that they value—that happen to suggest actions that will benefit the interest group in question. (Again, the theoretical sources of this concept are discussed in the appendix.) For example, business has exercised a great amount of ideological constraint over government officials through their beliefs about the economy and the role of vocational education. Even without business prompting, many government officials have strongly supported vocationally oriented community colleges because they believe that vocational education benefits society as a whole and groups that they value in particular. Most policymakers firmly believe that what is good for business is on the whole good for the entire community, for business constitutes the core of our economy and therefore of our society. Insofar as business's training costs are lowered through publicly subsidized vocational education, business clearly benefits, but so does the community at large in the form of increased employment, a larger tax base, and so on. And even if policymakers are dubious about business, they believe that vocational education helps disadvantaged students by making them more employable. Hence, policymakers need little prompting from business to provide programs that very directly benefit business.

It may seem at this point that the powers of participation and constraint are not all that different, for in both cases policymakers defer to interest groups' desires for reasons of ideology or material inducement. But a crucial difference is that constraint begins with the initiative of government officials and leaves them with more autonomy. They are responding to business interests that often have not been concretized in specific policy demands and may not even be conscious. This leaves government officials more latitude in forging the policy instrument that would meet a group's interests. As a result, government officials more often can pick policies that accord with their own interests as well as those of the interest group they are attempting to please. Typically, constraint has accounted for a larger proportion of the power exercised by business and students over community college policymaking at the state and national levels than at the local level, where business and student involvement has been more direct and active.

The Debate Over Why Community Colleges Were Vocationalized

The critics of the community college have been greatly interested in explaining the rapid vocationalization of the community college in the last three decades because they see occupational education as the quintessential expression of the community college's subversion of equality of opportunity. But the defenders of the community college, viewing this program in a much different light, provide a quite opposite explanation.

The Functionalists

In keeping with their functionalist and pluralist sympathies, the advocates offer a much more benign and economistic explanation of the rise of occupational education. They advance the oft-made argument that our economy has steadily eliminated unskilled jobs and created many new white-collar and skilled blue-collar occupations that require training falling between traditional college education and high school vocational education. As a result, students, parents, and business have demanded that community colleges provide training for these "middle-level" or "semi-professional" occupations (Cohen and Brawer, 1989: 22, 207–208; Fields, 1962: 31, 218, 297–298; Harris and Grede, 1977: 33, 292–293; Medsker, 1960: 19; Monroe, 1972: 13, 84–87, 92–93; Thornton, 1972: 54, 70–71). Norman Harris and John Grede, both long associated with the community college movement as scholars and administrators, argue for the centrality of student demand:

> Within community colleges in the big city districts, burgeoning enrollments increasingly have come from adults and the poor. Their average age of students is now 28, and more than half of their students come from families with incomes below the poverty level—and are strongly motivated to qualify for a better job. . . . These "new students," . . . have been the major factor . . . in the conversion of community college programs to a predominantly occupational orientation. (Harris and Grede, 1977: 293)

But while emphasizing demand by students and business, the advocates also note that community college officials have themselves taken some initiative to expand occupational education. They argue that, beginning with the Great Depression, community colleges increasingly took in students who were not traditional college material. Very few of them went on to the university. This required the institution to provide an alternative to the traditional academic education or run the risk of massive dropping out by these "nontraditional" students. And this shift was strengthened by the appearance of a significant degree of underemployment among college graduates in the early 1970s (Bogue, 1950: 185–190; Cohen and Brawer, 1989: 22; Fields, 1962: 59; Medsker, 1960: 23–24; Thornton, 1972: 70). Leland Medsker describes how community college officials sought to meet student needs through greater vocational education:

While the terminal function was not one of the original purposes of the junior college, this emphasis developed gradually as faculties realized that many students entering and graduating from their institutions did not transfer but went directly into employment or homemaking. (Medsker, 1960: 23–24)

The Instrumentalist Marxists

Where functionalists paint students as demanding occupational education, these critics describe students as opposing it.[11] In fact, drawing on their Marxist roots, the critics describe students as an educational proletariat, resisting the vocationalization of the community college through "submerged class conflict" (Karabel, 1972: 548–550; Bowles and Gintis, 1976: 214–215; Nasaw, 1979: 233–235; Pincus, 1974: 30):

Just as the American working-class children at the turn of the century refused to accept the places prepared for them in vocational and industrial schooling tracks, so too did many of the students, newly admitted to higher education in mid-century, refuse to settle for the second-best schooling created for them. . . . Students, having discovered that the function of the community college is not so much to prepare them for transfer as to cool out their expectations, begin to abandon it, or resist being restricted to the nontransfer programs. (Nasaw, 1979: 233–234)

But if not students, who then demanded the vocationalization of the community college? The answer for the critics is business, along with its fellow travelers in government and the foundations. Bowles and Gintis note that "the continuing vocationalization of the community-college curriculum is now being actively pushed by the business community, the Federal Government, and major private foundations" and that "the connection between the needs of business and the curricula of community colleges is fostered by business representation on advisory boards" (Bowles and Gintis, 1976: 211–212).[12]

According to the critics, business has strongly supported occupational education as a means of securing publicly subsidized employee training (Bowles and Gintis, 1976: 206–208, 211–212; Karabel, 1972: 522, 543–544; Nasaw, 1979: 204–205; Pincus, 1980: 338–340). Jerome Karabel stated:

The interest of the business community in encouraging occupational training at public expense is manifest. With a changing labor force which requires ever increasing amounts of skill to perform its tasks and with manpower shortages in certain critical areas, private industry is anxious to use the community college as a training ground for its employees. (Karabel, 1972: 543)

Another reason for business interest, according to the critics, has been its fear of overeducation, and consequent radicalization, among college graduates (Bowles and Gintis, 1976: 205–206; Nasaw, 1979: 210–213, 235; Pincus, 1980: 341, 354–356; Zwerling, 1976: 55–59):

> Capitalism in the United States cannot always deliver what it promises. There are a limited number of decent, well-paid jobs, and most working-class and nonwhite young people are not destined to get them. . . . Business and government leaders— those at the top of the heap—regard postsecondary vocational education as a means of solving the political and economic problems created by the rising expectations of the working class. (Pincus, 1980: 355–356)

The Institutionalists

The institutionalists acknowledge the role of several of the actors cited by the functionalists and instrumentalists. But that said, they assign the pivotal role to community college and state university officials.

The institutionalists agree with the instrumentalists that, at least by the 1970s, business was strongly pushing vocational education, seeking to reduce its labor-training costs. Much of this business influence was indirect and structural, resting less on lobbying than on business's control of jobs that community colleges wanted for their students (Brint and Karabel, 1989: 15–17, 193–202, 209–210, 217–218). In addition, federal, state, and local governments supported the vocationalization of the community college through funds, legislation, and pronouncements in the hope that it would meet student needs, spur economic development, and prevent the overproduction of college graduates (Brint and Karabel, 1989: 68–72, 95–96, 108–111, 144–163, 185–186, 192–196, 199–200, 213; Labaree, 1990: 228). Moreover, institutionalists argue, the private foundations powerfully aided the development of vocational education through their financial and ideological support. Prompting this aid was a desire to prevent the appearance of too many overeducated college graduates and to protect the selectivity of the elite universities (Brint and Karabel, 1989: 47–51, 93–95, 103–7, 210; Labaree, 1990: 227–228). Finally, incited by the mass media, student demand played a role in the development of vocational education in the 1970s (Brint and Karabel, 1989: 116–119).

But in the end, the institutionalists refuse to attribute the vocationalization of the community college largely to the demands of students, business, or government policymakers. They note that occupational education was born and grew lustily before the appearance of any significant student or business demand for it in the 1970s. Moreover, even when student demand did become a strong factor in the 1970s, it was a demand that had been shaped by other forces, including community college efforts in the areas of public relations, counseling, and enrollment management (Brint and Karabel, 1989: 13–17, 29, 99–100, 149, 201–202, 209).

In the end, while acknowledging the role of noneducational forces, institutionalists instead stress the internal dynamics of the higher education system itself. They argue that the public universities have strongly favored vocationalized community colleges as a means of reducing admission pressure on themselves and of protecting the scarcity and thus the value of university credentials: "The university . . . was delighted at a policy that promised to strengthen the junior college's sorting function and thereby to channel students away from its gates" (Brint and Karabel, 1989: 213).

At the same time, the community colleges cooperated in this division of labor, playing a key role in vocationalizing themselves. On this point, the institutionalists are in agreement with the functionalists. Where they disagree is in the motives. The functionalists stress the desire to meet student needs for an alternative to baccalaureate education. The institutionalists have a more cynical explanation: organizational self-interest. They argue that community colleges, seeing that the universities and four-year colleges had snapped up the best occupational-training markets, tried to carve out a market of their own, supplying middle level or semiprofessional occupations. While inferior to that of the universities, this market nonetheless was open territory:

> [E]ducational institutions may be viewed as competing for training markets—the right to be the preferred pathway from which employers hire prospective employees. . . . Community colleges, by their very location in the structure of higher education, were badly situated to compete with better-established institutions for their training markets. . . . The best that the community colleges could hope to do, therefore, was to try to situate themselves favorably for the next available market niche. Therein resided the powerful organizational appeal for the two-year college's long-standing vocationalization project . . . (Brint and Karabel, 1989: 16–17)

The main vehicle through which the community colleges worked out the terms of their "anticipatory subordination," to use Brint and Karabel's (1989) evocative term, was their national association, the American Association of Community Colleges. Beginning in the 1920s, its leaders began to develop and then militantly proselytize for a vocationalized community college. And in time, this vision proved persuasive not only to AACC members but also to external supporters such as state university heads, government officials, business, and foundations:

> Locked into a subordinate position in the academic hierarchy . . . , some leaders of the two-year college movement began to develop in the 1920s and 1930s an alternative strategy to enhance their institutions' low status. . . . Their solution . . . was to transform the junior college . . . into [an institution] principally dedicated to providing terminal vocational education. . . . After decades of strenuous effort, the vocationalization project finally began to yield dividends in the late 1960s. By this time, outside sponsors—among them, major private foundations and the federal government—had joined the push for expanded occupational training in the community college. (Brint and Karabel, 1989: 208, 210)

The State Relative Autonomy Perspective

The preceding explanations provide us with various plausible instigators of the vocational movement in the community college. The functionalists give us students demanding training opportunities, assisted by sympathetic community college administrators. Instrumentalist Marxists award the laurel wreath to capitalists—and their allies in government and the foundations—seeking publicly subsidized training for company employees. And the institutionalists highlight entrepreneurial community college presidents searching for new markets for their institutions within the constraints set by the universities' dominance of the educational market and business's command over jobs.

There is some validity to all these perspectives, particularly that of the institutionalists. But this still leaves a very large explanatory vacuum. All three of the preceding schools fail to sufficiently acknowledge the pivotal participation of self-interested, relatively autonomous government officials. To be sure, the institutionalists correctly note that community college heads, and their American Association of Community Colleges, were at the epicenter of efforts to vocationalize the community college. Yet even the institutionalist theory does not give an equally central role to state governors, legislators, chief state school officers, U.S. presidents, and members of Congress, even though they were also master vocationalizers. Political pressure and serving the social good partially explain why state and federal officials were involved. But of equal or more importance was their interest in securing economic growth, with all its electoral bounty for incumbent elected officials.

A second defect of the explanations that precede mine is that they misconstrue the real nature of business's influence in the vocationalization of the community college. Business certainly played the important role that the advocates and critics of the community college claim. But the functionalists and instrumentalists are wrong in viewing this business influence as primarily founded on business's direct participation in vocational policymaking. In fact, the bulk of business's influence was founded on its power of constraint. The institutionalists are aware of this power, noting that community college officials have heeded business's desires because it controls jobs that their graduates need. This formulation, however, draws too narrow a boundary around business's power of resource dependence. It neglects the fact that state and national elected officials have also been constrained by business's control over capital for investment and thus the ability to influence the pace and distribution of economic growth. Furthermore, the institutional school ignores the ideological side of constraint: the fact that government officials have served the interests of business and students in part because they subscribe to values and beliefs that suggest the social value of aiding those groups.

Summary and Conclusions

The functionalist advocates and instrumentalist and institutionalist critics of the community college capture several key features of its origins and impact. But their analyses are also one-sided and incomplete. Like the blind men in the parable of the blind men and the elephant, they each grasp part, but only part, of the truth about that contradictory institution, the community college. As Chapter 3 shows, the community college has indeed democratized access to higher education as functionalists claim, but it has also hindered the success of baccalaureate aspirants as instrumentalists and institutionalists argue. Moreover, although both the critics and defenders are correct that the community college has become perhaps the major trainer of middle-level workers, they also fail to note that the community college often undershoots and overshoots the shifting curve of labor market demand, producing more graduates than needed in some fields and fewer than demanded in others.

The incomplete functionality and contradictory effects of the community college stem from the fact that it has been the product of many different actors with quite varying interests. The advocates and critics of the community college have illuminated parts of this creation story, correctly noting the role of students, business, state universities, and community college officials. But as Sections III and IV demonstrate, these explanations largely ignore the crucial participation of government officials—ranging from local school superintendents to state governors and members of Congress—pursuing interests and values of their own. In contrast, my "state relative autonomy" argument puts the autonomous— but only relatively autonomous—actions of government officials at the heart of the explanation of the rise and vocationalization of the community college. Because of this governmental autonomy, the community college has features that cannot be explained by the interests, much less the demands, of private interest groups alone. At the same time, however, government officials were constrained by the fact that they shared the values and beliefs of certain interest groups, above all business, and needed access to resources controlled by those interest groups. This power of resource and ideological constraint allowed interest groups to exercise great influence over community college policymaking even when they did not participate.

My analysis is intended to speak most directly to the debate over the origins and outcomes of the community college. But its relevance is not restricted to that area. Other spheres of educational scholarship have also been divided by the debate between functionalists and instrumentalist Marxists and would benefit from the third way that I have termed the state relative autonomy approach. (For more on this, see Chapter 16.)[13]

Appendix: Theoretical Antecedents of My Concept of Constraint

An important starting point for my concept of constraint is Raymond Murphy's (1982) contrast between the "power of constraint" and the "power to command":

> Although the autonomy of the school is mutually exclusive with the power of society's dominant groups to command the school, it is not mutually exclusive with their power . . . to constrain it in the course of their other activities, e.g., their economic activities. External constraints on the school may make certain alternatives appear less sanguine than others to educators, students, and parents, and thereby influence their choices and subsequent actions, without denying them the possibility of choosing and taking independent initiative, and without obliging them to obey commands from external sources. . . . The school is . . . far from being fully autonomous because it is informally and indirectly subject to con-

straints which result from the actions of society's dominant groups. . . . (Murphy, 1982: 200)

Murphy in turn draws on Carl Friedrich's (1963) concept of "influence" and its tie to "anticipated reaction." Friedrich describes influence as usually existing "when the behavior of B is molded by and conforms to the preferences of A, but without the issuance of a command" (p. 200). This influence "rests upon the capacity of human beings to imagine and thus to anticipate the reactions of those who are affected by their actions. Influence flows into the human relation whenever the influencer's *reac*tion might spell disadvantage and even disaster for the actor, who foresees the effect the action might have and alters it more or less in accordance with this foresight" (p. 201).

Murphy and Friedrich do not systematically lay out the bases of the power of constraint. Murphy suggests that it lies in a group's command of economic resources, while Friedrich hints that it lies in its capacity to inflict penalties. These suggestions are valuable and are explored in my discussion of that facet of constraint that I call "resource dependence." But first let us explore another side of the power of constraint, one that I call "ideology."

In recent years, Steven Lukes (1974) and his student John Gaventa (1980) have particularly called attention to ideology as a form of power:[14]

> [I]s it not the supreme and most insidious exercise of power to prevent people, to whatever degree, from having grievances by shaping their perceptions, cognitions, and preferences in such a way that they accept their role in the existing order of things, either because they can see or imagine no alternative to it, or because they value it as divinely ordained and beneficial? (Lukes, 1974: 24)

I argue that an interest group exercises ideological constraint over government officials when the latter hold beliefs—about what is desirable either for themselves or another group that they value—that happen to suggest actions that will benefit the interest group in question.

My conceptualization of resource dependence as a facet of the power of constraint is indebted to several approaches in the field of complex organizations: resource dependence theory (Aldrich and Pfeffer, 1976; Pfeffer and Salancik, 1978) and its cousins, political economy (Benson, 1975; Walmsley and Zald, 1973) and dependence exchange (Jacobs, 1974) theory. The resource dependence approach describes organizations as constrained but not determined by their environment:

The resource dependence model proceeds from the indisputable proposition that organizations are not able to internally generate either all the resources or functions required to maintain themselves, and therefore organizations must enter into transactions and relations with elements in the environment that can supply the required resources and services. . . . The resource dependence model portrays the organization as active, and capable of changing, as well as responding to, the environment. . . . The presumed result of such strategies is the acquisition of resources and the survival of the organization, as well as the stabilization of relationships with environmental elements. (Aldrich and Pfeffer, 1976: 83)

Although this theory has largely been applied to nongovernmental organizations, it applies quite nicely to government as well. Government agencies and officials also depend on their environment for the resources they need in order to function effectively. This has been brought out by recent work in the theory of the state. Fred Block (1987) and Theda Skocpol (1979, 1980) note that in order to maintain their power government officials, particularly chief national executives, must preserve internal order, effectively compete against other states, and maintain reasonable levels of tax revenues and popular support.[15] Block goes on to note that in order to realize these interests government officials need a healthy economy:[16]

[T]hose who manage the state apparatus—regardless of their own political ideology—are dependent on the maintenance of some reasonable level of economic activity. . . . First, the capacity of the state to finance itself through taxation or borrowing depends on the state of the economy. . . . Second, public support for a regime will decline sharply if the regime presides over a serious drop in the level of economic activity, with a parallel rise in unemployment and shortages of key goods. . . . (Block, 1987: 58)

Aware that their stay in power greatly depends on the state of the economy, government officials actively promote economic growth. But to secure it, they must typically make concessions to business, for it holds the capital that finances this growth:

In a capitalist economy the level of economic activity is largely determined by the private investment decisions of capitalists. This means that capitalists, in their collective role as investors, have a veto over state policies in that failure to invest at adequate levels can create major political problems for the state managers. . . . It also means that state managers have a direct interest in using their power to facilitate investment, since their own continued power rests on a healthy economy. (Block, 1987: 58)

As a result of government's dependence on resources monopolized by business, in this case, capital to finance economic growth, business exercises a quiet, but immense, power of constraint over government officials. Robert Alford and Roger Friedland (1975) make this clear in their description of what they call business's "systemic power":

> The fiscal capacity of all units of government is contingent upon the locational, production, and investment decisions of increasingly concentrated corporations. Given their frequently superior financial resources, especially when compared to cities and states, and their locational flexibility, corporations present a constant constraint on city, state, and even national attempts to increase tax rates, to change the tax structure, or to cut back on the subsidies available to corporations in other political units. Thus the absence of corporate participation in political decision making does not indicate the extent of corporate systemic power. (Alford and Friedland, 1975: 447)

Block (1987) and Alford and Friedland (1975) speak of cases quite different from that of the development of the community college. However, I will show in Sections III and IV that the power of constraint founded on resource dependence that their theories suggest is very much at work in the case of the community college as well. At the same time, my research also suggests ways in which Block's state manager perspective needs to be revised and extended. We need a broader concept of state officials and their interests. Chapter 16 will discuss the needed changes in the theory of the state that are suggested by my analysis of the development of the community college.

Section II
Outcomes

CHAPTER 3

The Community College's Impact on Students, the Economy, and the Universities

Is the community college a gateway of opportunity for disadvantaged students or is it a blind alley? This is the main issue dividing the community college's defenders and critics. For its functionalist defenders, the community college is "perhaps the most effective democratizing agent in higher education" (Medsker, 1960: 4). But for its institutionalist and Marxist instrumentalist critics, it constitutes "a new form of tracking within higher education" (Pincus, 1980: 334).[1]

This debate over the community college's effects is highly important for educational policy. Over the last 30 years, state and federal higher education policymakers have designated the community college to be the main artery for broadening higher education opportunity and providing postsecondary vocational education. This policy emphasis shows up in the central place it is given in state master plans for higher education. For example, the renowned 1960 California Master Plan for Higher Education assigns the community college the task of harboring that multitude of high school graduates who fall below the top third of their high school graduating class and thus are ineligible to directly enter either the University of California or the California State University (Liaison Committee, 1960). Clearly, this central role given to the community college should be called into question if the critics of the community college are correct that it greatly hinders the success of many students.

This chapter will concentrate on resolving the competing claims of the critics and defenders of the community college regarding its impact on students. At the same time, the opposing camps make additional claims about the community college's effect on elite universities and on business and the economy that also need to be addressed. Interestingly, these additional claims do not divide the critics and advocates of the community college. Albeit in very different tones, the two sides agree that the community college has met the economy's needs for "middle-level" or "semiprofessional" workers and has allowed elite state universities to remain selective in the face of mass demand for college access. But is this consensus a guarantee of the correctness of these two claims?

This chapter shows that the functionalist defenders and the Marxist instrumentalist and institutionalist critics of the community college grasp much, but also miss much, of its manifold and contradictory nature. The community college opens the door to opportunity for many, but also closes it for others. It dances to the music of the labor market but does so only clumsily. It is a Janus-faced institution, but its critics and defenders, each looking from different perspectives, have wrongly insisted that it has only one profile.

The Impact on Business and the Economy

Although their language differs, the advocates and critics agree that the community college meets the labor market's demand for "middle-level" or "semiprofessional" workers, such as computer operators, nurses, and technicians. I find, however, that the community college is much less responsive to the demands of the labor market than either school postulates.

Evidence is easily found of the community college's great willingness to train people in these middle-level occupations. Business leaders often laud the community college for meeting their training needs at a low cost to business (Beckwith, 1980; Broman, 1981; Fields, 1987a, 1987b; Maryland State Board for Community Colleges, 1990: 100; Pincus, 1989). For example, a survey of employers of community college associate and certificate degree holders one year after graduation found that across the 1980–1988 period, the percentage of employers rating the graduates' training as good and very good averaged 89% (Maryland State Board for Community Colleges, 1990: 100). And in Illinois, the manager of the Education Department of the Illinois State Chamber of Commerce praised the community colleges' efforts in the area of vocational training customized to the needs of specific firms:

> We're working on a program right now that touches into the hearts of many community colleges. It's called the High Impact Training Service, . . . which would train people for new or expanding positions, train them for a specific industry for a specific job role within that industry. . . . That HITS program has even encouraged some industries to come into Illinois . . . by knowing that they can get training services without having to use their own resources. . . . (Beckwith, 1980)

But on closer examination, the community college appears to be much less functional to the economy than either side claims. Like the sorcerer's apprentice, the community college has been a willing, but unreliable, instrument of the invisible hand. Grubb (1988) has found that the community college's output of vocational graduates is only poorly correlated with the state of the labor market. In a cross-state regression analysis, he tried to predict state-by-state differences in the number of associate degree graduates in each of six different vocational fields (such as computer programming and health technologies). Using states as the unit of analysis, he regressed a state's number of associate degree graduates in 1980–1981 in a given field on the state's community college enrollments in 1979, its tax effort, five different measures of labor market conditions, and four measures of state demographic characteristics.[2] Only two of the five labor market variables proved to be significant in any of the six regression equations (one for each of the vocational fields): proportion of the labor force in a related occupation in 1980 (significant in two equations); and the earnings differential between those with some college and those with only a high school diploma (significant in one).[3] Grubb concludes that

> these results do not support the view that community college completion is related to labor market conditions. Differences among states in occupational composition have little effect. . . . Other labor market conditions—earnings differential, opportunity costs, and unemployment rates—are similarly without effects. . . . The dominant finding is one of rigidity and unresponsiveness: programs once established tend to perpetuate themselves, and adjustment to new conditions is likely to be relatively slow. (Grubb, 1988: 312)

Other evidence also gives testimony to the community college's clumsy dancing to the rhythms of the labor market. In California and Washington, business leaders have been loudly complaining that many of their training needs go unmet so that they have had to establish brokering agencies to forge a stronger connection between their demand and community college supply (Fields, 1987b). At other times, the problem is one of overproduction (Grubb, 1984). In Washington State, for example, the community college system trains large numbers of people in several traditional occupations in which the supply of vocational graduates exceeds the demand by at least 200%: auto mechanics, diesel engine repair, computer programming and analysis, food production, welding, and electrical and electronic technology. In fact, in food production, the community college system alone graduates three times as many people as the field can employ (Mitchell, 1986). This overproduction of vocational graduates may be one cause of the repeated finding that on the average only about 50 to 70% of the graduates of community college vocational programs find jobs directly related to their training (Cohen and Brawer, 1989: 213; Maryland State Board for Community Colleges, 1990: 100; Pincus, 1980: 348).

This oversupply of graduates in various vocational programs may explain why community college vocational graduates fail to strongly outpace high school graduates in income. Using the 1986 follow-up of the National Longitudinal Survey of the High School Class of 1972, Grubb finds that in 12 comparisons—involving hourly pay and annual income for men and women with three different community college credentials (vocational associate's degree, vocational certificate, and vocational credits but no degree)—community college students outperformed high school graduates with comparable backgrounds, high school perform- ance, and job experience on 6 of 12 comparisons, but only 4 of those positive comparisons were statistically significant (Grubb, 1994a, b). Similarly, analyzing the 1986 follow-up of the High School and Beyond 1980 high school graduating class, Lyke, Gabe, and Aleman (1991) found that men and women who had completed community college degrees made *less* money hourly and monthly (three out of four comparisons) than high school graduates with similar social and educational backgrounds (Lyke et al., 1991: 69–72). (For the methodological characteristics of Grubb's and Lyke et al.'s studies, see Appendix Table A3–5.)

How do we reconcile this evidence that occupational training does not coincide all that well with labor market demands with employers' fre- quent praise for community college vocational graduates? The key may lie in the fact that employers and others who praise occupational educa- tion in the community college are focusing on whether their labor de- mands are being met and if the graduates are sufficiently well trained. They are not paying attention to whether vocational graduates are finding jobs, especially ones that are well-paying and commensurate with the students' training. As a result, occupational education can be quite inefficient and yet still please employers.

In summary, the community college does indeed provide business and students with vocational training. But contrary to the claims of both the defenders and critics of the community college, this vocational output appears to be only weakly connected to labor market demand (particularly for clearly postsecondary skills).[4] As we will see in Section IV of the book, this loose coupling reflects the fact that the community college's vocational effort has been governed by nonmarket as well as market criteria. In particular, community college officials and state elected officials have promoted occupational education for self-interested reasons that often have little to do with the demands of business or of students. We will explore these reasons in depth in Chapters 11 through 13.

The Impact on the Elite State Universities

Has the community college indeed reduced admissions pressure on the top state universities and allowed them to maintain their admissions selectivity, as both its advocates and critics have claimed? The answer is yes.

University officials in California and Washington State have noted and lauded the community college's role as a safety valve. For example, Robert Sproul, who presided over the University of California from 1930 to 1958, stated:

> [T]he University of California . . . , without the excellent junior colleges that have been developed, would hardly have been able to establish and maintain its present high standards of admission and graduation. . . . Certainly class size could not have been held to a reasonable level, nor could the need for land and buildings have been kept within bounds. (Sproul, 1958: 101)

And 20 years later, Sproul's successor as university president, Clark Kerr, made a very similar statement (Kerr, 1978). Meanwhile, in Washington State, officials of the University of Washington echoed the sentiments of Sproul and Kerr (Waldo, 1981).[5]

Testimony to the community college's diversionary effect comes not only from the words of university officials but also from the actions of college students. Orfield and Paul (1992: 86–88), in a study of five states with different kinds of higher education systems (California, Wisconsin, Florida, Indiana, and Illinois), found that the ones with community college systems—especially large community college systems—have lower rates of transfer from two-year to four-year colleges and lower rates of baccalaureate attainment. Unfortunately, they did not control for differences between the states in the composition of their populations. But another study did. Controlling for population social composition, characteristics of the higher education systems, and state labor market conditions,[6] Grubb (1989) found that states with large community college systems tend to have smaller proportions of their female high school graduates getting baccalaureates—that is, going on to four-year colleges—than states with smaller community college systems. (In the case of men, the evidence is inconclusive, with different indicators pointing in opposing directions.)

One of the main reasons community colleges pull students away from universities is that tuitions are lower at community colleges than at state universities. In 1991–1992, the average tuition and fees for state residents were $962 at public two-year colleges and $2,134 at public four-year colleges (U.S. National Center for Education Statistics, 1992a: 307–308). These lower tuitions at community colleges draw students away from four-year colleges. Three different studies have found that, even with controls for other variables, states with lower community college tuitions have significantly higher community college enrollments than states with higher community college tuitions. They estimate that the price elasticity of community college tuition falls between –0.44 and –0.69: that is, for every 1% decrease in community college tuition, community college enrollments rise, other conditions held equal, by one-half to two-thirds of 1% (Corman and Davidson, 1984; Grubb, 1988; Sulock, 1982). This finding of the impact of tuition differences is not restricted to the community college. A wealth of studies on college choice generally testify to the significant impact of tuition differences, even with other variables controlled, on where students go to college (Manski and Wise, 1983: 19–20; Rosenfeld and Hearn, 1982: 140–141).

Grubb (1988) provides a good example of the methods used in the studies of community college pricing. Analyzing differences across states, he regressed state community college enrollments in 1979–1980 as a percentage of the population age 18 to 30 over three tuition variables (average community college tuition, average public four-year college tuition, and average private four-year college tuition), five labor market variables, three state demographic characteristics, and three variables measuring college enrollments in 1970. He found that community colleges' average tuition had a strong and statistically significant negative effect on their enrollments: a 1% decrease in community college tuition led to a little over 1/2% increase in community college enrollments. (The results of these studies on the effects of community college tuition are summarized in Table 3–1. Further details, including the precise control variables analyzed, are provided in Appendix Table A3–1.)

The shared view of both defenders and critics of the community college—that it has served as a safety valve for the top state universities—holds up better on examination than their earlier common claim that it smoothly meets the needs of business and the economy. Both statistical and testimonial evidence does strongly indicate—although it might be too strong to say "prove"—that the community college has indeed drawn students away from the top state universities and allowed them to be more

TABLE 3–1
The Impact of Community College Tuition on College Choices[a]

	Grubb (1988)	Corman, Davidson (1984)	Sulock (1982)
Study Attributes			
Level of analysis	state	state	county or SMSA
Dependent variable	community college (CC) enrollments as percent of population age 18–30	CC enrollments as percent of high school graduates without B. A.	CC enrollments as percent of high school graduates in past 2 years
Findings			
Elasticity[b] of community college tuition, other variables controlled	–0.56*	–0.69* (women) –0.68* (men)	–0.44*

Notes:
* Statistically significant at *p* less than 0.05.
a. See Appendix Table A3–1 for a listing of the control variables.
b. Elasticity is defined as the percentage change in the dependent variable associated with a 1% change in the independent variable.

selective. This finding has major implications for the community college's impact on students' life chances, as we will see in the next section.

The Effect on Students

The tenuous consensus between advocates and critics on the community college's impact breaks down completely when we turn to the question of its effect on students' educational and economic attainment. The two sides disagree sharply not just on what this impact is but also on how it should be measured. Instrumentalists and institutionalists argue that the community college *reduces* its students' chances of getting a bachelor's degree. They use baccalaureate attainment as their standard because they hold that three-fourths of community-college entrants aspire to a bachelor's degree (Brint and Karabel, 1989: 216; Karabel, 1972: 530–536; Pincus, 1974: 21; Zwerling, 1976: 81).[7] The functionalist school rejects the use of baccalaureate attainment as the standard of community college effectiveness. They argue that the B.A. is not as crucial to success as the critics claim and that, in any case, only one-third to one-half of community college students wish to get a baccalaureate degree (Cohen and Brawer,

1987: 95; Richardson and Bender, 1987: 190). Instead, functionalists prefer to focus on the community college's contribution to broadening access to higher education, promoting the educational and economic attainment of students who do not (or cannot) aspire to a baccalaureate degree, and helping students meet their personal goals, whatever their content (Cohen and Brawer, 1989: 357–358, 363–364).

From this clash of claims, three questions emerge as important to answer. In comparison with other postsecondary institutions, how successful is the community college in widening access to higher education? How well does it promote its students' educational attainment, measured in terms of both years of education and baccalaureate attainment? Finally, how well do community colleges aid their students in getting jobs, and prestigious and remunerative jobs at that?

All three questions need to be answered with an awareness that community college students differ greatly from four-year college students in many regards. On average, they come from less advantaged backgrounds, perform less well in high school, and have lower educational and occupational aspirations. The task then is to compare community college and other institutions in their effects on *comparable* students: that is, ones similar in family background, high school achievement, educational and occupational ambitions, and so forth.

Access to Higher Education

The functionalist defenders vigorously claim that the community college provides significantly greater access to higher education than four-year colleges. Without community colleges, many students would not be able to enter higher education. But the instrumentalist and institutionalist critics counter that much of the community college's undoubted popularity rests on stealing students from the more expensive and distant four-year colleges. In short, community college enrollments do not so much add to higher educational opportunity as substitute for four-year college enrollments. In reviewing the available evidence, I find that it falls between these two positions: a significant degree of substitution does occur, but nonetheless the community college does provide higher education opportunities unmatched by other institutions.

As the functionalists claim, the community college expands opportunity more than do four-year colleges. Grubb (1989) found that in fall 1979 there was a statistically significant positive association (in the case of men but not women) between the relative size of a state's community college enrollments and the proportion of its high school graduates going on to college.[8] States that ranked high in the proportion of their college-age population that was enrolled in community college tended to also rank high in the proportion of that population going to college, even after controlling for differences between states in social composition, educational structure, and labor market conditions. (The control variables are largely the same as those in the Grubb (1988) study described in Table 3–1. See also note 6.)

Similarly, Medsker and Trent (1964) found that, among 16 cities in the Midwest and California, the 5 with community colleges had higher college attendance rates than did the 4 with state colleges, the 4 with extension centers of state universities, the 1 with a mixture of institutions, and the 2 with no college of any kind. These differences held not only in the aggregate but also across different kinds of students: for those high and medium in socioeconomic status (out of three SES levels), those high, medium, and low in ability (five categories), and six of nine combined socioeconomic status by ability categories.[9]

Several features of community colleges apparently lead them to provide greater access to college than do four-year colleges. Typically, community colleges are closer by, whereas many four-year colleges are located in distant rural areas. They are cheaper to attend, if only because they are commuter schools. And because of their open-door admissions ideal, they are more willing to take "nontraditional" students: high school dropouts, the academically deficient, vocational aspirants, and adults interested in leisure education.

But we must attach a major reservation to this finding about the community college's openness. As noted in our discussion of the community college's impact on elite state universities, a sizable proportion of the students enrolled by the community college are people who would still enter higher education even if a community college were not available. They are attracted away from four-year colleges by community colleges' lower tuitions and, possibly, greater proximity. These students, who might otherwise have gone to four-year colleges, tend to exceed other community college students in academic aptitude and socioeconomic status—and, most likely, in baccalaureate aspirations. Because of this "substitution effect" and because the community college is less effective in helping baccalaureate aspirants succeed (see the next section), the community college's undoubted attractiveness to students keeps baccalaureate attainment rates lower than they might otherwise be (Brint and Karabel, 1989: 91–92; Corman and Davidson, 1984; Grubb, 1989; Karabel, 1972; Orfield and Paul, 1992: 86–88; Tinto, 1974). As we saw in the discussion of the community college's impact on elite state universities, states with large community college systems tend to have lower rates of transfer and baccalaureate attainment than states with more four-year colleges and two-year branches of state universities (Grubb, 1989; Orfield and Paul, 1992: 86–88). This point leads us directly to the question of the community college's impact on its entrants' educational attainment, particularly their relative success in achieving baccalaureate degrees.

Educational Attainment

The instrumentalists and institutionalists argue that the community college significantly harms the educational success of baccalaureate aspirants, who they say represent the majority of community college students. The functionalist defenders counter that such students are actually in the minority in the community college and in any case suffer little or no ill effects at its hands. More importantly, the community college is much superior to the four-year college for the real majority of community college students: those *sub*-baccalaureate aspirants who come to college looking for vocational education, avocational adult education, and remedial education. Furthermore, the community college is superior to other sub-baccalaureate institutions such as postsecondary vocational schools and proprietary schools.

I find that each camp is correct, but only partially. Baccalaureate aspirants are neither as common as the critics argue nor as rare as the defenders claim. However, as the critics argue, these students are significantly hindered by entering a community college. On the other hand, there is intriguing evidence that the defenders are correct that sub-baccalaureate students do better at the community college than at four-year colleges or at other sub-baccalaureate colleges.

Community Colleges and Four-Year Colleges Compared

Social surveys routinely find a large gap between community college entrants and four-year college entrants in proportions attaining a bachelor's degree. Three different national surveys found that, on the average, 70% of four-year college entrants had received a baccalaureate degree when followed up 4 to 14 years later, whereas only 26% of two-year college entrants had achieved the same goal (Astin et al., 1982; Bayer, Royer, and Webb, 1973; Velez, 1985). One of these surveys also indicates that four-year college entrants on the average secure one-half more years of education than two-year entrants (Anderson, 1984).[10]

Community college defenders have responded that this "baccalaureate gap" is largely rooted in the fact that community college students differ greatly from four-year college entrants in family background, high school academic record, and educational aspirations (Cohen and Brawer, 1989: 44). This is true, and it does account for a good part of that gap. Community college students are poorer, more often nonwhite, less academically apt, and less ambitious than are four-year college students. Compared with students at four-year colleges, students at public two-year colleges are more likely to have below-average family incomes, have family heads with a high school education or less, be nonwhite and female, and have lower high school grades. (See Table 1–1 in Chapter 1.) And community college entrants are less oriented toward receiving a baccalaureate degree. Whereas about 85% of four-year college entrants aspire to a bachelor's degree (Grubb, 1991: 205), only 20 to 35% of community college entrants do. Instead, the other 65 to 80% of community college students enter looking for new or enlarged vocational skills, a terminal general education, remedial education, or adult nonvocational education (Cohen and Brawer, 1989: 49, 51–52; Dougherty, 1987: 87; Grubb, 1991: 195; Pincus and Archer, 1989: 10–11).[11]

These differences in student characteristics in turn account for a considerable part of the gap in educational attainment. When these characteristics are controlled (see below), the baccalaureate gap is reduced by as much as three-fifths and the difference in years of education attained by one-half.

Nonetheless, even after controlling for these differences, the baccalaureate gap between two-year and four-year college entrants remains large and statistically significant. Despite differences in sampling, follow-up period, and analytic method, several careful quantitative analyses based on nationally representative data find that students who enter community colleges receive significantly fewer bachelor's degrees and years of education than students of similar background, ability, and aspirations who enter four-year colleges. Even when we control for these characteristics, we find that students entering the community college receive 11 to 19% fewer bachelor's degrees than similar students entering four-year colleges. (See Table 3–2.) The fact that community college entrants get many fewer bachelor's degrees than comparable four-year college entrants means that we can no longer dismiss the baccalaureate gap as due to students' personal traits. We must now also give a sizable role to the *institutional characteristics* of the college they have entered.

Nunley and Breneman (1988) analyzed the 1979 follow-up of students in the National Longitudinal Survey of the High School Class of 1972 (hereafter NLS-72) who entered college in fall 1972.[12] They found that community college entrants received 11.4% fewer baccalaureate degrees than students similar in background, aspirations, and high school record

TABLE 3–2

Educational Attainment of Four-Year College versus Two-Year-College Entrants[a]

	Nunley, Breneman (1988)	Lavin, Crook (1990)	Nunley, Breneman (1988)	Velez (1985)	Anderson (1984)	Astin et al. (1982)
Study Attributes						
Data set used	NLS-72	CUNY	NLS-72	NLS-72	NLS-72	ACE
Year respondents began college	1972	1970–72	1972	1972	1972	1971
Year respondents followed up	1979	1984	1979	1979	1979	1980
Aspirations of respondents	any higher educ.	any higher educ.	B. A. and above	college academic program	college academic program	B. A. and above
Findings[b]						
Difference in Percentage Attaining B. A.						
No controls	NA	42.0%	NA	48.0%	23.9%	44.0%[c]
With controls	11.4%*	17.0%*	11.5%[d]	18.7%*	14.0%*	NA[e]
Difference in Average Years of Education Attained						
No controls	NA		NA		0.46	
With controls	0.12*		0.16[d]		0.25*	

Notes
* Statistically significant at the *p* less than 0.05 level.
a. See Appendix Table A3–2 for a description of the nature and sources of the data and a listing of the control variables.
b. Positive score indicates that four-year colleges are higher than community colleges on the statistic in question.
c. Figures are for whites only. Does not report figures for all races together.
d. Level of statistical signficance not reported; only reported for comparison with those not entering college.
e. Reports *partial correlations* between college type and attainment of a baccalaureate for five racial/ethnic groups. The partial correlations for public two-year college entrants range from 0.01 to –0.20 (with four of five correlations significant at *p* less than 0.05), while the correlations for public four-year nonuniversity college entrants range from –0.08 to 0.08 (with only one being significant). See discussion in text.

who entered four-year colleges. This finding is not restricted to the NLS-72 and to a follow-up 7 years after college entrance. Attesting to this is a 14-year longitudinal study by Lavin and Crook (1990) of students who entered the community colleges and four-year colleges of the City University of New York (CUNY) between 1970 and 1972 and were followed up in 1984. Although the CUNY community colleges make strong efforts to facilitate transfer to the senior colleges, community college entrants still received 17% fewer bachelor's degrees than four-year college entrants with similar personal characteristics. (See Appendix Table A3–2 for the particular background and other characteristics controlled in these studies.)

This average finding sits astride an important interaction, however. Students aspiring to a baccalaureate degree or higher are very clearly hindered by entering a community college. On the other hand, there is evidence, although less conclusive, that *sub*-baccalaureate aspirants seem to get more years of higher education if they enter a community college rather than a four-year college or postsecondary vocational school. Let us explore this interaction between aspirations and the effect of community college entrance on educational attainment.

Four studies illuminate the impact of type of college entered on baccalaureate aspirants. Their results are reported in Table 3–2. Using the NLS-72, Nunley and Breneman (1988) examined the educational records of *baccalaureate aspirants* who entered college in October 1972 and were followed up in October 1979. They found that community college entrants still received 11.5% fewer bachelor's degrees and averaged 0.16 fewer years of education than four-year college entrants even after controlling for differences in family background, high school record, and educational aspirations (pp. 80–81).[13] These findings were replicated in two other studies using the NLS-72 1979 follow-up but focusing instead on students who entered the *academic* programs of community colleges and four-year colleges in fall 1972.[14] Velez (1985) found that, even after controlling for prematriculation differences, community college entrants still received 18.7% fewer baccalaureate degrees than comparable four-year college entrants (Velez, 1985: 199).[15] Anderson (1984), meanwhile, found that students who entered community college academic programs secured 14.0% fewer bachelor's degrees and 0.25 fewer years of education than comparable students who entered state four-year colleges (Anderson, 1984: 33–34).[16]

It could be argued that these findings are peculiar to the NLS-72. But an analysis of an entirely separate survey discovered the same pattern. Alexander Astin and colleagues in 1980 followed up freshmen surveyed in 1971 as part of the American Council for Education's yearly national survey of full-time freshmen. Concentrating on those aspiring to at least a bachelor's degree, they found that 9 years later the two-year college entrants were uniformly less likely to have attained a baccalaureate degree than were four-year college entrants, even after controlling for their differing personal characteristics. For example, for whites, the partial *correlation* between community college entrance and attaining a bachelor's degree was –0.14, but the partial correlation between entrance to one or another four-year college and attaining a bachelor's degree was largely positive, ranging between –0.04 and 0.15. (This pattern held as well for blacks, Chicanos, and Indians, although not for Puerto Ricans.)

Students with uncertain educational aspirations may also benefit more from attending a four-year college than a community college. Crook and Lavin (1989) found that students who were unsure of their educational plans at the time they entered the City University of New York between 1970 and 1972 were more likely to have attained a baccalaureate degree by 1984 if they had entered a four-year college rather than a community college at CUNY. Crook and Lavin explain this pattern by suggesting that uncertain students at community colleges largely receive support for pursuing a sub-baccalaureate degree, whether a terminal associate's degree or certificate, whereas similar students at four-year colleges more often receive support for pursuing a bachelor's degree.

Baccalaureate aspirants clearly fare less well if they enter a community college than a four-year college. But as many functionalist defenders of the community college have claimed, the community college seems to be superior for students with *sub-baccalaureate* aspirations. Breneman and Nelson (1981: 90) estimated that, among NLS-72 respondents who entered college in fall 1972 and were followed up in 1976, 44% of the community college entrants (and 20% of four-year college entrants) would have attained more *years of education* by entering a community college rather than a four-year college. These students were more likely to be nonacademically oriented, nonwhite, and of low socioeconomic status than students who would benefit more from entering a four-year college.[17] This finding is reinforced by an analysis of the NLS-72 showing that fall 1972 college entrants who aspired to less than a baccalaureate degree were *less* likely to have dropped out of higher education by fall 1974 if they had entered a two-year college rather than a four-year college in fall 1972 (U.S. National Center for Education Statistics, 1977b: 71, 74).

Educational aspirations are not the only student characteristics that may condition the impact of community college entrance on educational attainment. Breneman and Nelson (1981: 90–92) found that students who are of low social class, male, black, and with poor high school grades receive more years of education if they enter a community college rather than a four-year college. Looking at baccalaureate attainment, Crook and Lavin (1989) found a similar community college benefit for students who are low in socioeconomic status and have poor grades, but they found that blacks do better in four-year colleges. However, none of these interaction effects proved statistically significant in their analysis. Clearly, this is an area deserving considerable research.

But if community colleges fare somewhat badly in comparison with four-year colleges in promoting their students' educational attainment, they do better than postsecondary vocational schools, whether public or private. Focusing on baccalaureate aspirants entering community colleges and vocational-technical schools, Nunley and Breneman (1988) found that the former received 31% more bachelor's degrees and 0.88 more years of education than the latter, despite extensive controls for socioeconomic background and academic aptitude (pp. 80–81). Similarly, surveying 1967 graduates of various kinds of vocational programs, Godfrey and Holmstrom (1970) found that 37.9% of the graduates of 62 community colleges, but only 4.2% of the graduates of 16 public vocational-technical institutes and none of the graduates of 13 public vocational-technical centers, had received a baccalaureate degree by 1969 (pp. 164, 129).

Focusing on dropout rates and using the High School and Beyond survey, Grubb (1993) found a similar community college advantage. He estimated that, among 1980 high school seniors who entered college that fall, those entering community colleges had a dropout rate by 1984 of somewhere between 42.0 and 45.9%, whereas the rate was between 46.5 and 50.1% for public vocational school entrants and 42.2 and 51.3% for proprietary school entrants. Furthermore, community colleges had a much higher percentage of their High School and Beyond entrants transferring to four-year colleges by 1984: 20.2% versus 8.6 and 8.0% for the other two kinds of schools (Grubb, 1991: 200–202; idem, 1993: 20–21). These results are summarized in Table 3–3. For a detailed rendering of the findings and the characteristics of the studies from which they emerge, see Table A3–3 in the appendix to this chapter.

In sum, the community college has a contradictory impact on the educational futures of its students. Baccalaureate aspirants clearly attain fewer bachelor's degrees and years of education than if they had entered a four-year college. But counterbalancing this, students who aspire to less than a bachelor's degree appear to receive more years of education, but perhaps fewer baccalaureate degrees, if they enter a community college rather than a four-year college. Furthermore, community college entrants receive more education than students entering public and private postsecondary vocational schools.

Economic Attainment

For many, however, the true test of college is how it advances not its students' educational careers but rather their economic prospects. Gazing

TABLE 3–3

Educational Attainment of Entrants to Community Colleges versus Other Two-Year Colleges[a]

	Nunley, Breneman (1988)	Godfrey, Holmstrom (1970)	Grubb (1991, 1993)
Study Attributes			
Data set used	NLS-72	own	HS & B
Year students began college	1972		1980
Year students ended college		1967	
Year students followed up	1979	1969	1984
Aspirations of students	B. A. or higher	any higher educ.	any higher educ.
Findings			
Difference in Percentage Attaining B. A.			
Graduates of community colleges versus			
public vocational technical schools			
No controls	NA	33.7%	
With controls	31.3%[b]	NA	
Difference in Percentage Transferring			
to Four-Year Colleges			
Entrants to community colleges versus			
public postsecondary vocational schools			
No controls			11.6%
With controls			NA
Entrants to community colleges versus			
proprietary schools			
No controls			12.2%
With controls			NA
Difference in Percentage Dropping out			
Entrants to community colleges versus			
public postsecondary vocational schools			
No controls			0.6–8.1%[c]
With controls			NA
Entrants to community colleges versus			
and proprietary schools			
No controls			0.2–9.3%[c]
With controls			NA

Notes:

a. See Appendix Table A3–3 for a description of the nature and sources of the data and a listing of the control variables.

b. Level of statistical significance not reported; only reported for comparison with those not entering college.

c. Dropout rate is lower for community college entrants. Figures given are based on low and high estimates.

at studies on this question, we discover a pattern that is similar to that for educational attainment. In the main, students—particularly if they are baccalaureate aspirants—fare less well economically if they enter a community college than a four-year college. On the other hand, community college entrants and graduates do better—though with some exceptions—than similar students entering public and private postsecondary vocational schools.

Community Colleges Compared with Four-Year Colleges

Four-year college entrants and graduates enjoy a considerable advantage over their community college counterparts on a variety of economic yardsticks, including occupational status, hourly and yearly income, and protection from unemployment. Three studies using different data sets found that community college students average 2 to 7 points lower in occupational status (on a 96-point scale) than do comparable students at four-year colleges. Using the National Longitudinal Survey of Labor Market Experience, Elizabeth Monk-Turner (1983) studied men who entered college between 1966 and 1968 and were followed up in 1976 and 1977.[18] She found that, among men working full-time 10 years after entering college, those who entered four-year colleges held occupations that averaged 3.5 points higher in occupational status than those who entered community colleges, even when their differences in social background, educational aspirations, high school record, educational attainment, and job experience were controlled (Monk-Turner, 1983: 395, 401).

Monk-Turner's (1983) findings are buttressed by Kristine Anderson's (1984) analysis of the NLS-72. Examining the occupations in 1979 of students who had entered college in 1972, she found that community college students had reached occupations that ranked 2.4 points lower— even after controlling extensively for differences in social background, high school performance, and so on—than the jobs attained by comparable entrants to public four-year colleges (Anderson, 1984: 17–18, 36, Tables 5 and 9).

Finally, continuing his intensive study of students who entered the City University of New York (CUNY) in the years 1970–1972, David Lavin found that by 1984 baccalaureate graduates of CUNY outranked associate's degree graduates by 6 to 7 points in occupational status (Lavin and Hyllegard, 1991: Tables 5.3–5.5).[19] (See Table 3–4 for a summary of the results of these three studies. Appendix Table A3–4 gives a detailed rendering of the characteristics of these studies, including the control variables used.)

TABLE 3–4
Economic Attainment of Entrants to Community Colleges versus Four-Year Colleges[a]

	Monk-Turner (1983)	Anderson (1984)	Grubb (1993, 1994a, b)	Lavin, Hyllegard (1991)
Study Attributes				
Data set used	NLSME	NLS-72	NLS-72	CUNY
Year students began college	1966–68	1972	1972	1970–72
Year students followed up	1976–77	1979	1986	1984
Aspirations of students	any higher educ.	college academic program	any higher educ.	any higher educ.
Findings				
Difference in Mean Status of Current Occupation				
Entrants to four-year versus public two-year colleges				
No controls	11.8	5.4		
With controls	3.5*	2.4*		
Graduates of four-year versus community colleges				men women
No controls				7.8 7.3
With controls				7.2[b] 5.8[b]
Difference in Mean Earnings in Current Job: Hourly				
Entrants to four-year versus public two-year colleges				
No controls		$0.03		
With controls		–$0.05		
Graduates with B. A. versus two-year public college degrees				
No controls			men women	
Vocational AAs				
Certificates				
With controls				
Vocational AAs			$2.69[b] $0.72[b]	
Certificates			$4.49[b] $2.52[b]	
Difference in Mean Earnings in Current Job: Yearly				
Graduates with B. A. versus two-year public college degrees				
No controls				men women
All associates				$4,358 $2,965
			men women	men women
Vocational AAs				
Certificates				

TABLE 3–4 continued
Economic Attainment of Entrants to Community Colleges versus Four-Year Colleges[a]

	Monk-Turner (1983)	Anderson (1984)	Grubb (1993, 1994a, b)	Lavin, Hyllegard (1991)
With controls				
All Associates				$5,533[b] $2,571[b]
Vocational AAs			$ 4,268[b] $1,454[b]	
Certificates			$11,566[b] $3,278[b]	

Notes:
* Statistically significant at the .05 level.
a. See Appendix Table A3–4 for a description of the nature and sources of the data and a listing of the control variables.
b. Level of statistical significance not reported; only reported for comparison with those not entering college.

It is often claimed that community college students graduating from community college programs can make as much money as baccalaureate graduates. But this claim is not backed up by careful analyses of the NLS-72 and City University of New York (CUNY) data. Students graduating with community college associate's degrees and certificates on average make considerably less money than bachelor's degree holders, even after one has controlled for differences in social background, high school achievement, college experiences, and occupational traits. Lavin and Hyllegard (1991) estimated that among their CUNY students followed up 12 to 14 years after they entered college, those who graduated from a community college but did not go on for a baccalaureate degree earn, depending on their sex, from $2,571 to $5,533 less than their counterparts who earned a baccalaureate degree (Lavin and Hyllegard, 1991: Tables 5.4–5.5). This finding is not restricted to CUNY. W. Norton Grubb (1993; 1994a, b) arrived at essentially the same finding in his analysis of the 1986 follow-up of the NLS-72. However, he also noted some interesting variations within this general theme. Men receiving vocational certificates are particularly hard hit, falling $11,566 behind their baccalaureate counterparts in yearly income. Meanwhile, women earning vocational associate's degrees lag behind their baccalaureate counterparts by only $1,454 a year.

But if it is clear that community colleges do not afford their students the same economic opportunities as do four-year colleges, how well do community colleges compare with other two-year colleges in ensuring their students' economic futures?

Community Colleges Compared with Other Two-Year Colleges

Community colleges are by no means the only two-year colleges. Although they are the dominant species in their ecological niche, they share
it with public postsecondary vocational schools and proprietary (private,
usually for-profit) business and technical colleges. Although the evidence
is rather heterogeneous and contradictory, it appears to indicate that
community colleges lag behind proprietary schools in securing stable and
well-paid employment for students and at best equal public postsecondary
vocational schools.

Community college graduates appear to secure higher status positions than graduates of public postsecondary vocational schools. However, this conclusion is based on only one study: Gerald Somers, Laure
Sharpe, and Thelma Myint's 1969 survey of 1966 graduates of 61 junior
colleges (321 student respondents) and 54 postsecondary schools (725
student respondents) (Somers, Sharpe, and Myint, 1971: 9–10, 19–21).
We have more extensive but also more contradictory data on income.
Community college students earn more money than students of comparable background and ability graduating from public postsecondary vocational schools, according to two different studies: Somers et al.'s (1971:
134, 150) 1969 survey; and Goodwin's (1989: 61–69) analysis of the 1986
follow-up of the High School and Beyond class of 1980. However, two
other analyses conclude that community college entrants earn less money
than do comparable postsecondary vocational school entrants (Kane and
Rouse, 1993; Lyke et al., 1991: 69–72). Completing this contradictory
picture, Grubb (1993, 1994a, b) finds that—in 12 different comparisons,
involving male and female vocational credit earners, certificate holders,
and vocational associate recipients—5 favor the community college and
7 public vocational schools. This split in findings appears as well on the
question of protection from unemployment. One study finds that community college students have a lower unemployment rate than their
postsecondary vocational school peers (Somers et al., 1971: 86), whereas
another concludes that they have a higher unemployment rate (Goodwin,
1989: 61–69). These results are summarized in Table 3–5 and Appendix
Table 3–5.

Vis-à-vis proprietary schools, community college graduates have a
lower unemployment rate than comparable proprietary school graduates
(Goodwin, 1991: 61–69). However, proprietary school graduates appear
to have an edge in income. Four studies find that proprietary school
graduates secure higher incomes (Kane and Rouse, 1993; Lyke et al.,
1991; 69–72; Goodwin, 1991: 61–69; Wilms, 1980), while only one gives
the nod to community colleges (Grubb, 1993; 1994a, b).

TABLE 3–5

Economic Attainment of Graduates of Community Colleges versus
High Schools and Other Two-Year Colleges[a]

	Grubb (1993, 1994a, b)		Lyke et al. (1991)		Goodwin (1989)	Somers et al. (1971)
Study Attributes						
Data set used	NLS-72		HS & B		HS & B	own
Year students began college	1972		1980		1980–84	
Year left college						1966
Year followed up	1986		1986		1986	1969
Population involved	men	women	men	women	both sexes	both sexes
Findings						
Difference in Mean Status of Current Job						
Graduates of community colleges versus postsecondary vocational schools						
All vocational grads.						
No controls					6.1	
With controls					NA	
Difference in Mean Current Earnings: Hourly						
Community colleges versus public postsecondary vocational schools						
College entrants						
No controls					$0.29	
With controls					$0.73*	
All graduates			men	women		
No controls			−$0.22	−$0.54		
With controls			−$0.49[b]	−$0.82[b]		
All vocational grads.						
No controls					$0.50	
With controls					$0.29[b]	
Vocational AA grads.	men	women				
No controls						
With controls	−$0.34[b]	$1.44[b]				
Voc. certif. grads.						
No controls						
With controls	−$2.72[b]	−$0.71[b]				

TABLE 3–5 continued
Economic Attainment of Graduates of Community Colleges versus
High Schools and Other Two-Year Colleges[a]

	Grubb (1993, 1994a, b)		Lyke et al. (1991)		Goodwin (1989)	Somers et al. (1971)
Community colleges versus proprietary schools						
College entrants						
No controls					−$1.56	
With controls					−$0.77	
All graduates			men	women		
No controls			−$0.76	−$0.41		
With controls			−$0.96[b]	−$0.61[b]		
Vocational AA grads.	men	women				
No controls						
With controls	$1.25[b]	$0.82[b]				
Voc. certif. grads.						
No controls						
With controls	−$3.33[b]	−$1.50[b]				
Community colleges versus high schools only						
All graduates			men	women		
No controls			$0.27	$0.60		
With controls			−$0.43	$0.11		
Vocational AA grads.	men	women				
No controls						
With controls	−$0.61	$1.32*				
Voc. certif. grads.						
No controls						
With controls	−$2.41	−$0.48				
Difference in Mean Current Earnings: Yearly						
Community colleges versus public postsecondary vocational schools						
Vocational AA grads.	men	women				
No controls						
With controls	−$1,148[b]	−$570[b]				
Voc. certif. grads.						
No controls						
With controls	−$6,816[b]	−$430[b]				
Community colleges versus proprietary schools						
Vocational AA grads.	men	women				
No controls						
With controls	$1,381[b]	$8,304[b]				

TABLE 3–5 continued
Economic Attainment of Graduates of Community Colleges versus
High Schools and Other Two-Year Colleges[a]

	Grubb (1993, 1994a, b)		Lyke et al. (1991)	Goodwin (1989)	Somers et al. (1971)
	men	women			
Voc. certif. grads.					
No controls					
With controls	$5,009[b]	$1,447[b]			
Community colleges versus high schools only					
Vocational AA grads.	men	women			
No controls					
With controls	$1,298	$3,187*			
Voc. certif. grads.					
No controls					
With controls	–$6,000	$1,363			
Difference in Unemployment Rate					
Community colleges versus public postsecondary vocational schools					
College entrants					
No controls				4.3%[c]	
With controls				2.4%[c]	
All vocational grads.					
No controls					–4.4%
With controls					NA
Community colleges versus proprietary schools					
College entrants					
No controls				–9.3%	
With controls				–8.8%	

Notes:
* Statisticaly significant at the *p* less than 0.05 level.
a. See Appendix Table A3–5 for a description of the nature and sources of the data and a listing of the control variables.
b. Level of statistical significance not reported; only reported for comparison with those not entering college.
c. Positive difference means the unemployment rate is *higher* for community colleges.

Community College Compared with Stopping with High School

The question has been raised whether students benefit at all by attending community college rather than terminating their education with high school. No clear answer can be given, however, because the evidence is quite mixed, yielding at best a very slight edge to the community college.

At the most positive end, Kane and Rouse (1993) found that— comparing the yearly incomes of male and female high school graduates and socially similar community college students who had accumulated vocational credits or academic credits or both but no degrees—4 of the 6 comparisons favored community colleges, but only one was statistically significant.[20] Less positively, Grubb (1993, 1994a, b) made 20 different comparisons between male and female high school graduates and community college students who either had acquired vocational credits or academic credits but no degree or had received either a vocational certificate, vocational associate degree, or associate of arts degrees. He found that on 11 of these matchups community college students did better than high school graduates with similar backgrounds, high school performance, and job experience. However, only 6 of the 11 positive differences were statistically significant. On the remaining nine comparisons, community college students did no better or even worse than their high school counterparts. Grubb's figures also indicate that students—especially men—do worst if they secure vocational certificates rather than other degrees or even simply accumulate credits. Finally, at the more negative end of the continuum, Lyke et al. (1991) found that in three of four comparisons involving hourly and monthly income community college graduates did *worse* than socially similar high school graduates. However, none of these differences was statistically significant. (See Table 3–5.)

Interestingly, women apparently benefit more from community college attendance than do men. Across the 16 instances in the three studies above in which community college students made more money than comparable high school graduates, 10 of the comparisons involved women, while only 6 involved men.

Summary and Conclusions

Neither illusion nor illogic explains why the community college's critics and defenders are so opposed in, yet each so convinced about, their assessments of that institution's effects. The community college is quite contradictory in its effects, and each camp has grasped different parts of that manifold impact.

The critics and defenders are both correct on one point. As both claim, albeit in quite different tones, the community college has indeed protected the elite state universities from the onrushing tide of mass higher education. Without the community colleges, those universities probably would have had to become much larger and less selective in their admissions.

But past this point, the community college presents contradictory faces to its observers. For it responds but also reneges on the demands of the economy, and it retards as well as advances the prospects of students.

As both critics and defenders claim, the community college does respond to labor market demand, whether viewed—depending on one's ideological predilections—as the needs of society or the command of capital. The community college is indeed a central supplier of trained workers across a wide variety of "middle-level" or "semiprofessional" occupations. But its response to the labor market's call is much more clumsy than is acknowledged by both its defenders and critics. The community college often under- and overshoots the demands of the labor market: in many cases training far more people than the labor market can absorb and in other cases producing fewer workers than business would like. In short, the community college indeed dances to the rhythms of the labor market, but it rarely keeps very good time. As we will see in Section IV of the book, this loose coupling reflects the fact that the community college's vocational effort has been governed by nonmarket as well as market forces. In particular, community college officials and state elected officials have promoted occupational education for reasons apart from the demands of business or of students.

The community college also presents contradictory faces to students, for it closes as well as opens educational opportunity. Its instrumentalist Marxist and institutionalist critics are correct that students—particularly baccalaureate aspirants—do less well educationally and economically if they enter a community college than a four-year college. But its functionalist defenders also appear to be correct that the community college is superior to the four-year college in opening the doors of higher education to students generally and in facilitating the educational success of students who do not aspire to a baccalaureate. However, community colleges are apparently no better than public postsecondary vocational schools or proprietary schools in helping students advance economically.

Despite the mixed nature of these findings, it is important to underscore the finding that community college students—even if we restrict our focus to baccalaureate aspirants—secure significantly fewer baccalaureate degrees than four-year college entrants. This result is so cruel given the fact that so many students (particularly among working-class and minority youth) enter the community college in the belief that it will greatly assist their pursuit of the baccalaureate degree. In order to remove this obstacle, we need to determine precisely how the community college hinders the attainment of baccalaureate degrees. This is the task of the next chapter.

Appendix

APPENDIX TABLE A3–1

The Impact of Community College Tuition on College Choices

	Grubb (1988)	Corman, Davidson (1984)	Sulock (1982)
Control Variables			
Other Tuition Variables			
Average for four-year colleges			X
Average for public four-year colleges	X	X	
Average for private four-year colleges	X		
Average for noncollegiate postsecondary schools		X	
Labor Market Variables			
Difference in family income between head with B.A. and one with H.S. degree			X
Ratio of earnings of those with 13–15 years of education to those with 12	X		
Average earnings of 18–24-year-olds with 12 years of education	X		
Change in percentage of labor force in professional and managerial jobs	X		
General unemployment rate	X	X	
Ratio of unemployment rate for managers and professionals to clerical and craft workers		X	
Female labor force participation rate	X		
Per capita income		X	
Average hourly wage in manufacturing			X
Demographic Variables			
Percentage of population black	X		
Percentage of population Hispanic	X		
Percentage of population rural	X		
18–24-year-olds as a percentage of all people over 18		X	
Persons over 65 as a percentage of all people over 18		X	
Median family income			X
Other Variables			
Percentage of associate degrees in fields other than general or academic	X		
Community college enrollments 10 years before	X		
Private two-year college enrollments 10 years before	X		
Four-year college enrollments 10 years before	X		
Proximity of four-year colleges			X
How old community college is			X

Educational Attainment of Entrants to Two-Year and Four-Year Colleges

	Nunley, Breneman (1988)	Nunley, Breneman (1988)	Lavin, Crook (1990)	Velez (1985)	Anderson (1984)	Astin et al. (1982)
Study Attributes						
Data set used	NLS-72	NLS-72	CUNY	NLS-72	NLS-72	ACE
Year respondents began college	1972	1972	1970–72	1972	1972	1971
Year respondents followed up	1979	1979	1984	1979	1979	1980
Aspirations of respondents	any higher educ.	B.A. and above	any higher educ.	college academic program	college academic program	B.A. and above
Findings						
Percentage Attaining B.A.						
Four-year colleges						
Public and private	NA	NA		79.0%		73.0%[a]
Public only			73.0%			
State college only					NA	
Two-year colleges						
Public and private				31.0%		29.0%[a]
Public only	NA	NA			NA	
Community colleges			31.0%			
Differences						
No controls	NA	NA	42.0%	48.0%	23.9%	44.0%[a]
With controls	11.4%*	11.5%[b]	17.0%*	18.7%*	14.0%*	NA[c]
Average Years of Education Attained						
Four-year colleges						
Public and private	NA	NA				
State college only					14.49	
Two-year colleges						
Public	NA	NA			14.03	
Differences						
No controls	NA	NA			0.46	
With controls	0.12*	0.16[b]			0.25*	

Educational Attainment of Entrants to Two-Year and Four-Year Colleges

	Nunley, Breneman (1988)	Nunley, Breneman (1988)	Lavin, Crook (1990)	Velez (1985)	Anderson (1984)	Astin et al. (1982)
Control Variables						
Social Background						
Sex	X	X	X	X	X	X
Race	X	X	X	X	X	X
Socioeconomic status	X	X	X	X	X	X
Age			X			X
Language spoken at home	X	X				
Religion				X	X	
Marital status	X	X				
Location of home	X	X				
Kids while in college	X	X				
Married in college	X	X				
Aspirations						
Student's educational aspirations	X	X[d]	X	X	X	X[d]
Student's occupational aspirations					X	X
Parents' educational aspirations for respondent	X	X		X	X	
Peers' post–high school plans	X	X				
College decision date	X	X				
Student's perception of college ability	X	X	X		X	
Importance of general education			X			
High School Experiences						
Test scores				X	X	X
Grades or class rank	X	X	X	X	X	X
Curriculum or track	X	X	X	X	X	X
Hours spent on homework	X	X				
Hours spent at job	X	X				
Location of high school	X	X				
High school racial mix						X

Educational Attainment of Entrants to Two-Year and Four-Year Colleges

	Nunley, Breneman (1988)	Nunley, Breneman (1988)	Lavin, Crook (1990)	Velez (1985)	Anderson (1984)	Astin et al. (1982)
College Experience						
Enrollment status						
(FT/PT)	X					
Living arrangement	X	X		X		
Hours spent on campus	X	X	X			
Work on campus				X		
College program	X		X	X[e]	X[e]	
Number of remedial						
courses			X			
College grades	X			X		

Notes
* Statistically significant at the *p* less than 0.05 level.
a. Figures are for whites only. Does not report figures for all races together.
b. Level of statistical significance not reported; only reported for comparison with those not entering college.
c. Reports *partial correlations* between college type and attainment of a baccalaureate for five racial/ ethnic groups. The partial correlations for public two-year college entrants range from 0.01 to –0.20 (with four of five correlations significant at *p* less than 0.05), while the correlations for public four-year nonuniversity college entrants range from –0.08 to 0.08 (with only one being significant). See discussion in text.
d. The sample included only those aspiring to a baccalaureate degree.
e. The sample included only those in the academic program.

APPENDIX TABLE A3–3
Educational Attainment of Entrants to Community Colleges
Versus Other Two-Year Colleges

	Nunley, Breneman (1988)	Godfrey, Holmstrom (1970)	Grubb (1991, 1993)
Study Attributes			
Data sets used	NLS-72	own	HS & B
Year students began college	1972		1980
Year students ended college		1967	
Year students followed up	1979	1969	1984
Aspirations of students	B.A. or higher	any higher	any higher
Findings			
Percentage Attaining B.A.			
Community colleges	NA	37.9%	
Public vocational			
technical schools	NA	4.2%	
Differences			
No controls	NA	33.7%	
With controls	31.3%	NA	
Percentage Transferring			
to Four-Year Colleges			
Community colleges			20.2%
Public postsecondary			8.6%
vocational schools			
Proprietary schools			8.0%
Gap between community colleges			
& public postsec. voc. schools			
No controls			11.6%
With controls			NA
Gap between community colleges			
and proprietary schools			
No controls			12.2%
With controls			NA
Percentage Dropping Out			
Community colleges			42.0–45.9%
Public postsecondary			
vocational schools			46.5–50.1%
Proprietary schools			42.2–51.3%

APPENDIX TABLE A3–3 continued
Educational Attainment of Entrants to Community Colleges
Versus Other Two-Year Colleges

	Nunley, Breneman (1988)	Godfrey, Holmstrom (1970)	Grubb (1991, 1993)
Gap between community colleges & public postsec. voc. schools			
No controls			0.6–8.1%
With controls			NA
Gap between community colleges and proprietary schools			
No controls			0.2–9.3%
With controls			NA
Control variables			
Social Background			
Sex	X		
Race	X		
Socioeconomic status	X		
Language spoken at home	X		
Marital status	X		
Location of home	X		
Kids while in college	X		
Married in college	X		
Aspirations			
Student's educational aspirations	X		
Parents' educational aspirations for respondent	X		
Peers' post-high school plans	X		
College decision date	X		
Student's perception of college ability	X		
High School Experiences			
Grades or class rank	X		
Curriculum or track	X		
Hours spent on homework	X		
Hours spent at job	X		
Location of high school	X		
College Experience			
Living arrangement	X		
Hours spent at job	X		

Sources: Nunley and Breneman (1988: 80–81); Godfrey and Holmstrom (1970: 164, 129); Grubb (1993: 20–21).

Economic Attainment of Entrants to Community Colleges
Versus Four-Year Colleges

	Monk-Turner (1983)	Anderson (1984)	Grubb (1993, 1994a, b)[a]	Lavin, Hyllegard (1991)
Study Attributes				
Data set used	NLSME	NLS-72	NLS-72	CUNY
Year students began college	1966–68	1972	1972	1970–72
Year students followed up	1976–77	1979	1986	1984
Aspirations of students	any higher educ.	college academic program	any higher educ.	any higher educ.
Findings				
Mean Status of Current Occupation				
Entrants to four-year versus two-year public colleges				
Four-year colleges				
All types	61.1			
State colleges only		54.1		
Two-year colleges				
Public	49.3	48.7		
Graduates of four-year versus community colleges				
Four-year colleges				men women
Public B.A.'s				62.0 60.2
Community colleges				
All associates				54.2 52.9
Differences				
No controls	11.8	5.4		7.8 7.3
With controls	3.5*	2.4*		7.2[b] 5.8[b]
Mean Earnings in Current Job: Hourly				
Entrants to four-year versus two-year public colleges				
Four-year colleges				
State Colleges Only		$5.96		
Two-year colleges				
Public		$5.93		
Differences				
No controls		$0.03		
With controls		–$0.05		
Graduates of four-year				

APPENDIX TABLE A3–4 continued
Economic Attainment of Entrants to Community Colleges
Versus Four-Year Colleges

	Monk-Turner (1983)	Anderson (1984)	Grubb (1993, 1994a, b)[a]		Lavin, Hyllegard (1991)	
versus two-year public colleges						
Four-year colleges			men	women		
All B.A.'s			$10.30	$8.74		
Two year public colleges						
Vocational AAs			$ 9.59	$8.42		
Vocational certificates			$ 7.08	$8.42		
Differences between B.A.'s and two-year public college degrees						
No controls						
Vocational AAs						
Vocational certificates						
With controls						
Vocational AAs			$2.69[b]	$0.72[b]		
Vocational certificates			$4.49[b]	$2.52[b]		
Mean Earnings in Current Job: Yearly						
Graduates of four-year versus two-year public colleges						
Four-year colleges			men	women	men	women
All college B.A.'s			$34,208	$19,831		
Public college B.A.'s					$31,121	$24,020
Two-year public colleges						
All associates					$26,763	$21,055
Vocational AAs			$29,173	$19,075		
Vocational Certificates			$24,186	$17,700		
Differences between B.A.'s and two-year public college degrees						
No controls			men	women	men	women
All associates					$4,358	$2,965
Vocational AAs						
Vocational certificates						
With controls						
All associates					$5,533[b]	$2,571[b]
Vocational AAs			$ 4,268[b]	$1,454[b]		
Vocational certificates			$11,566[b]	$3,278[b]		

APPENDIX TABLE A3–4 continued
Economic Attainment of Entrants to Community Colleges
Versus Four-Year Colleges

	Monk-Turner (1983)	Anderson (1984)	Grubb (1993, 1994a, b)[a]	Lavin, Hyllegard (1991)
Control Variables				
Social Background				
Sex	X	X	X	X
Race	X	X	X	X
Socioeconomic status	X	X	X	X
Religion		X		
Location of home	X			
Size of hometown	X			
Marital status	X			
Aspirations				
Student's education aspirations	X	X		
Student's occupation aspirations		X		
Parents' educational aspirations for respondent		X		
Student's perception of own college ability		X		
High School Experiences				
Test scores	X	X	X	
Grades or class rank		X	X	
Curriculum or track		X		
College Experience				
College program		X		
Educational Attainment	X			
Occupational Traits				
Job experience	X		X	X
Hours worked per week	X			
Economic sector				X

Notes:
* Statistically significant at the .05 level.
a. Grubb's estimates of the net (after control) returns for different kinds of degrees are from his 1994a, b correction of mistakes in his 1992a and 1993 articles. The gross (before control) figures are from the 1993 article.
b. Level of statistical significance not reported; only reported for comparison with those not entering college.

Sources: Monk-Turner (1983: 395, 401); Anderson (1984: 17–18, 36, Tables 5 and 9); Grubb (1993: 24; 1994a, b); Lavin and Hyllegard (1991: Tables 5.3–5.5).

APPENDIX TABLE A3–5
Economic Attainment of Graduates of Community Colleges Versus High Schools and Other Two-Year Colleges[a]

	Grubb (1993, 1994a, b)[a]		Lyke et al. (1991)		Goodwin (1989)	Somers et al. (1971)
Study Attributes						
Data set used	NLS-72		HS & B		HS & B	own
Year students began college	1972		1980		1980–84	
Year left college						1966
Year followed up	1986		1986		1986	1969
Findings						
Mean Status of Current Job						
College graduates						
All vocational grads						
Comunity colleges						49.0
Public voc.-tech.						42.9
Gap between community colleges and public postsecondary voc. schools						
No controls						6.1
With controls						NA
Mean Current Earnings: Hourly						
	men	women	men	women		
High school only	$8.13	$6.25	$6.82	$5.46		
College entrants						
Community colleges					$7.03[b]	
Public voc.-tech.					$6.74[b]	
Proprietary					$8.59[b]	
College graduates						
All graduates			men	women		
Community colleges			$7.09	$6.06		
Public voc.-tech.			$7.31	$6.60		
Proprietary			$7.85	$6.47		
All vocational grads.						
Community colleges						$3.20
Public voc.-tech.						$2.70
Proprietary						NA
Vocational AA grads.	men	women				
Community colleges	$9.59	$8.42				
Public voc.-tech.	$8.62	$6.21				
Proprietary	$7.77	$6.24				
Voc. certif. grads.	men	women				
Community colleges	$7.08	$8.42				
Public voc.-tech.	$7.10	$7.22				
Proprietary	$8.93	$7.71				

Economic Attainment of Graduates of Community Colleges Versus High Schools
and Other Two-Year Colleges

	Grubb (1993, 1994a, b)[a]		Lyke et al. (1991)		Goodwin (1989)	Somers et al. (1971)
Gap between community colleges and high schools only						
All graduates	men	women	men	women		
No controls			$0.27	$0.60		
With controls			−$0.43	$0.11		
Vocational AA grads.						
No controls						
With controls	−$0.61	$1.32*				
Voc. certif. grads.						
No controls						
With controls	−$2.41	−$0.48				
Gap between community colleges and public postsecondary vocational schools						
College entrants						
No controls					$0.29	
With controls					$0.73*	
All graduates			men	women		
No controls			−$0.22	−$0.54		
With controls			−$0.49[c]	−$0.82[c]		
All vocational grads.						
No controls						$0.50
With controls						$0.29[c]
Vocational AA grads.	men	women				
No controls						
With controls	−$0.34[c]	$1.44[c]				
Voc. certif. grads.						
No controls						
With controls	−$2.72[c]	−$0.71[c]				
Gap between community colleges and proprietary schools						
College entrants						
No controls					−$1.56	
With controls					−$0.77	
All graduates			men	women		
No controls			−$0.76	−$0.41		
With controls			−$0.96[c]	−$0.61[c]		
Vocational AA grads.	men	women				
No controls						
With controls	$1.25[c]	$0.82[c]				

APPENDIX TABLE A3–5 continued
Economic Attainment of Graduates of Community Colleges Versus High Schools
and Other Two-Year Colleges

	Grubb (1993, 1994a, b)[a]		Lyke et al. (1991)	Goodwin (1989)	Somers et al. (1971)
	men	women			
Voc. certif. grads.					
No controls					
With controls	−$3.33[c]	−$1.50[c]			
Mean Current Earnings: Yearly					
	men	women			
High school grads. only	$24,006	$13,301			
College graduates					
Vocational AA grads	men	women			
Community colleges	$29,173	$19,075			
Public voc.-tech.	$26,171	$12,049			
Proprietary	$21,019	$7,042			
Voc. certif. grads.	men	women			
Community colleges	$24,186	$17,700			
Public voc.-tech.	$23,012	$19,453			
Proprietary	$27,763	$14,322			
Gap between community colleges and high schools only					
Vocational AA grads.	men	women			
No controls					
With controls	$1,298	$3,187*			
Voc. certif. grads.					
No controls					
With controls	−$6,000	$1,363			
Gap between community colleges and public postsecondary vocational schools					
Vocational AA grads.	men	women			
No controls					
With controls	−$1,148[c]	−$570[c]			
Voc. certif. grads.					
No controls					
With controls	−$6,816[c]	−$430[c]			
Gap between community colleges and proprietary schools					
Vocational AA grads.	men	women			
No controls					
With controls	$1,381[c]	$8,304[c]			
Voc. certif. grads.					
No controls					
With controls	$5,009[c]	$1,447[c]			

Economic Attainment of Graduates of Community Colleges Versus High Schools
and Other Two-Year Colleges

	Grubb (1993, 1994a, b)[a]	Lyke et al. (1991)	Goodwin (1989)	Somers et al. (1971)
Unemployment Rate				
College entrants				
Community colleges			17.0%[d]	
Public voc.-tech.			12.7%[d]	
Proprietary schools			26.3%[d]	
All vocational graduates				
Community colleges				3.3%[e]
Public voc.-tech.				7.7%[e]
Proprietary schools				NA
Gap between community colleges and public				
postsecondary vocational schools				
No controls			4.3%[f]	–4.4%
With controls			2.4%	NA
Gap between community colleges				
and proprietary schools				
No controls			–9.3%	
With controls			–8.8%	
Control Variables				
Social Background				
Sex	X	X	X	X
Race	X	X	X	X
Socioeconomic status	X	X	X	X
Age				X
Location of home		X	X	X
Size of hometown		X[g]		X
Marital status		X	X	X
Educational expectations			X	
Psychological orientation		X		
Military status		X[h]		
Prior military service		X[h]		
High School Experiences				
Test scores	X	X	X	
Grades or class rank	X	X		
High school program			X	
Cooperative educ. program			X	
High school diploma		X[g]		

Economic Attainment of Graduates of Community Colleges Versus High Schools
and Other Two-Year Colleges

	Grubb (1993, 1994a, b)[a]	Lyke et al. (1991)	Goodwin (1989)	Somers et al. (1971)
College Experience				
College program			X	X
Type of college degree			X	
Duration since left school			X	
Occupational Traits				
Worked during high school			X	
Worked before college			X	
Worked last college semester			X	
Job experience	X	X[h]		
Hours worked per week		X[h]		
Job relatedness of educ.				X
Nonschool job training	X	X[h]	X	
Labor Market Conditions				
Local unemployment rate			X	
Employment growth rate			X	
Average manufacturing wage			X	

Notes:
* Statistically significant at the .05 level.
a. Grubb's estimates of the net (after controls) returns for different kinds of degrees are from his 1994a, b correction of mistakes in his 1992a and 1993 articles. The gross (before control) figures are from the 1993 article. The returns for post-secondary vocational schools and proprietary schools must be taken as rather tentative given the small cell sizes involved.
b. Excludes students who took less than 15% of their postsecondary credits in vocational or technical courses.
c. Level of statistical significance not reported.
d. Unemployment is measured in terms of occurrence anytime in previous year.
e. Unemployment is measured in terms of incidence at time of survey.
f. Positive difference means that the rate is higher at community colleges.
g. Appears in monthly income equation only.
h. Appears in hourly income equation only.

Sources: Grubb (1993: 24; 1994a, b); Lyke et al. (1991: 27, 70, 72); Goodwin (1989: 61–69); Somers et al. (1971: 80, 86, 119, 134, 150).

CHAPTER 4

How Does the Community College Hinder
Baccalaureate Attainment?

The finding in Chapter 3 that baccalaureate aspirants secure less education and poorer jobs if they enter a community college rather than a four-year college is very troubling. We are talking about something that affects as many as one-third of all community college students (and one-ninth of all college students). For reasons both of scholarship and policy, we should try to find out precisely how this effect is produced. A clear understanding of the mechanisms generating this outcome bolsters our certainty that we are not dealing with a defective observation or a transient phenomenon. Moreover, it can guide us in removing the obstacles baccalaureate aspirants encounter when they enter the community college. (Specific policy recommendations are taken up in Chapter 15.)

As much as two-thirds of the baccalaureate gap described in Chapter 3 is explainable by the fact that community college students are more often working class, minority, female, less prepared academically, and less ambitious than four-year college students. But even after we control for these differences in student composition, community college entrants still receive 11 to 19% fewer baccalaureate degrees than *comparable* four-year college students (see Table 3–2 in Chapter 3).[1] Hence the popular tendency to dismiss the gap in baccalaureate attainment between community college and four-year college students as simply a product of their different backgrounds simply will not suffice. We must move beyond an individualistic analysis to also examine the impact of more structural factors.

In this chapter, I will offer an "institutional obstacles" theory of why baccalaureate aspirants garner less education if they first enter a community college rather than a four-year college. I will examine the contributions of the institution of the community college and the system of higher education to creating this baccalaureate gap.

I conceive of community college students' progress toward the baccalaureate as consisting of a series of clearly predictable crises that students must negotiate in order to continue. For this concept, I draw on

Rosenbaum's (1976) concept of "tournament mobility." He describes the career of high school students in the college prep track as involving a series of trials. If students survive one, they only secure passage to the next. But if they fail at any point, they are forced out of the tournament (that is, out of the college prep track). I modify Rosenbaum's concept to make failure less damning: if one fails to succeed at a certain stage one is not thereby forbidden from ever pursuing the baccalaureate. But I do retain his notion that the student career has certain essential stages that cannot be skipped but must be negotiated in order to reach the desired end.

In order to attain a baccalaureate degree, a community college entrant has to survive the following trials (these are described in brief here and developed in depth below):

1. Staying in college during the first two years, when dropout is at its highest. As it happens, community college entrants suffer a higher dropout rate in the first two years than do comparable four-year college entrants. One institutional reason is that community college students receive less financial aid than four-year college students. In addition, community colleges are less able than four-year colleges to integrate their students into the academic and social life of the institution. Two primary reasons are community colleges' lack of dormitories and their lower academic selectivity and thus weaker expectations for students.

2. Transferring to a four-year college. Unfortunately, even if community college entrants survive the first one or two years of college, they are less likely to continue on to the upper division of four-year colleges than comparable four-year college entrants. Two reasons stand out. Even if they enter the community college aspiring to transfer, community college entrants less often try to move on to the upper division, and even if they do try, they less often succeed in doing so. Community college entrants are less likely to try to move up to the junior and senior year than four-year natives because transfer involves a difficult move to a new and foreign institution and potential transfer students receive too little encouragement from community colleges. But even if they still make the effort, would-be transfers less often succeed in moving up because they find it harder to secure financial aid and because they are more often turned away by four-year colleges.

3. After transferring to a four-year college, surviving there. Even after transfer, community college entrants are at risk, dropping out more often than comparable four-year college entrants. Key causes are their difficulty in becoming integrated academically and socially into four-

year colleges. Community college transfers are less well prepared by the community college for upper-division work. And their social integration is hindered by their difficulty in receiving financial aid, their greater need to work, and the poor efforts of four-year colleges to incorporate them socially.

Let us review each of these crises in depth, examining how various institutional impediments crop up in turn as community college students try to fight their way toward the baccalaureate degree.

Attrition in the Freshman and Sophomore Years

The first years in the community college are lethal to the hopes of many baccalaureate aspirants. Several studies, using a variety of data sources, show that community colleges suffer higher rates of dropout from higher education than four-year colleges.[2] For example, the High School and Beyond survey of 1982 high school graduates found that 42.6% of those entering two-year colleges (public and private) had by 1986 left higher education without receiving a degree. Meanwhile, the comparable figure for four-year college entrants was 30.6% (U.S. National Center for Education Statistics, 1990: 19–20).

A good part of this difference is attributable to the lower aspirations and social and academic disadvantages of community college entrants (Cohen and Brawer, 1989: 54–57). Community college students are disproportionately working class, nonwhite, or academically weak, and these are the very students most likely to drop out of a community college (Astin, 1972; U.S. National Center for Education Statistics, 1977b: 22, 135–136, 150; idem, 1989b: 5). Moreover, many community college dropouts are simply people who do not intend to go on for a four-year college degree or even to secure a community college associate's degree or vocational certificate. They may want to take only one or two courses for purposes of personal exploration or occupational upgrading and leave college once they have achieved this limited ambition (Cohen and Brawer, 1989: 55–57, 60; Grubb, 1991; Riesman, 1980: 186–189).[3]

But several studies show that the divergences in background and interests between community colleges and four-year colleges cannot fully account for the gap in attrition. A sizable gap remains even after one compares students who are similar in their prematriculation characteristics. It is this divergence among institutions that remains after we have factored out differences in student composition that I would like to explain here.

An analysis of the National Longitudinal Survey of the High School Class of 1972 (NLS-72) found that 32.3% of students entering public two-year colleges in fall 1972 with the aim of eventually securing a baccalaureate degree had dropped out of higher education by fall 1974. Meanwhile, the comparable figure for four-year college entrants was 20.2% (U.S. National Center for Education Statistics, 1977b: 22–26, 50–51, 74, 135–136, 191–192, 197–198). This gap does not disappear even if a wide array of control variables is used. Looking at NLS-72 entrants to academic programs in two-year and four-year colleges, Kristine Anderson (1981) found that—even with controls for family background, educational and occupational aspirations, high school record, whether students worked in college, and whether they lived on campus—fall 1972 two-year college entrants were 5% less likely than four-year college entrants to still be enrolled in an academic program in fall 1973 and 14% less likely to be so enrolled in fall 1974 (Anderson, 1981: 9–12).[4] These results are reported in Table 4–1 and the control variables are listed in Appendix Table A4–1.

Alexander Astin (1975) replicated these findings from the NLS-72 using a different data set. In 1972, he followed up students who in 1968 had filled out the annual freshman survey administered by the American Council on Education. He found that male and female community college entrants were 10% and 18%, respectively, more likely to drop out of higher education than their four-year counterparts. This gap occurred despite controlling for differences between the two- and four-year entrants in sex, race, socioeconomic status, religion, educational aspirations, and high school record.

 The evidence above clearly demonstrates that the greater dropout rate of community college students is not due just to their more modest backgrounds and academic aptitudes. Something about community colleges causes greater attrition even when we control for the ways in which their students differ from those entering four-year colleges. But what precise features of the community college cause this institutional effect?

Answers to this question are still incomplete, because almost all research on dropouts has focused on those withdrawing from four-year colleges (Astin, 1975, 1977; Pantages and Creedon, 1978; Pascarella and Terenzini, 1991; Spady, 1970, 1971; Tinto, 1975, 1987). But this research does provide us with a useful framework for analyzing the community college's impact on attrition.

One simple, but important, institutional factor is that community college students receive less financial aid than four-year college students, despite being poorer (Breneman and Nelson, 1981; Grubb and Tuma, 1991; Orfield et al., 1984: 25, 288). The National Postsecondary Student Aid Study found that in 1986 only 28.5% of public two-year college

TABLE 4–1

Differences in Attrition from Higher Education Experienced by Entrants to
Two-Year and Four-Year Colleges

	U.S. National Center for Education Statistics (1990)	Ibid.	U.S. National Center for Education Statistics (1977b)	Ibid.	Astin (1975)	Anderson (1981)[a]
Study Attributes						
Data set used	HS & B		NLS-72		ACE	NLS-72
Year began college	1982		1972		1968	1972
Year followed up	1986		1974		1972	1973–74
Aspirations	any higher education	B.A. and above	any higher education	B.A. and above	B.A. and above	college academic program
Findings						
Differences at End of One Year						
No controls			13.6%	7.9%		NA
With controls			NA	NA		5.0%**
Difference at End of Two Years						
No controls			15.8%	12.1%		NA
With controls			NA	NA		14.0%**
Difference at End of Four Years						
No controls	12.0%	4.4%			18.4% (men) 27.3% (women)	
With controls	NA	NA			10.0%[b] (men) 18.0%[b] (women)	

Notes:
** Significant at .01 level.
 a. Anderson counts as withdrawal not only dropping out of higher education but also moving out of the academic program into the vocational program.
 b. No significance level reported.

students received any student aid from nonfamilial sources, whether public or private, whereas the comparable percentages for students attending public universities and public nonuniversity four-year colleges were 46.8% and 47.3%, respectively (U.S. National Center for Education Statistics, 1989a: 286). This 18 to 19% gap in receipt of student aid drops when one controls for tuition costs, family background, race, sex, age, and aspirations. But at the end it still remains quite sizable: 12.1% (Grubb and Tuma, 1991: 373).[5]

Another powerful institutional factor is that community colleges are less able than four-year colleges to integrate their students into the academic and social life of the institution. Tinto (1975, 1987) holds that dropout decisions are most immediately the product of a breakdown in commitment to staying at a given college (in the case of withdrawal from an institution) or in commitment to securing a college degree (in the case of dropout from the higher education system as a whole). This breakdown in turn is precipitated by inadequate *academic integration* (marked by poor college grades, low attendance, weak academic contact with teachers and students, and lack of a sense that one is developing intellectually) and poor *social integration* (evidenced by low participation in extracurricular activities, little extra-academic contact with faculty, and few friends on campus).[6]

Various studies demonstrate that community colleges indeed do not integrate their students socially and academically as strongly as do four-year colleges. Socially, community college students are much less involved in extracurricular activities and have less extra-academic contact with faculty and peers (Chapman and Pascarella, 1983: 316). Although this in good part reflects the attitudes and interests of community college students themselves, it also reflects the nature of the institution. The most important institutional feature is that community colleges very rarely afford their students the opportunity to live on campus, whereas the majority of four-year colleges do. An analysis of the 1986 National Postsecondary Student Aid Study found that only 1.9% of public two-year college students live in school-owned housing, whereas the comparable percentages are 30.2% for public doctoral-granting universities and 46.5% for private doctoral universities (Choy and Gifford, 1990: C5–7). Living on campus has been found to have a significant positive effect on students' persistence into the sophomore year, even with controls for student background, aspirations, and high school achievement and various characteristics of the college (Anderson, 1981: 12; idem, 1984: 15–18; idem, 1988: 173; Astin, 1975: 91–92, 165–168; idem, 1977: 109, 217; Pascarella and Terenzini, 1991: 400, 402, 419; Velez, 1985: 196–197).

On-campus residence powerfully contributes to student social integration into collegiate life by fostering wider contact with faculty and other students, greater participation in extracurricular activities, and deeper satisfaction with campus life. This greater social integration in turn promotes greater commitment to staying at the institution for the full course and securing a degree. Campus residence fosters this effect in good part by weakening home and neighborhood obligations and allegiances, which often divert time and energy from schoolwork. More positively, campus residence exposes students more to fellow students and college faculty and thus enhances involvement in college activities (Astin, 1977; Pascarella and Chapman, 1983a, 1983b; Pascarella and Terenzini, 1991: 400, 402; Tinto, 1975: 107, 109–110; Velez, 1985: 198–199).[7]

Community colleges also less strongly integrate their students academically than do four-year colleges. To be sure, community college students report more contact with their teachers than do many four-year college students, and their grades are comparable.[8] However, community college students are more surrounded by an institutional culture that discourages good academic work than are four-year college students. Consider, for example, a conversation that sociologist Howard London had with a student while doing fieldwork in a northeastern urban community college:

> Frank tells me [London] Larry is generally disliked by "the guys" even though he used to be part of their group. He complains Larry now studies too much, that he takes school as if it were the "only thing around."
>
> Frank: "He's pushy and always browning the teachers."
> London: "What do you mean, he's pushy?"
> Frank: "He doesn't want to go to U_____ [the state university]. He wants to go to _____ or _____ [small private colleges with excellent reputations]. Do you think he can get in there?"
> London: "I don't know, really."
> Frank: "Well if he does, bye-bye Larry. Have a good time." (London, 1978: 102–103)

Student characteristics certainly play a role in generating this antiacademic student culture. Many working-class and minority students are quite ambivalent about higher education. They may want to do well, but they are also afraid of failing. Furthermore, they tend to view academic success as requiring them to take on the culture of an alien group and to repudiate (and be repudiated by) their family and peers. Hence, working-class and minority students often develop powerful norms against taking academic work seriously (Brint and Karabel, 1989: 180; London, 1978: chaps. 3–4; Neumann and Riesman, 1980: 58; Weis, 1985: 102, 122, 134–137, 153–154).[9]

At the same time, community colleges play a role in this process. They are less selective academically because of their open-door admissions policy. This goal is admirable, but it has an unanticipated consequence: it causes lower persistence. Several studies have pointed to the positive impact of college selectivity on persistence, even when controlling for student traits and other college characteristics (Anderson, 1984: 15–17, 33, 36; Astin et al., 1982: 101–102; Cohen and Brawer, 1982: 55–56; Pascarella and Terenzini, 1991: 374–375; Tinto, 1975: 114–115). This selectivity effect occurs on two fronts. As noted above, low selectivity means that community colleges take in many students who are not terribly interested in academics and discourage those who are. This factor is then amplified by the fact that community college teachers, noting the low academic interest of the bulk of their students, lose their motivation to encourage the academic interest of all but a few students.

Many observers have noted that community college teachers tend to have low expectations of their students, perceiving them as largely lacking academic ability and motivation (Brint and Karabel, 1989: 179; Cohen and Brawer, 1989: 65, 82–84, 242; London, 1978: chaps. 2, 5; Neumann and Riesman, 1980: 61; Richardson and Bender, 1987: 36; Seidman, 1985; Slutsky, 1978: 9; Weis, 1985: 84, 89–90, 93). For example, a survey of community college humanities instructors in 1975 found that only 12% rated their students' enthusiasm for learning as excellent and 39% put it as fair or poor (Cohen and Brawer, 1977: 139, 148). And another nationwide survey of community science instructors found that—when asked, "What would it take to make yours a better course?"—over half responded, "Students better prepared to handle course requirements" (Brawer and Friedlander, 1979: 32). And this attitude has continued to this day. A nationwide survey of college faculty in 1989 found that 85% of two-year faculty agreed with the statement that "the undergraduates with whom I have close contact are seriously underprepared in basic skills" and 73% endorsed the statement that "this institution spends too much time and money teaching students what they should have learned in high school" (Carnegie Foundation for the Advancement of Teaching, 1990: 25). (The equivalent percentages for four-year faculty were 70% and 65%, respectively.)

These assessment have a good bit of truth, and they have prompted community college faculty and administrators to make admirable efforts to remedy the academic deficiencies of their students. But this disappointment in students also breeds actions that deepen the problem. To blunt the sharp edge of their frustration, many community college teachers concentrate on reaching a few students and largely give up on the rest (London, 1978:

chaps. 2, 5; Weis, 1985: 84–93). Two teachers interviewed by Howard London (1978: 117, 143) conveyed this attitude of unhappy resignation:

> [A history teacher:] "The thing that was most *shocking* about the year I was here. . . . was to deal with students to whom the concept of college was alien, to deal with students who *really* didn't understand what college was all about, to deal with students who didn't just apply high school standards to what was going on, but applied poor high school—lower-level high school—standards to what was going on." [A social science teacher:] "I think that if I didn't rationalize I would probably go stark, raving loony at times. . . . And the only thing that saves me are my better students. . . . I know that if I couldn't relate to the better students I would quit. I would have resigned, because I would not have been helping even them."

The sad irony is that these low expectations feed a self-fulfilling prophecy. In a process well described by labeling theorists within the sociology of education (Rist, 1973; Persell, 1977), low expectations tend to lead teachers to withdraw attention and praise from poorer students, which in turn reinforces the very poverty of the student performance that is being decried. Demoralized teachers not only teach badly but also tend to provoke students to react to teachers' restricted expectations by curtailing their own effort and treating teachers and courses with disrespect (London, 1978; Weis, 1985: 106–108).

Although pernicious in their effects, community college teachers' diminished expectations for their students are an all-too-human response to difficult circumstances. Their low expectations reflect the difficulty of teaching students who arrive at college bereft of many of the skills that colleges traditionally expect and that make teaching go smoothly. As Howard Becker (1952) pointed out, good students make teachers feel good themselves. Thus when faced with poor students, teachers find it hard to keep up their self-esteem. A very frequent defense is to find fault with the students. Community college teachers' unhappiness with their students' abilities also reflects the low status assigned by society and the academy to colleges dealing with nontraditional students (Cohen and Brawer, 1987: 78, 80, 85; Neumann and Riesman, 1980: 61). A community college teacher has written eloquently about this:

> Like their students, community-college teachers are stereotyped as second-rate laborers in the college hierarchy. . . . Community-college professors teach the production-line introductory courses to a total of 250 to 300 students, while university professors may have as few as 75 to 100 students, as well as the freedom to develop unusual courses, frequent sabbaticals, and time for creative research. "I feel like a leper," one Oregon community-college professor admitted at a conference. (Bauman, 1990)

Bauman's commendable reaction to such stigmatization has been to challenge it by celebrating the rich variety of his nontraditional students. But for many of his colleagues a very natural way to neutralize this "spoiled identity" is to displace the sense of stigma onto students.

Although we have moved down to social-psychological causes of the greater attrition among community college students, we have to remain firmly aware that they are anchored in institutional realities: particularly, the community college's lack of dormitories and consequently weak social integration of its students, and its unselective admissions policy and consequently weak academic integration. This effect of an open-door admissions policy does not mean that community colleges should abandon it. Far from it: it is one of the glories of the community college. But we do need to find ways to neutralize its harmful side-effects. Possible solutions to this and other institutional problems of the community college are discussed at length in Chapter 15.

Failure to Transfer to Four-Year Colleges

Even when community college entrants survive the early college years, they move on to the junior year in four-year colleges at a lower rate than do four-year college natives. The best estimate of the transfer rate of community college entrants is around 15 to 20%.[10] This transfer rate is much lower than the continuation rate for four-year college natives. The NLS-72 indicates that 76.4% of those who entered four-year colleges in fall 1972 were still enrolled in fall 1974 (U.S. National Center for Education Statistics, 1977a: 6–9, 72–74; idem, 1977b: 22–26, 191–192).[11] This discrepancy in continuation rates particularly hurts female, minority, and working-class students because they depend disproportionately on the community college for access to higher education (see Chapter 1) (Nora and Rendon, 1990: 237; Orfield et al., 1984; Rendon, 1992: 2).

But defenders of the community college point to this very concentration of disadvantaged students in the community college to justify the difference in continuation on to the upper division between community college and university entrants. They note—and research backs them up (Grubb, 1991: 206; Holmstrom and Bisconti, 1974: 71–76, 79–86; Lee and Frank, 1990; U.S. National Center for Education Statistics, 1977a: 28, 32, 70, 73; Van Alstyne, Henderson, Fletcher, and Sien, 1973: 1–5; Velez and Javalgi, 1987: 86)—that students who are female, working class, nonwhite, or have weak high school academic records are both more common in community colleges and less likely to transfer to four-year colleges.

However, this rebuttal is not fully convincing. It seems quite unlikely that controlling for these differences in student body characteristics will wipe out the gap in rates of continuation on to the upper division. For instance, if we restrict our analysis to students who are likely prospects for upper-division work—they aspired to a baccalaureate degree on entering college *and* have survived the first two years of college—we still find a considerable discrepancy in continuation. In the NLS-1972, 96.2% of four-year college entrants fitting these criteria were still in college in fall 1974 (two years after entering college), but only 49.3% of similar two-year college entrants had transferred to a four-year college by then (U.S. National Center for Education Statistics, 1977a: 8, 11, 13; idem, 1977b: 135–136, 50–51).[12] Such a sizable remaining gap suggests that institutional as well as individual student factors are also at work.

But even that part of the continuation gap that is attributed by the community college's defenders to students' background quite likely also reflects the operation of institutional causes. As we will see below, the lower transfer rate of disadvantaged students stems not just from their tendency to be less motivated and prepared academically but also the tendency of four-year colleges and community colleges to respond to disadvantaged students in ways that interfere with their chances to transfer.[13]

So what are these institutional factors that interfere with transfer? What characteristics of the community college and the higher education system hinder students' passage from two- to four-year colleges? The impediments lie in two areas. Many community college baccalaureate aspirants fail to transfer because their desire to do so is diminished ("cooled out") or not encouraged (not "warmed up"). And even if students still wish to transfer, they often are denied financial aid or even turned away by four-year colleges.

Students lose their desire to transfer in part because transfer involves a difficult readjustment. Community college entrants have to move to a new school, perhaps in a different community, where they might stay only two or three years (Zwerling, 1976: 240n). Four-year college entrants find no such chasm lying between their sophomore and junior years. Moving from the lower to the upper division is simply a matter of registering for the next semester's classes at what now is a familiar institution. Hence, four-year college natives need very little encouragement from their college teachers and counselors to continue into the junior year.

But far from arming their students to cross the moat, most community colleges provide little encouragement to their baccalaureate aspirants.

Baccalaureate aspirants entering the community college fail to have their transfer hopes strongly bolstered and in fact are pulled in the opposite direction by the community college's strong promotion of vocational education.

Various studies testify to the negative impact that an emphasis on vocational education has on transfer rates. The California state community college board has found that vocationally oriented community colleges have significantly lower transfer rates to the University of California than transfer-oriented community colleges, even controlling for differences in student body composition (race and grades) and proximity to the university (California Community Colleges, 1984: 17–19). Similarly, using the 1979 follow-up of the NLS-72, Anderson (1984: 16–17) found that two-year and four-year colleges that offer a high proportion of vocational majors tend to rank low in the proportion of their students achieving a baccalaureate degree, even when differences among the colleges in average student background and high school and college achievement are controlled. And at the systemic level, Grubb (1989) found that the more vocational a state's community college system was (as measured by the proportion vocational of its associate degree output in 1970–1971), the lower the proportion of its high school graduates receiving baccalaureate degrees 10 years later, even with controls for differences between states in their population composition and labor market conditions. This negative association was statistically significant in the case of women but not of men (Grubb, 1989: 367).

In what ways has the growing vocationalization of the community college weakened transfer? One way is by drawing more students into programs that largely do not encourage transfer. Another is by demoralizing the academic programs that do encourage transfer.

Community colleges have attracted many students who enter with baccalaureate ambitions or are undecided into vocational-education programs because they are seductively packaged and aggressively promoted. Community colleges spread before students a vast array of well-designed vocational programs in attractive fields such as radiologic technology, computer operations, and engineering technology. They give these vocational-education programs new facilities. They blur the distinction between academic and vocational-education programs by housing their faculty together and requiring the same prerequisites (Harris and Grede, 1977: 382–385). They proclaim that vocational-education graduates do as well as baccalaureates (although the evidence is to the contrary). And they market vocational programs with extensive commentary in college catalogs and in brochures that are numerous, visible, and glossy, in contrast to the often paltry, poorly displayed, and low-quality advertisements for transfer programs (Richardson and Bender, 1987: 40; Orfield et al., 1984: 216). (For more on this, see Chapter 11.) Richard Richardson and Louis Bender (1987) vividly describe the press in favor of vocational education:

> In one college that served a large minority clientele, a small bulletin board in an obscure corner of the counseling center displayed several dated announcements from four-year institutions. . . . In more prominent locations around the center and on bulletin boards at the entrance were displayed many attractive materials on career opportunities, job placement, and personal development. . . . In another college a large display rack, prominently located in the counseling center, had more than sixty brightly colored brochures, each describing a different occupational program. (Richardson and Bender, 1987: 40)

Once in vocational programs, students are not strongly encouraged to consider transfer. The main goal of these programs is still to prepare students for immediate employment. The teachers and administrators in these programs are often recruited from the trades for which they train students and have relatively little interest in and knowledge about transfer.

This is not to say that enrolling in a vocational program is an insurmountable hurdle to transferring. As several commentators have pointed out, many community college vocational students do transfer to four-year colleges, particularly in California (Cohen and Brawer, 1989: 217; Palmer, 1990: 22). Among 1980 community college entrants involved in the High School and Beyond Survey, 23.2% of those who received a vocational associate's degree and 6.7% of those receiving a vocational certificate ended up transferring to a four-year college by spring 1984 (Grubb, 1991: 200–201).[14] But if pursuing a vocational degree is not an *absolute* impediment to transferring, it is still a *relative* impediment. The same analysis of the High School and Beyond survey also finds that students completing vocational associate's degrees are less than half as likely to transfer as those with academic associate's degrees: 23.2% versus 48.9% (Grubb, 1991: 200–201). Similarly, Crook and Lavin (1989) found that community college students who enrolled in vocational-education programs in the community colleges of the City University of New York were 13% less likely to eventually receive a baccalaureate degree than those who enrolled in a liberal arts curriculum, even with controls for students' background, aspirations, and abilities at college entrance, college freshman grades, number of remedial courses taken in college, and employment record in college.

But a community college's commitment to vocational education undercuts transfer not just by drawing students into vocational education but also by demoralizing the academic program. As the community college has steadily increased its interest in and spending on vocational education over the last three decades, it has also stopped mentioning transfer as an important option. Students have not been strongly intro- duced to the idea and given adequate preparation. The liberal arts curricu- lum has steadily shriveled, with many fields abandoned and sophomore or postintroductory courses becoming rare (Cohen and Brawer, 1989: 288– 296, 304–305; Richardson and Bender, 1987: 38–39). As a result, fewer students have been getting the academic associate degree, the traditional route to the baccalaureate. Instead, they "mill" around with no particular major or direction (Grubb, 1991: 202, 213).[15]

But even if they take liberal arts courses, students still receive little encouragement to transfer. Many of those who teach these courses have lost interest in encouraging transfer (Zwerling, 1976: 229). A 1984 nationwide survey of 347 faculty teaching primarily *college transfer courses* at 24 community colleges nationwide found that only 19.2% believed that "the primary function of the community college should be to prepare students for transfer to four-year colleges or universities" and only 34.1% agreed with the statement that "first time freshmen in commu- nity colleges should be encouraged to earn, at the very least, the baccalau- reate degree" (Cohen and Brawer, 1987: 81–82; Cohen, Brawer, and Bensimon, 1985: 71, 82, 88). This lack of faculty and administrative interest in transfer has had a clear behavioral impact. The faculty survey described above found that only 27% of community college faculty hold frequent meetings with students to discuss transfer, and only 33% know their students' transfer intentions (Cohen, Brewer, and Bensimon, 1985: 78–82). Students corroborate that faculty and staff have provided them with little encouragement to transfer. A companion survey of 1,613 students at the same 24 community colleges nationwide found that only 38% reported that their instructors had played an important role in providing information on transfer opportunities, only 21% took part in orientation activities for potential transfers, and only 21% met with college recruiters. In 55% of these cases of nonparticipation, the reason students gave for not taking part was not lack of interest or time but lack of awareness that orientation and other activities were available (Cohen, Brawer, and Bensimon, 1985: 82, 122, 124).[16]

But even if community college entrants retain a desire to transfer, they encounter several obstacles to actualizing this goal. As two-year colleges, community colleges do not control an upper division to which they can pass on whom they wish. Rather, they depend on four-year colleges to accept their transfer students. And there is evidence that four-year colleges are less willing to take in community college transfers than to admit freshmen, especially if those would-be transfers are in vocational programs and/or largely minority community colleges (Brint and Karabel, 1989: 172; Richardson and Bender, 1987: 81; Willingham and Findikyan, 1969: 5–6, 25; Zwerling, 1976: 247–249).[17] Universities' distaste for community college transfer students does not take the form only of simple denial of admission. It also shows up in the poorer financial aid they typically give transfer students than new freshmen and continuing students (Brint and Karabel, 1989: 172–173; Sandeen and Goodale, 1976: 7; Zwerling, 1976: 246). According to the NLS-72, students who transferred from two-year colleges received fewer scholarships and other grants than students who initially entered four-year colleges (19.3% versus 38.9%), although they received as many loans (22.1% versus 23.8%) (U.S. National Center for Education Statistics, 1977a: 34).[18] This aid gap has an impact. A study of transfer applicants to the University of California who were accepted but did not matriculate (19% of those accepted) found that a major reason was finances (Baratta and Apodaca, 1984: 6). Meanwhile, a survey of minority transfers with high GPAs found that one-third could not have transferred if they had not received a scholarship (Pincus and Archer, 1989: 34).

Even when four-year institutions are committed to accepting transfers, as in the case of the University of California, this does not mean that transfer students are home free. Eligible students may still be denied admission to the campus of their choice because of insufficient room in the junior year, particularly in highly popular majors. And if offered an alternative campus, many accepted transfer students refuse either because the second campus has different requirements or because they cannot move due to family and other obligations (California Postsecondary Education Commission, 1989: 7; Illinois Community College Board, 1989: 8).

Attrition after Transfer

Even after transferring to four-year colleges, community college entrants are still at greater risk of failing to secure a baccalaureate than are four-year natives. Several studies—some national and some specific to large states such as California, Florida, Illinois, and Pennsylvania—have found that community college transfers have a high rate of attrition, one that is considerably higher than that for four-year college natives entering the junior year. Within one year of transfer, about one-fifth of community college transfers have been felled. And five years after transfer, about two-fifths of transfer students have left higher education without a baccalaureate degree. Meanwhile, the comparable percentage for four-year college natives entering the junior year the same year as the community college transfers is about one-quarter after five years. These patterns emerge clearly in Table 4–2. (For more information on the studies, see Appendix Table A4–2.)

A good part of this difference in dropout rate is no doubt due to the lower average aptitude and weaker motivation of two-year college transfers compared with four-year natives. For example, only 37.8% of transfers participating in the NLS-72 were in the top quartile in academic aptitude, versus 53.5% of four-year juniors (U.S. National Center for Education Statistics, 1977a: 32, 70–75). But these student-centered factors are unlikely to explain the entirety of this difference. Other evidence indicates that several features of the U.S. higher education system contribute to the higher mortality of community college transfers.[19] Compared with four-year college natives, transfer students less often receive financial aid, their lower-division credits are less often recognized by senior colleges, and they are not as well integrated socially and academically into four-year colleges. Let us review each of these factors in turn.

As stated in the section on transfer difficulties, transfer students less often receive financial aid than native four-year college students (U.S. National Center for Education Statistics, 1977a: 34). Moreover, transfer students transferring between the fall and spring semesters often find that, even when they do receive financial aid, this aid is not increased to reflect the sharp increase in tuition and living expenses accompanying the move to a four-year college (Richardson and Bender, 1987: 56–57, 112). This gap in financial aid increases the probability that transfer students will have to withdraw for lack of money. This is the main reason given by transfer students who withdraw of their own volition (Knoell and Medsker, 1965: 71). In addition, as we will see below, lack of financial aid hinders transfer students' academic and social integration into four-year colleges.

A sizable number of transfer students lose credits in transit to four-year colleges, thus slowing their educational progress and endangering their ability to finance their college career (Cohen and Brawer, 1989: 54; Pincus and DeCamp, 1989; Richardson and Bender, 1987: 80).[20] A recent study of community college transfers at nine urban universities across the country found that 58% reported losing credits in transferring, with 29% losing 10 or more credits. In addition, 25% reported that even when the university gave them credit for certain courses, those credits were not counted toward their majors. For 11%, this loss of major credit involved 10 or more credits (Richardson and Bender, 1987: 148). Similarly, a

TABLE 4–2
Attrition at Four-year Colleges for Transfers from
Two-Year Colleges and Four-Year College Natives[a]

	U.S. National Center Educ. Stats. (1977b)	Holmstrom, Bisconti (1974)	California Community Colleges (1984)[b]	Florida State Educ. Dept. (1983)[c]	Illinois Community College Board (1986b)	Martinko (1978)
Study Attributes						
Population covered	U.S.	U.S.	Calif.	Fla.	Ill.	Penn.
Data set used	NLS-72	ACE	own	own	own	own
Year respondents began college	1972	1968	NA	NA	NA	NA
Year respondents transferred	1973	NA	1975	1976	1979	1976
Year respondents were followed up	1974	1972	1980	1978	1984	1977
Findings						
Percentage Dropping Out within One Year after Transfer						
Two-year college transfers	17.7%		27.8%	16.9%	24.3%	18.0%
Four-year college native juniors				8.0%		
Percentage Dropping Out within Two Years after Transfer						
Two-year college transfers		14.3%		32.0%	34.1%	
Four-year college native juniors				19.8%		
Percentage Dropping Out within Three Years after Transfer						
Two-year college transfers					39.0%	
Percentage Dropping Out within Four Years after Transfer						
Two-year college transfers					42.0%	
Percentage Dropping Out within Five Years after Transfer						
Two-year college transfers			35.6%		43.2%	
Four-year college native juniors			23.9%			

Notes

a. See Appendix Table A4–2 for a description of the nature and sources of the data.

b. The California data compare fall 1975 transfers to the California State University system (CSU) who came in as juniors and CSU natives who became juniors the same year.

c. The Florida data are for fall 1976 transfers to three state universities who came in as juniors and for university natives who became juniors at the same time.

recent study of transfers from Maryland community colleges found that 6% lost 13 or more credit hours (that is, at least one semester) (Maryland State Board for Community Colleges, 1983: 12). And several national studies conducted during the 1960s discovered that 10 to 12% of community college transfers lost at least a semester's worth of credits (Godfrey and Holmstrom, 1970: 167; Knoell and Medsker, 1965: 61; Willingham and Findikyan, 1969: 30).

This credit loss appears to be particularly pronounced among students transferring from community college vocational programs. Students transferring with academic courses are often protected by state requirements that public universities accept community college general education courses (Bender, 1990: 9; Illinois Community College Board, 1989: 21; Kintzer, 1989: 15).[21] But nongeneral education courses get much tougher scrutiny. They are more often denied any credit or they are counted only toward free electives rather than major requirements. Vocational courses receive a particularly unfriendly response from universities. In the City University of New York system, an evaluation by the senior colleges of the entire course offerings of the community colleges in the system found that only 48% of vocational courses, but 90% of liberal arts courses, were transferrable. Also, whereas 63% of liberal arts credits met degree requirements, only 23% of vocational credits did as well (Bowles, 1988: 29–31).

Credit loss stems from several sources. Community colleges have been criticized for often making little effort to ensure that their transfer courses indeed parallel university courses in credit hours, course sequencing, and prerequisites. Moreover, community college faculty and staff frequently do not know which courses are transferrable (Richardson and Bender, 1987: 40, 159–160, 164). As a result, students often do not know which courses are appropriate for transfer and choose the wrong ones. For example, a 1984 survey of students at 24 community colleges nationwide found that, among transfer-oriented students, 11% of those surveyed said they did not know which courses were transferrable (Cohen, Brawer, and Bensimon, 1985: 120).

At the same time, four-year colleges deserve a share of the blame for denying credit for transfer students' community college courses. Some of this credit denial is quite understandable when it involves community college courses that differ in rigor and content from four-year college courses (Bowles, 1988: 32–35; Orfield et al., 1984: 225). But universities also often deny credit to community college courses that do closely parallel university courses simply because the universities consider such courses inappropriate for community colleges to teach. This has been a major problem in the area of business education. The American Association of Collegiate Schools of Business discourages university students from enrolling in business courses until their junior year, when they have gotten their general education requirements out of the way. As a result, university business schools rarely give credit for community college business courses, because they are considered as having been taken out of proper sequence (Blood, 1987; Florida State Department of Education, 1988: 30–31; Savage, 1987). Also, many four-year colleges refuse to give credit for more than two years of courses (Kintzer and Wattenbarger, 1985: chap. 2; Knoell and Medsker, 1965: 61; Maryland State Board for Community Colleges, 1983: 12; Richardson and Bender, 1987: 193; Winandy and McGrath, 1970: 189–190). Of 541 four-year colleges surveyed in 1982, 22% limited the number of courses students could transfer for credit to two years' worth (Walton, 1984: 224–225). Beyond these clearly disputable university practices, there is also a grey area that deserves reconsideration. Four-year colleges routinely refuse credit for community college courses that may be up to university standards but simply have no direct counterpart in the university curriculum: this often happens with interdisciplinary courses and vocational education (Bowles, 1988: 32–35).[22] Furthermore, four-year colleges often give no credit or only partial credit for community college courses for which a student has received a D, whereas four-year college natives are not so penalized. A random survey of 541 four-year institutions in 1982 found that 64% refused to give even credit toward the general residence requirement (quite apart from credit toward the major) for transfer courses carrying a D (Walton, 1984: 222).

But the travails transfer students face are not just financial and academic but also social. For various reasons, transfer students have a hard time integrating themselves into the social life of four-year colleges (Astin, 1975: 154, 168; Knoell and Medsker, 1965: 68).[23] Because many have difficulty getting sufficient financial aid, transfer students more often have to work to support themselves and thus have less time for mixing with their peers on campus. Orientation programs directed specifically to transfer students are rare, and clubs and other extracurricular activities at four-year colleges usually focus their recruitment efforts on freshmen.[24] In addition, transfer students often fail to get campus housing because many four-year colleges give first priority to freshmen. These various impediments lead transfer students to often complain that they find it difficult to join student activities and take part in the general social life of the college (Richardson and Bender, 1987: 82–83, 161; Sandeen and Goodale, 1976: 7–9).

Poorer social integration leads in turn to greater likelihood of academic failure. Pincus and DeCamp (1989) found, in a study of high-achieving minority students who transferred to four-year colleges in the early 1970s and were followed up in 1986, that those who failed to graduate were less often members of student clubs or organizations at the four-year college and were less likely to report that their classmates encouraged them to graduate. Similarly, a study of Los Angeles community college transfers to UCLA found that those who dropped out were significantly less likely than those who remained to have most of their friends within UCLA (Kissler, Lara, and Cardinal, 1981: 9–10).[25]

Finally, transfer students run afoul of obstacles to integrating themselves academically into four-year colleges. Studies repeatedly find that they tend to suffer a sharp drop in grades in the first year after transfer (Cohen and Brawer, 1987: 101–102; idem, 1989: 53; Hills, 1965; Kintzer and Wattenbarger, 1985; Knoell and Medsker, 1965: 27–28). For example, the GPAs of fall 1982 community college transfers to the University of California and California State University systems dropped by an average of one-half point at UC and one-third point at CSU from their community college GPAs (California Community Colleges, 1984: 26, 30, F–2). Similarly, fall 1979 Illinois community college transfers to Illinois public and private universities suffered an average drop of about one-third grade point between their community college GPAs and their first-year university GPAs (Illinois Community College Board, 1984: 11; idem, 1986b: 12).

It is often claimed that transfers' upper-division grades soon recover from "transfer shock." However, this claim is misleading. It is based on comparing the grades of students two or three years past transfer to those of students in the first year of transfer. Even when the same cohort is involved, no correction is made for the fact that the older students no longer include the many students who did badly after transfer and dropped out. In fact, a study of Illinois transfers found that, while those who eventually graduated with a baccalaureate largely did rally from their transfer shock, those who dropped out never did recover. On average, the transfer students who eventually graduated saw their GPA drop from 3.04 at the community college to 2.78 in their first semester after transfer, but by the end their cumulative university GPA had risen back to 2.96. However, among the 43% of Illinois 1979 transfer students who had dropped out by 1984, the average GPA plummeted from 2.79 at the community college to 2.27 in the first semester at a four-year college.

Post-transfer GPAs then slowly recovered the longer students stayed on. But even those dropouts who had lasted until 1984, five years after transferring, had raised their average cumulative university GPA only to 2.42, still 0.37 point below their community college GPA (Illinois Community College Board, 1986b: 12–15, 69).

As the Illinois data indicate, transfer shock in the form of bad grades after transfer is significantly associated with greater attrition, whether through academic dismissal or voluntary withdrawal. Two other studies further document this connection. Kissler et al. (1981: 9–10) found that Los Angeles Community College transfers to UCLA who dropped out had significantly lower grades at UCLA than those who continued. Similarly, Johnson (1987: 324–325) found that community college students transferring to a large urban commuter university in the Southwest in fall 1984 were significantly less likely to return for the spring semester if they had lower grades, even if one controlled for educational aspirations, academic self-concept, perception of practical value of education, rating of academic difficulties, academic satisfaction, and degree of academic integration.[26]

Clearly, a good part of the grade shock encountered by transfer students stems from a collision between their abilities and the tougher standards of the four-year colleges. But it also stems from institutional factors: particularly, less access to financial aid and poorer academic preparation in the community college.

As noted above, transfer students receive less financial aid than four-year college natives. And this exclusion significantly depresses their upper-division grades and persistence rates. A study of fall 1977 transfers from Los Angeles community colleges to UCLA found that the students' grades at UCLA were negatively and significantly associated with their amount of unmet financial need, even when their community college GPAs and community college preparation were controlled (Kissler et al., 1981: 6–8).

Community college transfers also get poorer upper-division grades than four-year college natives because their lower-division preparation is, on average, inferior (Aulston, 1974: 116–118; Bernstein, 1986: 36–38; Kissler et al., 1981: 12–13; Knoell and Medsker, 1965: 60, 98; Richardson and Bender, 1987: 27–28, 34–36, 46–48). Those who do well in the community college do less well after transfer than university native students with comparable grades. For instance, Crook and Lavin (1989) found that, for 1970–1972 entrants to the City University of New York, freshman grades were significantly less predictive of B.A. attainment by 1984 among community college entrants than four-year college entrants. In separate regressions, an increase of one point in first-year GPA increased the probability of getting a baccalaureate degree by 20% among four-year entrants but only by 11% among community college entrants, even when their differences in background, aspirations, high school record, and college experiences were controlled.

Programs ostensibly designed to prepare students for eventual transfer to four-year colleges have become essentially open-door programs with virtually no entry or exit requirements. Many transfer courses do not have prerequisites, with the result that students do not have to progress in their learning and can avoid difficult courses. As a result, transfer courses are often not up to university standards of instruction (Bernstein, 1986: 38; Bowles, 1988: 32–35; Cohen and Brawer, 1987: 100; Orfield et al., 1984: 210, 213, 226–228). Moreover, community college instructors often do not communicate and enforce high academic expectations for their students. They more often grade relative to the class norm (rather than an abstract standard) than do university instructors. They cover less material in class. And they less often assign difficult readings and essay exams (Bernstein, 1986: 36–37; Richardson and Bender, 1987: 27–28, 34–36, 46–48). In a survey of 1977 community college transfers to UCLA, only one-third reported that in the community college they frequently had to write papers integrating ideas from various parts of a course; yet two-thirds stated that at UCLA they had to do this frequently (Lara, 1981: 2, 8–9). A similar pattern of neglect of higher order cognitive skills appears in national data. The previously mentioned 1984 national survey of 347 community college instructors in university-parallel courses found that 45% did not use essay exams and only 27% allocated more than a quarter of the final course grade to essay exams. Moreover, 39% did not assign outside papers and only 23% based more than a quarter of the final grade on them (Cohen et al., 1985: 84). Although only part of their academic malpreparation, community college students' lack of writing experience nonetheless has a seriously deleterious effect. Among the UCLA transfers described above, lack of writing experience in the community college had a significant impact on upper-division grades and persistence rates, even after controlling for students' social background, community college grades, and course-taking and study habits in the community college (Lara, 1981: 2, 8–9).

A major reason for the declining academic rigor of community college transfer preparation is that community colleges have seen an influx of students who are less prepared academically, often are not interested in transfer, and yet enroll in transfer programs. As a result, such courses lose their rigor as the student culture becomes less academic and community college instructors become discouraged (McCabe, 1981: 8;

Orfield et al., 1984: 231; Palmer, 1986: 55). Also, community college transfers are taking fewer university-parallel courses before transferring. Instead, they increasingly concentrate on vocational education or take a melange of courses of no particular academic content and rigor and transfer without an academic associate's degree (Grubb, 1991: 202, 209; Palmer, 1990: 23). Students who enter vocational programs are not being prepared as well for university work. A study of transfers from Illinois community colleges to Illinois four-year colleges finds that the number receiving a baccalaureate within five years after transferring in 1979 was only 48.4% for those entering with a vocational degree (the Associate in Applied Science) as compared to 67.0% for those entering with a prebaccalaureate degree (the Associate in Arts or Associate in Science) (Illinois Community College Board, 1986b: 20, 26, 53).

The declining rigor of the community college's transfer preparation efforts reflects a change not just in the institution's clientele but also in its self-conception. As the community college fell in love with vocational and community education in the 1960s and 1970s, it stripped the transfer program of resources, energy, and elan. As a result, community colleges truncated their liberal arts offerings to the point that few postintroductory courses were left (Cohen and Brawer, 1989: 288–289; Palmer, 1986: 56). For example, Gary Orfield and his colleagues found that by 1982–1983 the Chicago City Colleges were offering only 39% of the mathematics and science courses listed in their catalogs (Orfield et al., 1984: 219–224). In addition, community colleges largely abandoned in the 1970s their responsibility to assess, place, motivate, and monitor their students, so as to determine which ones should go into transfer courses and what kind of progress they should show (Grubb, 1991: 213; McCabe, 1981: 7). Again using Chicago as an example, Orfield and colleagues found that 10 of 13 Chicago area community college districts had no standards listed in their catalogs regulating admission to their university-parallel programs (Orfield et al., 1984: 210, 213).

Summary and Conclusions

When we go to explain why the community college hinders its baccalaureate aspirants, we find a wide variety of often unintended factors that nonetheless concatenate in a surprisingly systematic way. In their pilgrimage toward Zion, baccalaureate aspirants face three main tests: surviving their years in the community college; successfully transferring to a four-year college; and surviving in the four-year college. At each stage, aspirants are beset by certain *institutional* features of community colleges and of four-year colleges that threaten their progress. Their persistence in the community college is jeopardized by community colleges' lower social integration (due in good part to a lack of dormitories) and lower academic selectivity and prestige. Their successful traversal of the straits between the community college and the four-year college is threatened by the community college's emphasis on vocational education, the sheer difficulty of moving to a strange new college, and the difficulty of securing acceptance and financial aid from four-year colleges. Finally, even in the university, baccalaureate aspirants face the trials of little financial aid, loss of credits, and poor social and academic integration.

The wide range and malignant effectiveness of the hurdles community college entrants face in pursuing a baccalaureate can easily lead one to assume that these obstacles are deliberate. It seems plausible that because the community college's *effect* is to hinder baccalaureate attainment that this has been its *intent*. However, this assumption of a symmetry between effects and intents is mistaken. As we will see in Sections III and IV, the features of the community college that impede baccalaureate attainment are almost wholly not the result of a desire by private interest groups and government officials to block students' life chances. Rather, these hindrances emerge from the community college's attempt to reconcile many different and often antithetical goals. It has contradictory effects because it has contradictory goals.

Appendix

APPENDIX TABLE A4–1
Differences in Attrition from Higher Education
Experienced by Entrants to Two-Year and Four-Year Colleges

	U.S. National Center for Education Statistics (1990)	Ibid.	U.S. National Center for Education Statistics (1977b)	Ibid.	Astin (1975)	Anderson (1981)[a]
Study Attributes						
Data set used	HS & B		NLS–72		ACE	NLS–72
Year began college	1982		1972		1968	1972
Year followed up	1986		1974		1972	1973–74
Aspirations	any higher education above	B.A. and	any higher education above	B.A. and above	B.A. and program	college academic
Findings						
Percentage Dropping Out at End of One Year						
Public two-year colleges			30.1%	16.9%		NA
All four-year colleges			16.5%	9.0%		NA
Difference						
No controls			13.6%	7.9%		NA
With controls			NA	NA		5.0%**
Percentage Dropping Out at End of Two Years						
Public two-year colleges			39.3%	32.3%		NA
All four-year colleges			23.5%	20.2%		NA
Difference						
No controls			15.8%	12.1%		NA
With controls			NA	NA		14.0%**
Percentage Dropping Out at End of Four Years						
Two-year colleges						
Public and private	42.6%	31.8%			men women	
Public					56.0% 59.0%	
All four-year colleges	30.6%	27.4%			37.6% 31.7%	
Difference						
No controls	12.0%	4.4%			18.4% 27.3%	
With controls	NA	NA			10.0%[b] 18.0%[b]	

APPENDIX TABLE A4–1 continued
Differences in Attrition from Higher Education
Experienced by Entrants to Two-Year and Four-Year Colleges

	U.S. National Center for Education Statistics (1990)	U.S. National Center for Education Statistics (1977b)	Astin (1975)	Anderson (1981)[a]
Control Variables				
Social Background				
Sex			X	X
Race			X	X
Socioeconomic status			X	X
Religion			X	X
Aspirations				
Student's educational aspirations			X	X
Student's occupational aspirations				X
Parents' educational aspirations for respondent				X
Peers' college plans				X
Student's perception of college ability				X
High School Experiences				
Test scores				X
Grades or class rank			X	X
Curriculum or track				X
College Experience				
Living arrangement				X[c]
Job while in college				X
Work on campus				X

Sources: U.S. National Center for Education Statistics (1990: 19–20, 24–26); idem (1977b: 22–26, 50–51, 74, 135–136, 191–192, 197–198); Astin (1975: 112–113); Anderson (1981: 9–12).

Notes:
** Significant at .01 level.
  a. Anderson counts as withdrawal not only dropping out of higher education but also moving out of the academic program into the vocational program.
  b. No significance level reported.
  c. In equation for persistence into third year (dropout after two years) but not for persistence into second year (dropout after one year).

Educational Outcomes at Four-Year Colleges for
Transfers from Two-Year Colleges and Four-Year College Natives

	National Center Educ. Stats. (1977b)[a]	Holmstrom, Bisconti (1974)[b]	California Community Colleges (1984)[c]	Florida State Educ. Dept. (1983)[d]	Illinois Community College Board (1986)[e]	Martinko (1978)[f]
Study Attributes						
Study coverage	U.S.	U.S.	Calif.	Fla.	Ill.	Penn.
Data set used	NLS-72	ACE	own	own	own	own
Year respondents began college	1972	1968	NA	NA	NA	NA
Year respondents transferred	1973	NA	1975	1976	1979	1976
Year respondents were followed up	1974	1972	1980	1978	1984	1977
Findings						
Percentage Dropping Out						
Within one year after transfer						
Two-year college transfers	17.7%		27.8%	16.9%	24.3%	18.0%
Four-year college native juniors	NA		NA	8.0%	NA	NA
Within two years after transfer						
Two-year college transfers		14.3%[g]		32.0%	34.1%	
Four-year college native juniors		NA		19.8%	NA	
Within three years after transfer						
Two-year college transfers					39.0%	
Four-year college native juniors					NA	
Within four years after transfer						
Two-year college transfers					42.0%	
Four-year college native juniors					NA	
Within five years after transfer						
Two-year college transfers			35.6%		43.2%	
Four-year college native juniors			23.9%		NA	

APPENDIX TABLE A4–2 continued
Educational Outcomes at Four-Year Colleges for
Transfers from Two-Year Colleges and Four-Year College Natives

	National Center Educ. Stats. (1977b)[a]	Holmstrom, Bisconti (1974)[b]	California Community Colleges (1984)[c]	Florida State Educ. Dept. (1983)[d]	Illinois Community College Board (1986)[e]	Martinko (1978)[f]
Percentage Attaining Baccalaureate						
Within two years after transfer						
Two-year college transfers	40.8%[g]			21.9%	18.2%	
Four-year college natives	57.2%[g]			NA	NA	
Four-year college native juniors	NA			38.0%	NA	
Within three years after transfer						
Two-year college transfers					41.3%	
Four-year college native juniors					NA	
Within five years after transfer						
Two-year transfers			61.1%		53.8%	
Four-year college native juniors			67.8%		NA	
Percentage Still in College						
Two years after transfer						
Two-year college transfers	44.9%[g]			46.1%	47.7%	
Four-year college native juniors	NA			42.2%	NA	
Three years after transfer						
Two-year college transfers					19.7%	
Four-year college native juniors					NA	

APPENDIX TABLE A4–2 continued

Educational Outcomes at Four-Year Colleges for

Transfers from Two-Year Colleges and Four-Year College Natives

	National Center Educ. Stats. (1977b)[a]	Holmstrom, Bisconti (1974)[b]	California Community Colleges (1984)[c]	Florida State Educ. Dept. (1983)[d]	Illinois Community College Board (1986)[e]	Martinko (1978)[f]
Five years after transfer						
Two-year college transfers			3.3%		3.0%	
Four-year college native juniors			8.3%			

Sources: U.S. National Center for Education Statistics (1977b: 136, 142, 146, 150); Holmstrom and Bisconti (1974: 106–107); California Community Colleges (1984: 29; F–7, 9, 11–12); Florida State Department of Education (1983: 12–13); Illinois Community College Board (1986b: 9, 52); Martinko (1978: 1–3).

Notes:
a. The attrition rate is for withdrawal from higher education as a whole.
b. The Holmstrom and Bisconti data are from the American Council of Education's annual survey of entering *full-time* freshmen. The attrition rate is for withdrawal from higher education as a whole.
c. The attrition rate is for withdrawal from the particular university entered rather than from higher education as a whole. The California data pertain to fall 1975 transfers to the California State University system (CSU) who came in as juniors and to CSU natives who became juniors the same year. The CSU enrolls about 60% of all California community college transfers to public and private four-year colleges (California Community Colleges, 1984: 1–2, 33, A–1).
d. The Florida data are for fall 1976 transfers to three state universities (University of Florida, University of South Florida, and Florida Technological University) who came in as juniors and for university natives who became juniors the same year (Florida State Education Department, 1983: 2). The attrition rate is for withdrawal from the particular university entered.
e. The Illinois data come from a survey of Illinois community college students entering Illinois public and private four-year colleges in fall 1979 and followed up over the next five years. The survey had a response rate of 95%. The attrition figure is for withdrawal from the particular four-year college entered rather than from higher education as a whole.
f. The Pennsylvania data come from a survey of Pennsylvania community college students entering Pennsylvania public and private four-year colleges in fall 1976. The survey has an estimated response rate of 57%. The attrition figure is for withdrawal from the particular four-year college entered rather than from higher education as a whole.
g. Holmstrom and Bisconti (1974) did not report the time elapsed between the year transfer students entered four-year colleges and the year they were followed up. I therefore assumed that on average it came two years after they transferred.

Section III
The Origins and Expansion
of the Community College

CHAPTER 5

The Founding of Community Colleges: Introduction

If the advocates and critics of the community college are divided over its effects, so are they over its parentage. The functionalist defenders, believing that the community college has egalitarian effects, posit in turn that it has had an unimpeachably democratic birth. But finding evidence that the institution has inegalitarian effects, its institutionalist and Marxist instrumentalist critics have countered that it is of elitist issue. (For more on these three positions, see Chapter 2.)

These explanations are too simple. Just as Chapter 3 found that the community college's impact is more contradictory than is acknowledged by either the critics and defenders, the chapters in this section demonstrate that its origins are similarly complex. Based on an analysis of developments at the national, state, and local levels, this section shows the insufficiency of interest-group pressure, whether democratic or capitalist in origin, in explaining why community colleges proliferated across this country. Although interest groups have profoundly shaped the development of the community college, they have not acted alone. Government officials have also played an absolutely key role. The institutionalist theory has highlighted one of these government actors—the state universities—but there are many more than it acknowledges. From local superintendents to state governors and members of Congress, government officials have been at the center of the politics of community college expansion, often acting in service not of interest-group demands but of interests and values of their own.

Before moving to examine the forces behind community college foundings, we should first establish the outlines of what is to be explained.

The Stages of Community College Growth

The first community college appeared in Joliet, Illinois in 1901, and the second in Fresno, California in 1910. From that point on, community colleges multiplied rapidly, but unevenly. (See Table 5-1.) Growth was

TABLE 5–1
Number and Enrollments of Community Colleges, 1901–1991[a]

	1901	1919	1940	1950	1960	1970
United States						
Number	1	39	217	256	345	654
Enrollments						
Academic year			107,553	296,816	712,224	
Fall semester					606,171	2,101,972
Percentage of all higher						
educ. enrollments						
California						
Number	0	21	47	66	62	94
Enrollments						
Academic year	0		79,818	235,323	357,715	
Fall semester					272,799	715,689
Percentage of all higher						
educ. enrollments						
Illinois						
Number	1	3	12	14	20	47
Enrollments						
Academic year			16,574	25,635	38,896	
Fall semester					28,820	150,729
Percentage of all higher						
educ. enrollments						
Indiana[b]						
Number	0	0	1	1	1	1
Enrollments						
Academic year	0	0	128	287	729	
Fall semester					577	
Percentage of all higher						
educ. enrollments						
New York[c]						
Number	0	0	0	1	16	45
Enrollments						
Academic year	0	0	0	367	24,630	
Fall semester					21,656	186,157
Percentage of all higher						
educ. enrollments						
Washington						
Number	0	1	8	9	10	27
Enrollments						
Academic year	0		1,398	14,166	26,966	
Fall semester						95,521
Percentage of all higher						
educ. enrollments						

TABLE 5–1 continued
Number and Enrollments of Community Colleges, 1901–1991[a]

	1980	1991
United States		
Number		999
Enrollments		
Academic year		
Fall semester	4,328,782	4,937,663
Percentage of all higher	35.8%	36.0%
educ. enrollments		
California		
Number		113
Enrollments		
Academic year		
Fall semester	1,212,810	1,385,137
Percentage of all higher	67.7%	67.7%
educ. enrollments		
Illinois		
Number	47	54
Enrollments		
Academic year		
Fall semester	347,964	380,646
Percentage of all higher	54.0%	47.6%
educ. enrollments		
Indiana[b]		
Number	1	3
Enrollments		
Academic year		
Fall semester	5,174	9,255
Percentage of all higher	2.1%	3.5%
educ. enrollments		
New York[c]		
Number	45	50
Enrollments		
Academic year		
Fall semester	234,165	318,200
Percentage of all higher	23.6%	26.5%
educ. enrollments		
Washington		
Number	27	28
Enrollments		
Academic year		
Fall semester	171,760	150,714
Percentage of all higher	56.6%	57.2%
educ. enrollments		

TABLE 5–1 continued
Number and Enrollments of Community Colleges, 1901–1991[a]

Notes:
a. Academic-year enrollments are for year ending May of year listed. October enrollments are for year listed (except 1960, when they are for October 1959). The figures for number of community colleges exclude two-year university branches and entirely vocational postsecondary schools (going by such names as vocational-technical institutes, technical institutes, and technical colleges). They are restricted to public two-year colleges that offer academic programs (with or without vocational education) and are autonomous of the universities. For the individual states I use data compiled by the American Association of Community Colleges (under its earlier name, American Association of Junior Colleges) because they allow one to exclude two-year institutions that are not community colleges strictly speaking.
b. Excludes the Indiana vocational-technical schools.
c. Excludes the institutes for applied arts and sciences and the agricultural and technical colleges.

Sources:
1990: McDowell (1919: Appendix K).
1919: McDowell (1919: 47).
1940: American Association of Junior Colleges (1941); and U.S. Office of Education (1954: chap. 4, p. 7). The Washington figures above differ from those in the AAJC publication because in that year it listed the community colleges in Washington as private institutions.
1950: American Association of Junior Colleges (1950); and U.S. Office of Education (1954: chap. 4, p. 7).
1960: American Association of Junior Colleges (1961); U.S. Office of Education (1962: Pt. 3, 13; 1964: 15); and U.S. National Center for Education Statistics (1987: 122). October figures are for October 1959.
1970: American Association of Community and Junior Colleges (1971); and U.S. National Center for Education Statistics (1971: 13).
1980: U.S. National Center for Education Statistics (1982: 84, 91); American Association of Community and Junior Colleges (1982: 62).
1991: U.S. National Center for Education Statistics (1992a: 170); American Association of Community Colleges (1992: 58).

particularly rapid in the 1920s, 1930s, and 1960s. In 1919, 39 community colleges were operating in eleven states: seven in the Midwest, three in the West, and one in the South (Texas) (McDowell, 1919: Appendix K). By 1940, this number had risen by a factor of 5, to 217. During the 1960s, rapid growth gave way to explosive growth. A third of the total expansion of the community college in enrollments and numbers of campuses occurred during that decade alone. In the 1970s, however, this swift pace slowed, with community colleges growing in numbers and enrollments at only half their 1960s rate. This deceleration reflected the fact that state governments were facing increasing fiscal stringency and community colleges were running out of new populations to reach. Finally, in the 1980s, community college growth nearly ceased.[1]

This national, average pattern of community college growth obscures considerable variation by state. Some state community college systems developed more quickly than average: most notably California. Its first community college was founded in 1910. By 1919 it already had 21. And entering the 1960s, it had already accumulated three-fifths of the community colleges it has today. But other states lagged considerably.

The most noticeable delay was in the Northeast. Many northeastern states lacked community colleges for many years, developing them only within the past few decades. New York, for example, did not establish any community colleges until 1950, and by 1960 it had accumulated only two-fifths of its current number and 9% of its present enrollments. This absence reflected the strength of its existing higher educational system and the fact that its colleges were within easier reach than was typical in the large, more recently settled midwestern and western states.

Six states, meanwhile, have never developed community colleges at all. Two have preferred university branches combined with vocational-technical institutes (Indiana and Maine), three have opted for two-year colleges organized under the aegis of the state university (Hawaii, Kentucky, Alaska), and one has neither community colleges nor university branches (South Dakota). Meanwhile, several states have established both community colleges and two-year university branches: for example, Connecticut, New Mexico, Ohio, and Pennsylvania.

Studying the Founding of Community Colleges

Any study of the development of the community college must grapple with the fact that it is the product of policy made at all three levels of our government—national, state, and local. Moreover, because states and localities vary greatly in their social, economic, and political ecologies, the development of community colleges in any one state or locality cannot be taken as representative of the experience of other states and localities. As a result, in order to capture the myriad facets of the community college's development across the United States, a study of the origins of the community college must range extensively, both vertically and horizontally. Vertically, one must study policymaking at all three levels of government, for each level has played an important and distinct role in the development of the community college. Horizontally, a study aiming at comprehensiveness must examine the experience of several different states and, within each state, several different localities, with these states and localities preferably varying greatly in their social, economic, and political characteristics.

In pursuit of this methodological desideratum, this section analyzes developments at the national level, at the state level in five states, and at the local level in several different locales within each state. The national-level analysis examines the genesis of four key congressional acts advancing the community college: the Higher Education Facilities Act of

1963, the Vocational Education Act of 1963, the Higher Education Act of 1965, and the Higher Education Amendments of 1972.

The state-level analysis is focused on legislation and other policy initiatives in five states: California, Washington State, Illinois, Indiana, and New York. My choice of states largely follows the "method of agreement" and the "method of difference" discussed by Skocpol (1984: 378–379). My concern is to develop an explanation that explains not only why community colleges were established but also why they were *not* established. Four states were selected because they developed flourishing community college systems but took different paths to that result: California, Illinois, New York, and Washington State. But the fifth state— Indiana—was selected in contrast, for it has developed only one community college (Vincennes University, which started as a private institution). While similar to Illinois in many regards, Indiana has elected instead to expand its higher education system through university branches and state vocational-technical institutes.

This mixture of states provides a safeguard against spurious causation. Our confidence that a certain factor *caused* community college development and is not just associated with it is raised if it is present in four different states with large community college systems but absent in one without them. Moreover, this research design allows for a plurality of causes of community college expansion to exhibit themselves. There is no reason to assume that the same set of causes would be present in all states, given the large regional variations across the United States. My research design allows for discovering these variations on a main theme by sampling states that, although similar in developing community college systems, vary considerably on other characteristics.

The states differ greatly in how rapidly they developed their systems. California, Illinois, and Washington moved quickly, establishing community colleges by World War I. New York, however, did not establish any community colleges until 1950. Hence, a different constellation of political forces should be present in New York than in California, Illinois, and Washington.

Furthermore, the four states differ in the degree to which their community college systems attract working-class and minority students. This variation has direct relevance to the clash between the functionalist and instrumentalist explanations. One would hypothesize that the instrumentalist argument that community colleges are intended to track working-class and minority students should hold best in states where minority and working-class *college entrants* have been considerably more likely to attend community colleges than are white, middle- or upper-class college entrants. Illinois is such a state. Among college goers in 1972, there was a 30% difference in rates of community college attendance between those in the bottom and top quartiles in socioeconomic status (SES) and a 7% differences between nonwhites and whites. (See lines 5 and 6 of Table 5–2.) Conversely, the instrumentalist argument should hold least well for states such as Washington and California, where there has been little SES and race difference in community college attendance among college entrants. In 1972, the gap in community college entrance rates between students in the bottom and top quarters in socio-economic status was only 10% in Washington and 14% in California: that is, less than half of the gap in Illinois.

In addition, the states differ in their political cultures. These complexes of attitudes and beliefs about government and public policy have been found to influence strongly whether and how issues are raised in state and local politics (Elazar, 1984; Marshall, Mitchell, and Wirt, 1989). In his influential typology of state political cultures, Elazar (1984: 124–125) has classified Washington State's political culture as largely moralistic (issue oriented), Illinois and Indiana's as mostly individualistic (patronage oriented), and California and New York's as mixed. Because moralistic states are more supportive of welfare-state redistributive policies, one would expect that Washington should evidence greater concern about equality of educational opportunity for the poor and minorities than individualistic states such as Illinois.

Finally, the states vary in their industrial structures, that is, how their labor forces are distributed across different industries. (See item 9 in Table 5–2.) This variation, it is hypothesized, would cause the participation of certain economic interest groups to vary across the states. For example, Washington and California have particularly large primary sectors (agriculture, forestry, and mining). One would therefore expect farmers and other primary-sector interest groups to play an important role in community college politics in those states.

The local-level analysis examined at least four community colleges in each of the states that developed large community college systems. These community colleges represented four different kinds of locale: metropolitan center city, metropolitan suburb, small city, and rural small town. The community colleges are listed in Table 5–3. This range of political ecologies allows a broad-based and inclusive examination of the local politics of community college expansion.

To determine the actors and motives behind the expansion of the community college and occupational education, I focused on the key decisions made at each level: at the local level, to establish community

TABLE 5–2

The Five States' Educational and Socioeconomic Characteristics

	California	Illinois	New York	Washington	Indiana[a]
1. *Number of community colleges* (fall 1991)	113	54	50	28	3
2. *Date community college first established*	1910	1901	1950	1915	1801
3. *Community college enrollments* (fall 1991)	1,385,137	380,646	318,200	150,714	9,255
4. *Community college students as percentage of all higher education students* (fall 1991)	67.7%	47.6%	26.5%	57.2%	3.5%
5. *Tracking by social class:* percentage of freshmen of given socioeconomic status enrolling in public two-year colleges (fall 1972)					
Lowest SES quartile	74.2%	56.1%	47.9%	48.8%	
Top SES quartile	60.2%	26.2%	26.8%	38.9%	
Difference	14.0%	29.9%	21.1%	9.9%	
6. *Tracking by race:* percentage of collegians of given race enrolling in two-year colleges (fall 1978)					
Minority	67.7%	53.3%	31.3%	57.5%	
White, non-Latino	61.2%	46.1%	27.8%	62.3%	
Difference	6.5%	7.2%	3.5%	–4.8%	
7. *Tracking by sex:* percentage of collegians of given sex enrolling in two-year colleges (fall 1989)					
Women	61.5%	51.0%	24.6%	59.2%	
Men	57.3%	44.7%	22.4%	51.8%	
Difference	4.2%	6.3%	2.2%	7.4%	
8. *Political culture*[b]	M, I	I	M, I	M	I
9. *Occupational mix:* percentage of employed civilians in these occupational sectors (1980)					
Primary sector	3.5%	2.9%	1.3%	4.1%	3.4%
Secondary sector	26.0%	30.4%	24.6%	26.5%	35.9%
Service sector	70.5%	66.7%	74.1%	69.4%	60.7%

Notes:
a. Figures are for the one community college (Vincennes University).
b. M = moralistic, issue oriented; I = individualistic, patronage oriented; M, I = mixture of the two.

Sources:
1, 3: American Association of Community Colleges (1992).
4: U.S. National Center for Education Statistics (1992a: 170); American Association of Comunity Colleges (1992: 58).
5: My analysis of the National Longitudinal Survey of the High School Class of 1972.
6: U.S. National Center for Education Statistics (1981a).
7: U.S. National Center for Education Statistics (1991b: 11–12).
8: Elazar (1984: 124–125).
9: U.S. Bureau of the Census (1983: Tables 58 and 69).

TABLE 5–3
Local Community Colleges Studied[a]

	California	Illinois	New York	Washington
Metropolitan center city	Los Angeles	Chicago	New York City	Seattle
Metropolitan suburb	Contra Costa (San Francisco Bay Area)	DuPage (Chicago) Lake County (Chicago)		Shoreline (Seattle)
Small city	Fresno San Bernardino Fullerton	Belleville Joliet Blackhawk (Moline)	Schenectady	Everett Yakima Grays Harbor (Aberdeen) Olympic (Bremerton) Columbia Basin (Pasco)
Small town (less than 20,000 in population)	Cuesta (S.L. Obispo)	John Logan (Carterville) Southeastern (Harrisburg) Kaskaskia (Centralia) Shawnee (Ullin)	Genesee (Batavia) Orange (Middletown)	Wenatchee Centralia Skagit (Mt. Vernon) Clark (Vancouver) Lower Columbia (Longview)

Note:
a. The location is identified in parentheses only when it is not included in the name of the community college.

colleges; at the state level, first permitting their establishment and later enacting state aid; and at the national level, providing federal aid. These key decisions provided excellent occasions to read the alignment of forces in the community college policy arena because they constituted occasions in which authoritative decisions were made on the community college and its supporters and opponents were most stimulated to act. But to guard against the well-known pitfalls of a "decisionist" approach (Lukes, 1974), I also sought to find instances of "nondecisions" in which critics of, and alternatives to, the community college were suppressed and prevented from entering public discussion. For example, an effort was made to determine why the states other than Indiana chose to rely not on university branches but on community colleges as a way of extending higher educational opportunity.

At all three levels of government, data were gathered by interviewing a wide range of government officials, private interest group leaders, and political observers. In addition, a multitude of documents by and studies of these groups were analyzed.

Explaining Community College Expansion

The functionalist advocates of the community college argue that it arose to meet the fundamental needs of society as a whole. The agent of this policy development was a broad coalition centered around students and their parents, although also including business, local educators, university heads, and state and federal officials. Animating their efforts above all was the desire to promote equality of opportunity. In addition, the state university heads wished to protect the academic integrity of their institutions, and businesses wanted vocational training for their employees (Cohen and Brawer, 1989; Medsker, 1960; Monroe, 1972; Thornton, 1972). (For fuller descriptions of the arguments of the advocates and critics of the community college, see Chapter 2.)

The Marxist instrumentalist critics, meanwhile, move business from a supporting to a leading role. Driven by a desire to secure publicly subsidized employee training and maintain educational differentials between the classes, it was the principal creator of the community college. It has dominated the policymaking process both through its own direct action and through those of its fellow travelers in government and the great philanthropic foundations (Bowles and Gintis, 1976; Karabel, 1972; Pincus, 1974, 1980; Zwerling, 1976).

The institutionalists, finally, deny that student or business pressure was fundamental to driving the expansion of the community college. Far more important were the dynamics of a higher education system in which institutions compete for an exclusive clientele. More particularly, state universities actively fostered the development of the community college in order to keep down university enrollments and thus preserve the scarcity and selectivity of their degrees (Brint and Karabel, 1989; Labaree, 1990).

As we will see, parts of these arguments are borne out by the evidence. As the functionalists hold, students did support the rise of the community college. However, their participation was far less significant than functionalists argue. Similarly, business was an important actor, as the Marxist instrumentalists claim. But while business pressure was more pronounced than that of students, it still was too weak to explain the breadth and depth of community college policymaking.

To fill this theoretical vacuum, we have to recognize the key role played by government officials. They often acted in the absence of any significant interest-group pressure in order to realize values and interests of their own. The institutionalists and functionalists have partially acknowledged this, pointing to the self-interested role of the state universities and the American Association of Community Colleges. But their theoretical opening is too narrow. They fail to perceive how wide was the initiative of government officials. It was not dominated by state university and AACC officials alone but also included local school superintendents, state governors, legislators, departments of education, and Congress members and presidents in central roles.

Pursuing interests and values of their own, these government officials put their unique stamp on the community college. Several different kinds of institutions could have met students' desire for college opportunities and business's wish for publicly subsidized employee training. But government officials favored the community college among a range of functional alternatives—such as more four-year campuses, two-year university branches, or vocational-technical schools—because it facilitated their own pursuit of such goals as prestige and reelection. For local educators, founding a community college brought prestige as educational innovators and offered access to such jobs as college presidents and teachers. For state and federal elected officials, the community college offered a cheap way to meet the demand for college opportunities and to stimulate politically popular economic growth (by providing business with publicly subsidized employee training). And for university heads, the community college promised to preserve and even increase university admissions selectivity by drawing away less prepared students.

At the same time, this governmental initiative was not untrammeled. Government officials operate within the constraints set by a democratic polity and a capitalist economy. To hold on to power, governors, legislators, and presidents and Congress members have to maintain a healthy economy and mobilize the support of voters. The community college has seemed like a good means to ensure both because it offers business the carrot of publicly subsidized employee training and students the benefit of cheap and accessible education. These constraints on government officials have allowed business and students to shape the development of the community college even when they have not participated in policymaking on it. For however much the community college has met the interests of government officials, it also has addressed the needs of business and (less so) students. Government officials, in short, have shaped the community college in a situation of *relative autonomy* from the desires of private interest groups. (For a detailed discussion of the concepts of state relative autonomy and power as constraint, see Chapter 2.)

The next three chapters develop my alternative to the functionalist, Marxist instrumentalist, and institutionalist explanations of the rise of the community college. They examine the key decisions at the local, state, and federal levels that shaped the institution, analyzing the precise role of students, business, and government officials. Chapter 9 then summarizes my findings and shows how they diverge from the claims of the pluralist functionalist, Marxist instrumentalist, and institutionalist accounts of the rise and expansion of the community college.

CHAPTER 6

Local-Level Institution Building: The Centrality of Local Educators

Local community colleges make up the vast bulk of public two-year colleges. Other kinds of two-year colleges—state community colleges, two-year university branches, or public vocational-technical institutes— are much rarer. In almost all cases, local community colleges were begun at local initiative. In fact, states generally required local initiative and governance as a way of ensuring that localities would be prepared to help support them. Of the 28 states in 1963–1964 that had laws pertaining to local community colleges, only two allowed for the state to alone initiate their establishment. In the remaining 26 states, the initiative was supposed to come either from local citizens alone (9 states), local school boards or local governments alone (9), or either one (8). Moreover, whatever the mode of initiation, 14 states required approval by a vote of the people (Morrison and Witherspoon, 1966: 12–21).[1]

Local efforts to establish a community college ordinarily followed one of two paths in California, Illinois, New York, and Washington. The first path, one I call "circumscribed initiation," was dominant in the early decades of this century. Local school administrators (or occasionally members of school boards) would come up with the idea of a community college and then secure the approval of the school board. With that, the community college was opened, usually as a department of the local high school. This was a very self-contained process, with very little if any consultation of outside interest groups or the public at large. Of the 34 community college foundings I studied, 13 took this route.

Among the earliest and best-known examples of circumscribed initiation were the community college foundings at Joliet, Illinois (1901) and Fresno, California (1910). The spark for founding a community college in Joliet, a small city just south of Chicago, came from the superintendent of the local township high school district, J. Stanley Brown.[2] Inspired by the vigorous advocacy of the junior college by William Rainey Harper, president of the University of Chicago and a fellow Baptist, Brown founded Joliet Junior College in the modest form of a "postgraduate

127

department" of the high school, with students who were recent graduates of the high school and faculty who taught regular high school fare in addition to their college courses. Although most date the college's inception to 1901, if not earlier, the township board of education did not formally recognize the college until 1902, when it decided that "graduates of the high school may take post-graduate work without any additional charge being made" (quoted in Fretwell, 1954: 11). This quiet start gave way to an equally sober and gradual institutional development. It was not until 1912 that a Junior College Committee of teachers was formed. The title "Junior College" supplanted the term "postgraduate program" only in 1937. And the junior college remained part of the high school until the 1960s, when governance was shifted to an independent district with its own board and tax base.

Fresno Junior College, the first to be established in California, came into the world in a similarly modest manner.[3] The local high school superintendent, C. L. McLane, circulated a letter to parents in his district and to principals in adjoining districts explaining the advantages of a community college. When "over two hundred favorable replies were received with not one adverse opinion" (McLane, 1913: 163), he asked his board of education to establish the community college as a department of the high school. With the board's approval, the community college started with 20 students and three instructors, who taught high school courses as well as college courses. It was to be many years before the community college broke away from the high school to form its own district.

With time, the relatively self-contained process of initiation described above gave way to a more open and politically complicated process. In order to prevent community colleges from wildly multiplying and developing an overwhelming appetite for state aid, state governments began to require that community college foundings be approved in advance by a designated state agency and, typically as well, by the local citizenry through referendum. Moreover, the increasing number of college aspirants and the consequent increase in the cost of operating a community college broadened the list of interested private parties.

These new conditions gave rise in the 1930s and 1940s to the second path to community college founding, which we might term "popular mobilization." It was characterized by a much more broadly based politics. Again, local school administrators were the main initiators, although school board members and local businesspeople often were co-initiators. (Table 6–1 gives the frequency of participation of various actors in the founding of community colleges.) In order to secure the approval of the voters, local initiators typically established a "citizens' committee" to

TABLE 6–1
Local-Level Stances Toward the Community College in Four States:
Percentage of Community Colleges in Which Actors Participated in Indicated Way[a]

	In Favor, Strong Participation	In Favor, Weak Participation	In Favor, Unknown Degree of Participation	Opposed	Ambivalent	No Role
Nongovernmental Actors						
Students[b]		23%	2%			75%
PTAs	11%	12%	6%			72%
Business	62%	6%		4%		27%
Civic clubs[c]	23%	34%				43%
Labor unions	15%	41%				44%
Farmers	5%	11%		15%	3%	68%
Minority groups		8%		6%		86%
Private colleges[d]	10%	4%				87%
Taxpayer groups		3%		13%		85%
Foundations						100%
Governmental Actors						
K-12 educators	72%	11%			6%	12%
State universities	22%	20%			4%	55%
State educ. depts.	28%	3%			4%	65%
State community college boards	21%	5%				74%

Notes:
a. The four states are California, Washington, Illinois, and New York. Each statistic reported is an average of the percentages for each state. Hence, the statistic reported corrects for the fact that the number of community colleges I studied varied by state: California (6); Washington (14); Illinois (10); New York (4). However, in each state, I studied at least one community college in each of these locales: metropolitan center city; metropolitan suburb; small city; and small town. (See Table 5–3 in Chapter 5.) The percentages (which read across) do not add up to 100% because of rounding error. Actors are classified as strong participants in favor if they not only announced strong support but backed it up with active involvement, such as working to pass a community college referendum or lobbying the state government to approve a community college. If their support only took the form of endorsements, without active support, they are classified as weak participants. If an interest group was split, it is put as ambivalent.
b. Only conventional student participation is listed. Participation in the form simply of enrolling in community college is excluded. See text for more.
c. Often civic clubs such as the Lions and Jaycees were largely composed of businesspeople. Hence, they cannot be taken as an entirely separate actor.
d. In Illinois, there were reports of extensive local private college opposition to community college foundings other than those I studied.

spearhead a referendum drive. The key participants in this committee, in addition to educators, usually were school board members and businesspeople (who often were one and the same). Less important participants were the local newspapers, service clubs and civil organizations (such as the Rotary Club and the League of Women Voters), labor unions, and occasionally officials of the state universities and the state department of education.

The founding of John A. Logan College in Carterville, Illinois provides a good example of this second path to founding a community college. The college is nestled deep in southern Illinois in an area called "Little Egypt." Nearby are the towns of Marion (the site of the federal penitentiary), Carbondale (the home of Southern Illinois University), Herrin, West Frankfort, and DuQuoin.[4] The idea for a community college was first raised in 1964 by a loose group of educators and local businesspeople. In early 1965, educators from a four-county area formed a steering committee to assay how much support there was for a community college among school board members and local notables in their districts and to develop a proposal to the state for a community college district. In fall 1965, the committee decided that enough support existed to present a proposal for a community college district to the Illinois Community College Board (ICCB). The ICCB had been established under the 1965 Illinois Public Junior College Act to ratify local proposals to establish community college districts, hold local referenda on their establishment, and then regulate the newly established community colleges. Community colleges had long existed prior to this, of course, but almost all took the form of high school divisions. The 1965 act provided strong incentives for localities to transfer control over existing community colleges to newly formed independent community college districts and to establish community college districts in areas otherwise lacking a nearby community college. The ICCB held hearings on the Logan College proposal in May 1966 and approved it in February 1967. A referendum was held on the proposal in September 1967, with the community college winning.

With a good idea of the form local decisions to establish community colleges took, let us examine whether the actors highlighted by the functionalist, instrumentalist, and institutionalist explanations adequately explain that policymaking. Was the participation of students and their parents, business, or the state universities sufficiently extensive and strong to make them deserving of the leading roles they are assigned by the contending theories? Or are their performances so weak that other actors, left hidden in the wings, should be brought center stage?[5]

Private Interest Group Pressure Was Not the Main Cause

The Role of Students

The functionalist advocates, while mentioning a number of actors, give the central role to demands by students and parents in explaining the proliferation of community colleges. The precise form this political participation took is often not specified clearly, so we will look at two forms. One is conventional participation, involving the formulation of opinions and their insertion into the policymaking process by such means as joining groups that mobilized support for the community college, endorsing the efforts of such groups, or at minimum, simply expressing favorable opinions in polls that policymakers took note of. The second, and much weaker, concept of political participation is simply enrolling in community colleges once they are established: that is, voting with one's feet rather than one's mouth.

As Table 6–1 shows, students only occasionally participated in one of the various conventional ways in local-level policymaking on the community college. Averaging across the four states that developed community colleges (California, Illinois, New York, and Washington), I find that only one-quarter of community college foundings involved the conventional participation of students.[6] This participation took various forms. In San Bernardino, California in 1926, high school students endorsed a proposal to establish a community college (Fretwell, 1954). In Wenatchee, Washington, during the Depression, graduates came back individually to their high school to ask if they could take additional courses. According to the first dean of Wenatchee Valley College,

[A]t the time, this was Depression time, the young men and women of the town wanting to get further education had no money to go on to college and they couldn't find jobs. So they kept coming back to me to ask if they could take courses in the high school that they hadn't had. (Van Tassell, 1982)

In other localities—such as Seattle (Washington), Carterville (Illinois), and Batavia and Schenectady (New York)—high school students participated politically by indicating in polls conducted by community college advocates that they would enroll in substantial numbers at a local community college, if one were made available (Chestnut, 1973: 355; Hill, 1978: 311; Peters, 1969: 78–80; Seattle Schools, 1964: 1–4). As we can see, student participation was not particularly strong. In the majority of foundings, student did not participate. And in the cases they did, their involvement was not concerted and persistent but rather took the weaker forms of endorsement and simple expression of opinion.

Parental participation is hard to pin down. Parents of would-be college students could agitate for a community college in their capacities as members of the local chamber of commerce or labor council. But in that case, it would be hard to know in what guise they were participating: was it as parents or as businesspeople or unionists? To get a more direct measure of parental participation, I have looked at the involvement of groups that more clearly represent parents qua parents: for example, Parent-Teachers Associations (PTAs). Admittedly, this is a crude measure, since PTAs do not enroll most parents and tend to be dominated by teachers and administrators (Wirt and Kirst, 1982). Nonetheless, did PTAs evidence any greater involvement than did students in local policymaking on the community college? Essentially, the answer is no. PTAs were involved in only one-quarter of the community college foundings I studied, with their most typical involvement being to endorse a proposal made by others for establishing such a college. To be sure, in 11% of these foundings, PTAs did play a strong role. For example, in San Bernardino, California in 1926 the local PTA was one of the groups involved in the coalition mobilizing voter support for a community college referendum (Fretwell, 1954). But in no case did PTAs ever spearhead a community college drive.

Because it could be argued that conventional political participation is too narrow a concept, I also wish to examine whether rising college enrollments, particularly in the community college, constituted a kind of student participation in community college policymaking. By flocking to community colleges once they were established, students could be taken as voting with their feet for further expansion. A major problem with this formulation is that it loses the specificity of the pluralist concept of political participation, which centers on the self-conscious formation, articulation, and mobilization of political sentiments. But let us set this objection aside and examine the evidence in the light of this looser definition of political participation. Again we find that students and parents played a not insignificant role in the development of the community college, but this role was still not determinative. The rapid escalation of the number of students going to college certainly influenced local activists to think of establishing community colleges. At the same time, why did that rapid enrollment escalation suggest establishing community colleges rather than four-year colleges? It could be argued that community colleges would be cheaper and more accessible than four-year colleges. But the problem with this answer is that these characteristics were matters of political decision rather than intrinsic institutional nature. Community colleges tuitions (as well as other features of the community college) were largely determined not by student demand but by governmental decision, typically at the state level. Four-year colleges could have been made as cheap and accessible as two-year colleges. But as we will see below, government officials found it not in their interest to do so. They much preferred to have community colleges rather than four-year colleges absorb the bulk of the enrollment wave of the 1960s and 1970s. And a prime way they ensured this result was to make community colleges the cheaper and more accessible of the two institutions.

These considerations do not lead to the conclusion that student desire played no role in local decisions to found community colleges. But they certainly suggest that the functionalist emphasis on the centrality of student and parental demand is misplaced. This case is particularly weak if we focus on conventional political participation, whether in the form of lobbying, joining pressure groups, or expressing support in opinion polls. Student and parental participation in these forms was at best moderately strong at the local level. If we relax the definition of student participation to simply equate it with student enrollment in community colleges, a stronger case can be made for the importance of student influence on the policymaking process. But this still does not validate the central role functionalist theory gives to student demand for college access, because it does not explain why the community college was favored over other postsecondary institutions such as four-year colleges, university branches, or postsecondary vocational schools.

Business

But if student and parental demand leaves much of community college policymaking unexplained, how are we to fill this explanatory vacuum? The instrumentalist critics of the community college have an answer: the commands of a capitalist class centered in the business elite but with fellow travelers in the higher circles of the foundations and government.

This left-wing version of the thesis of interest-group pressure fares better than the functionalist argument. Business pressure indeed played a significant role in local decisions to establish community colleges, but again it was not determinative. Businesspeople—whether as individuals, firms, or organizations such as chambers of commerce—supported the establishment of an average of 68% of the community colleges studied across the states of California, Illinois, New York, and Washington.[7] And in nearly all of these cases their support was strong (see Table 6–1).[8]

Along with local educators, businesspeople usually provided a major part of the membership and often the leadership of local community college committees. These committees were established in many areas, often at the behest of local educators, to drum up support for establishing a community college. Usually business served as a junior partner of local educators. But occasionally businesspeople were the main sparkplugs, as in the cases of the community colleges at San Bernardino, California (1926), Orange County, New York (1950), and Schenectady, New York (1969) (Chestnut, 1973; Fretwell, 1954; Schuilling, 1978). In the case of Schenectady Community College, the County Chamber of Commerce began to study the idea of a community college in 1957, 12 years before the college was founded. It gathered information from the State Department of Education and the State University of New York and published in 1961 a booklet calling for a feasibility study. In 1965, the Chamber of Commerce recommended to the County Board of Supervisors that a committee be established to study the feasibility of a community college. Closely monitored by the Chamber of Commerce, the Community College Study Committee recommended in 1966 that a community college be established, and one finally opened its doors in 1967 (Chestnut, 1973).

Business's championing of the community college had considerable impact because businesspeople usually hold a sizable proportion of the seats on the local board of education.[9] Moreover, local chambers of commerce are typically among the best organized and financed private interest group locally. In fact, local chambers of commerce frequently function as the voice of their communities, often overshadowing local governments.

Local business strongly supported the community college in part because it shared the general interest in educational opportunity. But three other interests were as or more important: securing publicly subsidized employee training, fostering local economic development, and burnishing local pride. Donald Carlson, a banker who helped found the College of DuPage in a suburb of Chicago, stated the interest in employee training:

> We felt a need—having discussed it with people in manufacturing and the business world—that they needed people not necessarily having finished a four-year accredited college but at least several years. . . . Many people were not prepared for jobs. This is what we kept hearing from people in the business world. (Carlson, 1982)

Business also saw a local community college as an engine of economic development. Roland Sax, editor of the *Belleville [Ill.] News Democrat,* noted that one reason local business supported Belleville Junior College was that

> increased educational opportunities for all . . . is an asset to the community and would at least be a factor in permitting growth and expansion. . . . Because if you have a college it's like having a good highway to your town. If you have a highway to your town somebody's going to come through and may be attracted to establish a business or an industry. It's an asset, a community asset, by serving all kinds of people.

Business's interest in economic growth was tied to the fact that several key local industries have a direct stake in the state of the local economy. As Molotch (1976) has argued, banks, utilities, real estate firms, and newspapers—what he calls the "growth coalition"—prosper when land values rise. And land values rise as the population and business investment rise. In the eyes of local growth coalitions, a community college would stimulate the local economy by attracting outside industry through its occupational-education program, by attracting students (and their spending) from neighboring towns, and by purchasing goods and services in the local economy.

The desire to foster local economic development was intertwined and legitimated by another motive: local pride. Many chambers of commerce and civic clubs (which largely enroll small-business people and local professionals) supported a community college in part as a way of putting their towns on the map and successfully competing, culturally and economically, with neighboring towns. Alexis Lange, dean of the University of California School of Education and one of the earliest of community college advocates, noted the role of local pride: "The rapid multiplication of junior colleges, since the first one was established at Fresno, is partly owing to inter-communal bellwether-and-sheep relations, combined with the spirit of emulation" (Lange, 1916: 4).[10]

But despite the evident importance of business in supporting and occasionally leading local efforts to found community colleges, we must not exaggerate its influence. Business did not participate with the breadth and depth claimed by instrumentalist Marxist theory. Business was not a factor in the founding of several important community colleges: Chicago, Joliet, Los Angeles, New York City (Cox, 1971; Eells, 1931; Fretwell, 1954; Gordon, 1975; Hoffland and Evans, 1976; Reid, 1966; Smolich,

1967). And even in those foundings where it played a major role, its participation was usually catalyzed and organized by local educators. Usually business served as a junior partner of local educators. James Walker, a businessman and the first president of the board of trustees of John A. Logan College in Carterville, Illinois described the typical relationship between educators and businesspeople involved in founding a community college:

> In those first early things it was school people that I ran into. When we began to know that we had a district and got out then and developed a referendum to create a district, then we began to see other individuals getting in. . . . The steering committees, the blue-ribbon committees, that were in each of the towns, I would say that they were steered to a large extent by your school people—county superintendents and various unit or school principals. But rather quickly the business community got behind it, maybe out of civic pride, economic benefit, a little do good. It was a mixed bag. (Walker, 1982)

The Key Role of Local School Officials and Other Educators

Government officials did not just wait for private interest groups to press them to act. They often acted in the absence of interest-group involvement, seeking the realization of values and interests of their own. The institutionalist and functionalist explanations have pointed to one such governmental actor, the state universities. They indeed played a key role, but so did local educators and state departments and boards of education. In fact, if anything, we must give pride of place to local educators.

Local Educators

Local school superintendents and high school principals were the master builders of the community college at the local level.[11] Averaging across the four states establishing community colleges, they were involved in 83% of the 34 community college foundings I studied. In fact, in 72% of the cases, local educators were strongly involved, usually acting as the initiators of the local effort to establish a community college. (See Table 6–1.) This key role of local educators becomes especially clear if we examine specific cases. Let us begin with the founding of John A. Logan College in Carterville, Illinois. Leslie Stilley, the chair of the steering committee leading the effort and the superintendent of schools of Williamson County, Illinois, described educators' key role:

All the school principals, superintendents, and business managers in the county met once a month . . . to discuss their problems, get better acquainted, and have a better working relationship for all of us. And at one meeting . . . is when I discussed with the Williamson County administrators the [just passed 1965 Illinois Public] Junior College Act: what it amounted to, our needs. . . . Everybody was enthused by the program. We met then and organized the steering committee to work on the junior college. . . . Our steering committee was made up of all unit superintendents (we had five units in the county ...), all high school principals, business managers, the county superintendents, and the assistant superintendents. We had around 23, 24. (Stilley, 1981)

It could be argued that, as an educator, Stilley exaggerated his colleagues' role in the Logan effort. But as we have seen in the previous section, James Walker, a businessman active in the same effort, concurred that local educators were the key actors: "The steering committees, the blue-ribbon committees, that were in each of the towns, I would say that they were steered to a large extent by your school people—county superintendents and various unit or school principals."[12]

The establishment of Shoreline Community College, in the northern suburbs of Seattle, also illustrates the key role of local educators in leading efforts to found community colleges.[13] According to several different participants and observers, the superintendent of schools, Raymond Howard, sparked and led the effort to found a community college in the Shoreline area. Howard had been nursing the idea of a community college from the early 1950s, after having taught in California and seen their community college system:

I taught in California during the summer of '51 and the summer of '53 at San Jose State College courses in school administration. I spent a considerable time around Stanford, particularly with the new community colleges that were established around there. . . . And I talked with a lot of people. I visited community colleges. . . . So in the 1960s, when the population pressure came . . . I had filed that in memory and it came out so easily. (Howard, 1981)

As college enrollments began to rise rapidly in the late 1950s, Howard began to mobilize support for a community college among his school board members and teachers. With the school board's permission, the Shoreline School District applied for state approval of a community college, which came in 1963. Meanwhile, Howard secured local approval in a 1962 referendum of a bond issue to fund the community college. He mobilized support for the bond issue through a Citizens' Advisory

Committee consisting of school board members, teachers, and laypeople. According to Howard, the citizens' committee allowed him to advance the community college idea without always having to be in the forefront:

> I was there to really run with the ball and provide the leadership, the encouragement that here was something that was really needed for the north end of Seattle, and we needed to work together. And once the people came in, this [school] board was so outstanding, I could take a back seat once they understood. (Howard, 1981)

Local educators—stretching from district superintendents to high school principals to teachers—supported the community college for a host of different reasons. One certainly was the very strong value they put on enlarging educational opportunity. As educators, they were passionately committed to broadening college opportunity. They were very aware of escalating student interest in college opportunities. As the high school expanded rapidly in the early decades of this century, it rapidly began to produce many more graduates, with many of these graduates eager to go on to college.[14] In California, for example, the number of high school graduates roughly tripled every 10 years, rising from about 1,000 in 1900 to 4,247 in 1910, 11,787 in 1920, and 35,236 in 1930. And in Illinois the number of 16- to 17-year-olds attending school rose by 283% between 1920 and 1940 in four localities that established community colleges in the period—Joliet, Chicago, Cicero (Morton Junior College), and Centralia—while rising by only 88% in the rest of the state (U.S. Bureau of the Census, 1923; idem, 1943). In both cases, this rapid increase in numbers soon overwhelmed the available number of college places at the state's public and private colleges and led to considerable interest in expanding college places.

Local educators were also committed to meeting the training needs of the "community." Especially after 1960, the community college came to be seen as a "comprehensive" institution, providing vocational education as well as academic education. Local educators saw the beneficiaries of this vocational education to be both students of limited ambition or ability and businesses needing trained employees. Raymond Howard, the Shoreline school superintendent, stated:

> The attitude of most people in Shoreline was that they viewed the college as the transition opportunity to help their kids into a large university. They therefore viewed it essentially from an academic standpoint. But there were those of us including the board [of education], many of our citizens too, who recognized that the population could change and that increasingly crafts and technologies [would be important]. (Howard, 1981)

Both needs were united in the concept of the needs of the "community" (Howard, 1981; Seattle Schools, 1964: 1).

The values of local educators provided a powerful impetus for action even in the absence of strong pressure from students or business. But they do not explain why those educators favored the community college over other means of meeting students' wish for college opportunities and business's desire for publicly subsidized vocational training, such as four-year colleges and vocational schools, respectively. The secret lies in educators' self-interests. Local educators were attracted by the prospect of a college that, unlike the others, would be locally controlled and thus provide them access to college-level teaching and administrative jobs and prestige as educational innovators.

The superintendent of the Shoreline (Washington) public schools, Raymond Howard, noted that high school teachers and administrators were attracted to the idea of founding a community college by the prospect of college-level jobs:

> As they began to appraise it—to see that maybe this was going to be a really outstanding community college . . . —we found then that the head of the math department of the high school, the head of the science department, began to express an interest and attend the planning sessions. And sure enough a number of those heads of departments at Shoreline College are former secondary school people. (Howard, 1981)

In fact, very often the first administrators and teachers of a community college were the teachers and administrators of the local high school.

Local educators also favored the community college over other kinds of institutions because it was a route to garnering prestige as educational innovators (Reid, 1966: 294; Cothran, 1979: 297). For example, after spearheading the establishment of a community college in his town, Centralia (Washington) school superintendent C. L. Littel found himself invited to describe his achievement to a group contemplating doing the same in Aberdeen, Washington (Crawfurd, 1959: 85, 91). In fact, the pleasures of starting a community college could be so great that Frederick Bolton (1926: 294), dean of education at the University of Washington and a key supporter of the community college movement, was compelled to admonish community college advocates on the dangers: "No junior college should be launched in any community unless there is enthusiastic and whole-hearted support of the movement by the community. A college should not be started to gratify the ambitions of the superintendent [and] the board of education. . . . " More recent testimony to this desire for prestige comes from Shoreline superintendent Raymond Howard, as he describes how he interested his teachers in forming a community college:

> We have a space needle in Seattle. And I came on a happy thought that really caught. I said to them: "Look. Sure, we've got a good school system. But what we need in this school system is a space needle. And a community college can provide that space needle." Well, they kind of caught hold of that. (Howard, 1981)

Local educators' interest in being educational innovators stemmed in good part from their membership in a profession in which, as in most professions, success is defined in terms of winning the good regard of its leaders. In this case, these leaders often were faculty members at the leading university schools of education (Tyack and Hansot, 1982). The leaders' approbation could be won through pioneering a new educational program, particularly one such as the community college that many university presidents and faculty members had conceived of and propagandized for (Eells, 1931; Koos, 1925). Not surprisingly, then, many colleges were founded by local educators who had close ties to the centers of power of the educational profession. For example, J. Stanley Brown, the school superintendent who founded the Joliet Junior College (1901), cited as his inspiration William Rainey Harper, president of the University of Chicago, vigorous advocate of the junior college, and a fellow Baptist:

> Joliet takes no particular credit for it [its founding], but concedes it to the man of vision, Dr. William R. Harper, the first president of the University of Chicago. Superintendent Soldan of St. Louis, President Butler of Columbia University, and one or two others met at the University of Chicago in 1899, and during that meeting clearly set forth that the first two years of college is secondary school work. . . . They said, Why should not centers be established where the first two years of college work should be given? Accordingly a junior college was started at Joliet with five or six students. . . . (Brown, 1922: 27)

A similar process of influence was at work in Washington State. C. L. Littel and Arthur Nelson—the school superintendents who founded the Centralia and Mt. Vernon (Washington) community colleges, respectively—were both doctoral students at Stanford University, a leading fount of community college sentiment. Its presidents, David Starr Jordan and Ray Wilbur, and professors of education, Walter C. Eells and Ellwood P. Cubberly, were vigorous advocates of the community college idea (Reid, 1966: 140, 359; McLane, 1913: 166–167). And A. C. Roberts, the high school principal who founded the Everett (Washington) Junior

College in 1915, claimed to have been inspired by his teacher at the University of Washington, Frederick Bolton (Crawfurd, 1959: 54).

For local educators interested in college-level jobs or professional prestige, a community college was much more attractive than a vocational-technical school because it carried the cachet of being a "real" college, one that led toward the baccalaureate degree. But a community college was even superior to a four-year college or university. It was more likely to recruit its staff among local high school teachers and administrators than would a new four-year college, which would be much more likely to advertise nationally for new staffers. Moreover, unlike a four-year college, it could be established without requiring the approval of the state legislature (the exception was Washington during the 1960s).

But although quite real, local educators' autonomy of action was not unconstrained. Like all government officials, they were only relatively autonomous. Even when pursuing their own values and interests they also served those of other groups. The constraints were both ideological and material. Educators' values benefited other groups because they were ideologies: that is, belief systems that implicitly advanced the interests of certain groups. Educators' attachment to equality of opportunity benefited students desiring college chances. Similarly, the value they put on meeting the needs of the "community" for vocational education benefited business because it was usually seen as a central element of that community. Furthermore, educators found themselves serving the interests of students and business for reasons of resource dependence. To stay in office, they needed the political support of school board members and those voting for them. Even when business and students groups were not demanding specific actions, educators were mindful of the fact that they would be attracted by the prospect of a cheap, vocationally oriented college.

State Universities

Local educators were the most important, but not the only, governmental actors intervening in local decisions to found community colleges. As the institutionalists and functionalists have noted, the state universities were early and powerful champions of the community colleges. As early as the turn of the century, they exhorted local educators and citizens to establish community colleges (Bolton, 1926: 294; Griffith, 1945: 245–246; University of Illinois, 1947; McLane, 1913: 166–167). Once a community college was established, all the leading state universities were quick to provide assistance, which in turn encouraged the efforts of community college advocates elsewhere. The universities accredited community colleges if they met certain minimum requirements (Crawfurd, 1959: 72, 78–80, 83, 98, 159). More importantly, they gave university credit for courses taken at community colleges, thus allowing students to begin working on a baccalaureate degree at a community college and complete it at the university (Lange, 1916: 7; McDowell, 1919; Ross, 1963: 145; Smolich, 1967: 193–194; Stewart, 1922: 44).

But the universities did not rest with this general assistance. They also intervened directly in an average of 42% of local community college foundings (22% of them strongly). (See Table 6–1.) In 1907, the dean of education at the University of California, Alexis Lange, wrote to the Fresno School Superintendent, C. L. McLane, announcing the university's support of the latter's efforts to found a community college in Fresno (McLane, 1913: 166–167). Forty years later, the university publicly supported the effort to establish the Contra Costa Community College east of San Francisco (Fretwell, 1954: 70–71). Farther up the Pacific Coast, the dean of the School of Education at the University of Washington, Frederick Bolton, encouraged the champions of a community college in Yakima by guaranteeing that it would receive provisional accreditation from the university if it satisfactorily met certain conditions (Crawfurd, 1959: 83). And in Illinois, the University of Illinois, faced with the onrushing tide of World War II veterans entering college, invited local school boards to set up extension centers of the university, suggesting that these centers could become community colleges. In fact, 31 of these centers were set up by local school boards, with 4 eventually transmuting themselves into community colleges (Smith, 1980: 1–2, 10–18).

State Education Departments and Boards

The state universities were not the only state agencies intervening in the local politics of the community college. State chief school officers and their state education departments participated in an average of 31% of local community college drives, typically offering local proponents advice and encouragement.[15] In New York, a representative of the state department of education met with the Schenectady Chamber of Commerce to present the case for establishing a community college (Chestnut, 1973: 44). In California, state education officials suggested to local notables in the Contra Costa area near San Francisco that they consider establishing a community college. In fact, these officials went further: the state superintendent of schools publicly urged Contra Costa voters to approve such a college when it was put to referendum three years later

(Fretwell, 1954: 63, 73; Stoker, 1971: 22, 28). And jumping to Illinois, we find that the founders of the John A. Logan (Carterville) and Southeastern (Harrisburg) community colleges first encountered the idea of establishing a community college district when this was suggested by the state department of education (Hill, 1978: 94–96; Szymczak, 1977: 55). In the late 1950s, the state department had created the post of junior college specialist and an Inter-University Bureau to assist communities with the mechanics of founding community colleges.

After 1965, the newly established Illinois Community College Board (ICCB) took up the state education department's role of intervening in local decisions on the community college. The ICCB actively brokered the formation of several community colleges in southern Illinois. In this poor, thinly populated region, community colleges had to be based on geographically large districts. But this imperative ran counter to the fierce competitiveness of the many small towns in this area. Many towns would not join a district if their hated rival, which might be only 15 miles away, would be the site of the community college. The state board emerged as a key mobilizer in the face of these local impediments to action. It met with local advocates to provide advice, encouragement, and not infrequently, rebuke. It conducted studies to determine which boundaries would yield a community college district capable of supporting a community college. And it mediated disputes among the small towns (Hill, 1978; Idisi, 1979; Smith, 1980; Szymczak, 1977). (See Chapter 7 on state-level policymaking for more on the role of state community college boards.)

It might be argued that the state universities, departments of education, and community college boards intervened in local policymaking simply at the behest of interest groups at the state level rather than at their own volition. To see that this was not the case, let us move to examining policymaking at the state level and the forces impinging on state officials.

CHAPTER 7

State-Level Advocates: The Interests of Governors and State University Officials

Local community college efforts were spurred and shaped by state-level policy decisions. This influence reflected the central role that state government plays in educational policymaking. Under the reserve clause of the United States Constitution, state governments exercise original jurisdiction over education. For the most part, they delegate the day-to-day administration of education to local school districts and higher education institutions. But this delegated power is hedged around by a host of state restrictions (Campbell, Cunningham, Nystrand, and Usdan, 1985: chap. 3; Wirt and Kirst, 1982: 192–197, 215–221, 229–239).

State governments began to intervene in the process of community college expansion by granting to localities permission to form community colleges if they met certain conditions. California inaugurated such legislation in 1907. Illinois followed in 1937 and Washington in 1941 (although the first community college had been founded in 1901 in Illinois and in 1915 in Washington). But New York waited to give state permission until 1948 (with the first community college not opening its doors until 1950). Looking across all 50 states, we find that by 1948 half the states had a law regulating the establishment of public two-year colleges. By 1964, 43 states had such laws (Martorana, 1963: 34; Morrison and Martorana, 1962: 13; Morrison and Witherspoon, 1966: 11; Simms, 1948: 16).

State aid to community colleges came next. Usually it began in the indirect form of allowing school districts to include community college enrollments in the calculation of general state school-aid apportionments. In time, states enacted grants directed specifically to community colleges. Again, California was a pioneer, initiating indirect aid in 1917 and direct aid in 1921. Washington and New York followed in 1941 and 1948, enacting direct aid. And Illinois brought up the rear, passing indirect aid in 1951 and direct aid in 1955. Across all 50 states, we find that by 1961, 21 had enacted aid specifically for community colleges and 23 had allowed community college enrollments to be included in calculating

TABLE 7–1
State Aid to the Community College, 1920s–1990

	1920s	1949–1950	1957–1958	1969–1970	1978–1979	1989–1990
Absolute amount (in millions)		$26.3	$47.7	$755.9	$3,100	
Percentage of all community college current income	5%	30%	30%	41%	49%	49%

Sources: Cohen and Brawer (1989: 128); U.S. Office of Education (1954: chap. 4, sec. 2, p. 36); idem (1962: chap. 4, sec. 2, p. 24); U.S. National Center for Education Statistics (1973a: 14–15); idem (1981a: 14–15); idem (1992b: 16).

school-aid apportionments (Levine, 1986: 175; Morrison and Martorana, 1962: 37–70; Simms, 1948: 49–52).

Standing at 5% of the current revenues of community colleges in the 1920s, state aid jumped to 30% in 1950 and 49% in 1989–1990 (Cohen and Brawer, 1989: 128; U.S. Office of Education, 1954: chap. 4, sec. 2, p. 36; idem, 1962: chap. 4, sec. 2, p. 24; U.S. National Center for Education Statistics, 1973a: 14–15; idem, 1981a: 14–15; idem, 1992b: 16).[1] (See Table 7–1.) This aid was very important because it reduced the price to localities of maintaining a community college. It made economically depressed areas such as the southern part of Illinois and the eastern part of Washington able to consider community colleges. But state aid played a role even in affluent areas. The citizens' committee leading the drive to establish the College of DuPage in a suburb of Chicago gave as one argument for establishing a community college the ready availability of state aid.

The capstone to these legislative efforts typically was the establishment of a state community college system, headed by a state board to govern, but not directly administer, the local community colleges. Illinois established its state community college system and board in 1965, with California and Washington following in 1967.[2] In the case of Illinois, this new legislation provoked a major upsurge in community college foundings. Nearly as many community colleges were established after 1965 as in all the years previous. It provided new fiscal incentives to localities to establish a community college. It also installed a state community college board that actively brokered the formation of local community colleges (see Chapter 6 for more). But perhaps the most important effect was ideological. The 1965 act made local community college advocates feel that they were part of a broad-based, statewide movement that was a necessary response to the times. In my interviews, these advocates often explained why they established a community college by simply noting the passage of the 1965 act and saying, "Well, the time had just come."

Some areas in Illinois did not heed the trumpet call of the zeitgeist, however, so the state legislature gave them an extra push by passing a law in 1971 that required the Illinois Community College Board to assign every "out-of-district" area to a new or existing community college district, with the proviso that these areas be allowed to hold referenda on whether they wished to remain in those districts (Smith, 1980: 189–194).

Other forms of state-level encouragement overlapped in time with the legislative encouragement described above. From the very beginning, state universities encouraged local community college activists by offering advice on how to establish a community college, providing university credit for community college courses, and passing up the opportunity to develop statewide systems of university branches that would substitute for community college development (Brint and Karabel, 1989: 25–27, 208; Eells, 1931; McDowell, 1919: 102). (See Chapter 6 for more.)

With a firm sense of the scope and importance of state policymaking to encourage community college expansion, let us turn to examining how well pressure from students, business, and the foundations explains these state efforts.

How Involved Were Nongovernmental Actors?

Students

Conventional political participation by students and parents was almost entirely absent at the state level. I have found no evidence that students lobbied, issued endorsements, or expressed their opinions in polls on any of the major decisions detailed above: permitting community colleges to be established, enacting state aid, establishing a state community college system, providing university credits for community college courses, or forgoing the development of two-year university branches. (See Table 7–2.) To be sure, parents, at least in the form of the PTA, were not entirely uninvolved. The PTA did lobby state officials in Illinois and Washington to facilitate the spread of community colleges. However, such participation in state-level policymaking occurred on only two occasions in Illinois and one in Washington and was powerful only in the latter state (Browne, 1981: 2; McKinney, 1967: 219–220; Pedtke, 1979: 18).

Because it could be argued that conventional political participation is too narrow a concept, I also wish to examine whether rising college enrollments, particularly in the community college, constituted a kind of

TABLE 7–2
State-Level Stances Toward the Community College in Four States:
Percentage of States in which Actors Participated in Indicated Way[a]

	In Favor, Strong Participation	In Favor, Weak Participation	In Favor, Unknown Degree of Participation	Opposed	Ambivalent	No Role
Nongovernmental Actors						
Students[b]						100%
PTAs	25%	25%				50%
Business	25%[c]					75%
Labor unions		100%				0%
Farmers					25%	75%
Minority groups						100%
Private colleges		25%		50%		25%
Foundations		50%	50%			0%
Governmental Actors						
State universities	75%					25%
State educ. depts.	50%	25%			25%	
State higher educ. and community college boards	50%					50%
Governors					100%[d]	0%
Legislators	100%					0%
State K-12 associations	50%	25%				25%
State community college assns.	75%					25%
AACC		100%				0%
Federal government		100%				0%

Notes:
a. The states are California, Washington, Illinois, and New York. Actors are classified as strong participants in favor of the community college if they not only announced strong support but backed it up with active involvement in such forms as lobbying the state government to pass community college legislation. If their support only took the form of endorsements, without active support, they are classified as weak participants.
b. Only conventional political participation is listed here. Participation in the form simply of enrolling in community college is not included. See text for more.
c. This 25% represents business in Illinois. It could be argued that it should be put down as ambivalent, because while the Illinois State Chamber of Commerce strongly supported the community college after 1955, the other business associations were uninvolved and even slightly opposed.
d. This rating is somewhat deceptive. Before World War II, governors were typically opposed to the community college, but after World War II they were almost invariably supportive of it.

student participation in community college policymaking. Here we find that students and parents played a not insignificant role, but it was still not determinative. The rapid escalation of the number of students entering higher education institutions, especially community colleges, certainly influenced state policymakers to think of expanding the community colleges still further. At the same time, that rapid escalation in community college enrollments was itself the product of earlier decisions by policymakers to offer students the community college in place of other kinds of institutions. Many students enrolled in community colleges not necessarily because they wanted this institution in particular but because they were looking for colleges with certain characteristics: for example, accessibility and low cost. Testimony to the importance of cost in student choice was given in Chapter 3, which cites several studies that find that the lower community college tuitions are relative to four-year college tuitions, the more likely students will attend community colleges, all other things being equal (Corman and Davidson, 1984; Grubb, 1988; Sulock, 1982).[3]

But if community colleges are simply cheaper and more accessible, should we not then treat the desire for a cheap and accessible institution as tantamount to a desire for a community college? This would be a mistake, for these characteristics were matters of political decision. Community college tuitions (as well as other features of the community college) were largely determined not by student demand but by governmental decision, typically at the state level. Four-year colleges could have been made as cheap and accessible as four-year colleges. But, as we will see below, state officials did not find it in their interest to do so. They much preferred to have community colleges rather than four-year colleges ingest the bulk of the enrollment wave of the 1960s and 1970s. And a prime way they ensured this result was to make community colleges the cheaper and more accessible of the two institutions.

A final indication of the weakness of student influence is found in Grubb's (1988) study of the political determinants of community college enrollments. He found that states with high proportions of college-age voters (between ages 18 to 30) were no more likely to have high community college enrollments than states with lower proportions of young voters. This null effect occurred despite controls for a wide variety of social and economic differences between the various states (Grubb, 1988: 310).

Business

Was the weak participation of students and parents at the state level counterbalanced by strong pressure from business, thus saving the thesis of the primacy of interest-group pressure? The answer is no. Although largely not opposed, business for the most part absented itself from state-level decisions to expand the number of community colleges in California, New York, and Washington.[4]

In California, business was not involved in the key state-level decisions to promote the community college: the 1907 act permitting their establishment, the laws in 1917 and 1921 extending state aid, the 1961 act recognizing them as part of the higher education system, and the 1967 law bringing them under a state board (Reid, 1966; Simonsen, 1950). Even as late as the 1960s, by which time the community college system had largely been built, business was still largely uninvolved (Brown, 1986; Mussatti, 1986). James Mussatti, longtime general manager of the California Chamber of Commerce (1939–1961), made business's relative disinterest clear:

> We didn't pay much attention to the community colleges unless they came in with an attempt at a big increase in appropriations, in which case we insisted on finding out exactly what was going on. . . . Once the community college idea got going, it had the support of the business community overall during the years I was there. [Did this support ever take the form of actively lobbying for appropriations?] No, not that I know of. (Mussatti, 1986)

The New York business community was no more enthusiastic. It expressed some interest in postsecondary vocational centers (the Institutes for Applied Arts and Sciences) established in 1946. Local businesspeople showed up and made supportive statements at virtually all the public hearings held across New York by the state commission charged by the legislature to determine the degree of public interest in establishing these vocational centers (Donovan, 1952: 129). But when it came to the passage of the 1948 act authorizing the establishment of community colleges and providing them with state aid, business took no role, according to the first president of the State University of New York, Alvin Eurich (1985) and the leading scholar of the 1948 act, O. C. Carmichael (1955). In fact, the community colleges were not mentioned at all in the *Monthly Bulletin* of the state chamber of commerce in the period between May 1947 and April 1950.

And in Washington, business's participation was absent when the key state decisions on the community college were made. There is no mention of business participation in the passage of the 1941 act that authorized community colleges in 1941 and extended them aid (Crawfurd, 1959: 151–152; McKinney, 1967: 222). Moreover, by the admission of its own spokespeople and other observers, business largely sat on the sidelines in 1961, when the state legislature removed the prohibition on establishing community colleges in counties with existing four-year colleges, and in 1967, when a state community college system and state coordinating board were created. To be sure, there was some involvement by Boeing and the King County (Seattle) Chamber of Commerce in 1961, but this involvement was weak by all accounts. Moreover, the Association of Washington Business took no role, even according to its own head (Bruno, 1981; Crawfurd, 1959; Gordon, 1982; McKinney, 1967; Swain, 1982).

Only in Illinois was business actively involved and supportive. Beginning in the mid-1950s, the Illinois State Chamber of Commerce steadily increased its support for community college expansion, according to both its own officials and observers in government and other interest groups. In 1955, the chamber supported, although not all that avidly, the first act to provide direct state aid to community colleges. And 10 years later, it very strongly advocated the 1965 Public Junior College Act, which established a state community college system coordinated by a state board and committed Illinois to the statewide expansion of community colleges (Broman, 1981; Browne, 1981; Clabaugh, 1981; Scott, 1981; Smith, 1981).

The Illinois Chamber's support was largely self-interested. To be sure, it pledged allegiance to the American educational creed of providing greater opportunity for higher education (Illinois State Chamber of Commerce, 1966: 8, 10; Broman, 1981; Scott, 1981). But its main reasons for supporting the community college were to keep down state spending on higher education (and thus keep down taxes) and, above all, to secure business access to publicly supported occupational training (Broman, 1981; Illinois State Chamber of Commerce, 1966: 2, 7, 12). According to the manager of the Chamber's education department,

> they [the State Chamber] ranked the business-vocational function as having the main thrust. . . . To have the opportunity to mold the occupational programs, which in effect will subsidize their [business's] training for the local plants, is a pretty attractive incentive for an industry. I would say that was the main selfish motive [for supporting the 1965 Public Junior College Act]. (Broman, 1981)

But the Chamber's activism was exceptional, even in Illinois. The other Illinois state business associations—such as the Illinois Taxpayers' Federation, the Illinois Manufacturers' Association, and the Chicago Association of Commerce and Industry—were neutral or even slightly opposed to state support of the community college (Broman, 1981; Clabaugh, 1981; Page, 1981; Scott, 1981; Smith, 1981).[5] Moreover, however active the Chamber was in 1955 and after, it did not play a role in the passage of the 1931 and 1937 acts authorizing the establishment of community colleges in Chicago and downstate and the 1951 law allowing community college enrollments to be counted in the formula determining the apportionment of state secondary school aid (Hardin, 1975: 57–58, 90–94).

The Private Foundations

But if business cannot fill the leading role assigned to it by instrumentalist theory, could another of its change masters, the private foundations, answer the casting call? The answer again is no. To be sure, the private foundations had a significant influence on the development of the community college, as they have had on other areas of educational policy (Arnove, 1980; Lagemann, 1983; Scott, 1983). Through their pronouncements and research and program funding, the foundations did focus the attention of state policymakers on the community college and entice their efforts in certain directions (Brint and Karabel, 1989: 47–51, 93–95, 103–107, 210). In its 1956 annual report, the Carnegie Corporation endorsed the community college as "an extremely significant element in the diversity of our system, and its role in the future may be increasingly prominent" (Carnegie Corporation, 1956: 31–32). Fourteen years later, the Carnegie Commission on Higher Education was even more emphatic: "The community college has proved its great worth to American society. Community colleges should be available, within commuting distance, to all persons throughout their lives" (Carnegie Commission on Higher Education, 1970: 1).[6]

These endorsement were widely heeded by state policymakers. The Joint Committee on Higher Education of the Washington State Legislature, when treating the question of what should be the admissions policy of the Washington State community colleges, openly mulled over the Carnegie Commission's recommendation that community colleges should maintain an open-door admissions policy (Washington State Legislature, 1971a: 61–67).

In addition to endorsements, the Carnegie Corporation and the Kellogg Foundation funded research that shaped the rationale for the community college and drew it in certain directions. The Carnegie Corporation granted $400,000 to the University of California in 1955 to establish the Center for the Study of Higher Education. The grant carried the stipulation that the center was to study the diversification of higher education, giving particular attention to the role of the community college in allowing a differentiated higher education system that would preserve selective universities (Carnegie Corporation, 1956: 31–32, 64; idem, 1959: 39; Darknell, 1980: 393–394). Among the studies produced were these now classic books: Leland Medsker's *The Junior College* (1960), Burton Clark's *The Open Door College* (1960), and T. R. McConnell's *A General Plan for Higher Education* (1962). In emphasizing that the community college should be an open-door, vocationally oriented institution that would allow the university to be more selective in its admissions, these studies influenced many state higher education policymakers nationwide. These included the architects of the famous California Master Plan for Higher Education for 1960–1975, which called for massively expanding open-door community colleges and making them the main port of entry into higher education, while restricting admissions to the University of California (Liaison Committee, 1960: 4, 6, 9, 13–14, 59).

The foundations also influenced policymakers indirectly by providing funds to develop the organizational capacities of the American Association of Community Colleges (AACC), thus allowing it to become a major influence in its own right.[7] (See Chapter 8.) Beginning in 1959, the Kellogg Foundation made almost yearly contributions to various programs of the AACC, with these funds totaling $3.5 million by 1980. Meanwhile, the Carnegie Corporation offered $1.2 million between 1963 and 1978. These funds allowed the AACC to conduct research, publish reports, convene meetings, and offer technical consultation on how to establish and run community colleges and develop new programs in such areas as vocational education, guidance and personnel services, lifelong learning, community services, and education of "nontraditional" students (American Association of Junior Colleges, 1967; Brint and Karabel, 1989; Carnegie Corporation, 1963–1978; Kellogg Foundation, 1959–1980).[8]

The private foundations publicly premised their support of the community college on its value in enlarging equality of opportunity and increasing the availability of vocational education to meet the needs of both the economy and of less academically oriented students. The community college's contribution to educational opportunity lay in its low cost and high proximity: "It [the junior college] is important because of the hope it holds out, through geographical accessibility and relatively low costs, for so many young Americans—and especially for those from poor and minority group backgrounds" (Carnegie Corporation, 1968: 21. See also Carnegie Commission on Higher Education, 1970: 1; Kellogg Foundation, 1960: 34). And in the area of vocational education, the community college was praised as addressing the laborpower needs of the economy and providing economic opportunities for students who would otherwise be unable or unwilling to enter higher education (Carnegie Corporation, 1963: 20; Carnegie Commission on Higher Education,

1970: 1; Kellogg Foundation, 1963: 2). The Kellogg Foundation noted:

> We view this area [of semiprofessional and technical education, particularly in community and junior colleges] as one having relation to employment and manpower problems, retraining programs, and population growth, and as being of vital importance to the long-range development of the nation's economy and to the salvaging of many of its youth. (Kellogg Foundation, 1963: 2)

But beyond these much publicized commitments, the foundations also supported the community college for other, less public and more controversial reasons. The foundations also approved of the community college as a means to protect the selectivity of the elite universities (Brint and Karabel, 1989: 104; Carnegie Commission on Higher Education, 1973: 30; Carnegie Corporation, 1956: 31–32; Kellogg Foundation, 1960: 34–35). For example, in its final report in 1973, the Carnegie Commission on Higher Education stated:

> "Elite" institutions of all types—colleges and universities—should be protected and encouraged as a source of scholarship and leadership training at the highest levels. They should not be homogenized in the name of egalitarianism. . . . they should be protected by policies on differentiation of functions. (Carnegie Commission on Higher Education, 1973: 30)

It is well known, of course, that such "policies on differentiation"—such as the much imitated California Master Plan crafted by the Carnegie Commission's chairman, Clark Kerr, in his former capacity as president of the University of California—typically use community colleges to protect the selectivity of the elite state universities. (For more on this, see below.)

The ultimate interests that the foundations pursued are hard to pin down. Many have charged that the foundations essentially serve as the "organic intellectuals" of the capitalist class, determining its interests in the rear areas away from the prime battleground of the shop floor (Arnove, 1980; Karabel, 1972). Certain statements by the foundations give this argument immediate plausibility. The Kellogg Foundation, for example, has openly cast itself as a defender of capitalism: "[F]oundation giving presents the opportunity to show some of the benefits from benevolent capitalism, for most philanthropic organizations, of course, derive their funds directly or indirectly from industrial profits" (Kellogg Foundation, 1960: 2). But this sentiment cannot be applied with any such ease to the Carnegie Corporation. Alan Pifer, its president during the tumultuous 1960s and 1970s, suggested that his conception of the foundation's role during this period was as a mechanism for reforming society so that it could meet its emerging needs:

> Many observers, while denying the foundation a role as *active leader* of the more militant movements of social change, would say that its chief value to society today lies in its capacity to anticipate the need for institutional transformation and help bring these about by speedy deployment of its funds to critical points of leverage and potential breakthrough. (Carnegie Corporation, 1968: 1)

However, to the degree that the Carnegie Corporation has not questioned the institution of capitalism, the effect of its actions has been to rationalize the relationship between the educational system and the capitalist economy with which it coexists (Brint and Karabel, 1989: 48, 105, 213). In essence, the foundations indeed may play the role that instrumentalists assign them, but their motivation may not be as instrumentalists claim.[9]

But while acknowledging the foundations' influence on state-level policymakers, we must not overestimate it. The foundations only began to exert really significant influence in the 1960s, long after the community college movement had begun. State policymakers were already making important decisions on the community college by the 1910s. Hence, although the foundations undoubtedly exerted an important influence, they fail, either alone or as allies of business, to explain the full breadth and depth of policymaking on the community college.

Government Agencies and Officials Weigh In

The interest-group pressure argument again leaves us with an explanatory lacuna. And again we find that to fill it we must acknowledge the key role of self-motivated and self-interested government officials. The institutionalists and functionalists anticipate us by quite rightly pointing out the crucial involvement of state universities. But they have failed to equally note the key roles of state governors, legislators, state departments and boards of education, and state educational associations. These state officials gave state policymaking on the community college the power and completeness it could not have achieved on the basis of private interest group pressure alone. Motivated by reasons of their own, they strongly promoted state assistance to the community college even when students, business, and the foundations were silent.

The experience of different states illustrate the importance of state officials. The states that were quick to develop community college systems—California, Illinois, and Washington—were characterized by the early and strong support of the leading state university, the governor and legislature, and the state educational department. Conversely, in the states that misfired in their community college development, one or more of these key state officials were neutral or even opposed. Indiana—the one state among the five I studied that failed to develop a community college system—evidenced the early, strong, and sustained opposition of the leading state universities (Indiana University and Purdue University) and a lack of support from the governor, legislature, and state department of education. And New York—which was very slow to develop a community college system, not enacting one until 1948—was characterized by the absence of a state university until midcentury, the strong opposition of the state department of education for many years, and the disinterest of the governor and legislature until late.

State Universities[10]

As both the institutionalist and functionalist schools claim, the so-called flagship state universities indeed played an important role in mobilizing state support for the community college (Brint and Karabel, 1989; Cohen and Brawer, 1989; Labaree, 1990).[11] The University of California Board of Regents has been supportive of community college legislation throughout this century (Lange, 1916; Reid, 1966; Simonsen, 1950; Sproul, 1931b). It has usually not intervened on particular bills. However, the university did call for the passage of legislation in 1957 and 1959 to provide capital aid to the community colleges. And in 1960, it endorsed all 63 recommendations in the California Master Plan of 1960, which made the community colleges part of higher education and declared them as the main port of entry to college (Liaison Committee, 1960: iii; Medsker, 1960: 211).

Going north, we find that the University of Washington—in the person of the dean of education, Frederick Bolton—endorsed the 1941 act authorizing the establishment of community colleges and offering state aid. In fact, he also testified before the legislature in favor of similar bills in 1927 and 1929 (Crawfurd, 1959: 78; McKinney, 1967: 212–213). And the University of Washington strongly endorsed the 1961 law that finally allowed community colleges to be established in urban areas and the 1967 act establishing a state community college system (Odegaard, 1980; University of Washington, 1960: 76–77).

Moving to the Midwest, the University of Illinois publicly endorsed state aid in the 1950s and testified in its favor before the School Problems Commission, an advisory group chartered by the Illinois Legislature (Hardin, 1975: 115; Henry, 1956: 1, 5).

One of the least noticed but most important forms of assistance the leading state universities in California, Illinois, and Washington rendered the community college cause was inaction. The public universities in these states, unlike those in Indiana, chose to forgo the development of systems of university branches that would substitute for statewide community college development.[12] This was an extraordinarily important "nondecision," for most trace Indiana's failure to develop community colleges to the decision by Indiana University and Purdue to construct statewide systems of university branches (Holmstedt, 1967: 64; Medsker, 1960: 231; Spilley, 1986; Usdan, Hurwitz, and Minar, 1969: 71–72). These branches absorbed the students that in other states were directed toward community colleges. Nationally, public two-year colleges today enroll 36% of all college students. In Indiana, however, the 10 branches of Indiana University, Purdue, and Indiana State University (not counting the main campuses) account for 26% of all Indiana higher education enrollments, and the 13 state vocational-technical institutes (established in the 1960s) and the one state community college add another 13%, for a total of 39% (U.S. National Center for Education Statistics, 1984a: 45–46; idem, 1984b). The main reason Indiana University and Purdue sponsored the two-year branches was a fear of competition from the community colleges. President Herman B. Wells of Indiana University was quite explicit on this:

> A *special* word of caution is in order with respect to the establishment of junior or community colleges. . . . junior colleges are frequently subjected to pressure from the local chamber of commerce and other groups to change their character. As a result, they gradually develop into four year institutions, thus competing with already established colleges. (Wells, 1956: 6)

The flagship state universities in the other states were not immune from this fear of competition. In the late 1920s and early 1930s, with funds tight and enrollments slipping, the Universities of California, Illinois, and Washington pulled back for a while from their previous stance of undiluted support of the community college. The University of California opposed legislation in 1929 to expand state aid to the community colleges (Brenner, 1979: 263; Cothran, 1979: 266). Frederick Bolton, the dean of the School of Education at the University of Washington, was warned by his president in 1930 that his championship of the community college was not in the university's best interests (Crawfurd, 1959: 89–90). And the University of Illinois fought the 1937 act that authorized the establishment of community colleges outside of Chicago because it feared the bill would spawn a horde of community colleges statewide

(Hardin, 1975: 94–101; Pedtke, 1979: 18). Moreover, the university seriously considered in the late 1930s setting up branches throughout the state (Hardin, 1975: 94, 100–103). The issue for all three universities was enrollment competition. In the case of the University of Illinois, its enrollments fell from 13,370 in 1929–1930 to 10,675 in 1933–1934, while community college enrollments tripled from 6,181 in 1929–1930 (8.2% of all college enrollments) to 19,782 (17.4%) in 1939–1940 (U.S. Office of Education, 1932: II, 343, 387, 419, 525; idem, 1937: II, chap. 4, 50, 122, 218; idem, 1947: II, chap. 4, 20, 110, 250).[13]

But in the end, the elite state universities in California, Illinois, and Washington were dissuaded from starting two-year branches because they feared that these would pull away too many resources from the main campus (Henry, 1981; Odegaard, 1980). Moreover, by the 1950s, they had found many positive reasons to support the expansion of the community college. As educators, they clearly valued its potential as a means of extending opportunity to students who would otherwise not go to college, in part by providing postsecondary vocational education (Bolton, 1926: 271; Griffith, 1945: 162–165, 244; Lange, 1916: 3–5, 8; Sproul, 1958: 101–102; University of Washington, 1960: 6).

And by the 1950s and 1960s, university officials saw the community college as a politically expedient way of relieving overcrowding at the universities and preserving their academic selectivity (Brint and Karabel, 1989: 24–26, 86–87; Kerr, 1978; Labaree, 1990: 223–224; Nasaw, 1979: 228–229; Sproul, 1958; Waldo, 1981). This second set of interests is key to explaining why university officials preferred to meet the challenge of expanding educational opportunity less through opening their doors wider than through supporting the expansion of another institution: the community college. Fear of overcrowding the university was particularly acute beginning in the mid-1950s. University officials began to warn that their institutions would be engulfed by a "tidal wave" of enrollments when the baby boom generation reached college. Though willing to expand their own institutions to some degree, the heads of the elite universities far preferred to divert the tidal wave toward other institutions, particularly the community college. For example, David Henry, president of the University of Illinois (1955–1970), declared in 1956:

> Although we have not yet adequately translated the statistics of the new college enrollments into human terms, . . . it is obvious that we shall have to utilize all the educational resources at our command. In any measure of the load ahead for higher education, the development of the junior college takes on unusual significance. . . . These proposals [for state aid for local junior colleges and

legislation which will permit an enlargement of the tax base for local support], in principle, have my personal endorsement, for I believe the junior college under local auspices provides a sound and economical way to help extend post-high school education service to the youth of the State of Illinois. (Henry, 1956: 1, 5)

Although particularly acute in the 1960s, admission pressure on the state universities was nothing new.[14] Similar admission pressure built up in the late 1940s with returning veterans surging into college under the G.I. Bill (Olsen, 1974). Again, state universities encouraged the formation of community colleges in order to provide an enrollment safety valve (Griffith, 1945: 245–246; Fretwell, 1954: 70–71). In fact, fears of over-crowding were present around World War I. Between 1900 and 1920, undergraduate enrollments at the Universities of California, Illinois, and Washington rose by 608%, 811%, and 1990%, respectively (U.S. Office of Education, 1901: 882ff; idem, 1923: 31ff). Not surprisingly, university officials encouraged the formation of community colleges in order to reduce the clamor at their gates (Cole, n.d.: 2; Smolich, 1967: 193–194). In a speech urging the Mount Vernon (Washington) Chamber of Commerce to support the establishment of a community college, the dean of the School of Education at the University of Washington declared: "The junior college has come as a sorely needed relief for the overtaxed universities and colleges" (Cole, n.d.: 2). And in Illinois, a faculty member of the Chicago City Colleges noted that the University of Ilinois also strongly encouraged the formation of community colleges in order to relieve their enrollment burden right after World War I:

> [T]he courses [at the Chicago City Colleges] were organized under their [the University of Illinois's] direction and under very close inspection of the faculty of the University of Illinois. . . . the university is very much overcrowded in the first year and is very glad indeed to "shunt" some of its students into other institutions where they can get training for the senior college. . . . (Stewart, 1922: 44)

These recurrent "tidal waves" of enrollments alarmed university officials not simply because they would strain the facilities of the universities and force them to grow to Brobdingnagian proportions. They also threatened the elite universities' capacity to preserve or, even better, raise their academic selectivity. Beginning in the latter part of the 19th century, the Universities of California, Illinois, and Washington stated a desire to become "real" universities on the German model, which would entail taking students only after the first two years of college, once they had proven their ability and maturity (Bogue, 1950: 81–82; Brint and Karabel,

1989: 24–26; Cohen and Brawer, 1989: 5–8; Eells, 1931: 45–52; Labaree, 1990: 223–224; Lange, 1916: 4; idem, 1917: 473). Hence, university leaders encouraged the formation of two-year colleges with the hope that they could eventually relegate to them the first two years of college education. And in later years, the Universities of California and Washington moved to restrict their admissions to the more able high school graduates by diverting less able students to the community colleges (Kerr, 1978; Sprul, 1931b, 1958; Waldo, 1981).[15] Clark Kerr, president of the University of California (1958–1967), described the community college as if it were a moat protecting the elite universities:[16]

> When I was guiding the development of the Master Plan for Higher Education in California in 1959 and 1960, I considered the vast expansion of the community colleges to be the first line of defense for the University of California as an institution of international academic renown. Otherwise the University was going to be overwhelmed by large numbers of students with lower academic attainments or attacked as trying to hold on to a monopoly over entry into higher status. (Kerr, 1978: 267)

The director of government relations for the University of Washington, Robert Waldo, echoed Kerr's sentiment: "In 1961, the University raised its basic admission requirement from a 2 point [grade point average] to a 2.5 for a high school graduate. That created all kinds of flap. . . . [Were the community colleges one way of easing this flap?] Yes" (Waldo, 1981).

It could be argued that the elite universities could have addressed their desire to widen educational opportunity yet preserve their selectivity and avoid overcrowding by promoting the expansion of the lesser universities and four-year colleges. But certainly in California—and possibly in Illinois and Washington also—the flagship university was concerned that this would make the lesser state universities and colleges even more formidable competitors (Brenner, 1979: 250–251, 264–268; Cothran, 1979: 101; Sproul, 1931b: 113–114). Moreover, the elite universities may have worried that this would potentially devalue the baccalaureate by enormously expanding its supply (Labaree, 1990). Hence, the University of California preferred to sponsor instead the development of an institution that offered a different and subordinate degree and would never attain the same degree of prestige and power.

So far we have recapitulated, though with different emphases and more detail, territory charted by the institutionalists and functionalists. But now we must enter lands that they left unexplored.

State Education Departments and Boards

In California and Washington, chief state school officers and their departments of education emerged as champions of the community college almost as early as the elite state universities. In California, the State Department of Education began its long career of support by proposing to the legislature what became the landmark 1917 and 1921 acts extending state aid to the community colleges and permitting them to be established on the basis of independent districts (California State Department of Education, 1920: 50–55; Eells, 1931: 97, 106–107, 118; Reid, 1966: 201–203). This support continued through the 1960s, when the department jointly framed with the University of California the Master Plan for Higher Education, which gave community colleges the leading role in broadening access to higher education (Liaison Committee, 1960: iii, 8).

The Washington State Education Department was an equally energetic champion of the community college. It endorsed a bill in 1929 to provide state recognition and aid to the community college and the 1941 act that finally realized these goals (Crawfurd, 1959: 87). It took the lead in proposing what became the 1961 law that finally lifted a 20-year prohibition on establishing community colleges in areas already having four-year colleges (McKinney, 1967: 212–213, 262; Washington State Department of Education, 1960: 2). The only major break in its long history of support came in 1967, when it opposed the bill to establish a state community college system under a state board, for it would strip the state department of education of its jurisdiction over the community colleges (Bruno, 1981).

The community college cause was greatly strengthened by the support of the state education departments. Until the 1970s, the education departments and their powerful allies, the state educational associations, constituted an educational lobby that largely decided the policy agenda for secondary education (which included the community colleges until the last 30 years) (Campbell and Mazzoni, 1976: 35–41, 103–106, 115: Iannaccone and Cistone, 1974: 44–47; Wiley, 1966: 14–18, 29–36, 120–123; Wirt and Kirst, 1982: 218–219).[17]

The power exercised by chief state school officers and departments of education is attested by the halting development of community colleges in New York State. New York did not permit community colleges or extend state aid until 1948. This delay stemmed from the opposition of the New York State Department of Education and Board of Regents.[18] The New York State Department of Education feared that community colleges would undermine the private colleges and universities, which openly regarded the community college as a potential competitor (Abbott, 1958: 146; Gulick, 1938: 59; Miller, 1937: 332; New York State Department of Education, 1935). In the mid-1930s, a member of the Board of Regents, the governing body of the education department, made this fear of the community college explicit:

> The State should go very slowly in assuming direct material obligation for the support of junior college education and should embark upon no plan which would handicap or weaken the established private institutions. . . . The enlargement of the University scholarship system . . . would enlarge educational opportunity for capable students and be generally acceptable to the established colleges of the State. (New York State Education Department, 1935: 260–261)

Even when the Board of Regents finally proposed in 1944 a system of public two-year technical institutes, creating the preconditions for the 1948 community college law, it had in mind the interests of private higher education. The proposal was developed in consultation with the private colleges with the aim of undercutting the rising sentiment for establishing a State University of New York, which of course would constitute formidable competition for the private colleges (Abbott, 1958: 199; Carmichael, 1955: 28–29, 38–39n). The proposed institutes were to be two-year, vocationally oriented institutions so that they themselves would not pose a threat. The private colleges were repeatedly assured that the institutes would not become four-year institutions or offer liberal arts or general education (Abbott, 1958: 198–199; Carmichael, 1955: 38–39; Eurich, 1985; Stoddard, 1944a: 61).[19]

   In the Land of Lincoln, the department of education took a more ambivalent and less disruptive stance. It supported the 1955 state aid act (Scott, 1981; Smith, 1981). Moreover, it recommended in 1960 the idea of establishing a system of state-operated community colleges that would be vocationally oriented (McLure et al., 1960: 136–140), a proposal that served as one of the main ideological tributaries of the 1965 Illinois Public Junior Act. But for reasons that are unclear, the department opposed the 1937 bill permitting localities outside of Chicago to found community colleges (Hardin, 1975: 57–58, 90–94). Moreover, in the mid-1960s, it apparently floated an idea that could have severely damaged the prospect of vocationally oriented community colleges: establishing a system of regional vocational centers that would be tied to the public schools and would provide postsecondary as well as secondary occupational training. Observers at the time were mystified by the department's action, but took it as an indication of great ambivalence toward the community colleges (Browne, 1981).

In recent decades, the state departments of education have largely ceded their oversight of higher education to state boards of higher education. In 1948, The State University of New York was established and given control over the existing public colleges and the soon-to-emerge community colleges.[20] The Illinois Board of Higher Education was founded in 1961, to be followed by the Community College Board in 1965. California and Washington completed this train in 1967, when both established state higher education and community college boards. The boards in California and Washington came too late to exert much influence over the establishment of community colleges; by the time they were established, most community colleges had been built. But in New York and Illinois, the state boards exerted great influence.[21] Beginning in 1950, the State University of New York issued a string of state master plans that called for greatly increasing the number of community colleges in the state (State University of New York, 1950a: 34–35; 1961: 19, 39–40; 1964: 16–17; 1968: 24–25, 41). Shortly after its founding, the Illinois Board of Higher Education issued the first state master plan for Illinois higher education. At the behest of the board's senior staff, the master plan concentrated on the community colleges. It called for blanketing the state with open-door, vocationally oriented community colleges, which would be run by their own locally elected boards but overseen by a state community college board (Illinois Board of Higher Education, 1964). These proposals were swiftly translated by the governor and state General Assembly into the 1965 Public Junior College Act. Once established in 1965, the Illinois Community College Board also became a powerful advocate for the community college. Not only did it lobby the state legislature, but it also forcefully intervened to encourage localities to establish community colleges (Smith, 1980). (See Chapter 6.)

The state departments of education and boards of higher education shared much the same motives for supporting the community college. Certainly, they viewed the community college as a means to broaden educational opportunity (Allen, 1959: 233; California State Department of Education, 1920: 50; Illinois Board of Higher Education, 1964; State University of New York, 1961: 10; Washington State Department of Education, 1961a: 19). Moreover, the state education departments and boards hailed the community college's usefulness in providing vocational education that would meet the needs of both students and the economy (California State Department of Education, 1920: 50; Illinois Board of Higher Education, 1964: 39–40; New York State Education Department, 1947: 16–17, 38–41, 74–75; State University of New York, 1964: 16; Washington State Department of Education, 1961a: 19). These words by the Washington State Department of Education were typical:

Because a high proportion (approximately 70–80%) of our high school graduates have their attention centered upon and are motivated toward continuing their education in a college, it will be the responsibility of Washington's community-junior college system to develop the necessary technical and sub-professional curricula and effective counseling services to properly guide the post-high school educational experiences of a substantial proportion of Washington's youth. . . . The responsibility of Washington's community-junior colleges in the expansion of technical education programs essential to the industrial development of the State is clearly evident. (Washington State Department of Education, 1961b: 1–2)

But other, more self-interested motives also entered in. The Illinois state education department supported state aid to the community college in part as a means of relieving the financial burden on part of its constituency: local educators who were operating community colleges (Smith, 1981). Furthermore, the education departments and boards in Illinois, New York, and Washington also championed the community college as a means of reducing the financial pressure on state government (Allen, 1959: 234; Bruno, 1981; Illinois Board of Higher Education, 1964: 28, 57; New York State Education Department, 1957: 31; State University of New York, 1969: 6). For example, the Illinois Board of Higher Education (1964: 57) reported that if all additional students entering public higher education were to attend community colleges, the savings within seven years would be nearly $260 million. The state departments of education especially did not want state higher education expenditures to get so large that they would imperil elementary and secondary education budgets. Community colleges attracted their attention because they seemingly educated students at a considerably lower cost to state government than four-year colleges. As two-year, commuter institutions, they did not require residential facilities, expensive upper-division or graduate programs, and large athletic budgets. Moreover, in California and Illinois until recently, they were largely financed by local taxes and student fees rather than by state funds.[22] Louis Bruno, former Washington State superintendent of public instruction (1961–1973), force-fully made this case for the community college when lobbying the state legislature:

We showed [the legislature] how it would only cost X number of dollars to educate someone in English at a community college and for the same student at a senior institution it might be $1000 instead of a few hundred. (Bruno, 1981)

These sentiments were echoed by state education officials in New York. For example, James Allen, the commissioner of education of New York

State, stated: "Experience is showing that a tax dollar will buy more education in this type of higher institution [the community college] than any other" (Allen, 1959: 234).

In addition, chief state school officers may have supported the community college because it constituted an attractive issue. Because in California, Illinois, and Washington they are elected to office, chief state school officers in this state may have been looking for a way to address the popular interest in college opportunities. They could do little about expanding four-year opportunities, because those were not within their jurisdiction. But they could expand two-year college opportunities, for the community colleges still fell under their jurisdiction until the state community college boards were established in the mid-1960s.

Governors and Legislators

State legislators and, especially, governors were much slower than officials of the state universities and departments of education to emerge as strong supporters of the community college. They could not be counted as strong supporters until the late 1950s. In prior years, particularly before World War II, governors were often opposed to the expansion of the community college. In Washington, they vetoed community college aid legislation in 1929 and 1937, with state aid passing only in 1941, when the governor chose to remain neutral (Crawfurd, 1959: 85–86, 143–147, 151; McKinney, 1967: 212–222). In Illinois, community college aid bills were first introduced in the 1920s, but none passed until 1955, when the governor finally came out in support (Hardin, 1975: 122–124, 147–149; Smith, 1981). And in California, the governor vetoed state aid in 1909, and even after it was passed in 1921, other governors kept it from rising rapidly during the 1930s and 1940s (Cothran, 1979: 303; Eells, 1931: 106; Reid, 1966: 198; Rolph, 1931: 184). In each case, this opposition arose from governors' fear that state aid would stimulate the proliferation of community colleges, which in turn would put pressure on already tight state budgets.

Legislators, meanwhile, were passing legislation in favor of the community college, even in the face of gubernatorial opposition. But these efforts did not reflect any great interest or knowledge on the part of legislators. Rather, they were tribute to the lobbying efforts of state university officials, state departments of education, and state associations of local educators. (See below for more.)

By the late 1950s, state governors and legislators had warmed to the community college. They heard the anxious alarums of state universities, departments of education, and boards of higher education confronted by an exponentially rising demand for higher education. They noted the increasing pressure that higher education expenses were putting on state budgets, and they found suddenly attractive the community colleges' lower cost. This change of heart had an immediate impact on the community college movement, for it transformed a frequent opponent into an often strong advocate.

This turnabout was particularly evident in Illinois. In 1953, a bill to provide direct state aid to community colleges failed because of the opposition of Governor William Stratton, who was afraid of the bill's impact on the state's finances. But two years later he enlisted in the ranks of supporters, and the bill passed handily (Hardin, 1975: 147–149; Stratton, 1981; Smith, 1981). This new stance continued under Stratton's successors. Otto Kerner (1961–1968) strongly supported the 1965 Public Junior College Act, which established a statewide community college system (Broman, 1981; Browne, 1981).

In Washington, with the endorsement of Governor Albert Rosellini (1957–1965) and Daniel Evans (1965–1977), several legislators hammered out the 1961 law removing a 20-year prohibition on establishing community colleges in areas already possessing four-year colleges and the 1967 Community College Act that established a statewide system coordinated by a state board (Brouillet, 1980: 2; Crawfurd, 1959: 266–267, 272; McKinney, 1967: 262, 272–273; Rosellini, 1961). Never to be outdone, New York's Governor Nelson Rockefeller (1958–1974) was a formidable supporter of the community college, often speaking out in its favor and strongly pushing for more aid (Duryea, 1985; Eurich, 1985; Rockefeller, 1961; idem, 1970). And in the Eden of the community college, California, state legislators played a key role in crafting the 1960 law that enshrined the community colleges as a key constellation in the higher education firmament. Meanwhile, Governors Edmund Brown, Sr. (1958–1966), and Ronald Reagan (1966–1974) provided strong backing (Brenner, 1979: 217–218, 221, 234–235, 254–255, 285–286; Brossman, 1986; Brown, 1961: 71; Brown, 1986; Greenwood, 1971: 4; Trombley, 1970: 7; Tyler, 1965: 4)

Governors and legislators certainly supported community college expansion because they viewed it as a good political issue that would attract votes.[23] Even if students and their parents were not particularly demanding the expansion of the community college, they clearly were demanding more college opportunities, and the community college could be sold as just the solution to this need. Perry Duryea, a member of the New York State General Assembly between 1961 and 1978 and speaker in 1970–1978, noted the political attractiveness of the community college to legislators:

> [T]he community college concept was accepted by both the legislature and the various counties because it was something that was *tangible*, that a lot of political types could point to. If a community college was developed, let's just say in Suffolk County, . . . the state legislator could say, "here's something we've done that's very constructive." . . . This is a feather in our cap. (Duryea, 1985)

Besides finding the community college a quite salable good in the political marketplace, why else did state elected officials find it so attractive? Certainly, one reason was that it addressed their ideal of equality of opportunity. Illinois Governor William Stratton (1953–1961) stated that he supported the community college because

> our philosophy of education allowed the individual the greatest possible development. Funds spend on education were an investment rather than a cost that once paid went down the drain. Education is looked on as a great benefit for the future, for the individual, society, the community, and of course the state. (Stratton, 1981)

Other state officials shared this value (Duryea, 1985; Rockefeller, 1970; Rosellini, 1961: 32). A study of state legislators in nine states in the late 1960s found that one of the strongest reasons they gave for supporting community college expansion was its usefulness in expanding access to higher education (Eulau and Quinley, 1970: 117, 120).

But why did this valuation of equality of educational opportunity lead to support for community colleges rather than, say, four-year colleges? The main reason was self-interest. Governors and legislators found many benefits for themselves in supporting the community college. For one, they did not want to have the higher education budget grow so large or so rapidly that it would endanger their political position, and community colleges seemed to offer a workable means of cost containment. State budgets grew rapidly in the 1950s and 1960s. In Illinois, state expenditures rose 30.5% between the 1951 and 1954 fiscal years as the state sharply increased its appropriations for education, highway construction, and public assistance (Illinois Taxpayers Federation, 1955: 33). Similarly, the California state budget rose 54.9% between 1959 and 1964 (Fahey, 1966: 77–79). But while allowing their budgets to increase, state officials wanted to keep them under control. If expenditures on big-ticket items such as education grew too large, state officials feared that they might have to balance the state budget either by cutting other programs, thus alienating their beneficiaries, or by raising taxes, possibly alienating virtually all voters (Anton, 1966: 134; Brown, 1965; Fahey, 1966: 89–91; Lehner, 1972; Sabato, 1983).[24]

In order to avoid these dangers, state governors and legislators looked for ways of getting the maximum bang for their buck. In 1955, the Illinois legislature observed:

> The General Assembly recognizes that . . . enrollments in . . . public institutions will greatly increase in coming years . . . [and] that a solution to this problem should be found that will involve the least possible cost to the people of this state. (Illinois Higher Education Commission, 1957: 179)

The California State Assembly echoed these concerns in its 1959 resolution mandating the 1960 Master Plan for Higher Education: "it is in the interests of the students and of the taxpayers of the state to avoid unnecessary expenditures of state funds and the duplication of higher education facilities and curriculum" (California Legislature, 1959 Statutes, chap. 200, p. 5769).

With this pressure for cost-efficiency, governors and legislators appreciated the apparent cheapness of community colleges. They seemed to deliver entry-level higher education at a considerably lower cost than state four-year college and universities (Clabaugh, 1981; Duryea, 1985; Eulau and Quinley, 1970: 119; Greenwood, 1971; Post, 1960: 69; Stratton, 1982; Vahaplus, 1982; Wellman, 1982). For Illinois Governor William Stratton (1953–1961) it was "very important" that community colleges were cheaper to the state. "You didn't have to provide dormitories. That's a tremendous saving" (Stratton, 1982). And Albert Rosellini, governor of Washington State (1957–1965), added:

> As Washington faces the problems of fabulous growth in a technical age, it also faces the serious financial problems of finding adequate tax resources to furnish the public services demanded by a growing population. The economy and the sound educational services of the community junior colleges of necessity must be acknowledged and developed in the interests of the State and its citizens. (Quoted in Crawfurd, 1959: 272)

Besides expanding educational opportunity in a seemingly cost-efficient way, the community college also seemed to state elected officials to be an excellent means to foster economic growth. This desire for economic growth in part reflected ideology: the American belief in the benefits of a constantly expanding pie. But it also quite clearly stemmed from self-interest. Governors widely believe, and academic studies back them up, that economic conditions have a major impact on the outcome of state elections.[25] Good economic conditions aid governors' chances for reelection by providing jobs and rising incomes for citizens and rising tax revenues for new government programs. New York Governor Nelson Rockefeller (1958–1974) noted the importance of economic growth to state government:

> The ability of New York business to compete with those in other states and in foreign countries—the attractiveness of New York to new business enterprise—directly affects not only the individual but also the State's ability to provide public services—its schools, its highways, its hospitals, and other facilities vital to the general welfare. (Rockefeller, 1961: 358)

In the face of rapidly changing labor market demands and rising plant mobility in the 1960s and 1970s, state governments stepped up their efforts to assist economic growth, and education was a favored means of doing so (Glazer, 1989: 88). For example, Rockefeller (1958–1974) declared:

> [T]his administration has set as its goal the stimulation of the greatest economic expansion in the State's history—five hundred thousand new jobs in the next four years. . . . These new jobs can be achieved only by the encouragement of individual initiative, the creativity of private enterprise, and a more rapid rate of capital investment. It is the duty of government to shape its policies and actions so that these dynamic forces in the private sector are released to create employment and progress for all. (Rockefeller, 1963: 18)

Both in the states we are studying here and across the United States generally, one of the main ways state officials have tried to spur economic growth is by offering a well-developed system of postsecondary vocational education, centered on the community college. By providing publicly subsidized employee training, community colleges have promised to help native firms expand and to attract outside firms seeking better business conditions (Goodman, 1979: 25–31; Riles, 1986; Rockefeller, 1966: 1612; Wellman, 1982). Again, Governor Rockefeller:

> Our rapidly expanding community colleges are becoming a major source of trained technicians for staffing offices, factories, and labs in their respective areas. . . . They are playing an important role in the economic growth and development of our state by helping to fill the gap between the demand and supply of well-educated, well-trained manpower. (Rockefeller, 1966: 1612)

Finally, state elected officials were also motivated by what could be called a "bandwagon effect," in which states strive to keep up with policy

innovations in other states (Walker, 1969). California in particular provided the touchstone for many other states.[26] Gerald Smith, formerly
executive director of the Illinois Community College Board (1965–1970),
recalls:

> I don't think that there's any question that the Illinois legislature was influenced in
> 1965 by what was going on in legislation with regard to junior colleges across the
> country. They were very much aware of what had happened in Florida, in
> California. (Smith, 1981)

The bandwagon effect was propagated in part simply by observation.
One state noticed what other states were doing. But it was also spread by
more systematic means. In Washington State, the Arthur D. Little (1966)
consulting firm provided strong impetus for the 1967 legislation creating
a state community college system through a report commissioned by the
State Department of Education. Its recommendation that the community
colleges be open-door, vocationally oriented institutions carried great
weight because it was seen to be based on a review of the experience of
many other states.

The bandwagon effect stems in good part from uncertainty, particularly in the face of economic competition. When new needs appear and the
solution is not immediately apparent, policymakers often fall on the
example of other states, either in the superstition that the other states
somehow know what is right or out of a desire to not be caught out alone
in case something goes wrong.[27] Another source of the bandwagon effect
is status seeking. Many states wish to view themselves as modern,
progressive, in step, and so on, and therefore eagerly copy innovations in
other states.[28] Christopher Vahaplus, who had been press secretary to
Illinois Governor Kerner (1961–1968), described this status-seeking
process in Illinois:

> Everybody was pouring money into higher education. I can't help but believe that
> the material that came out of the Council of State Governments, Governors'
> Conferences that we attended, meetings and conferences that members of the
> bureaucracy attended—I'm sure that all that kind of feeling was being dissemi-
> nated. Everybody was feeling kind of high on higher education. We had kind of
> lagged in Illinois. Here we were a major industrial state and never really had a
> community college system. We always looked to California as a model. (Vahaplus,
> 1982)

Before moving on to examining the genesis of national-level
policymaking in favor of the community college, we should pause to

review the impact on state policymaking of state associations of local educators, state and national associations of community college officials, and federal agencies. Although not as important as the state officials we have just analyzed, they nonetheless had a sizable influence on state policy.

State Educational Associations

Local educators did not exhaust their role at the local level. They also pursued their interest in the community college at the state level through their state associations. This support had no mean impact, because until the 1970s the state educational associations were powerhouses in state education politics (Campbell et al., 1985; Wirt and Kirst, 1982). In Washington State, 29 members of the 1967 legislature were asked to list who had the most influence on their votes on six bills dealing with elementary and secondary education, and they ranked "professional education organizations" as first on each of three measures of influence (Saling, 1970: 65–66).

The Washington Education Association endorsed bills to provide state aid for community colleges in 1929 and 1940, with such aid passing in 1941. It also supported the 1961 act encouraging the spread of community colleges statewide (Bruno, 1981; McKinney, 1967: 212–213, 219–220; Washington Educational Association, 1929: 87; idem, 1939: 173). Similarly, the Illinois Educational Association (IEA) endorsed the 1955 bill enacting direct state aid to community colleges and the 1965 Public Junior College Act, which brought them within a state system (Smith, 1981).

According to a staffer, the IEA believed that state aid to the community colleges would advance the goal of college opportunity and, perhaps more importantly, afford financial relief to high school districts maintaining community colleges:

> By 1955, the community colleges had been made part of the common school system. . . . And this simply meant as far as the common schools were concerned that if there could be funding for the junior college program there would be that much total support for the total districts. Because without funding for the junior college, then the funding that they gave the community colleges had to be taken out of the elementary school money. (Smith, 1981)

State and National Community College Associations

The state and national associations of community college officials were perhaps less powerful politically than the state educational associations in conventional terms. They had fewer members and smaller war chests.

But they made up for these deficiencies with their missionary zeal. In California, Illinois, and Washington, the state associations worked tire-lessly to mobilize state support for the community college. The Illinois Association of Junior Colleges (IAJC) introduced the bills culminating in the 1931 and 1937 laws providing state recognition of community col-leges and the 1955 act establishing direct state aid. Moreover, the IAJC was involved in the task forces of the Illinois Board of Higher Education that drew up the 1964 Illinois master plan for higher education, which assigned the community colleges the central role in expanding opportu-nities for higher education (Browne, 1981; Hardin, 1975; 91–94, 155; Meisterheim, 1974: 53–54; Smith, 1981). Similarly, the Washington Junior College Association built support for the successful 1941 aid legislation by mobilizing not only that year but also in 1929, 1935, and 1937 (Crawfurd, 1959: 84–85, 143–144; McKinney, 1967: 214–215, 219–221, 228).

   The national association of community college officials, the Ameri-can Association of Community Colleges (AACC), rivaled the state asso-ciations in influence and persistence. Established in 1920 at a convention of community colleges that was called by the U.S. Office of Education (Zook, 1922), the AACC has been an energetic and influential evangelizer for the community college ever since (Brick, 1963; Brint and Karabel, 1989). Aided especially by grants from the Kellogg Foundation (see above), the AACC actively propagated the message, through reports and testimony, that community colleges were an excellent means of expand-ing access to higher education and providing postsecondary vocational education (American Association of Junior Colleges, 1962: 10–11; idem, 1964; U.S. Senate, 1965):[29]

> We believe that the educational and career goals of many Americans can be accommodated, that our new manpower needs can be met, and that many of our social ills can be effectively treated by worthwhile college experiences in two years or less. Furthermore, we believe that the kind of institution which should accept this responsibility has already been developed and nurtured in many parts of the country. It is the junior college. . . . Business, industry, and labor should project manpower needs so that appropriate programs can be planned in advance. . . . The junior college represents a means of providing high quality in-plant training that has as yet been untapped. (American Association of Junior Colleges, 1964: 5, 9)

Furthermore, in 1962 the AACC published a set of standards for state community college legislation prescribing that such legislation should provide for state supervision but local approval and control (American Association of Junior Colleges, 1962). The impact of these standards was attested by the Illinois State Community College Board: "This act [the landmark 1965 Illinois Public Junior College Act] incorporates all seven of the basic principles as set forth by the Legislative Commission of the American Association of Junior Colleges and approved by it in 1962" (Illinois Community College Board, 1967: 5).[30]

Federal Agencies

The federal government's intervention in state policymaking was indirect but noteworthy. As we have seen, the Office of Education in 1920 convened a meeting of community college and junior college heads that became the organizing ground for the American Association of Community Colleges (Zook, 1922). Furthermore, the federal government accelerated state and local efforts in favor of the community college by endorsing the institution in several reports issued by the U.S. Office of Education and various blue-ribbon commissions. For example, the 1947 "Truman" Commission on Higher Education and the 1957 "Eisenhower" Committee on Education Beyond the High School enthusiastically commended the community college (McDowell, 1919; U.S. President's Commission on Higher Education, 1947: I, 37, 68–69; U.S. President's Committee on Education Beyond the High School, 1957: 12–13, 21). In words that were widely noted by state officials, the Truman Commission declared:

> The time has come to make education through the fourteenth grade available in the same way that high school education is now available. . . . To achieve this, it will be necessary to develop much more extensively than at present such opportunities as are now provided in local communities by the two-year junior college. . . . (U.S. President's Commission on Higher Education, 1947: I, 37, 68–69)

But the federal government's influence went beyond encouraging words. It also took the form of hard cash. Let's trace that money back to its sources in Chapter 8.

CHAPTER 8

National-Level Reinforcement of Local and State Initiatives

Major federal assistance on behalf of the community college did not appear until the late 1950s and early 1960s. The federal government took a long time to interest itself in the community college, partly because of its long-standing lack of interest in education in general. State governments are constitutionally vested with the responsibility for sponsoring and regulating education (Campbell, Cunningham, Nystrand, Usdan, 1985; Wirt and Kirst, 1982). Hence, the federal government for many years largely restricted its involvement in education to funding research, subsidizing the land grant colleges established under the 1865 Morrill Act, and underwriting vocational education following the Smith-Hughes Act of 1917.

But in the late 1950s, the federal government moved to a much deeper involvement in educational policymaking, and the community college was a beneficiary of this intensified interest. In 1963, Congress passed the Higher Education Facilities Act, which provided aid for the construction of academic facilities. Nearly one-quarter (22%) of the funding under Title I, which provided grants for undergraduate facilities, was earmarked for community colleges and public technical institutes (Congressional Quarterly, 1963: 194–195).[1] The landmark Vocational Education Act, also passed in 1963, reserved one-third of the funds provided under Section 4 for the construction of area vocational schools (including community colleges) or the operation of programs for students who had left high school (Congressional Quarterly, 1963: 201–203).[2] And two years later, Title III of the Higher Education Act of 1965 authorized grants for strengthening "developing" institutions, with 22% of the funds set aside for two-year colleges (Congressional Quarterly, 1965: 294–297). In subsequent years, all these beachheads were enlarged when these acts were amended and supplemented as they came up for reauthorization.

With this burst of legislation, federal aid rose rapidly. Including student aid, federal funds rose from $10.9 million in 1949–1950 to $104.1 million in 1969–1970 and $462.2 million in 1978–1979 (7.3% of all current income received by community colleges) (U.S. National Center

175

TABLE 8–1
National-Level Stances Toward the Community College: Direction and Strength[a]

	In Favor, Strong Participation	*In Favor, Weak Participation*	*In Favor, Unknown Degree of Participation*	*Opposed*	*Ambivalent*	*No Role*
Nongovernmental Actors						
Students[b]						*
PTAs						*
Business						*
Labor unions		*				
Farmers						*
Minority groups						*
Private colleges						*
Foundations		*				
Governmental Actors						
Congress	*					
Presidents	*					
AACC	*					

Notes

a. Percentages are not reported since there is only one possible case: the U.S. as a whole. The asterisks indicate whether, and with what valence, an interest group participated in national-level policymaking. Actors are classified as strong participants in favor of the community college if they not only announced strong support but backed it up with active involvement in such forms as lobbying the federal government to pass community college legislation. If their support only took the form of endorsements, without active support, they are classified as weak participants.

b. Only conventional student participation is noted here. Participation simply in the form of enrolling in the community college is not included. See text for more.

for Education Statistics, 1973a: 14–15; idem, 1981a: 14–15; U.S. Office of Education, 1954: chap. 4, p. 36).

Why did the federal government suddenly discover the community college? Were the demands of students or of business and the foundations largely the cause, as functionalists and instrumentalist Marxists claim? Again the answer is no. As Table 8–1 shows, they were largely uninvolved at the national level.

The Limited Impact of Private Interest Group Pressure

Students

Students and the PTA on occasion did lobby Congress and federal officials on higher education policy. But these political interventions never involved the community college directly. Rather, they were principally focused on the issue of greater federal funding for higher education generally and for student aid.

As at the local and state levels, the thesis of student participation can be partially rescued if we wish to reconceptualize this participation to include the simple fact of enrolling in the community college. And indeed there is evidence that federal officials were quite aware of the rapid rise in community college enrollments and used this as justification for increasing federal aid (U.S. Senate, 1965: 1004). But while federal policymakers perceived student enrollments in the community college as an unbiased indication of student demand, we must again question this reasoning. Those enrollments were a product not just of student desires but also of decisions by local and state officials to favor community colleges over four-year colleges as the principal gateways into higher education. In any case, however we conceptualize student participation, it was not the only factor pushing federal officials to support the community college.

Business

These other factors did not include business pressure, however. Business's participation in federal policymaking was nil. A variety of observers—both from business and other groups—are unanimous that business organizations participated very little if at all in the push to secure federal support for the community college. To be sure, business had long been interested in vocational education, and occasionally it praised the community college (Business Week, 1972: 48; Rhine, 1972: v; U.S. House of Representatives, 1971a: 1043–1047, 1140–1141). But according to both its own representatives and those of labor and other organizations, business did not lobby at all for federal community college legislation (Halperin, 1985; Lee, 1985; Mallan, 1985; Mehan, 1987; and Radcliffe, 1985). For example, John Mehan, vice president for corporate relations of the U.S. Chamber of Commerce, describes the Chamber's role as very minimal:

> I don't recall where we specifically spelled out that we were for junior colleges per se. We also recognized in those days that not everybody could go to the university. I don't recall that we came out and had a specific policy supporting community colleges but we generally said there was a need for education for all kinds of people. (Mehan, 1987)

Kenneth Young, the AFL-CIO's leading lobbyist on educational matters in the years 1965 to 1977, recalls business's involvement in educational issues in Washington as, if anything, weaker than Mehan claims:

> I don't remember them having any role at all. In fact, if anything they were usually negative. I'm thinking now of funding. When we had our funding fights on appropriation bills, we always ran a coalition ... that tried to include all the various education groups. ... I don't recall the Chamber, the NAM [National Association of Manufacturers], the Business Roundtable, those groups, being involved at all. I suspect that, if they did anything, they were probably negative because they were concerned about the total size of the appropriations bills. I know they weren't part of the coalitions. (Young, 1985)

It could be argued that business exerted influence through the presence of a number of executives on the 1947 Truman and 1957 Eisenhower Commissions. But there is no evidence that these business people played any significant role in leading those bodies to their enthusiastic support of the community college and that their business connections were a factor in this.

Foundations

The instrumentalist theory fares better when it focuses on the role of the foundations. There is no doubt that they influenced federal policy toward the community college. The encomium the Carnegie Commission on Higher Education (1970) delivered to the community college (see Chapter 7) was certainly noted by federal officials. Representative John Brademas (D-Ind.) repeatedly asked those testifying at the House hearings on the Higher Education Amendments of 1972 to comment on the commission's recommendations (U.S. House of Representatives, 1971a: 222). Furthermore, one could note that former officers of the Carnegie Corporation— Francis Keppel and John Gardner—served as commissioner of education and secretary of health, education, and welfare, respectively, during the 1960s. However, there is no evidence that these two men played any particular role in the passage of the community college provisions in the Higher Education Facilities Act of 1963, the Vocational Education Act of 1963, and the Higher Education Act of 1965. In fact, Gardner took office in 1965, after these acts were passed. Moreover, as we will see below, the main initiative for these community college provisions came not from the administration but from Congress (Halperin, 1985). Hence, though it is fair to say there was some foundation influence, it is hard to argue that it was determinative.

Governmental Initiative

In the end, the major credit for the passage of federal aid to the community college must be given not to interest group pressure but to the efforts of government officials. More specifically, the laurels must be awarded to the president and members of Congress, with secondary honors going to the American Association of Community Colleges (AACC). The institutionalists have noted the role of these officials, but only in the case of the AACC have they explored it in depth, noting the deep vein of self-interest that runs through it.

Congress Members and Presidents

The federal laws during the 1960s and early 1970s that announced the federal government's commitment to the full-scale expansion of the community college had the support of the Kennedy through Nixon administrations (Kennedy, 1963: 977; Nixon, 1970: 38A). But, on the whole, the executive branch was only moderately interested in the community college (Gladieux and Wolanin, 1976; Halperin, 1985). According to Samuel Halperin, a top lobbyist for the Department of Health, Education, and Welfare (1961–1970), "in general, the executive branch did not view community colleges during all the ten years that I worked there as anything special or as deserving a higher priority than any other four-year or two-year institution" (Halperin, 1985). In fact, it was Congress that led the executive on this issue (Chavez, 1975; Halperin, 1985; Lee, 1985; Mallan, 1985). According to Halperin, "the initiative for treating community colleges differently I think came from the Senate, particularly from Senator [Wayne] Morse [D-Ore.] and the staff people that worked there" (Halperin, 1985). As early as 1959, Senator Clifford Case (R-N.J.) and Representatives Al Ullman (D-Ore.) and Rep. Melvin Price (D-Ill.) introduced bills to provide grants to build community colleges (Willits, 1968: 31–38). Senator Wayne Morse (D-Ore.), the chair of the Senate Education Subcommittee, picked up and completed these efforts. He wrote in the special allotments for community colleges in the Higher Education Facilities Act of 1963 and the Higher Education Act of 1965. Morse was aided in his efforts not only by the Congress members mentioned above, but also by Senator Harrison Williams (D-N.J.) and Representatives John Brademas (D-Ind.) and Albert Quie (R-Minn.). Senator Williams went on to sponsor the community college provisions (Part J) of the Higher Education Amendments of 1972. And Representatives Brademas and Quie were key framers of federal aid for postsecondary vocational education (Chavez, 1975; Halperin, 1985; Lee, 1985; Mallan, 1985; Price, 1964: 85, 91–92, 97; Radcliffe, 1985; Young, 1985).

Federal officials were motivated to act on essentially the same grounds as state elected officials: a belief in equality of opportunity and a desire to spur politically popular economic growth. Senator Morse stated during the Senate hearings on the Higher Education Act of 1965 his bedrock belief in the community college's contribution to equality of opportunity:

> [M]any of the students in the so-called two year colleges are the ones that come from very low-income families, and have no chance of going on to college if these two year institutions were not available to them. ... We are losing sight of tens upon tens of thousands of young men and women whose only hope for an education is through a community college. (U.S. Senate, 1965: 1004, 1006)

Presidents also shared this sentiment. In a statement that has been echoed by virtually every major federal and state educational policymaker of the last three decades, President John F. Kennedy declared:

> Education is the keystone in the arch of freedom and progress. ... For the nation, increasing the quality and availability of education is vital to both our national security and our domestic well-being. ... The opportunity for a college education is severely limited for hundreds of thousands of young people because there is no college in their own community. (Kennedy, 1963: 975)

He then offered the community college as a major solution to this need: "A demonstrated method of meeting this particular problem effectively is the creation of two-year community colleges—a program that should be undertaken without delay and which will require Federal assistance for the construction of adequate facilities" (Kennedy, 1963: 977).

But it was not just the golden prospect of equality of opportunity that attracted federal officials to the community college. They also noted that it seemed quite useful in spurring economic growth: a boon to the nation but also a boon to themselves. Presidents and Congress members believed—and political analysts have confirmed—that economic conditions have a considerable impact on their electoral chances (Jacobson, 1983: 126–128; Sundquist, 1968: 15, 20, 28, 34, 70–72, 433–435; Tufte, 1978: 5–8, 120–123). In explaining why he lost the 1960 election, Richard Nixon noted:

> The bottom of the 1960 dip did come in October and the economy started to move up in November—after it was too late to affect the election returns. ... All the speeches, television broadcasts, and precinct work in the world could not counteract that one hard fact. (Quoted in Tufte, 1978: 6)

In their quest to stimulate economic growth, one device that federal officials have turned to is the vocationally oriented community college (American Vocational Association, 1960; Brademas, 1963, 1967; Kennedy, 1963; Nixon, 1970; and Sundquist, 1968). For example, President Kennedy declared in 1963:

> There is an especially urgent need for college level training of technicians to assist scientists, engineers, and doctors. ... This shortage results in an inefficient use of professional manpower ... an extravagance which cannot be tolerated when the nation's demand for scientists, engineers, and doctors continues to grow. ... I recommend, therefore, a program of grants to aid public and private non-profit institutions in the training of scientific, engineering, and medical technicians in two-year college-level programs. ... (Kennedy, 1963: 977)

The American Association of Community Colleges

Though not yet the political force it was to become by the 1980s, the AACC certainly gave its local constituents influence over federal policymaking in the 1960s and 1970s (Brint and Karabel, 1988: 95–96, 111, 124–128). The AACC actively lobbied Congress in favor of more aid (U.S. Senate, 1965). In fact, it put the idea in Senator Morse's head of inserting a special "set aside" for the community college in Title III of the Higher Education Act (Halperin, 1985; Lee, 1985). As the national association of local and state community college officials, the AACC's advocacy of more federal aid was patently moved by self-interest as well as sincere belief in the democratizing effect of the community college. By enlarging the community college sector, every new community college enhanced the prestige, power, and revenues of its older siblings.

In the preceding discussion, we have seen that government officials have played a very important and independent sole in decisions to found community colleges. This goes against the grain of functionalist and instrumentalist Marxist arguments. But to tie down more precisely the theoretical implications of my findings, let us turn to Chapter 9.

CHAPTER 9

The Politics of Community College Founding:
Summary and Conclusions

The concept of government officials as operating in a situation of relative autonomy from the demands of civil society allows us to explain several features of the community college's development that go unexplained by its functionalist advocates and instrumentalist Marxist critics. The groups spotlighted by those two camps—students, business, and the foundations—simply did not participate strongly and systematically enough to satisfactorily explain the breadth and depth of community college expansion. This process involved major policy initiatives at the local, state, and national levels stretching over 70 years. Yet private interest group participation does not match in its temporal depth and spatial extent the timing and magnitude of community college policymaking. Students and business participated only weakly at the state and national levels, and their local participation was at best moderately strong. And the foundations, although moderately influential at the state and perhaps national level, had very little influence at the local level. Moreover, business and the foundations began to exert their largest influence only in the 1960s, many years after the expansion of the community college got under way.

In any case, even if one were nonetheless to credit these groups with strongly participating in all the major decisions that constructed the community college system that we know today, this thesis of the primacy of private interest group pressure would face the fact that the community college has several features that cannot be easily explained by business or student demands. For those emphasizing the importance of business pressure for publicly subsidized training, there is the conundrum of why this eventuated in an institution that is less vocationally oriented than another long established and readily available institution: the public vocational-technical school. Meanwhile, those stressing student demand for college opportunities confront the anomaly of explaining how this produced the expansion not of four-year colleges, which give students access to the most prestigious educational credentials and jobs, but of two-year colleges with a strong terminal component.

On the other hand, if we follow the grain of the evidence and conclude that private interest group pressure was not the decisive source of the community college, how do we then explain why the community college has been fairly responsive to interests of business and students despite their weak participation? Business was largely uninvolved in state and national policymaking on the community college. Yet a central concern of that policymaking was to ensure that business's training needs would be met.

The theory of the relative autonomy of the state provides the sword to cut this knot. It argues that government officials promoted community college expansion beyond the point needed to meet the demands of private interest groups because this met their own values and interests. Even when students were silent, government officials supported the community college out of their own belief in the value of higher educational opportunity. Even when business was mute, they supported postsecondary education in the name of the credo that government has a responsibility to meet the economy's needs. But this still leaves the question of why the community college was selected out of the range of institutions capable of providing college access or vocational education. Governmental self-interest provides the key. For local educators, the local community college was superior to a four-year college under state control because it better promised them access to college teaching and administrative jobs, and it was preferable to a vocational-technical school because it yielded greater prestige. State university officials, meanwhile, favored community college development over expanding their own institutions because it meant less crowding and better protection for selective university admissions. State governors and legislators, finally, preferred the community college to expanding the four-year colleges because it was cheaper for the state and would better yield vocational-education graduates who could attract business investment.

While government officials' values and interests explain features of community college expansion left unexplained by business or student or foundation pressure, they paradoxically also explain why business and students had greater influence than their weak participation would suggest. The solution to this paradox lies in the dual nature of government officials' interests and values: they are a source of constraint as well as autonomy. While leading government officials to act in the absence of private interest group demand and to choose policies that private interest groups do not call for, these values and self-interests also keep their actions within the horizon of private interest. The values of government officials serve as ideologies, for they motivate action that benefits private interest groups. The value government officials put on serving the economy's training needs clearly benefits business. Government officials almost unconsciously equate the economy with private business. Thus to meet the economy's needs for labor training means to provide business with publicly subsidized employee training, even if business does not demand it. (For more on this point, see Section IV.) Similarly, the value government officials put on greater higher educational opportunity benefits students. It leads government officials to widen college opportunities, even in the absence of conventional political demand by students.[1]

But even if government officials' values were not to incline them to serve business interests, their own self-interests would. Those self-interests put government officials in a situation of resource dependence. To realize their interests, they need to leverage resources that business controls. But to get that leverage, government officials have to pay a toll in the form of concessions to business. As we have seen above, state and federal elected officials are aware that good economic conditions greatly aid their chances for reelection by providing jobs and rising incomes for citizens and rising tax revenues for new government programs. They know also that to get a healthy economy one needs to provide incentives to attract business investment. One of the major incentives that government has provided business in order to get it to invest capital and thus spur economic growth has been to provide it with publicly subsidized employee training through the vocationally oriented community college. Elected officials are quite clear that they are doing business a favor. But they find it acceptable for two reasons: they believe in business's centrality to our economy; and they view favors to business as the necessary price of securing access to investment capital that can fuel politically popular economic growth.

Convergences and Divergences with the Institutional Perspective

The "state relative autonomy" argument made above converges on several points with the "institutional" perspective of Brint and Karabel (1989) and Labaree (1990). (See Chapter 2 for a fuller description of the institutional perspective.) Like the institutionalists, I find that student or business demand is insufficient to explain the rise of the community college. And like them, I give prominence to the efforts of the elite state universities, which promoted the expansion of the community college out of a desire to preserve their current size and selectivity and the relative value of their credentials.[2] Despite these points of convergence, the state relative autonomy argument also diverges greatly from the institutional argument in two main ways.

Using a broader range of data than the institutionalists, I find that many governmental actors besides the state universities were at the center of the development of the community college. Local school superintendents and high school principals were the central instigators of local drives to found community colleges. State governors, legislators, and education departments were as important in securing state aid for community colleges as were state universities. And at the national level, the president and Congress strongly supported the enactment of federal aid for the community college.[3]

Secondly, the state relative autonomy argument provides a more complete explanation in another area: the power of constraint that business and students have exercised over government officials. The institutionalists have focused on the power that business derives from its control of jobs that community college officials want to fill. This observation is valid, but too limited. The institutionalists miss the powerful influence business also exercises over state and national elected officials through its control over capital for investment and thus the pace and distribution of economic growth. Furthermore, the institutional school ignores the ideological side of constraint: the fact that government officials serve the interests of business and students in part because they subscribe to values and beliefs—such as equality of opportunity and serving the needs of the economy—that suggest the social benefit of aiding those groups.

From Diverse Origins to Contradictory Effects

Our awareness of the complex process by which the community college arose provides the basis for answering a puzzle that has lain at the heart of the community college debate: Why does an institution that professes such a strong commitment to equality of opportunity so significantly hinder the academic progress of its baccalaureate aspirants? Is this effect intentional?

The leaders and supporters of the community college are publicly—and, one has to conclude, for the most part genuinely—committed to helping its students succeed as much as possible. But several features of the community college militate against this in the case of baccalaureate aspirants. Because it lacks dormitories, many students drop out for lack of social integration. Because it is strongly committed to vocational education, many baccalaureate aspirants are seduced away from their initial ambitions. And because it is a two-year school, students wishing to get a bachelor's degree must transfer to a new institution—one that may be far away, deny many of their credits, refuse to give them as much student aid as they need, and fail to integrate them into the new institution. As a result, many fail to transfer or suffer academic death in the middle passage.

These barriers to success concatenate in such an effective way that it is very hard to avoid the conclusion of the instrumentalist critics of the community college that those barriers have been deliberately erected to ensnare the baccalaureate aspirants as they make their pilgrim's progress toward academic Zion. Operating on the basis of a principle of moral symmetry, the critics have concluded that, if the *effect* of the community college has been to hinder the social mobility of many students, then this must also have been the *intention* of its creators.

Although this is an understandable conclusion, it is also a mistaken one. We have long been warned about the frequency of unintended consequences of purposive action (Merton, 1968: 114–118) and the dangers of "normalizing" the relationship between actors and their consequences (Gouldner, 1979: 6). And this warning is of great applicability to the community college. Its deleterious consequences for baccalaureate aspirants are not due to malignant intention. They flow instead from the institution's attempt to serve many different and often contradictory goals on the part not only of private interest groups but also of a host of government officials. The reason community colleges lack dormitories is that this made them cheaper to operate, a potent consideration in the minds of the local educators founding them and the state officials having to finance them. The reason they are so strongly vocational is not so much to track students but to provide opportunities to less academically able and motivated students, meet business's need for trained employees, and satisfy government officials' desire for a nice incentive to offer business in order to secure its political support and economic investment. (For more, see Chapter 11.) And the reason community colleges are two-year schools is because university heads did not want the competition of four-year schools, state officials did not want the financial burden of a myriad four-year colleges, and local educators felt it would be easier to establish two-year colleges than four-year colleges. The precipitate of these varying desires is an institution that, unfortunately and unintentionally, is lethal to the educational ambitions of its baccalaureate aspirants, even as it opens up opportunities for other kinds of students.

Explaining the Homogeneity of Community College Expansion

A surprising feature of the process of community college expansion is how similar it has been across the four states that developed large community college systems (California, Illinois, New York, and Washington). None of the interstate differences anatomized in Table 5–2 proved to be associated with any systematic variation in community college politics, with the exception of the difference in how early the community college system was established. This difference was associated with a diversity of stances toward community college expansion on the part of state universities, state departments of education, and private colleges. Where they were opposed to the community college, its development was either prevented (Indiana) or significantly delayed (New York). Otherwise, differences among the states in political culture, industrial structure, and proportion of working class and nonwhite college students enrolled in community colleges in 1972 had no discernible impact on the process of community college expansion.

Furthermore, at the local level, the variable organizing the selection of localities—degree of urbanization—was not associated with local community college politics in any clear pattern. The only variation, and an obvious one, was that more rural areas were more likely to have farmers involved. But otherwise the role of various actors did not seem to vary across communities in any evident way.[4]

The functionalist, Marxist instrumentalist, and institutionalist theories have failed to adequate encompass the actors and motives behind the founding of community colleges. But will this change if we consider the forces behind the vocationalization of the community college, particularly in the last 30 years? Let's look at the five chapters in Section IV.

Section IV
The Origins of Occupational Education

CHAPTER 10

The Vocationalization of the Community College: Introduction

When they first appeared around the turn of the century, community colleges were largely liberal-arts-oriented institutions, providing many students with the first leg of their baccalaureate preparation and others with a terminal general education. But over the years, this orientation changed radically. Community colleges added programs in adult education, community education, remedial education, and most importantly, occupational education.[1] Today, vocational education is the dominant program in the community college, enrolling between 40 and 60% (depending on the estimate) of community college students (Cohen and Brawer, 1989: 209; Grubb, 1991: 203, n7; idem, 1992b; Palmer, 1990a: 22).[2]

The community college's vocationalization has become the most controversial facet of its transformation into a "comprehensive" institution. On few other issues are the critics and defenders of the community college so divided. Did it arise, as functionalists claim, out of the demand of students for remunerative work and of society for a trained labor force (Medsker, 1960; Monroe, 1972; Thornton, 1972)? Or are instrumentalist Marxists correct that occupational education stemmed from the demands of the capitalist class for publicly subsidized employee training and a means to maintain the educational gap between the social classes (Bowles and Gintis, 1976; Karabel, 1972; Pincus, 1980, 1983)? Or did the community colleges vocationalize themselves, as the institutionalists claim, in an effort to carve out a secure, if subordinate, training market for themselves (Brint and Karabel, 1989)?

Although this argument has produced great heat, it has shed much less light. The purpose of this chapter is to weigh the relative merits of these arguments and to bring a missing dimension to this debate. However opposed their positions seem to be, the combatants may be similarly blind, together missing much of the real origins of occupational education.

191

The Timing of Occupational-Education Development

Occupational education appeared at various community colleges in the early decades of this century. But for many years it grew slowly, blooming only in the late 1960s and early 1970s.

In California, Chaffey Junior College began in 1916 to offer courses in commerce, manual training, home economics, general agriculture, farm mechanics, and soils (Reid, 1966: 276–277). Meanwhile, in Illinois, the Medill branch of the Chicago Junior College began to offer business and commerce courses in 1919 (Smolich, 1967: 224, 235–236).

This modest beginning expanded in the 1930s. With the Depression, many community colleges began to offer vocational education to students who entered the community college less because of interest in higher education than because of the absence of jobs outside. By the late 1930s, occupational education was securely established in California. Terminal offerings (in liberal arts as well as vocational education) had risen from 16 courses in 1916–1917 to 1,725 in 1929–1930 and 4,116 in 1936–1937 (Hill, 1938: 14). In fact, by March 1939, 34.2% of *full-time* students in California community colleges were enrolled in semiprofessional programs (Lindsay, 1939: 303–308). (This percentage might vary if one were to take into account the already numerous part-time students.) But in other states, vocational education, although clearly discernible, was still a relatively minor offering in the community college's curricular portfolio. In Illinois, vocational programs enrolled 16% of community college students. And occupational-education enrollments in Washington State barely raised their head above the floor, standing at only 4% of all enrollments (American Council on Education, 1940).[3]

World War II modestly advanced the cause of community college vocationalization. During the war, community colleges lost most of their male students to enlistment and the draft. In order to survive, many institutions contracted with the military to offer training courses (Thornton, 1972: 54–55). For example, Wenatchee Valley Community College in central Washington kept the wolf from its door by beginning to offer courses in subjects such as aviation (Van Tassell, 1982). After the war, many of the returning veterans entered occupational education.

Despite its undoubted growth by this point, vocational education did not come to maturity until the 1960s and 1970s. Enrollments rose from 20% of all community college students in fall 1959 to 29% in fall 1968 and to 40 to 60% in the mid-1980s (Cohen and Brawer, 1989: 209; Grubb, 1991: 203, n7; idem, 1992b; Palmer, 1990: 22; U.S. Office of Education, 1964b: 15; U.S. National Center for Education Statistics, 1969: 7–8).[4]

Meanwhile, the proportion of community college graduates receiving vocational degrees and certificates rose from 49% in 1970–1971 to 65% in 1978–1979 (U.S. National Center for Education Statistics, 1973b: 39–43, 63, 298; idem, 1981b: 15–19).

Table 10–1 charts the trajectory of occupation education enrollments over the last 50 years.

Occupational education changed in content as it grew in enrollments. Community colleges often began by offering courses in commercial and semiprofessional subjects, such as secretarial work, accounting, and teaching. In time, preparation for blue-collar occupations, such as welding and auto repair, was added. In the 1960s, courses in technical and medical subjects became quite common: for example, computer programming, associate degree nursing, and medical technology. And recently, the favorite addition to the community college repertoire has been "contract" or "customized" training, in which community colleges provide training geared to the demands of specific employers, often at employers' work sites and using their employees as instructors (Fields, 1987a, b; Pincus, 1989). A survey commissioned by the American Association of Community Colleges[5] found that 75% of community colleges polled in 1985 said they were involved in providing some sort of contract employee training for the private sector (Schmidt, 1988: B6). (For more on this, see Chapter 11.)

Studying the Process of Vocationalization

The study reported in this section examines developments at the national, state, and local levels of government because the vocationalization of the community college was the product of decisions made at all three levels. Given the great variability of political ecologies across our country, this study analyzes several different state and local settings. And to counter the defects of any particular method of study, I have examined a wide variety of documents and conducted interviews with a host of public and private actors representing many different, and often opposed, interests.

The national-level analysis examines the genesis of federal legislation extending aid to occupational education, particularly the Vocational Education Act of 1963. The state-level analysis involves state decisions to stimulate and even mandate vocational education in the same four states as in Section III: California, Illinois, New York, and Washington. Furthermore, I also draw on the experience of Massachusetts as reported in Brint and Karabel (1989). The local-level analysis, finally, concentrates

TABLE 10–1
The Growth of Occupational-Education Enrollments

	1938–1939	1954–1955	Fall 1959	Fall 1968	1980s[a]
United States					
Headcount enrollments			122,091	477,333	
Percentage of all community college enrollments		13%	20%	29%	40–60%
California					
Headcount enrollments				200,573	
Percentage of all community college enrollments	34%			33%	43% (1980)
Florida					
Headcount enrollments					
Percentage of all community college enrollments					32% (1983–1984)
Illinois					
Headcount enrollments	1,621		6,095	27,225	132,697
Percentage of all community college enrollments	16%		18%	27%	39% (1985)
Michigan					
Headcount enrollments					
Percentage of all community college enrollments					46% (1983–1984)
Washington					
Headcount enrollments	43		2,174	24,670	
Percentage of all community college enrollments	4%		12%	37%	
FTE enrollments					37,262
Percentage of all community college enrollments					41% (1985)

Note:
a. The percentages for the 1980s are based on dividing occupational education enrollments by total enrollments (including adult, etc.).

Sources:
1938–1939: For California, Lindsay (1939). For Illinois and Washington, analysis of institutional reports in American Council on Education (1940).
1954–1955: U.S. Office of Education (1962: 43, 48).
1959: U.S. Office of Education (1964b: 15).
1968: U.S. National Center for Education Statistics (1969: 18–19).
1980s: National figure: Cohen and Brawer (1989: 209); Grubb (1991: 203, n7; 1992b); Palmer (1990: 22). State figures (in order of appearance): Sheldon (1982:3–6); Florida State Department of Education (1985:10); Illinois Community College Board (1986c: 9–10); Michigan State Department of Education (1985: 155, 268); Washington State Board for Community College Education (1987: B 1, 2).

on the two states on which I have the richest data on the local politics of vocationalization: Illinois and Washington. However, I also draw on material on developments in California, Massachusetts, and New York. In the case of Illinois and Washington, I examine the development of occupational education in four community colleges, each situated in a different kind of locale, ranging from metropolitan center city to rural area. These different community colleges are listed in Table 10–2.

Explaining the Expansion of Occupational Education

On the surface, the instrumentalist Marxist critics of the community college and its functionalist defenders provide very different explanations of the forces behind the vocationalization of the community college. Functionalists argue that students and their parents demanded occupational education in response to the changing requirements of the labor market. Instrumentalists stress the policymaking efforts of the capitalist class and its allies in the foundations and government. But despite their differences, these two camps provide essentially the same explanation: private interest group pressure on government policymakers. Both miss the fact that government officials often promoted occupational education even in the absence of demand from students or business, and they did so on the basis of values and interests of their own.[6]

The institutionalist school recognizes the key role of governmental actors, insofar as it highlights the role of community college and university heads in promoting occupational education. However, drawing on state relative autonomy theory, I will show that the range of governmental actors who substantially influenced the vocationalization of the community college is far wider than the institutionalist school acknowledges. These governmental activists included not just the community college and university heads emphasized by institutional theory but also state governors and legislators, state departments and boards of education, and Congress members and presidents.[7] Moreover, I will demonstrate that business has exercised a considerably broader power of constraint than institutionalists acknowledge. Business has constrained the actions of public officials not just through its command of jobs that community college officials want to fill, as institutionalists claim. It has also exercised constraint through two other means as well: its control over investment capital that state and federal officials need in order to stimulate politically popular economic growth; and the attachment of government officials to ideologies—such as the centrality of business growth to the social good—that legitimate probusiness educational policies. (For more

TABLE 10–2
Local Community Colleges Studied[a]

	Illinois	Washington
Metropolitan center city	Chicago	Seattle
Metropolitan suburb	DuPage (Chicago area)	Shoreline (Seattle area)
Small city	Belleville	Everett
Small town (less than 20,000 in population)	John Logan (Carterville)	Wenatchee

Note:
a. The location is identified in parentheses only when it is not part of the name of the community college.

on how my state relative autonomy explanation differs from functionalism, instrumentalist Marxism, and institutionalism, see Chapter 2.)

The next four chapters develop my analysis of the vocationalization of the community college in three stages. First, while showing that private interest group participation undoubtedly has had an impact, they also demonstrate that it fails to explain the breadth and depth of the vocationalization of the community college, a phenomenon that engaged policymaking efforts at all three levels of government over a protracted period of time. With the limits of the interest-group argument clarified, each chapter then demonstrates that a broad array of government officials put their independent stamp on the community college. The chapters then close by showing that, at the same time that their own values and interests led government officials to act autonomously, they also provided business and students with a backdoor influence that is missed by other explanations of the vocationalization of the community college.

CHAPTER 11

Local-Level Vocationalization: Community College Heads as Vocational Entrepreneurs

Although stimulated and guided by policy decisions at the state and national levels, occupational education has fundamentally been a matter of local initiative. For many years, community colleges simply decided on their own to establish or expand their vocational-education offerings. State and national interest was absent, and state regulation was virtually nil. But by the 1960s, this situation of decentralized initiation had given way to greater state regulation. However, even today, the balance of initiative will resides with the local community college.

The first offerings of the community colleges were quite scattershot and developed in an ad hoc manner. In time, however, community colleges invented several devices to rationalize the process of course creation. Fairly early on, they created advisory boards or committees, with members of various outside groups, especially business, to advise on which courses should be created or modified. Moreover, these committees were supplemented by periodic surveys of employers to identify emerging training needs and to assess the quality of existing courses.

Beginning in the 1970s, community colleges started to forge even more formal links to industry. Community colleges developed "contract" or "custom" training, in which programs are tailored to the desires of particular employers and are frequently offered on their premises using company employees as instructors (Deegan and Drisko, 1985; Fields, 1987a, 1987b; Jaschik, 1986; Pincus, 1989). A recent survey of California community colleges estimates that 60% provide some contract training (California Community Colleges, 1986: 1–13). In Illinois, 38 of 39 community college districts reported in 1986 that they were providing contract vocational training (Illinois Community College Board, 1986a: 6, 12). And nationwide, 75% of community colleges reported offering such training in 1985 (Schmidt, 1988: B6).

Increasingly, these training activities are part of large-scale economic development centers run by community colleges. Besides customized training, these centers may offer small-business incubation,

197

technology transfer, and business consulting and research. Under small-business incubation, community colleges will provide would-be entrepreneurs with classes and workshops on how to start a business, initial office space and clerical staff support, and consultation on management and finance once they are under way. Technology transfer, meanwhile, is addressed to existing firms that need advice on introducing new production technologies. Through Advanced Technology Centers, community colleges will keep track of new technologies, provide a space for demonstrating how they work, and train company employees in their use. The research and consultation activities that various community colleges have begun to offer include conducting brief evaluations of the competitiveness of small firms, researching export possibilities for area firms, and organizing conferences on how to compete for federal funds (Melville and Chmura, 1991; Nespoli, 1991; Smith, 1991; Waddell, 1990).

Business and Student Demand Are an Insufficient Explanation

Does interest-group pressure, whether from students or business, adequately explain these local initiatives? It certainly has been a significant factor. But, as I will show, it has been too spotty and too weak to be the dominant cause.[1]

Business

Business clearly benefits from occupational education. It is a means of securing trained employees at cut-rate prices, because the main cost of educating these workers is borne by students themselves through tuition and by the public at large through taxes. And business has openly realized and acted on this interest. As Table 11–1 indicates, it has participated in the vocationalization of *all* the community colleges I studied in Illinois and Washington. And there is evidence that it has played a sizable role also in California (Cloud, 1941: 154; Cox, 1971: 157, 161–163) and Massachusetts (Brint and Karabel, 1989: 175).[2]

California's community colleges started to forge relationships with employers quite early. Soon after its establishment in 1929, the Los Angeles Community College began to work with the aircraft industry and the medical and dental professions to offer courses in their fields (Cox, 1971: 157, 161–163). By 1939, a survey of 25 California community colleges found that 12 already had industry advisory committees (Cloud, 1941: 154).

TABLE 11–1
Local-Level Stances Toward Vocationalization in Illinois and Washington: Direction and Strength[a]

	In Favor, Strong Participation	In Favor, Weak Participation	In Favor, Unknown Degree of Participation	Opposed	Ambivalent	No Role
Nongovernmental Actors						
Students		38%		12%	12%	38%
Business	25%	75%				0%
Labor unions		50%			25%	25%
Farmers		38%				62%
Minority groups				12%	12%	75%
Private colleges						100%
Foundations[b]	12%	12%				75%
Governmental Actors						
Local community college admrs.	100%					0%
AACC	25%	50%				25%

Notes:
a. Actors are classified as strongly favorable participants if they enunciated strong support of local efforts to expand occupational education, took part in the occupational-education advisory committees of community colleges, and made frequent suggestions for new courses or programs. If they were not particularly active in suggesting courses, but only served on advisory committees or issued general endorsements of vocational education, they are classified as weakly in favor. If an interest group was split, with some members participating in favor and some in opposition to more occupational education, it is classified as "mixed."
b. The figure for foundations pertains to their direct participation. It does not include indirect participation through funding of the outreach efforts of the American Association of Community Colleges.

In Illinois, Washington, and Massachusetts, business was slower to develop links to the community college. Though the community colleges in Belleville and Moline, Illinois, began to work with business and local professionals in the late 1940s (Blair, 1981; Hall, 1982; Smith, 1980: 5), most Illinois community colleges did not develop any extensive relationships with employers until the 1960s.[3] In Washington, the 1960s were also the time when business involvement with occupational education flowered. The Boeing Corp. first approached Everett Community College in the early 1960s for help in securing people trained in drafting, engineering, and aviation mechanics (Nielsen, 1981). In subsequent years, it has entered into relationships with many other colleges as well (Swain, 1982).

In the last 15 years, business demands for occupational education have become even stronger. Faced with increasing competition and wishing to cut back their internal training costs, businesses have increasingly approached community colleges to provide training that is closely geared to the needs of particular firms or industries but yet is heavily subsidized by the public (Pincus, 1989: 84). For example, at the behest of area electronic companies, Edmonds Community College (Washington) has established an Applied Technical Training Center to provide contract training that is customized to the needs of those firms (Fields, 1987a: 21). Meanwhile, Monroe Community College (Rochester, New York) has established, at the request of the local division of General Motors, a series of courses for GM workers in "statistical process control" (Pincus, 1989: 85–86).

Business's requests for vocational programs tailored to its needs have carried weight because of its economic and political power. The large amount of financial support business can provide is always attractive to community colleges. Moreover, businesspeople typically make up a sizable portion—although not a majority—of local community college boards. Two surveys of trustees of Illinois community colleges found that business proprietors and managers represented 29% of the trustees in 1968 and 34% in 1972–1973 (Abell, 1974: 58; Ebbesen, 1969: 38–39). And similar results were reported in a 1976 national survey (Drake, 1977). In addition, business is heavily represented on the many advisory boards for occupational-education programs. Needless to say, these business representatives heavily favor occupational education. In 1968, 88% of the business trustees of Illinois community colleges agreed to the statement that community colleges should provide extensive technical and semitechnical programs (Ebbesen, 1969: 38–39, 46).[4]

Despite the above, we must not overestimate the significance of business's participation in local policymaking on occupational education. For the most part, it was not until the 1960s that business became a significant participant, yet occupational-education programs had been growing for many years before. Some community colleges in Illinois and California introduced occupational-education courses as early as the 1910s. By 1938–1939, 16% of Illinois community college students, and 34% of California students, were enrolled in occupational-education programs. And by fall 1959, 20% of community college students nationwide were enrolled in vocational education. (See Table 10–1.) But except in California, business did not begin to significantly press for vocational education until the 1960s. As a result, for many years community colleges encountered little interest by business in their occupational offerings (Boylan, 1940; Medsker, 1938). A staffer of the Chicago City Colleges, a pioneer in developing occupational education, recounted the great difficulty the college had in interesting business in its vocational offerings:

The greatest difficulty encountered by the placement counselor has been the extreme reluctance of industry in general to experiment with graduates on the junior college level. . . . a vigorous campaign to educate industry concerning the worth of our junior colleges, the courses we give, and the value to industry of the services we render [should] be instituted immediately. (Boylan, 1940: 426, 428)

Similarly, the head of the Belleville (Illinois) Junior College in the late 1940s and early 1950s noted that the initiative for occupational education came much more from the community college than from business: "We would take initiative to find out what was needed. The initiative of the community college people was a big factor. Groups in the community . . . probably did not know too much about the community college" (Hall, 1981).

But even when business's involvement did become significant by the 1960s, it was still not of surpassing importance. Although it was a factor in all eight of the community colleges I studied in Illinois and Washington, business participation was strong in only two cases.[5] Typically, although business has willingly advised on existing courses, it has less often lobbied for new courses. William Gooch, the dean for vocational-technical education at the College of DuPage (Illinois), noted in 1980 that at his college

very little of new programs comes from industry or business. What they do through our advisory committees is to encourage us to expand or offer different options once a program is approved. If you're talking about a new program, we get very little from the community . . . ; an existing program, we'll get much input from the community, business, and industry. (Gooch, 1980)

These findings for Illinois and Washington can be extended as well to New York State. A survey in the early 1970s of officials of 25 community colleges in New York found that they ranked business only 14th out of 34 groups in influence, with a mere 3% saying it had major influence. Moreover, business virtually never secured even this weak effect through reward or coercion. According to the survey, its dominant channels of influence were the use of information or persuasion and a sense of identity or mutual interest that community college officials shared with it (Ensign, 1972: 108, 322, 38, 340).[6]

In sum, the instrumentalist argument for the centrality of capitalist *participation* in the vocationalization of the community college does not fare well when confronted with the evidence. To be sure, business certainly has participated notably in local-level efforts to expand occupational education, with the aim of securing publicly subsidized employee training. But that said, business participation does not begin to approximate the central role that the instrumentalist school assigns it. Local efforts to develop occupational education began well before extensive business pressure first appeared. And even at its height, business pressure at the local level has not been exceedingly forceful in many cases. Moreover, as we will see, business pressure has been quite weak at the state and national levels.

The only moderate strength of business *pressure* over the historical span of local vocational-educational development does not mean that business has not powerfully influenced the vocationalization of the community college. But this influence has rested far more on its power of *constraint*, based on the resource and ideological dependencies of government officials, than on the direct participation stressed by instrumentalist Marxists. We will explore this in detail in the section below on the role of local community college officials.

But if business pressure cannot rise to the star turn it has been given by instrumentalist theory, what about that other actor instrumentalists have also mentioned: the foundations?

Private Foundations

The private foundations deserve careful attention, for they have played an important role in reforming many areas of American education (Arnove, 1980; Lagemann, 1983). But on close examination, they do not live up to the billing assigned them not only by the instrumentalist school but also by others.

The direct influence of the foundations was weak. Occasionally, they would make grants that had a considerable impact on individual community colleges. For example, the General Education Board in 1940–1941 funded nine community colleges (including Chicago and Los Angeles, two pioneers in vocational education) to study the implementation of terminal education (General Education Board, 1940: 45; 1941: 54). And in the 1960s, the Kellogg Foundation advanced many community colleges the money to establish programs for training associate degree nurses (Grede, 1981; Smith, 1981). Finally, the foundations funded various programs to train administrators for the burgeoning vocational curriculum. In 1965, the Carnegie Corporation granted $115,000 to the St. Louis Junior College District and $24,000 to the University of Michigan to train vocational-technical leaders (Carnegie Corporation, 1965: 26, 37–38, 68, 72).

On the whole, however, the foundations exercised no *direct* influence on vocational policymaking in three-quarters of the community colleges I studied in Illinois and Washington. On the other hand, the foundations exercised a considerable *indirect* influence on local policymaking through intermediaries such as the American Association of Community Colleges. Massive and repeated grants, especially from the Kellogg Foundation, built up the AACC's capacity to serve as a national resource center and cheerleader for vocationalization efforts at the local level. These grants allowed the AACC to conduct research, publish journals and reports, hold workshops, and hire staff members to do outreach with community colleges. With this help the AACC was able to exert considerable influence on local decisions to vocationalize (Brint and Karabel, 1989). (See below for more.)

The private foundations had several immediate motives for supporting occupational education. Their most public motive was to address the needs of the labor market and of many students. They subscribed to the common belief that our economy needed a large increase in its supply of semiprofessional workers. This belief was coupled with a concern to provide economic opportunities for students who did not appear to have the ability or the ambition for a traditional college education. And in a characteristic American belief that what is good for the economy is good for the individual and vice versa, the foundations found the solution to both needs in the expansion of occupational education (Carnegie Corporation, 1963: 20; Carnegie Commission on Higher Education, 1970: 21; Kellogg Foundation, 1963: 2). In a statement repeating the conventional wisdom of the age, the Kellogg Foundation declared:

> We view this area [of semiprofessional and technical education within community colleges] as one having relation to employment and manpower problems, retraining programs, and population growth, and as being of vital importance to the long-range development of the nation's economy and to the salvaging of many of its youth. With studies indicating the need of from one to four technicians for every professional or scientist employed, opportunity is seen for pioneering experimentation to develop courses and curriculums which will enhance the skills and value of auxiliary workers. (Kellogg Foundation, 1963: 2)

In sotto voce, however, the foundations subscribed to other goals as well. In the early 1970s, the foundations sought in occupational education a solution to the recently discovered problem of underemployment among college graduates (Brint and Karabel, 1989: 106). Moreover, in the 1960s, they also supported occupational education as a way to divert less able students away from the university, thus protecting the university's academic selectivity (Brint and Karabel, 1989: 104; Carnegie Commission on Higher Education, 1973: 30; Kellogg Foundation, 1960: 34–35). For example, the Kellogg Foundation stated:

> When this image of the role of the community college [as an institution offering vocational, transfer, and continuing education] is more widely accepted, it should assure the "citadel of learning," the American university, of a chance to preserve its character and to concentrate on advanced and professional education. (Kellogg Foundation, 1960: 34–35)

(For a discussion of the ultimate meaning of these sentiments for our view of the foundation's relationship to the capitalist class, see Chapter 7.)

Despite the foundations' undoubtedly important role, much of the development of occupational education is still left unexplained. To be sure, foundation grants clearly advanced the efforts of local colleges to vocationalize themselves. At the same time, these funds were not the source, but a supplement, to these efforts. The foundations only began to exert a large impact on the community college in the early 1960s, but vocational education had been developing since the 1910s and already enrolled one-fifth of all community college students by the beginning of the 1960s.

Students

If the instrumentalist challenge has proved less compelling than claimed, does this mean that functionalists were right all along, that parental and student demand was the essential spring of occupational education? An examination of the evidence does show that students and their parents did measurably participate in local vocational policymaking, using conventional measures of political participation: lobbying government officials, voting for candidates, endorsing legislation, and most weakly, simply expressing views in public form such as opinion polls. As Table 11–1 indicates, students supported the vocationalization of three of the eight (38%) community colleges I studied in Illinois and Washington. For example, in southern Illinois, 6,012 ninth through twelfth graders were asked by advocates of the proposed John A. Logan College (Carterville) about their opinions on the community college. Some 1,546 (26%) expressed an interest in occupational education (Hill, 1978: 311). Similarly, a statewide survey of community college students in Washington State in the early 1970s found that 60% of them agreed with the statement that the community college's goal should be to prepare two-thirds of its students for employment immediately following their community college training (Corrick, 1975: 62). Moving beyond Illinois and Washington, a survey of high school juniors and seniors in the three-county area to be served by the proposed Genesee Community College (near Buffalo, New York) found that 63% of those interested in the community college wished to take a vocational program (Peters, 1969: 180). However, after the community college opened its doors, a 1971–1972 poll of its students found that only 36% of entering students said they were interested in a two-year degree or less (Baron, 1982: 158).

Did these student sentiments influence policymakers or were they simply chaff in the wind? There is some evidence of influence. A survey of 21 California community colleges in the late 1940s found that in 16 of these colleges officials stated that past or present student desires were a source of information on vocational education needs and of revision in courses (Johns, 1948: 266–267). And a number of community college heads I interviewed in Illinois and Washington State held that they had promoted vocational education in part because of student wishes (Grede, 1981; Steward, 1982; White, 1981). For example, in response to my question of what outside pressures influenced his efforts in the area of vocational education, William Steward, president of Wenatchee Valley Community College (Washington), answered:

> Students of course. . . . Several of the students came in wanting vocational educa-
> tion. They had not been successful in their college preparatory work in the high
> school. And also about that time the high school began to put emphasis on farm
> mechanics so we had more students calling for it. . . . It was the awakening, I think,
> that not every person who finishes high school is a failure unless he completes at
> least a baccalaureate degree in some four-year college or university. . . . And also
> wages. . . . People began to realize that they didn't have to be a doctor or lawyer
> to make a decent living. (Steward, 1982)

But despite this evidence of student participation, we also have good reason to conclude that students and their parents simply did not play the central role in the local vocationalization of the community college that functionalists try to assign them. Whether we define student political participation in conventional or unconventional terms, it simply cannot explain the full extent of the development of vocational education.

First, student and parental participation in conventional politics (such as lobbying, voting, and articulating opinions) was at best weak at the local level. Although students supported the vocationalization of the community college in 38% of the community colleges I studied in Illinois and Washington, their participation was quite weak, involving no more than expressing interest in vocational education when asked in opinion polls. Besides being weak in spatial breadth, students' political participation has been restricted in temporal depth. Occupational education began to grow well before there was any significant student demand for it (Brint and Karabel, 1989: 119). Virtually all the evidence we have of student sentiment in favor of vocational education is restricted to the late 1960s and 1970s. There is very little evidence of significant student interest in prior years. There were no opinion poll results, no endorsements, no lobbying. Yet, before the 1960s, occupational education had already grown significantly.

Advocates of the functionalist theory might reply that student participation must be broadened to include looser and less conventional forms, such as exerting influence through the simple fact of enrolling in large numbers in vocational-education programs. But even this loose form of student participation fails to satisfactorily explain the vocationalization of the community college. Many community college officials complained of the difficulty in getting students to enroll in occupational education programs, particularly outside such attractive fields as nursing and computer technology (Johns, 1948: 239; Karabel, 1972; Monroe, 1981; Reid, 1966: 283–284; Steward, 1982; Terry, 1981). Officials of Salinas Community College in California said that "an ever present difficulty with respect to terminal courses is that of getting the better students to take them" (Reid, 1966: 283–284). Black students have tended to be the most resistant, because of black people's recurrent experience that separate is not just different but usually unequal.[7] In Chicago, Charles Monroe, one of the early pioneers of occupational education, said that he had great difficulty overcoming the fears of black students that vocational education was a form of tracking (Monroe, 1981). Similarly, at Seattle Central Community College, many occupational programs simply attracted no demand from black students (Terry, 1981; McKinney, 1981). "Because of the history of blacks being relegated to menial positions of all kinds," a former president of the college argued,

> there was a feeling among them that vocational education was a step below academic education. And their families encouraged them not to be pushed into a vocational track. In fourteen years, we have had three black students in machinist courses. . . . Still can't get them into voc-tech programs. (Terry, 1981)

Still, despite such resistance, beginning in the late 1960s, students enrolled in large numbers in vocational programs that promised interesting and well-paying jobs (Brint and Karabel, 1989: 116–117). For instance, a study by Washington State found that 4,746 students were on waiting lists for vocational education courses in fall 1972 (Leister, 1975: 147–149), and officials at Shoreline (Washington) Community College noted that their program in dental hygiene was attracting large enrollments (White, 1981). No doubt these large enrollments were taken by policymakers as evidence that they should expand vocational education offerings.

But this student enrollment is deceptive. It is as much due to the efforts of policymakers as the demands of students. Faced for many years with student disinterest in and even resistance to occupational education, its champions gradually worked out a variety of techniques for changing student sentiment. They developed the claim that vocational education is less elitist and, in any case, pays off as well baccalaureate training (Brint and Karabel, 1989: 14, 102, 113–117; Haberacker, 1981; Middleton, 1980; Steward, 1982).[8] For example, Donald Middleton, the director of student personnel services (the advising office) at John A. Logan College (Illinois), told me:

> We make a concentrated effort to let these people know that it [blue-collar work] is an honorable profession, that many times the working conditions are much more attractive than in other occupations or they're just as attractive, and that their financial rewards will be the same or greater, and that they can do the things they may really want to do. (Middleton, 1980)

These appeals to financial interest have been backed up with advertising. Community college officials recruit students for their vocational programs by advertising in newspapers, visiting high schools, and holding open houses on their campuses (Brint and Karabel, 1989: 174; Haberacker, 1981; Middleton, 1980; Monzhimer, 1980).

But financial appeals and advertising do not always succeed in reconciling community colleges' supply of, and students' demand for, occupational education. William Steward, president of Wenatchee Valley Community College (Washington) between 1963 and 1977, noted that many of his students have "been brought up with this all their lives . . . the idea that I want my son to go to college so he doesn't work like I've had to work all my life. I tell you, that's a toughie" (Steward, 1982). In response, community college administrators have turned to counseling (Brint and Karabel, 1989: 169–172; Clark, 1960; Gooch, 1980; Haberacker, 1981; Steward, 1982). President Steward noted that to get students to think about vocational education his college often has had to resort to pulling out their academic records through high school and pointing out what were the possibilities of coming into the community college and succeeding. Most of them came in wanting to be a brain surgeon or be an engineer to build a bridge across the Atlantic Ocean. It's pretty hard to convince these people that maybe their strong suit is in auto mechanics. . . . (Steward, 1982)

To further erase the stigma of vocational education, community college officials have often given occupational-education programs the newest and most attractive facilities. They have blurred the distinction between academic and occupational-education programs by, for example, making certain courses such as mathematics required for both academic and occupational programs. Rodney Berg—former president of Everett Community College (Washington) and, later, the College of DuPage (Illinois)—stated:

We almost made a fetish out of not differentiating between the occupational and the academic or transfer. These were words we tried to expunge. . . . We did not separate a math course for technical work as versus math work for academic transfer. . . . By not having a separate math for technical students and for the academic transfer students, he was able to go either direction . . . without loss of time. (Berg, 1982)

Furthermore, as at many other community colleges, academic and occupational faculty at DuPage have been put in adjoining offices and even in the same departments. Theodore Tilton, the provost at the College of DuPage, noted:

We work very hard trying not to separate vocational-technical programs from others, even to the extent where we assign office space to those in various disciplines—the vocational-technical, maybe one in English, maybe one in mathematics—to keep them from getting separated like that, establishing their own little empires. (Tilton, 1980)

Finally, if all else fails, community colleges have occasionally set enrollment limits on transfer programs in order to shunt students over to vocational programs (Bradley, 1981). At Bunker Hill Community College in Massachusetts the president deliberately limited liberal arts transfer enrollments to 25% of all matriculants in order to get the vocational program off the ground (Brint and Karabel, 1989: 173).

In sum, the political participation of students and parents simply cannot bear the explanatory weight given it by the functionalist school. Students' conventional participation—whether lobbying, voting, endorsing, or simply expressing opinions—simply has not coincided sufficiently in time and space with the instances of vocational policymaking to allow student and parental demand to be the fundamental factor that functionalists claim. In the bulk of community colleges, students and their parents have not lobbied for or otherwise demanded vocational education. And even when they have participated in vocational policymaking, their efforts have been restricted to the last 25 years, well after community colleges began to make major efforts to vocationalize themselves. Moreover, their enrollment demand has been powerfully shaped by the efforts of community college administrators. Finally, students not infrequently have been skeptical of or even opposed to vocational education.[9]

Community College Officials Take the Lead

We have seen above that local community colleges did not simply act in response to interest-group pressure for occupational education. To a considerable degree they created this pressure. Their actions illustrate a more general aspect of governmental policymaking: that government officials do not simply register and transmit the demands of civil society, but act with great initiative. That is, they operate with relative autonomy from the demands and interests of civil society. In examining this relative autonomy of the state, let us look in greater detail at the actions and motivations of local community college officials and their national association, the American Association of Community Colleges. The institutionalists have powerfully analyzed the important role of these actors (Brint and Karabel, 1989), but there is still much more that we can learn about the content and motivations of their actions.

Local Community College Officials

In the vocational arena, community college officials were entrepreneurs. They did not just administer programs established at the behest of other groups. Instead, they often were the very initiators of those programs (Brint and Karabel, 1989: 124–125, 156–157, 165–168, 199–200; Monroe, 1972: 92; Moe, 1980; Polis, 1980). Roland Stemmer, vocational instructor at Everett Junior College, notes that community college staffers were the main initiators of new occupational curricula at his college:

> The development of our program seemed to be a function of our Dean of Instruction. The more active he was, if he was really a get up and goer, then we referred to these as periods of expansion. If he wasn't, we would kind of

drag. . . . We had a dean who was a hot shot and we started all kinds of programs while he was dean. (Stemmer, 1981)

William Gooch, dean for vocational-occupational education at the College of DuPage (Illinois), agrees that the initiative for new programs mostly has come from within the community college. He describes his main stimulus for new programs as his own reading: "You read everything you can: papers, journals, projections" (Gooch, 1980). He then goes on to trace the typical origins of a program:

A good example is laser tech. A year ago we started investigating this program. We found that Waco, Texas had a program. We also found another program in Wisconsin. We sent an associate dean to visit each of them. He picked up all the information he could from them. . . . We then read everything we could. We started writing to industry to ask if there were jobs [in laser technology] and it seemed there were. . . . We then developed an advisory committee, which is working now. (Gooch, 1980)

This process of investigation also occurred at the Los Angeles City College. In the early 1930s, well before business began to demand occupational education, the college began to set up meetings with leaders in various industries to assay their needs and interests (Cox, 1971: 99, 161; Orme, 1950: 122–127; Snyder, 1930; idem, 1933). The college's first president stated: "we have had many conferences with leaders of each of different occupations we have endeavored to investigate" (Snyder, 1933: 237). Other California community colleges soon emulated this entrepreneurial search for opportunities to offer vocational training. A survey of 21 California community colleges in the 1940s found that 16 had faculty members and staff specifically in charge of keeping abreast of occupational developments by doing surveys of employment opportunities and watching employment needs (Johns, 1948: 266–267, 269).

In fact, one can argue that business interest in occupational education was as often the consequence as the cause of community college officials' efforts to encourage occupational education. The president of Shoreline Community College near Seattle made this clear:

The Shoreline area has a relatively young Chamber of Commerce that's only four years old. I'm a member of that Chamber of Commerce. We push them into being interested in what's going on here. We try to get them to realize that there are things here that we might be able to do for them in the way of providing seminars, workshops, short courses geared to the small business community. (White, 1981)

Philip Swain, former director of education relations for the Boeing Corporation, corroborates that community college contact with business has often been at the initiative of the community colleges themselves:

> We had countless discussions [with community colleges] regarding appropriate curricula, equipment needed for them, qualifications of instructors. I won't say that we never initiated those conversations, but overwhelmingly they were initiated by the schools themselves, who were enfranchised and now looking for useful areas of effort. (Swain, 1982)

But if local community college officials often have led the efforts to establish vocational programs and make connections to business, what motives have fueled these actions? Certainly a firm belief in the worth of occupational education has been at work. A survey of 27 administrators and faculty in the Los Angeles Community College in the 1950s found that 96% said that vocational education was a major function of the community college, but only 71% gave similar status to college preparation (Given, 1957). And in Illinois in the late 1960s, 96% of community college administrators said that vocational education was always a purpose of the community college, a higher percentage even than the board members from business (87%) (Brandt, 1968). In fact, this belief in the primacy of occupational education is firmly entrenched among community college faculty across the country. A 1984 survey of 342 faculty members primarily teaching *in college transfer courses* at 24 community colleges nationwide found that 68.1% agreed with the statement that "to attract students, community colleges have to expand occupational/vocational programs in high demand areas" (Cohen, Brawer, and Bensimon, 1985: 94).

This belief in the worth of vocational education has been rooted in both the values and self-interests of community college administrators and faculty. One value has been the social desirability of meeting the training requirements of the labor market. Often couched in terms of meeting the needs of the "community," community college officials have repeatedly stressed the importance of providing postsecondary training for emerging occupations (Chicago School District, 1956: 2, 39; Hill, 1938: 77; Seattle Community College District, 1970: i, 23; Smith, 1981: 33).[10] Robert Tarvin, president of John A. Logan College (Illinois), stated this ideal in clear terms:

> We set a goal to hit 50-50 [occupational education and college transfer] in five years. . . . Our area has very few opportunities for people with four-year degrees.

It had a lot of work opportunities for technically trained people. I looked at the characteristics of our student body, and 95% said they wanted to live in Southern Illinois the rest of their lives. So we were trying to meet area employment needs, and we were trying to provide students with the skills that they would need to live where they wanted to live. (Tarvin, 1980)

Tarvin's statement makes clear that, besides feeling a commitment to meeting the demands of the labor market, community college officials have also believed that they should address the needs of students who are not bound for the university. Community college officials have long felt that these students would benefit academically and economically more from vocational education than traditional academic education (Brint and Karabel, 1989: 36, 54, 58, 96, 209; Reid, 1966: 465–466). During the Depression, many community colleges augmented their vocational offerings in response to an increasing number of nontraditional students who entered the community college in order to keep busy in the face of unemployment or in the hope they might somehow pick up training that would help them get a job (Fretwell, 1954: 39–40; Hill, 1938: 23, 31, 45, 49; Himes, 1936: 86; Medsker, 1938: 109–110). Leland Medsker, then an official of the Chicago City Colleges, noted:

> Since the colleges opened, a number of factors have caused Chicago school officials to direct their attention to the need for and nature of other such [occupational] courses. Most significant of these has been the observation that only a small per cent of the students enrolling in the colleges are eventually going on to higher institutions, thus indicating the tendency to seek employment after junior college. . . . [O]nly 23 per cent of the students enrolled since the opening of the colleges has asked for transcripts to other institutions. (Medsker, 1938: 109)

In the 1950s and continuing to this day, community college officials developed even more courses in response to the needs of yet new populations, often black students fresh from the South (Grede, 1981; Monroe, 1981; New York City Board of Higher Education, 1962: 16–17; Starr, 1982). According to John Grede, former vice chancellor for occupational education of the Chicago City Colleges,

> There was always that feeling that there was a large group for which the transfer program didn't really suffice. . . . When we got into the middle '60s, we were really getting into the unserved elements in the high school: the high school dropouts, minority students. . . . The real shift to occupational education really came because we were dealing with an older, less academically oriented group who really needed some kind of menu other than straight transfer. (Grede, 1981)

James Starr, president of Wenatchee Valley College (1953–1963), concurred with this view that considerations of equality of opportunity were central in local efforts to promote occupational education: "There were lots of students coming out of high school without employable techniques or talents. The school districts, not the downtown people, felt the need to train kids beyond their high school graduation" (Starr, 1982).

Closely allied with the desire to open up college opportunities was a wish to reduce the number of students who were either dropping out or graduating without salable job skills. As with high school vocational education, it was hoped that occupational programs would retain students who otherwise had no reason for being interested in staying in school (Baron, 1982: 87–89; Crawfurd, 1959: 161; Grede and Korim, 1969: 2).

But with this belief in the importance of helping students persist in the community college, we being to move from motives that are other-regarding to ones that are self-regarding: that is, to self-interests. Community college officials in Chicago and elsewhere wished to reduce attrition and failure to acquire salable skills not just because of the harm to students. These problems also embarrassed the community college, because they raised the question of whether the community college indeed was a gateway to opportunity (Laney, 1981). This element of self-interest becomes even more obvious when we examine the remaining reasons why community college officials pursued the vocationalization of their institution.

For community college officials, occupational education has been a way of reinforcing the political position of their vulnerable institutions. Until recently, community colleges had little hold on people's attention and affection. As outgrowths of the high school, their collegiate identity was weak and insecure. And to the degree they were regarded as colleges, it was as "junior" versions of the four-year colleges (Clark, 1960; Jencks and Riesman, 1968: 491–495). By staking out a distinct training market for the community college, one separate from that of the university (Brint and Karabel, 1989: 16–17, 206–207; Labaree, 1990), occupational education has bolstered the community college's institutional position in several different ways: it has helped reduce an embarrassing dropout rate, created a new source of revenues, brought new prestige, and secured the support of the public and of political influentials.

John Grede, former vice chancellor for occupational education for the Chicago City Colleges (1970–1980), noted how occupational education created a new revenue source for community colleges:

The occupational people have always been criticized by the old-line liberal-arts transfer element for always responding to money, and I think it was true. The advent of getting some additional funding from the outside, both federal and state, was quite attractive. (Grede, 1981)

Community college finances were especially tight in the 1950s and early 1960s, when many were still part of local school districts and had to compete for budgets with the elementary and secondary schools. Occupational education offered a way out of this budgetary bind by providing community colleges with a means to attract federal aid (in the form of vocational education funds) and, occasionally, grants from local businesses.

This budgetary stringency has returned in the 1980s, providing a good deal of the impetus behind contract training. As federal and state aid to community colleges was frozen or even cut, community colleges began to beat the bushes for new sources of private funding. Contract training has allowed community colleges to secure from corporations not only funds to underwrite their operations but also state-of-the-art technical equipment (California Community Colleges, 1986: 1–13, 4–17, 4–18; Cohen and Brawer, 1989: 130, 141–142; Deegan and Drisko, 1985: 16; Ernst and Johnston, 1991: 24; Pincus, 1989: 85). For example, a survey of 402 community colleges in spring 1983 found that the most frequently cited benefits of contract training included "increased revenues to the college in times of enrollment stabilization and decreased public funding" (mentioned by 88 colleges) (Deegan and Drisko, 1985: 16).

Besides raising new revenues, occupational education has also allowed community college heads to define their institution in an attractive way. According to John Grede of the Chicago City Colleges, occupational education gave the community college "the possibility of getting into new programs, which would give us a new identification" (Grede, 1981). It could step out of its lowly position in the institutional prestige hierarchy, in which it was merely a "junior college," a two-year anteroom to the "senior" four-year colleges and universities (Brint and Karabel, 1989: 98–99). By developing programs in occupational education—as well as adult and community education and remedial education—it became a "community college." It now occupied a position in the educational system that was substantially outside the inflexible and invidious hierarchy of graded education.

Occupational education has also given community college heads a resource for political influence. It has attracted popular interest by reinforcing its divergence from what many judge to be the elitist model of the university. The community college can be portrayed as a unique institution, one that is more comprehensive and democratic than the more academically oriented and selective four-year college. Moreover, occupational education has given community colleges a carrot that they can use to entice the support of political influentials, most notably business and state and federal officials. Theodore Tilton, provost of the College of DuPage (Illinois), made this political equation clear:

All of them [local chambers of commerce] know that when they need any help with a program, any specialized service that we might have, all they have to do is give us a call and we'd be more than happy to help out. And they in turn are more than happy to help out when we need help too. . . . During our last referendum we really needed their support. . . . Les Braun, who was President of the state Chamber of Commerce, was the man who ramrodded our last referendum effort. And he got all the local chambers of commerce together to support that effort. (Tilton, 1980)

It might be thought that Tilton's statement is simply proof of Chicagoans' well-known political savvy. But we find in New York State that Genesee Community College has explicitly stated that it should expand its vocational advisory committees because the members of those committees serve as "goodwill ambassadors" for the college (Baron, 1982: 87–89). The president of one of the Los Angeles community colleges expanded on this point:

As a matter of long-term experience, advisory committees for specialized programs . . . play a vital role in college-community relations, bond elections, scholarships, and helping the college to create a good community image. . . . Extensive utilization of advisory committees should be encouraged and their relationships expanded at all colleges if more leadership in our communities is to become involved with our colleges. (Wilber, 1969: 28–29)

This use of vocational training as a way of attracting the support of business and high-level government officials has characterized contract training as well (Deegan and Drisko, 1985: 16; Ernst and Johnson, 1991: 24; Pincus, 1989: 86). The 1983 survey of community colleges mentioned earlier found that the most frequently cited benefits of contract training included "increased visibility resulting in greater community support" (mentioned by 56 of the 402 community colleges responding) and "beneficial public relations" (43 community colleges) (Deegan and Drisko, 1985: 16).

The fact that local community college heads have promoted occupational education as a way to secure the support of business demonstrates that business has powerfully influenced community college policy even when it has not participated in making it. It has exercised a great passive power of *constraint* over the community college's curriculum that has been missed by instrumentalist theory, with its emphasis on business's direct pressure on the community college. The institutionalist school has pointed to one such constraint: business controls jobs that students want. In order to attract these students and the revenues they bring, community colleges have tailored their training to business's requirements (Brint and Karabel, 1989: 17).

But the institutionalists miss two other forms of constraint that business has exercised. Business has also controlled great political resources in the form of social prestige and recognized political clout in the eyes of government officials, the mass media, and so forth. In order to draw on this power when they need to push state government or local taxpayers for more money, the community colleges have paid business a rent in the form of publicly subsidized employee training. In addition, institutionalists miss the fact that business has held ideological power over community college officials in the form of their willing adherence to values and beliefs that benefit business. The Seattle Community College District has given testimony to this ideological constraint:

> A community college which is not closely identified with the community which it serves is not fulfilling its high purpose. . . . Increasing technological demands, changing business and industrial patterns, and the ever-increasing complexity of social and economic conditions require effective lines of communication with business, industry, labor, and state and federal governmental agencies. (Seattle Community College District, 1970: i, 23)

Note how this commitment to meeting the needs of "the community" has the effect of making the community college quite responsive to the interests of business. Because community needs are defined in a way that puts business interests at the very center (changing "technological demands" and "business and industrial patterns"), it is very natural that the community college should develop "effective lines of communication with business [and] industry" (which are listed first, ahead of students, labor, or state and federal government agencies).

American Association of Community Colleges

The AACC, the national association of local and state community college officials, has not just served as their mouthpiece in Washington, D.C. Rather, as Steven Brint and Jerome Karabel have compellingly documented, the AACC also stoutly buttressed and even led the efforts of its local constituents (Brick, 1963; Brint and Karabel, 1989). Drawing on funds provided by various foundations, most especially the Kellogg Foundation, the AACC has powerfully promoted occupational education by disseminating information to its local affiliates on how to establish occupational programs.[11] Its monthly journal, a host of special publications, and numerous workshops vigorously spread the gospel of vocationalization (Bradley, 1981; Brick, 1963: 124–126; Brint and Karabel, 1989: 36–42, 61–66, 96–97, 125–126, 208–209; Gooch, 1980; Nielsen, 1981; Steward, 1982). According to William Steward, president of Wenatchee Valley College (Washington), "there were articles in the journals all the time telling you exactly how to set up advisory committees, how to set up curricula, how to talk to counselors in the high school" (Steward, 1982). Furthermore, the AACC established a corps of consultants to work with the colleges. John Grede, vice chancellor for occupational education at the Chicago City Colleges, testified to their effectiveness:

> At one point, they [the AACC] did catch fire and bring in a cluster of people who worked on special funding . . . in the middle 1960s. At that point, the [AACC] was really providing an impetus and support service for community colleges that wanted to develop occupational programs. . . . That cluster of consultants . . . helped in the middle 1960s to move community colleges more and more into the occupational field. (Grede, 1981)

In fact, the AACC did not just disseminate how-to information to its local members but also actively shaped their very goals. Most community colleges began as almost entirely liberal arts institutions. Beginning in the late 1920s, however, AACC officials began to urge their members to vocationalize because this allowed the community college to stake out an identity different from that of anteroom to the four-year colleges (Brick, 1963: 119–138; Brint and Karabel, 1989: 36–42, 61–66, 78, 96–97; Cohen and Brawer, 1982: 192–193). This view was actively resisted by many community college heads, but, as we can see above, the vocationalizers had largely triumphed by the 1940s.

More recently, the AACC has been urging its local affiliates to take the initiative in contract training and economic development (Schmidt, 1988: B8). For example, a president of the AACC has declared:

> AACC believes that immediate attention must be given to improve the United States' role in economic global competition. . . . We suggest that community

colleges . . . determine what they plan to do in cooperation with local industry to make manufacturing long-range competitive. Too often we have waited for an advisory committee or a local industry to establish goals. Now may be the time for community colleges to make the recommendations. . . . As a start, we suggest these initiatives: . . . [that local community college leaders] actively sell the community college high tech role to state and private decisionmakers. (Ponitz, 1989: 59)

But if local initiative has been key, it has been powerfully shaped by state governments, which are constitutionally vested with sovereign power over education. Let us turn to Chapter 12 to see the content and form of the politics of vocationalization at the state level.

CHAPTER 12

State Governors and Legislators Discover Occupational Education

State governments have been encouraging occupational education for many years. To some degree, this support was in reaction to the demands of business and students. But as we will see, it has been as much or more a response to the interests and values of government officials themselves.

As early as the 1910s, the University of California was encouraging local community colleges to offer more vocational education, and it was followed in the 1930s and 1940s by the Universities of Washington and Illinois (Bolton, 1933: 60; idem, 1940: 60; Griffith, 1945: 162–169: Lange, 1916: 7; Sproul, 1931a).[1] The state universities soon found their hymns to vocational education joined by those of chief state school officers and their state departments of education. Beginning in 1920, the California department of education became a persistent and powerful champion of occupational education. Even by 1922, it had ruled that it would approve courses only in community colleges that offered, among other things, vocational education (California State Department of Education, 1920: 50; 1922: 495–496; idem, 1928: 145–154; idem, 1933: 16–19; Simonsen, 1950: 84–85). The Washington State Board of Education soon began to emulate its southern neighbor. In 1945, at the request of the state superintendent of schools, it issued regulations requiring community colleges to offer courses in at least two vocational areas. And in the 1950s and 1960s, the state department's annual report on the community college routinely stressed the importance of vocational education (Crawfurd, 1959: 194–195, 276; McKinney, 1967: 233–235; Washington State Department of Education, 1960: 2).

By the 1960s, the states moved to much more direct control of the process of vocationalization. Many state governments decided to enclose their community colleges within state systems and install state boards to coordinate or even govern those systems. Illinois made this leap in 1965 and California and Washington in 1967. (New York, however, continued to rest state control with the State University of New York and the New York City Board of Higher Education.) These state boards strongly

219

pushed for more occupational education. Through state master plans and other publications, they made it very clear that they regarded occupational education as absolutely central to the community college's mission and that local officials should bend every effort to systematically vocationalize their institutions (Brint and Karabel, 1989: 155–158, 167; Brossman and Roberts, 1973: 44; Illinois Board of Higher Education, 1964: 39–40; State University of New York, 1964: 15–16; and Washington State Board for Community College Education, 1969: 6). For example, the first master plan of the Illinois Board of Higher Education recommended that

> the number and variety of technical and semi-technical programs leading directly to employment be greatly increased primarily through programs established in comprehensive junior colleges. . . . Nationally, the offering of technical education is considered a primary function of 2-year colleges. However, the junior colleges of Illinois offer only 28 different semi-technical and technical programs. . . . Illinois has a definite need for more variety in its opportunities for occupational training. (Illinois Board of Higher Education, 1964: 35, 40)

This imperative was sweetened by monetary incentives in the form of operating and capital aid specifically earmarked for vocational education (Baron, 1982: 92–93; Brint and Karabel, 1989: 84, 194–197; Illinois Community College Board, 1967: 14; Lape, 1980; Smith, 1981; Terrey, 1980). Community colleges were allocated more funds for operating their vocational programs than their academic programs.[2] In addition, the state boards provided community colleges with more capital aid for building and equipping vocational facilities than academic facilities. The Illinois Community College Board arranged that a number of community colleges get large capital grants specifically earmarked for vocational education (Smith, 1981). A similar incentive was deployed in Washington State and proved quite effective, according to the president of Shoreline Community College:

> Funds were provided by the Legislature, the State Community College Board, and the federal government . . . to enable institutions to do planning for new occupational programs and, more than that, to provide facilities which were costly in many cases and to buy initial equipment. We learned early on that if we had a need for additional building space that we could have a better chance of getting space if we were to gear up our requests to occupational education. (White, 1980)

Most community colleges went with the grain of state government sentiment. But the few that chose to ignore this sentiment and dawdled in their efforts to vocationalize were quickly warned that this would not be tolerated. If action were not forthcoming, they might have their state aid sharply cut (Smith, 1980).

More recently, state governments have been strongly pushing community colleges in the direction of contract training and economic development. Many have formed programs that provide funds to community colleges specifically for customized training: for example, the High Impact Training Services Program and Industrial Training Program in Illinois, the Employment Training Panel in California, and Bay State Skills Corporation in Massachusetts (Brint and Karabel, 1989: 195–197; Jaschik, 1986: 14; Nespoli, 1991: 21; Osborne, 1990).

Business and Student Pressure Are Not the Explanation

How well do the functionalist and instrumentalist Marxist theories fare in explaining state-level policymaking? Were students and business any more influential than they were on the local level? The answer, in fact, is no: they were even less influential in the state house than in the hometown.

Students

At the state level, student and parental political participation was quite weak. A careful review of the evidence on California, Illinois, New York, and Washington yields only one case of conventional participation by students or parents: the endorsement by the Parent-Teacher Association in Washington State of a bill in 1939 that would have established a program of limited aid to community colleges with a strong vocational orientation (McKinney, 1967: 219–220; Washington Educational Association, 1939: 92). Other than this case, the written record and my interviews disclose no cases of student or parental involvement in those four states. (See Table 12–1.) This finding is buttressed by Brint and Karabel's (1989: 149) finding that students and their parents did not participate in state-level policymaking in Massachusetts either.

As at the local level, we have to consider the possible impact of student enrollments, conceptualized as a form of student demand, on state policymakers. There is no doubt that the latter were aware in the late 1960s and 1970s that increasing numbers of students were enrolling in occupational education and that this awareness spurred further state support for occupational education. At the same time, the points made in Chapter 11 about the influence of student enrollments on local policymaking hold here as well. State governments were encouraging vocational education as early

TABLE 12–1
State-Level Stances Toward Vocationalization in Four States:[a]
Direction and Strength[b]

	In Favor, Strong Participation	In Favor, Weak Participation	In Favor, Unknown Degree of Participation	Opposed	Ambivalent	No Role
Nongovernmental Actors						
Students						100%
PTAs						100%
Business	25%	50%	25%			0%
Labor unions		75%			25%	0%
Farmers		50%				50%
Minority groups						100%
Private colleges	25%					75%
Foundations		25%	75%			0%
Governmental Actors						
State universities		75%				25%
State educ. depts.	100%					0%
State higher educ. and community college boards	100%					0%
Governors	75%	25%				0%
Legislators	100%					0%
State community college assns.	25%	25%				50%
AACC		25%	75%			0%
Federal government		100%				0%

Notes:
a. The states are California, Illinois, New York, and Washington.
b. Actors are classified as strongly favorable participants only if they actively lobbied legislative and executive officials in favor of occupational-educational legislation. They are classified as weakly favorable participants if they only issued verbal endorsements.

as the 1920s and 1940s, well before the great upsurge in student enrollments. Moreover, when this upsurge came in the 1960s and 1970s, it was stimulated in part by state officials, who eagerly seconded the efforts of local policymakers to break down student resistance to vocational education.

Business

The thesis of the primacy of business influence fares no better than that of the centrality of student demand. Business has been much less of an influence at the state level than at the local level. To be sure, in Massachusetts, business strongly influenced the State Board for Regional Community Colleges, which led the effort to vocationalize the Bay State's community colleges (Brint and Karabel, 1989: 146n, 193–195). And in Illinois, the State Chamber of Commerce has eagerly encouraged state support of occupational education, including contract education (Beckwith, 1980; Broman, 1981; Browne, 1981; Clabaugh, 1981; Scott, 1981; Smith, 1981; Wellman, 1981). For example, Robert Beckwith, manager of the State Chamber's Education Department, has made clear that the chamber is strongly supportive of the state's program to encourage contract training in the community colleges:

> We're working on a program right now that touches into the heart of many community colleges. . . . It's called the High Impact Training Service—where in . . . 95% of the cases, the community college is the training institution identi-fied—which would train people for new or expanding positions, train them for a specific industry, for a specific job role within that industry. . . . We're very optimistic and enthusiastic about that program and about once or twice a year make mention of it in our publications and draw the attention of our chambers of commerce and our own members. (Beckwith, 1980)

Fred Wellman, former executive director of the Illinois Community Col-lege Board (1970–1980), corroborated that the State Chamber of Com-merce has actively participated in vocational policymaking: "We worked closely with him, Bob Beckwith. Frequently, on our advisory committees, we had him. Also on the Board of Higher Education advisory committees, he would serve as their [business's] representative" (Wellman, 1981).

But Beckwith's enthusiasm notwithstanding, business leaders and government officials both note that the State Chamber of Commerce has been the only major Illinois business association involved to any signifi-cant degree in occupational-education policymaking at the state level. The Illinois Manufacturers Association and the Chicago Association of Commerce and Industry are forces to reckon with. But top business leaders and state officials agree that they have not been involved in policymaking on the community college curriculum (Beckwith, 1980; Bruce, 1980; Netsch, 1980; Scott, 1981; Springer, 1982). Meanwhile, in Washington and California, none of the business associations played a significant role in state-level occupational policymaking, according to their own leaders and well-placed observers (Brown, 1986; Gordon, 1982; Moe, 1981; Mussatti, 1986).

Private Foundations

The private foundations have also influenced state-level policymaking, but again this impact has not been so sizable as to rescue the instrumentalist thesis of the central role of the capitalist class. As early as 1939, the General Education Board provided the California State Department of Education with funds to commission a study of terminal education in the community college (Reid, 1966: 475). But the bulk of foundation influence came considerably later and rested less on finance than on persuasion. The most explicit and publicized statement of the foundations' approbation of occupational education came in the Carnegie Commission on Higher Education's report, *The Open Door College:*

> Occupational programs should be given the fullest support and status within community colleges. . . . The health-service professions, in particular, will be expanding rapidly, and training for many of them can best be given in the community college. . . . The Commission recommends coordinated efforts at the federal, state, and local levels to stimulate the expansion of occupational education in community colleges and to make it responsive to changing manpower requirements. (Carnegie Commission on Higher Education, 1970: 1, 21)

It is hard to assess the impact of such pronouncements, however. There is no doubt that many state officials were aware of the Carnegie Commission's recommendations. For example, the Washington State Board for Community College Education stated that it reviewed the reports of the Carnegie Commission in developing its initial six-year plan for the state's system of community colleges (Mundt, 1973: 40; Washington State Board for Community College Education, 1970). But did this review change any state officials' mind or implant a new idea? Some state officials in fact noted that, although aware of the Commission's recommendations, they were not influenced by them (Kelley, 1981).

In any case, even if we were to assign a very heavy influence to the foundations, we run into the same problem of temporal disjuncture that befell the thesis of student influence. The foundations only began to speak on vocational education in the late 1950s, but state officials had begun to promote it 20 to 40 years earlier. This leaves a great part of the vocationalization of the community college out of the reach of foundation influence.

The Interests of Government Officials

The foregoing clearly suggests that state policy was primarily not the resultant of interest-group pressure. But let us tie down this point more explicitly. Why have state officials eagerly supported occupation education even when it has not been demanded by students, business, or foundations? The answer lies in their values and self-interests.

State Officials

The state universities in California, Illinois, and Washington stimulated the process of vocationalization wittingly by verbal praise and unwittingly by preempting training for the best jobs, leaving community colleges with the area of "middle-level training" (Brint and Karabel, 1989).[3] State departments of education and, later, state community college boards and higher education boards redoubled the words of the universities and put teeth on them by offering special funds for occupational education and by mandating action when community colleges were unresponsive.[4]

And still later, governors and legislators jumped on the bandwagon (Brint and Karabel, 1989: 145, 191; Brossman, 1986; Duryea, 1985; Rockefeller, 1970: 452–453). Soon after the Illinois community colleges were drawn together in a state system in 1965, Governor Otto Kerner of Illinois sent a letter to the newly established Illinois Community College Board asking it to give special attention to occupational education (Illinois Community College Board, 1966: 38). And in the years following, all of Kerner's successors repeated his call, as would numerous Illinois legislators (Illinois Community College Board, 1970: 135; Jepson, 1980; Wellman, 1981). In fact, Governor James Thompson (1979–1991) was a particularly strong supporter of contract training (Jaschik, 1986: 14).

In Washington, Governor Daniel Evans (1965–1977) repeatedly commended the virtues of vocational education, and a survey of 20 legislators found that 70% favored more vocational education (Corrick, 1975; Washington State Governor's Office for Program Planning and Fiscal Management, 1976: 70). In order to give weight to its wishes, the Washington legislature added a provision to the 1971 Appropriation Act declaring that two-thirds of new students entering the community college should be enrolled in vocational education (Washington State Legislature, 1971b: chap. 275, sec. 77, pp. 1308–1309).

In Massachusetts, Governors Edward King and Michael Dukakis and prominent members of the legislature were very strong supporters of contract education through the Bay State Skills Corporation (Brint and Karabel, 1989: 195–196, 199; Osborne, 1990: 206).

Several sentiments have united these state officials in favor of a vocationalized community college. All have put great value on enhancing the eonomic and academic opportunities of students who ordinarily would not enter college, for lack of either ambition or aptitude. Many have believed that occupational education would help these students by providing programs that are short, vocationally relevant, and not unduly demanding intellectually.[5]

In addition to enhancing equality of opportunity, state officials have viewed vocational education as a means of meeting the training needs of the labor market.[6] Fred Wellman, executive director of the Illinois Community College Board between 1970 and 1980, noted the very strong interest of Illinois legislators in the labor-training uses of occupational education:

> The majority of the legislators were very supportive of the community colleges, in particular the vocational-technical programs. . . . Once the legislators and other state agency heads realized that Illinois was having some economic problems, then anything that would help promote keeping jobs in Illinois or bringing new jobs into Illinois gained a lot of favor with the legislators and the agency heads. (Wellman, 1981)

State legislators' and governors' support for occupational education has certainly been rooted in a belief that it serves the social good: that educational opportunity and economic growth are of benefit to all. But there is reason to believe that this support has also been anchored in self-interest. Governors and legislators, like all elected officials, usually wish to be reelected, and here the vocationalized community college could help. As we have seen, there has been little student and parental demand for the expansion of occupational education. But students and parents might find state officials' support for occupational education quite attractive, if this program were well marketed and clearly offered as an answer to students' desire for economic opportunities. Moreover, occupational education could fuel economic growth, which is a great friend to incumbent politicians. State governors and legislators have long known that their electoral success often depends on their apparent success in generating rising employment, higher incomes, and increased tax revenues to finance politically popular programs (Chubb, 1988: 148; Lockard, 1969: 242; Osborne, 1990; Rockefeller, 1961: 358; Stein, 1990: 48–49).[7] Hence, state elected officials have a very lively personal interest in occupational education, for it promises to stimulate economic growth without the political costs of other means (Goodman, 1979: 25–31; O'Connor, 1973: 111–117). It does not require public employment or significant regulation of business investment decisions, both anathema in a capitalist society, particularly one as distrustful of government as ours (Lindblom, 1977;

O'Connor, 1973; Offe, 1984). Moreover, it has not seemed to be a giveaway to corporations. Although it subsidizes corporations (by substituting for internal training programs), it also appears to aid students by opening up job opportunities.

State officials' interest in occupational education has been fanned by the fact that state government associations, such as the Education Commission of the States and the National Governors' Association, have designated it as a highly appropriate policy for stimulating economic growth and providing educational opportunity for nonacademically inclined students (Education Commission of the States, 1970; Osborne, 1990). Moreover, individual state governments have incited each other to action through a competitive bandwagon effect. Illinois, New York, and Washington State have explicitly imitated the elaborate occupational education programs of California and other trailblazing states (Illinois Board of Higher Education, 1963: 25; Stoddard, 1944b: 1; Washington State Department of Education, 1960: 2–3).[8]

State governors and legislators have not been the only state officials with self-interested reasons for championing occupational education. So have state universities. The University of California vigorously urged vocationalization in good part because it hoped that it would pull less able students away from the university, thus allowing it to fulfill its promise as a great research institution. Alexis Lange, long the dean of the School of Education, enunciated this view as early as World War I:

> The Junior College will function adequately only if its first concern is with those who will go no farther, if it meets local needs efficiently, if it turns many away from the university into vocations for which training has not hitherto been afforded by our school system. . . . (Lange, 1916: 4–5)

The ultimate effect of diversion, Lange notes, is to "enable the universities to concentrate their efforts more and more on university work proper" (Lange, 1916: 8). Far from being ignored or even excoriated, Lange's academic elitism became a California tradition. His celebration of the diversionary role of occupational education was repeated by Robert G. Sproul, president of the university from 1931 to 1958, and Clark Kerr, president from 1958 to 1967. For example, Sproul declared in 1931:

> The real value of the junior college . . . rests in its attempt to meet the needs of those students whose talents and interests do not lie along the line of a university education but who *are* interested in further education. . . . From the junior college should come men trained not as agricultural scientists but as farmers . . . ;

men trained, not as engineers, but as highly skilled mechanics. . . . (Sproul, 1931a: 278–279)

Sproul repeated these sentiments in 1958 (Sproul, 1958), and they were further endorsed by Clark Kerr (1978) in the 1960s. (See Chapter 7 for more.)[9]

Chief state school officers have also had self-interested reasons for supporting the vocationalized community college. The New York State Department of Education supported vocationalization in the 1940s and early 1950s in good part to protect the private liberal arts colleges, to which it had many ties. It hoped that vocationalized community colleges would be less likely to cut into the enrollments of the private colleges than would more academically oriented public colleges (Abbott, 1958: 198–199; Carmichael, 1955: 38–39, 128, 133–134). (See Chapters 4 and 7 for more.) Meanwhile, in California, Illinois, and Washington, the vocationalizing interest of the state school superintendents might have been fanned by the fact that, as elected officials, they too had to come up with interesting programs to sell to voters.

State and National Community College Associations

Local community college officials have not been just the objects of state policies toward occupational education. They have also been the co-authors of those very policies. By the 1930s, local administrators had formed state associations that advanced their interest in occupational education at the state level. In California, for example, the state Junior College Association adopted a statement in 1941 calling for vocational education of a large proportion of community college students (Ricciardi and Harbeson, 1941). More recently, the association has pushed to have community colleges included among the program planners mandated by the California Work Site Education Training Act of 1979 (SB 132) (Perfumo, 1981: 79–80).

The American Association of Community Colleges (AACC) has vigorously buttressed the efforts of its state affiliates (Brick, 1963; Brint and Karabel, 1989: 36–42, 61–66, 96–97, 125–126, 208–209). The AACC's main contribution has been to develop a rationale for occupational education that has proved quite persuasive to state and national policymakers. The AACC posited the existence of a large and distinct class of occupations (variously labeled "semiprofessional," "technical," or "middle level") that required vocational education in neither the high school nor the university, but an institution located in between (American Association of Junior Colleges, 1964: 2–3; Brint and Karabel, 1989; Harris, 1964: 19, 28; Ingalls, 1939: 450; Koos, 1924: 44). Furthermore, it has argued that the vast bulk of community college students do not go on to the university and thus require this middle-level training (American Association of Junior Colleges, 1962: 10; idem, 1964: 5; Eells, 1941: 58–65; Parnell, 1984).

This rationale has reached the ears of influential state officials (Brint and Karabel, 1989). For example, the first master plan of the Washington State community college system states:

> Various lay and professional groups who have studied post–high school educational institutions and their potential for fulfilling today's great educational task are high-lighting the importance of the comprehensive community college. A national program of prominent citizens representing business, industry, and education, meeting in Washington, D.C. In December 1964 announced: "The community-centered junior college offers unparalleled promise for expanding educational opportunity through programs embracing job training. Occupational education initiated in junior colleges should be reinforced and new programs developed where necessary." (A. D. Little, 1966: 17)

The Washington State report is quoting a statement made originally by the AACC's National Advisory Commission on the Junior College (American Association of Junior Colleges, 1964: 5).

More recently, the AACC has been vigorously publicizing the idea that the community college is a key means of enhancing the nation's human capital and increasing its economic competitiveness. For example, Dale Parnell, the AACC's president, has declared:

> The missing link in current United States economic policy is systematic attention to human resource development. . . . America's success in meeting the challenges of uncertain but far-reaching economic change will depend, in part, on how well the knowledge, skills, and resources of community, technical, and junior colleges are used. . . . The work force of the future will require significant levels of postsecondary education and training. (Parnell, 1990: 9)

Hence, the AACC has committed itself to "helping national and state decisionmakers recognize community colleges as a major resource in economic development activities" and "prompting the development of college/employer partnerships" (American Association of Community and Junior Colleges, 1989: 25).

As we can see, state governments have played a very important role in the vocationalization of the community college, and state officials have been at the very center of that process. Will the same hold true for the federal government? Let us explore this question in Chapter 13.

CHAPTER 13

National-Level Support for Vocationalization

As early as 1947, the President's Commission on Higher Education (often called the Truman Commission) forcefully endorsed the national useful-ness of vocational education in the community college:

> [T]he commission recommends that the community college emphasize programs of terminal education. . . . Semiprofessional training, properly conceived and organized, can make a significant contribution to education for society's occupational requirements. In not providing this sort of training anywhere in existing programs, the educational system is out of step with the demands of the twentieth century American economy. (U.S. President's Commission on Higher Education, 1947: I 68–69)

But it was not until the 1960s that the federal government really became a force of note in the politics of occupational education. Beginning in 1958, a host of federal acts directly or indirectly extended aid to the community college for occupational education: the National Defense Education Act of 1958, the Manpower Development and Training Act of 1962, the Vocational Education Act of 1963, the Allied Health Professions Act of 1966, the Comprehensive Employment and Training Act of 1973, and various other pieces of legislation. Title VIII of the National Defense Education Act allowed community colleges to receive funding for their occupational education programs (Congressional Quarterly, 1958: 217–220). And the Vocational Education Act of 1963 explicitly earmarked one-third of its funds in Section 4 for postsecondary vocational education (Congressional Quarterly, 1963: 201–203; U.S. Office of Education, 1964a: 7).[1] As a result of these initiatives, federal aid for community college vocational education rose from $13 million in 1965 to $173 million in 1981 (U.S. Office of Education, 1968: 43; U.S. National Center for Education Statistics, 1983b: 6).

This aid strongly spurred state and local occupational-education efforts. Community college officials in California noted how federal funds accelerated the development of vocational education in their state (Peterson, 1962: 203). Similarly, in Illinois, while federal aid accounted for only a small part of total expenditures on vocational education, it nonetheless had a catalytic effect (Chase, 1969: 98–99; Grede, 1981; Grede and Korim, 1969: 2; Smith, 1981). Gerald Smith, former executive director of the Illinois Community College Board (1965–1970), noted that

> the stance of the federal government with its huge appropriations at the time . . . had a strong influence on some of the rapid development of vocational education programs in some of our community colleges. For example, in 1966–67, that office [the Illinois Department of Vocational Education and Rehabilitation] was able to give five of our big new junior colleges each a half million dollars apiece [in federal aid] for equipping their vocational facilities. That had an enormous influence on the five colleges. . . . (Smith, 1981)

Governmental Initiative

Congress Members and Presidents

Federal aid for occupational education rose rapidly during the 1960s and early 1970s at the initiative of certain members of Congress and, less so, the Kennedy through Nixon administrations (Halperin, 1985; Price, 1964: 97). Student, business, or foundation demand played very little role (see below).

In the early 1960s, Congress took the lead. Several members of the House of Representatives, most notably Representatives John Brademas (D-Ind.) and Albert Quie (R-Minn.), formed an "Advisory Group on Higher Education" to study the nation's needs in the area of postsecondary vocational education. In 1961, this group recommended that the federal government start funding programs to train semiprofessional technicians, and Brademas introduced a bill to this effect (Brick, 1963; Price, 1964: 85; U.S. House of Representatives, 1962). In the meantime, President Kennedy chartered a Panel of Consultants on Vocational Education (1963) to do a thorough evaluation of the federal government's program of aid to vocational education. The intersection of these legislative and executive initiatives produced the Vocational Education Act of 1963 and several subsequent labor-training acts (Halperin, 1985; Lee, 1985; Mallan, 1985; Radcliffe, 1985; Young, 1985).

Federal executive and legislative officials supported occupational education for the traditional reasons of broadening opportunity and meeting the training needs of the economy. But as elected officials they gave these common motives a particular twist.

By the early 1960s, the concern about educational quality that had dominated the 1950s began to give way to one about equality. A changing economy was rapidly eliminating many jobs for unskilled workers and stirring concern about the high dropout and low college-going rates of working class and nonwhite students (U.S. Panel of Consultants, 1963: 8–17, 217–221). In this context, occupational education was touted as a prime means of providing students of modest abilities and ambitions with enlarged economic opportunities (Brademas, 1963; idem, 1967; Kennedy, 1963: 977; Nixon, 1970: 38A; Sundquist, 1968: 72–73, 83–84). Representative John Brademas stated:

> In the next few years, employment in the professional, semi-professional, and technical fields will increase sharply, while job opportunities for unskilled and agricultural workers will continue to decline. . . . Vocational schools must move far more quickly to develop programs that prepare students not only for today's labor market but for tomorrow's as well. (Brademas, 1967: 12)

This concern about providing students was by no means entirely altruistic. Blacks were mobilizing politically and becoming a crucial source of votes for the Democratic party as it began to lose the affection of the South. Democratic officials looked for various ways of binding to their side this increasingly important black constituency. One major means was greater educational opportunity, including widened access to vocational education (Piven and Cloward, 1977; Sundquist, 1968). Federal officials' solicitude for the disadvantaged was also driven by the fear that unemployed high school dropouts could easily be set aflame by the rapidly escalating social turmoil of the time (Brademas, 1967: 12; U.S. Advisory Council on Vocational Education, 1968: 122; U.S. House of Representatives, 1968a: 197, 200, 239, 554, 663; idem, 1968b: 60, 63; U.S. Panel of Consultants on Vocational Education, 1963: 126). In 1963, the Panel of Consultants went so far as to describe such youth as "dynamite":

> Forgetting momentarily those needs of youth which are formally connected with special education and rehabilitation . . . there is a whole gamut of other needs which might be termed "special." These students are sometimes called potential dropouts, disinterested, reluctant, disadvantaged, alienated, or culturally deprived. Other youth problems are recognized in connection with the minorities, the migrants, the mentally retarded, the emotionally disturbed, and the delinquent. Altogether, the number represented in these classifications is very great; the "dynamite" generated as a result may be social, political, and economic, especially in large population centers. These young people are of grave concern to the Nation. (U.S. Panel of Consultants, 1963: 126)

By the early 1970s, this interest in social control took a new twist. The concern no longer was the disappearance of unskilled jobs for high school dropouts but the erosion of job openings for college graduates, with some federal officials fearing that this "overeducation" would fan the flames of political radicalism among well-educated youth. Occupational education again promised a solution: by diverting students from the pursuit of a baccalaureate degree, it would reduce the number of bachelor's degree holders to a level commensurate with the apparent number of "college-level" jobs in the United States (Brint and Karabel, 1989: 109; Green, 1970: 4; Nixon, 1970; U.S. House of Representatives, 1971a: 92; idem, 1971b: 74). Representative Edith Green (D.-Ore.), long a congressional leader on educational policy, stated:

> For too long, the educational system and the projections of our real manpower needs have been passing each other arrogantly and blissfully by like foreign ships in the night. . . . One of my two top priorities for the 1970s is more emphasis—much, much more emphasis—on vocational-technical education. . . . We must reject the utterly false assumption that a person, to be successful and happy, must be a lawyer or doctor. . . . In Congressional action, I predict increased financial aid to this fastest growing section—our community colleges and our technical institutes. (Green, 1970: 4)

Federal elected officials also favored occupational education as an engine of economic growth. As with state governors and legislators, this interest sprang as much from self-interest as altruism. Federal legislative and executive officials feared in the 1960s that insufficient numbers of semiprofessional and technical workers were being trained and that this would hamper economic growth (Brademas, 1963; U.S. Panel of Consultants for Vocational Education, 1963). Representative Brademas voiced this fear in the characteristic terms of the time:

> The second fastest growing category in our labor force is technical and semiprofessional jobs requiring 1 to 3 years of postsecondary education. . . . [F]or the maximum utilization of our professional, engineering, and scientific manpower, we should have 400 to 500 technicians for every 100 professional personnel. . . . Today the number of scientists and engineers engaged in civilian-oriented technology in Western Europe and England combined is greater than that in the United States. This is at least one of the reasons the rate of increase of our gross national product per worker is substantially less than the rate of increase of almost all other industrialized nations in the world. To enable our critically short supply of engineers and scientists and scientists to make a greater contribution to the civilian economy, we must back up our professionals with more semiprofessional technicians. (Brademas, 1963: 14958, 14959)

Federal officials felt they could not safely ignore these economic problems. Under the Employment Act of 1946, they are held responsible for maintaining economic growth. And this is no mere symbolic duty, for it is enforced by the electorate. Presidents and Congress members have found that their reelection depends heavily on the state of the economy (Jacobson, 1983: 126–128; Sundquist, 1968: 15, 20, 28, 34, 70–72, 433–435; Tufte, 1978: 5–8). For example, in winning election in 1960, John F. Kennedy had benefited in key states from the votes of the unemployed, with these votes often being greater than his total winning margin. To retain these votes the next time he stood for reelection, he had to improve the economy (Sundquist, 1968: 34, 72). (See Chapter 8 for more.) Faced with this political imperative to spur economic growth, federal officials have often turned to vocational education. For example, John F. Kennedy stated:

> Vocational education plays an important part in the program of the Democratic Party for acceleration of our nation's growth. Growing needs mean expansion of vocational education. As the skill of our workers increases, their contribution to the economy increases. (American Vocational Association, 1960)

As at the state level, occupational education has recommended itself as a cure for economic woes that is quite palatable politically. It apparently benefits students as much as business, and it spurs economic growth without requiring public employment or the regulation of business investment decisions. As a program for creating "human capital," it seemingly allows government officials to serve welfare goals without violating the rules of the game of a capitalist economy.

American Association of Community Colleges

The AACC has closely monitored and intervened in federal decisions on occupational education for many years. Beginning in 1937, it lobbied for the repeal of the provision in federal vocational-education legislation restricting aid to programs of "less than college" grade. It finally succeeded in getting such a repeal in the 1963 Vocational Education Act. This act also included, at the urging of the AACC, a substantial "set-aside" for the construction of vocational-education facilitates at community colleges and area vocational schools (Brick, 1963: 94–96; Ingalls, 1939).

TABLE 13–1
National-Level Stances Toward Vocationalization:[a] Direction and Strength[b]

	In Favor, Strong Participation	In Favor, Weak Participation	In Favor, Unknown Degree of Participation	Opposed	Ambivalent	No Role
Nongovernmental Actors						
Students						*
PTAs						*
Business						*
Labor unions		*				
Farmers						*
Minority groups						*
Private colleges						*
Foundations		*				
Governmental Actors						
Congress members	*					
Presidents	*					
AACC	*					

Notes

a. Percentages are not reported since there is only one possible case: the U.S. as a whole. The asterisks indicate whether, and with what valence, an interest group participated in national-level policymaking.

b. Actors are classified as strong participants in favor of vocationalizing the community college if they not only announced strong support but backed it up with active involvement in such forms as lobbying the federal government to pass community college legislation. If their support only took the form of endorsements, without active support, they were classified as weak participants.

The Limited Impact of Private Pressure

Interest-group pressure has been only a minor factor in the development of federal policy toward occupational education. Already weakening rapidly as it moved from the local to the state level, interest-group pressure virtually expires at the national level. (See Table 13–1.) There is no evidence that students or their parents, either singly or in association, have lobbied or otherwise pressured federal officials. Even the weakest form of conventional political participation is absent: there is no evidence that federal officials have consulted or even had access to national polls of student or parental sentiment on the desirability of occupational education. And student enrollment cannot be taken to have had much influence. When it surged in the late 1960s and early 1970s, this was already several years *after* federal officials had passed the Vocational Education Act of 1963.

Business participation in occupational-education policymaking has been similarly ephemeral. The major business associations occasionally have issued statements favoring vocational education. But they have not lobbied for it, according not only to their own staffers (Mehan, 1985) but also well-placed representatives of labor (Young, 1985), the American Association of Community Colleges (Mallan, 1985), Congress (Lee, 1985; Radcliffe, 1985), and the executive branch (Halperin, 1985). John Mehan, vice president of the U.S. Chamber of Commerce, notes the chamber's inactivity on this issue:

> It wasn't until the 70s that we began to suggest that in terms of meeting the technical skills necessary that you began to hear people talking more favorably about community colleges. Again, I don't recall that we came out with a specific statement. (Mehan, 1985)

The private foundations perhaps have been a bit more active than business. A member of the staff of the Ford Foundation testified before Congress in the 1960s in favor of occupational education (U.S. House of Representatives, 1968a: 446). And the Carnegie Commission on Higher Education (1970) commended occupational education to policymakers. But again, these initiatives were largely after the fact. The Carnegie Commission first spoke on occupational education seven years after the Vocational Education Act of 1963 had passed.

Having reviewed the politics of vocationalization at the local, state, and national levels, it is time to summarize our findings and draw their implications for the various theories we have been testing. This is the task of Chapter 14.

CHAPTER 14

The Politics of Vocationalization: Summary and Conclusions

In the end, we have to conclude that the functionalist and instrumentalist Marxist arguments fare little better in explaining the development of occupational education than they do the rise of the community college. Students and parents simply cannot bear the explanatory weight put on them by the functionalist defenders of the community college. If we begin with conventional participation—whether lobbying, voting, endorsing, or simply expressing opinions—we find that their participation was at best moderate at the local level and virtually nil at the state and national levels, where many important decisions were made. And if we define student demand in terms of the simple fact of enrollment, we face the fact that these enrollments did not precede or accompany, but come well after, the first efforts by policymakers to vocationalize the community college. In fact, when vocational enrollments finally rose sharply in the late 1960s, this surge stemmed not just from a preexisting student interest but also the energetic efforts of policymakers to provoke that interest. Moreover, as we have seen in Chapter 11, those efforts to evoke student interest sometimes had to confront rather sizable student *resistance* to occupational education.

The instrumentalist argument for the centrality of capitalist command in the vocationalization of the community college also falls short. To be sure, business did participate significantly in local-level efforts to expand occupational education, pursuing the goal of publicly subsidized employee training. At the same time, we must note that community colleges began to vocationalize well before extensive business pressure first appeared. Furthermore, business's participation has been at best moderate at the state level (largely due to the unusual vigor of the Illinois State Chamber of Commerce) and nonexistent at the national level.

The private foundations cannot bail out the thesis of capitalist dominance. Even if we accept the instrumentalist claim that the foundations have largely served as levers of capitalist power, we still face the fact that the foundations were simply not that influential. To be sure, they certainly had a significant degree of influence on the process of vocationalization after 1960, both directly through their own efforts and indirectly through their support for the American Association of Community Colleges. But this influence suffers from the same temporal disjuncture as the influence of students and business: it was largely restricted to the post-1960 period, long after the process of vocationalization began.

These observations do not add up to a conclusion that private interest groups played no significant role in the vocationalization of the community college. Far from it. But they deflate the functionalist and instrumentalist arguments that interest-group pressure was the primary motor and governmental activity simply a reflex of this pressure.

The central defect of the functionalist and instrumentalist positions has been their failure to acknowledge the centrality of relatively autonomous government officials in the development of occupational education. Granted, the two schools do mention several different government officials. But they entirely ignore the role of such important officials as state governors and legislators. More importantly, they fail to underscore that, rather than making educational policy solely in response to the demands of private interest groups, government officials to a great degree acted on their own initiative, pursuing their own self-interests. Local administrators of community colleges and their state and national associations have been long drawn to occupational education. It is a means of leveraging the political and monetary support of business and elected officials. It also protects their institution's reputation as an avenue of opportunity by providing salable job skills to students who leave without going on to four-year colleges. Meanwhile, state and national elected officials—ranging from state governors to U.S. Congress members—have supported occupational education in order to enhance their reelection chances by stimulating economic growth. State universities, finally, have seen occupational education as protecting university selectivity by channeling away the flood of students bidding for entry into the university.

The fact that government officials have promoted occupational education for reasons of their own has not precluded private influence. In fact, it is precisely government officials' values and self-interests that have given business and students a powerful influence over occupational education policymaking in spite of their limited degree of participation. Business has exercised a considerable power of constraint over government officials because those officials, in order to realize their own interests, need access to resources that business controls: for example, political clout with key political actors and the mass public, investment capital to fuel economic growth, and jobs for community college graduates. The probusiness bias created by this resource dependency on the part of public officials and other actors has been buttressed by ideology. Government officials have defined the ideal of community college service to the community in a way that puts business interests at the very heart. Government officials have also been predisposed ideologically to serve business interests in another way. They could try to secure economic growth by creating a large government-run economic sector or by forcefully regulating business. But this goes against a fundamental tenet of American belief: that the economy and private business are virtually coterminous and that government is not to trespass significantly on managerial prerogatives. Consequently, when public officials or other actors have sought to improve the economy or help students succeed economically, they have thought first, and usually last, of how this could be done not by regulating or replacing business but by providing it inducements to take desirable actions (Goodman, 1979; Lindblom, 1977; O'Connor, 1973).

Students, meanwhile, have influenced occupational-education policymaking far in excess of their participation through their ideological constraint over government officials. Those officials have supported occupational education to a significant degree because they are committed to providing greater educational opportunity for "nontraditional" college students and because they believe that occupational education would help such students remain in college and gain an economic payoff from it.[1]

But even as government officials' interests have transmitted business and student influence, they have acted as a source of independent policy initiative. Business's interest in postsecondary vocational education could have been met by vocational-technical schools as well as community colleges. But community college officials did not favor the former option because business favor would then flow not to them but to another institution. To be sure, community colleges could have converted themselves—and many are close to it now—into exclusively vocational-technical schools. But this would mean that community college officials would have to renounce the prestige that comes with being a "college." Hence, community college officials have fought to make sure that interest in postsecondary vocational education should remain focused on an institution offering both occupational education and an academic program: namely, the community college.

Convergences and Divergences with the Institutional Perspective

The "state relative autonomy" argument made above converges at several points with the "institutional" perspective of Brint and Karabel (1989) and Labaree (1990). We agree that the vocationalization of the community college cannot be explained largely in terms of student and business demand. To fill this explanatory gap, both the institutional and relative autonomy arguments highlight the actions of elite state universities, state community college boards, local community college heads, and the American Association of Community Colleges.[2]

Despite these points of agreement, the state relative autonomy argument also diverges sharply from the institutional argument in two main areas. Using a broader range of data, I find that several governmental actors that the institutional school does not mention or only mentions in passing played very important roles. Institutionalists do not mention the role of state school superintendents and departments of education, yet as early as the 1920s they were exhorting local officials to vocationalize and mobilizing support from the legislature. And they have continued this support to this day. Furthermore, although institutionalists do mention the role of federal officials and state governors, legislators, and boards of higher education, their coverage is not sufficiently systematic. The actions of these officials are described but the self-interests that drove them are not explained.[3]

Secondly, the state relative autonomy argument provides a broader analysis of the power of constraint that business exercised over government officials. Institutionalists focus on business's control of jobs in order to explain why community colleges catered to its interests. This is an important aspect of business's power of constraint, but there are two other major facets as well: business's control over investment capital and thus the volume of economic growth; and the fact that government officials subscribe to values and beliefs that suggest the social value of aiding business, quite apart from any political pressure that it might mobilize. These two forms of constraint, involving resource dependence and ideology, must be recognized in order to fully understand business's ability to influence policymaking over occupational education even when it was uninvolved in, or even unaware of, this policymaking.

Section V
Implications of the Research

From Research to Practice: The Policy Implications of the Community College's Impact on Students

Chapter 3 has shown that neither the defenders nor the critics of the community college have fully captured its multifaceted nature. Both grasp parts, but only parts, of this contradictory institution. This is particularly the case with regard to its impact on students. The functionalist defenders of the community college appear to be correct that it opens doors to higher education more widely than do four-year colleges and that it better facilitates the educational success of students seeking a *subbaccalaureate* education. Also, the community college is better than other two-year colleges in facilitating the educational and economic success of its students. However, the instrumentalist Marxist and institutionalist critics are also correct that the community college significantly hinders the education and economic attainment of its baccalaureate aspirants. They get significantly fewer bachelor's degrees, years of higher education, prestigious jobs, and (in the long run) high incomes than comparable students entering four-year colleges.

This last finding is highly disturbing and demands a dramatic policy response. We are not talking about an injury to a small group of people. Baccalaureate aspirants at the community college account for 20 to 35% of its entrants (and 7 to 13% of entrants to all colleges).

But if the community college's failure to serve the needs of this large group of students demands fundamental reform, do we know what direction this reform should take? In fact, we have been given useful suggestions by various policy scholars and advocates, but these proposals are also contradictory and flawed. Some of these commentators, whom I will call the "noncollegiate reformers," argue that the community college should recognize that it cannot and should not try to remain a major force in prebaccalaureate preparation. It should instead accelerate its shift away from transfer education by largely jettisoning it in favor of noncollegiate education, especially vocational education (Breneman and Nelson, 1981; Clowes and Levin, 1989; Cross, 1985; Gleazer, 1980; Kerr, 1980). Others, whom I will term the "collegiate reformers," forcefully reject this policy, calling instead for a major renewal of the community college's commitment to transfer and general academic education (Astin, 1983; Brint and Karabel, 1989; Cohen and Brawer, 1987, 1989; Eaton, 1988, 1990; McCabe, 1981, 1988; Pincus and Archer, 1989; Richardson and Bender, 1987; Zwerling, 1976).[1]

I will show below that, on both evidence and logic, the collegiate position is much more compelling. The recommendations of the noncollegiate reformers would seriously injure many students by crippling general education and fatally undercutting the transfer chances of those who aspire to a baccalaureate degree. But while the policies of the collegiate reformers are preferable, they are also insufficient. They would mitigate the obstacles encountered by baccalaureate aspirants but not eliminate or even drastically reduce them. Their reforms do not address the fact that these obstacles are rooted in fundamental features of the community college: as a vocationally oriented, two-year, commuter institution that is separate from the four-year colleges to which its baccalaureate aspirants must eventually transfer. Hence, we must transcend, while also subsuming, the collegiate reforms. We should seriously consider transforming large community colleges into four-year colleges and smaller, less urban ones into branches of the state universities. These "structural" reforms are not without their flaws, but they promise a more fundamental attack on the problem of educational inequality than the collegiate reforms alone.

The Noncollegiate Program

The noncollegiate reformers appeared in the late 1970s and early 1980s, at the height of the community college's vocationalizing surge (Breneman and Nelson, 1981; Clowes and Levin, 1989; Cross, 1985; Gleazer, 1980; Kerr, 1980). With the exception of Breneman and Nelson, they are not critics of the community college. In fact, they see themselves as defenders. Their reform suggestions stem from a desire to refine its emerging mission—focusing on vocational and community education—rather than to call for a return to a much stronger emphasis on transfer education.

The Reforms Detailed

The noncollegiate reformers argue that community colleges should address the apparent deterioration of transfer education by largely giving up this program and instead playing to their strength in noncollegiate education: vocational education, adult and community education, and remedial education. Breneman and Nelson (1981) cogently make this argument in a study commissioned from the Brookings Institution by the American Association of Community Colleges:

> [T]he demands of an era of limited growth and retrenchment in higher education will force state policymakers to consider institutional performance carefully in allocating limited resources for education. One area within the community college that is likely to be examined critically is the educational performance and productivity of academic transfer programs. . . . the performance data in many states are troubling. . . . One way to approach this question is to consider those areas in which a particular type of institution may have an educational comparative advantage over others. . . . We favor an educational division of labor among institutions . . . that would result in the community colleges enrolling fewer full-time academic transfer students of traditional college age and retaining a dominant position in those activities that four-year institutions have not undertaken tradition-ally and are likely to do less well. (Breneman and Nelson, 1981: 209, 211)

Breneman and Nelson are not alone in this recommendation. Their sentiments are shared by many prominent community college commenta-tors and officials, including the former executive director of the American Association of Community Colleges, Edmund Gleazer (1980), prominent community college scholars such as K. Patricia Cross (1985) and Darrel Clowes and Bernard Levin (1989), and the Carnegie Council on Policy Studies in Higher Education (1979) and its chair, Clark Kerr (1980).

For the noncollegiate school, the central program within a trans-formed community college would be vocational education. Remedial, adult, and community education would have an important place, but they would be orbiting the utilitarian sun of vocational education (Carnegie Council on Policy Studies in Higher Education, 1979: 25; Clowes and Levin, 1989: 353; Cross, 1985: 41–42, 46; Gleazer, 1980: 4–5, 10, 16; Kerr, 1980: 8–9). Darrel Clowes and Bernard Levin, prolific writers on the community college, put this pithily:

> [T]he only viable core function for most community colleges is career education. This is a function the society needs and supports, it is a function the institution can and does provide, and it can serve as the essential element, the core function—the *elan vital* about which community colleges may be restructured for a viable future. . . . career education is . . . perhaps the only possible choice given the inroads other institutions have made in the historic roles of the community college. A modified transfer and collegiate function could develop from this core and could provide the basis for maintaining some position within higher education. The

remaining functions could become satellites to the core of career education. (Clowes and Levin, 1989: 353)

Evaluation: These Reforms Would Exacerbate the Problem

The noncollegiate program has merit in that it recognizes that the community college's attempt to balance academic, vocational, adult, and remedial education has created a host of contradictions and difficulties. In trying to be a jack-of-all-trades, the community college often has ended being master of none. As we have seen in Chapters 3 and 4, the community college has failed to provide lower-division baccalaureate preparation of quality equal to that of four-year colleges. A major reason is that the community college's strong emphasis on vocational education interferes with effective transfer education by seducing baccalaureate aspirants from their original plans, by reducing the chances they will be accepted by four-year colleges (especially with full credits), and by distracting community colleges from mounting academically rigorous transfer or university-parallel courses (see Chapter 4).

Unfortunately, the proposal of the noncollegiate reformers to bring coherence to the community college by largely amputating its baccalaureate preparation program will itself cause major problems. It will leave the many baccalaureate aspirants homeless, and it will seriously undermine the capacity of the community college to provide general education even to its vocational aspirants.

Hindering Baccalaureate Aspirants

As many as a third of community college students today aspire to a baccalaureate degree (see Chapter 4). What will happen to them as the community college increasingly centers itself around vocational education?

Anticipating this problem, noncollegiate advocates have envisioned that baccalaureate aspirants would largely circumvent the community college and go directly to four-year schools (Breneman and Nelson, 1981). And those that remain would have a fallback path to the baccalaureate through the transfer of vocational credits:

> This modified transfer function would primarily be a technical/transfer function. . . . This technical/transfer function would also serve to sustain at least a vestigial social mission (ensuring access to higher education for those who might otherwise not attend). (Clowes and Levin, 1989: 353)

Unfortunately, this scenario falls afoul of obdurate reality. The hope that most baccalaureate aspirants will simply sidestep the community college ignores the reality of student choices. As we saw in Chapter 3, four-year colleges are considerably less accessible than community colleges, especially for the many poor, place-bound, and inadequately prepared students who attend community colleges. Typically, four-year colleges are farther away, often being located in distant rural areas. They are more expensive to attend, if only because they are farther away, so that one has to pay not only tuition but also room and board charges. And they are usually more selective academically, being less willing to take "nontraditional" students such as high school dropouts and the academically deficient.

But even if baccalaureate aspirants will have to continue going to community colleges in significant numbers, could they not transfer to the university? Clearly, this is unlikely if a major purpose of shifting the community college in a noncollegiate direction is to get it out of the failing business of transfer education. In addition, Chapters 3 and 4 find a great deal of evidence against the hope that many will transfer to four-year colleges from largely vocationalized community colleges. A study of the California community colleges finds that the more vocationalized ones have the lowest transfer rates, even when one controls for differences in student body composition (race and grades) and proximity to the university (California Community Colleges, 1984: 17–19). And studies using the National Longitudinal Survey of the High School Class of 1972 (NLS-72) and the High School and Beyond survey of the high school class of 1980 find that postsecondary vocational schools have much lower rates of transfer to four-year colleges and eventual attainment of a baccalaureate than do community colleges. Using the 1984 High School and Beyond follow-up of high school graduates who entered college in 1980, Grubb (1993) found that 20.2% of the community college entrants had transferred to a four-year college by 1984, whereas the comparable percentages for public postsecondary vocational school and proprietary school entrants were only 8.6% and 8.0%, respectively (Grubb, 1991: 202; 1993: 20–21). This difference in transfer shows up in turn as a difference in attainment of baccalaureate degrees. Using the 1979 NLS-72 follow-up of students who entered college in 1972 with the intention of getting a bachelor's degree, Charlene Nunley and David Breneman (1988) found that those entering community colleges earned 31.3% more baccalaureate degrees than students with comparable backgrounds, abilities, and aspirations entering public postsecondary vocational schools (Nunley and Breneman, 1988: 80–81). (See Chapter 3, Appendix Table A3–3.)

As Chapter 4 notes, a strong vocational orientation on the part of a community college hinders transfer in two ways. Baccalaureate aspirants are drawn away from their goal by the siren call of vocational training leading to a job immediately after leaving the community college. Students who enter with baccalaureate ambitions, or are undecided but could develop such ambitions, are seduced away from their ambitions by attractively packaged and aggressively promoted vocational programs. And if they do resist this temptation and continue their voyage toward the baccalaureate, transfer aspirants still face great obstacles. Four-year colleges are less willing to take in community college transfers than to pass on their own students, and they are especially reluctant to take in vocational students. Moreover, they often refuse to give credit for the vocational courses that students try to transfer.

Gutting General Education

The evisceration of the transfer program would not injure only baccalaureate aspirants. It would also greatly damage the general education of all community college students, vocational aspirants included. This would be a tragedy for our society, given the importance of general education for democracy and the fact that vast numbers of students and their formal education in the community college. As democratic theory has held for over 200 years, a democratic society requires citizens who are able and willing to participate actively and thoughtfully in governing their society and their lives. This active and informed citizenry needs to be able to think critically, appreciate its cultural traditions, and understand its social and natural environment (Apple, 1988: 189–190; Aronowitz and Giroux, 1985: 132–134, 255–266; Brint and Karabel, 1989: 230–231; Cohen and Brawer, 1989: 337). In short, a general education is a necessary, though not sufficient, element of the preparation of future clients.

But effective general education depends on a strong academic program, especially in the liberal arts (Cohen and Brawer, 1989: chap. 12). Taken alone, vocational education and adult education directed to literacy, job upgrading, or leisure activities cannot provide the critical literacy that is central to the democratic ideal. Their concern is largely practical rather than critical/theoretical. It is the liberal arts that have been the traditional home of the latter. To be sure, general education need not require taking separate courses in, say, philosophy, social science, history, or natural sciences; it may be best accommodated through interdisciplinary courses on broad subjects and the introduction of elements of the liberal arts in the form of modules into vocational courses (Cohen and Brawer, 1989: 334–340). But whatever the format, one still needs to have a strong liberal arts sector in the community college to provide the faculty and the culture that promote critical thinking for the entire college.

The Collegiate Program

Unlike the noncollegiate reformers, the collegiate reformers acknowledge, and worry about, the fact that the community college hampers the educational progress of their baccalaureate aspirants. Hence, they have called for the amplification, rather than amputation, of the "collegiate" function of the community college, centering on general education and college transfer preparation (Astin, 1983; Bernstein, 1986; Brint and Karabel, 1989; Cohen and Brawer, 1989; Eaton, 1988, 1990; Eaton, Hawk, Hirsch, and Terzian, 1988; McCabe, 1981, 1988; McGrath and Spear, 1991; Pincus and Archer, 1989; Richardson and Bender, 1987; Zwerling, 1976).

The collegiate reform movement owes its origins to the confluence of a variety of actors and motives. Many different states have been actively expanding the transfer capability of their higher education system: for example, California, Florida, Illinois, New Jersey, South Carolina, and Washington (Bender, 1987, 1990; California Community Colleges, 1984, 1989; California Postsecondary Education Commission, 1985, 1987; Illinois Community College Board, 1989; Kintzer, 1989; Knoell, 1987). In addition, the Ford Foundation has actively promoted efforts by local community colleges nationwide. In 1983, it established the Urban Community College Transfer Opportunity Program (UCC/TOP) to provide grants to 24 urban community colleges to encourage more students, especially from disadvantaged backgrounds, to transfer to four-year colleges (Donovan, Schaier-Peleg, and Forer, 1987: 1–3; Pincus and Archer, 1989: 37–42). The presidents and faculty members of these UCC/TOP community colleges provided key leadership for the collegiate reform movement, often writing its major texts: for example, Judith Eaton (1984, 1988, 1990), Dennis McGrath and Martin Spear (1991) of the Community College of Philadelphia; Robert McCabe (1981, 1988) of Miami-Dade Community College; Leslie Koltai of the Los Angeles community colleges (Koltai and Wolf, 1984); and Richard Donovan, Barbara Schaier-Peleg, and Bruce Forer (1987) of Bronx Community College. After leaving the Community College of Philadelphia, Eaton went on to become (until 1992) a vice president of the American Council on Education and head of its National Center on Academic Achievement and Transfer, which has received major funding from the Ford Foundation. In addition, the Ford Foundation has also funded leading community college scholars to study how transfer works and how to improve it (Cohen, Brawer, and Bensimon, 1985; Center for the Study of Community Colleges, 1988; Knoell, 1987; Pincus and Archer, 1989).

This interest in reviving transfer was spurred in part by the educational excellence and accountability movements of the 1980s. State policymakers began noticing that fewer and fewer students were transferring from community colleges to universities and eventually getting bachelor's degrees. Moreover, dropout rates have been high at community colleges. This concern has been particularly sharp in the case of minority students, given that a majority first enter higher education through the community college. In California, policymakers and business leaders have worried about the consequences of having few minority students receive baccalaureate degrees at the very time that the state's labor force is becoming increasingly nonwhite and requiring increasingly advanced skills (Bender, 1990: 8; Donovan et al., 1987: 1; Eaton, 1990: 18; Howard, 1990; 50; Kintzer, 1989: 20–45; Palmer, 1986: 53).

But if the collegiate reformers wish to revive transfer education and general education, how do they propose to do this?

The Collegiate Reforms Detailed

The proposals of the collegiate reformers are quite varied. In order to aid our critical understanding of them, I would like to classify them according to the theoretical framework I advanced in Chapter 4 for comprehending the ways in which higher educational institutions hinder the progress of baccalaureate aspirants entering the community college. Along the way, I will draw particular attention to proposals to improve the educational success of disadvantaged students.

Reducing Attrition in the Lower Division

Community college entrants are more likely to drop out than four-year college entrants, and, as we have seen in Chapter 4, this is due to the institutional characteristics of the community college as well as the personal traits of its students. Community colleges less well integrate their students academically and socially than do four-year colleges. Because they are less selective, community colleges are characterized by weaker student and faculty expectations that students will be successful academically. Moreover, because they are not residential colleges, community college are less able to insulate their students from the distractions of job and home life. Hence, community college reformers have suggested changes that address these institutional factors.[2]

One way that has been suggested to strengthen students' academic integration is to encourage greater faculty/student interaction outside of class, through both formal conferences in the office and informal contact outside the office (Astin, 1983: 132–133; Cohen and Brawer, 1987: 182). In addition, students' work lives should be integrated with their academic lives. Outside jobs absorb a great part of students' attention and time and may lead them to leave college entirely. Colleges can try to neutralize this competing influence by providing more jobs on campus and by academicizing outside work through paid internships (Astin, 1983: 132–133; Cohen and Brawer, 1987: 182; Tinto, 1987: 67–68).

Students' social ties are at least as important as their academic ties in binding them to their colleges. Perhaps the most potent way of building these social ties is by providing dormitories. However, most community colleges are unable to do so and therefore need to explore functional alternatives. Several have been suggested: keeping students on campus longer through cultural and social events in the evenings and on weekends; encouraging the formation of student clubs, study groups, and peer groups; holding weekend or even weeklong retreats for students; and scheduling the same students together in blocks of classes so that they bond together (Astin, 1983: 132–133; Cohen and Brawer, 1987: 182; Cohen, 1988: 397–398; Pascarella and Terenzini, 1991: 640; Pincus and Archer, 1989: 4).

Besides making efforts to better integrate students generally, collegiate reformers also urge community colleges to particularly reduce the high dropout rate among disadvantaged students. Community colleges, they argue, should work with high schools to improve the competence and motivation of students before they even reach the community college (Palmer, 1986: 54–55; Rendon and Taylor, 1989–1990: 19; Williams, 1989–1990: 16). In fact, several community colleges are offering disadvantaged high school students special courses not only in study skills and college survival but also regular academic fare (which is sometimes college creditable) in such areas as mathematics and literature (Donovan et al., 1987: 13–17, 47, 56, 66).

Once in the community college, disadvantaged students need to be offered intensive counseling and academic support programs (Nora and Rendon, 1990: 252; Palmer, 1986: 56–58; Rendon and Taylor, 1989–1990: 21–22; Williams, 1989–1990: 17). They should not be allowed to register in just any program, but should be tested and placed in programs appropriate to their level of preparation. Miami-Dade Community College has instituted this procedure for all students, and it is mandated by state law in Florida, New Jersey, and Georgia (Donovan et al., 1987: 28; McCabe, 1981: 9–10; Palmer, 1986: 57; Richardson and Bender, 1987: 60–61). Moreover, disadvantaged students should get intensive training in study skills and basic academic knowledge (Cohen and Brawer, 1987:

133–141; Richardson and Bender, 1987: 58–59). These efforts should not be provided only through the professional staff. Students can play an important role in their own preparation. Some community colleges have found study groups organized around students taking the same course and led by an older student very effective. And others have made good use of recent alumni as mentors and role models for younger students of a similar background (Donovan et al., 1987: 31, 54, 56, 58, 65).

This academic support and counseling should be backed up by close monitoring of students' course-taking patterns to make sure that they are taking the right courses and not registering for courses beyond their ability (Donovan et al., 1987: 21; Palmer, 1986: 56–59; Richardson and Bender, 1987: 61). A frequently cited model for such a student tracking program is Miami-Dade Community College's computerized Advisement and Graduation Information System (AGIS) and Academic Alert and Advisement System (AAAS). The first generates a sequence of recom- mended courses given the students' backgrounds and goals and keeps track of how well they are meeting graduation requirements. The second keeps track of students' grades and, when needed, recommends that they go seek a counselor (Kintzer, 1989: 56–57; Palmer, 1986: 59).

Increasing the Transfer Rate

If they survive their first or second year at the community college, baccalaureate aspirants then must leap over the chasm lying between them and the four-year college. Sometimes the problem is one of opportunity: though students may wish to transfer, they cannot, either because they are turned down or they are denied financial aid. Other times the problem is one of desire: students entering with transfer ambitions lose them in the course of the community college. In any case, low transfer rates play an important role in the low baccalaureate attainment rates for disadvan- taged students because they rely so heavily on the community college for college access (Nora and Rendon, 1990: 237; Rendon, 1992: 2).

As we have seen in Chapter 4, would-be transfer students often fail to receive financial aid from four-year colleges and consequently refuse the admissions offers of four-year colleges. Collegiate reformers therefore stress that aid programs need to give transfer students as much priority as freshmen or continuing students (Pincus and Archer, 1989: 7; Richardson and Bender, 1987: 56–57, 112, 209–210, 219). One way is to follow states such as Arizona, Florida, Illinois, and New York in reserving a certain amount of student aid for transfer students (Bender, 1990: 12).

In addition, universities not infrequently deny access to community college students. The cause sometimes is that the students happen to be applying to programs and campuses that are oversubscribed. Hence, collegiate reformers argue that universities need to engage in more careful enrollment planning order to allow eligible transfer students better access to popular programs and campuses (Bender, 1990: 16; Illinois Community College Board, 1989: 8; Kintzer, 1989: 33). Other times the cause for denial is that universities do not want to accept vocational graduates of community colleges, perhaps because they do not have a university program equivalent to the community college one. In order to open up transfer possibilities for such students, community colleges should work with four-year colleges to establish "capstone" programs, in which vocational education courses in the community college are credited by four-year colleges against a major in a technical field and the bulk of a students' upper-division course load is devoted to meeting the four-year college's general education requirements (Illinois Community College Board, 1989: 13; Richardson and Bender, 1987: 108–109, 173–174).[3]

But sometimes the issue is desire rather than opportunity. Baccalaureate aspirants lose their desire to transfer either because of trepidation or lack of support for their ambitions. In order to overcome students' fear of entering a new college, it is useful to have them experience four-year college life in advance. The collegiate reformers urge community colleges to encourage their students to take courses at four-year colleges, participate in university cultural events, and simply visit university campuses (Astin, 1983: 132–133; Cohen, 1988: 398; Donovan et al., 1987: 11–12, 52, 57, 64–66; Zwerling, 1976: 240–246). Conversely, four-year colleges should come to students. They should be given the names of potential transfer students whom they might wish to approach (Cohen, 1988: 397; Donovan et al., 1987: 10, 61). And university faculty and staff should be encouraged to visit community colleges to teach courses and lead programs that would familiarize students with what four-year colleges expect (Richardson and Bender, 1987: 210, 213). Some community colleges have united these two efforts in the form of dual admission programs in which community college students are also enrolled as university students and given certain university privileges (Donovan et al., 1987: 15–16, 47, 54, 57).

Besides providing encouragement, the collegiate reformers also argue that community colleges must avoid discouraging their students. They must improve their liberal arts programs and transfer advising. The liberal arts program, which still remains the best route to transfer, should be reinvigorated, with a reversal of the long-term tendency to offer fewer and fewer academic courses, particularly at the sophomore level (Cohen and Brawer, 1987: 180; Pincus and Archer, 1989: 3; Richardson and Bender, 1987: 38–39, 205–207). At the same time, community colleges should think of pulling back somewhat on their terminal occupational programs. This may seem quite objectionable, except for the evidence that too often community colleges are actually producing more vocational graduates than the market can actually bear (Grubb, 1989; Mitchell, 1986). (See Chapter 3 for more.)

Besides reinvigorating their academic program, community colleges must revamp their transfer advising. The collegiate reformers argue that advising should begin early, not waiting for students to announce their interest in transfer, but rather approaching those who might or should be interested in transfer (Cohen and Brawer, 1987: 180; Donovan et al., 1987: 38; Richardson and Bender, 1987: 181, 209–210). To heighten student awareness, they should expose students to more extensive, attractive, and up-to-date information about transfer opportunities, rather than the often desultory efforts made by community colleges. Community colleges need to name transfer officers to coordinate their transfer advisory program (Bender, 1987: viii, 46; Donovan et al., 1987: 40–41; Florida State Department of Education, 1988: 54). Special publications, orientations, and seminars should be provided to inform students about transfer possibilities and requirements (Bender, 1990: 13; Cohen, 1988: 397; Donovan et al., 1987: 39, 52, 57; Richardson and Bender, 1987: 210). Community colleges should follow California in establishing transfer centers, which would stock all available information on transfer, house special counselors, and provide a place to meet admissions officials from the universities (Bender, 1990: 16; Cohen, 1988: 399–400; Donovan et al., 1987: 39–40; Howard, 1990: 55). Meanwhile, the general faculty role in transfer advising must be revived (Donovan et al., 1987: 40–41, 54). This is particularly necessary in vocational education, where most instructors have little interest in and knowledge of transfer. But it is also required among liberal arts faculty, who have lost much of their commitment to transfer.

Besides not "cooling out" baccalaureate aspirations, collegiate reformers argue, the community college also needs to think about "warming up" sub-baccalaureate aspirations. This is particularly important in the case of disadvantaged students, who are more likely to enter the community college not wishing to pursue a baccalaureate degree. This will require intercepting students very early, even before they enter the community college (Donovan et al., 1987: 38, 47, 56, 66; Illinois Community College Board, 1989: 7; Palmer, 1986: 54–55; Rendon and Taylor, 1989–1990: 19). The process of warming up requires exploring careers carefully, developing skills in life planning, and coping with the emergencies all too common in the lives of disadvantaged students (Donovan et al., 1987: 39; Zwerling, 1976: 186–199, 213–224).

Reducing Post-Transfer Attrition

Even after they transfer, community college students still encounter obstacles that are traceable to their educational origins. As Chapter 4 shows, they often lose credits in transfer, are denied financial aid, are not integrated socially into the four-year college, and are poorly prepared for upper-division work.

To reduce the loss of credits, community college and university officials must come to explicit understandings about which courses are transferable and then transmit this knowledge to students. At its most extreme, this can be done on a very individualized basis: course by course, institution by institution. The difficulties and wastage involved are daunting, however. Hence, the collegiate reformers have typically recommended more systematic devices. They recommend that general education courses be accepted in a blanket fashion: approved community college general education courses should be accepted as meeting university general education requirements, as is the case now in New Jersey, Florida, Georgia, and Tennessee, or an associate's degree in approved majors should be made sufficient for junior-level standing, as it is now in Florida, Massachusetts, Illinois, and Ohio (Bender, 1990: 9: California Postsecondary Education Commission, 1989: 7; Cohen and Brawer, 1987: 161–162; Florida State Department of Education, 1988: 7–9; Illinois Community College Board, 1989: 2; Richardson and Bender, 1987: 169, 217).

For nongeneral education courses or in cases where the blanket general education policy does not work, the collegiate reformers have recommended other devices to ensure credit transfer. First, to ensure that universities adequately credit community college courses, they recommend regular formal consultation between university and community college personnel to reach agreements on which courses are transferable (Bender, 1990: 15; Donovan et al., 1987: 54, 58; Illinois Community College Board, 1989: 6). These agreements can then be concretized in the form of course equivalency guides and common course numbering. Each device declares which community college and university courses should be treated as equivalent, but common course numbering does this by giving the two kinds of courses the same number and sometimes even title. Florida and California have pioneered this device (Bender, 1990: 10–11; Cohen and Brawer, 1987: 160–161, 179–180; Florida State

Department of Education, 1988: 9–10, 29–30; Illinois Community College Board, 1989: 6; Kintzer, 1980: 29, 36–37; Richardson and Bender, 1987: 218–219). Moreover, states should follow Florida in developing a standard college transcript, which would make it easier to evaluate community college courses (Florida State Department of Education, 1988: 9, 28).

But it is not just university officials who must know what courses can transfer. Community college counselors, faculty, and students must be informed as well. Regular consultation with university officials and faculty helps keep key community college personnel aware (Richardson and Bender, 1987: 210–213). They can then transmit this information to the rest of the community college by using course equivalency guides and oral presentations and by indicating in the college catalog which courses are transferable (Donnovan et al., 1987: 64). But the collegiate reformers also strongly recommend the use of computerized advising systems such as Miami-Dade's AGIS (Advisement and Graduation Information System), Florida's SOLAR system, and California's ASSIST. They list the courses that the universities currently require, generate recommended course plans, and in some cases keep track of how well students are meeting those requirements (Bender, 1990: 11–12; Donovan et al., 1987: 42–43; Florida State Department of Education, 1988: 52; Illinois Community College Board, 1989: 9; Kintzer, 1989: 56; Palmer, 1986: 59).

Even after transfer, financial aid remains a problem for transfer students. Even when transfer students receive aid, it too often fails to reflect the fact that transferring is usually accompanied by sharp increases in tuition and living expenses. Hence, the collegiate reformers call for financial aid awards more closely tailored to transfer students' changing needs (Richardson and Bender, 1987: 56–57, 112, 209–210, 219).

Better financial aid can help students integrate themselves socially into the four-year school by lessening their need to work to pay their bills. At the same time, transfer students need other help as well. They need orientation programs directed solely to them, rather than ones that lump them with freshmen and other new students (Donovan et al., 1987: 41–42, 67; Florida State Department of Education, 1988: 45; Pincus and Archer, 1989: 4–5; Richardson and Bender, 1987: 82–83, 147, 213, 215).

The sharp drop that many transfer students suffer between their community college grades and their university grades, especially in the first year after transfer, is not a minor and transitory experience, as is often claimed. Instead, as Chapter 4 shows, it often slows and even stops many transfer students' pursuit of the baccalaureate. Several proposals have been made to combat the inadequate preparation in the community college that contributes to this "grade shock." Closer parallelism between university and community college standards can be fostered through greater interchange between university and community college faculty: for example, by having university and community college faculty team teach the same courses (Donovan et al., 1987: 11, 66). Moreover, potential transfer students need to be warned that university work will be tougher—requiring more self-directed work—and to have spelled out to them the specific competencies that universities expect (Richardson and Bender, 1987: 184–185). One means of doing this is to have community college students take university courses, perhaps on their own campus (Donovan et al., 1987: 64; Richardson and Bender, 1987: 214). Several scholars argue that this warning should be backed up by allowing entry into and graduation from transfer programs only if students pass exams, by requiring more intensive reading and writing, and by grading more toughly (Cohen and Brawer, 1987: 19, 181; Donovan et al., 1987: 28–31; Koltai and Wolf, 1984: 44–45; McCabe, 1981: 9–10; Richardson and Bender, 1987: 184–185, 207–209). Many states—for example, Florida and New Jersey—now require community colleges to test incoming students to determine if they need remedial education before they are allowed to take transfer courses (Florida State Department of Education, 1988: 21–22; Palmer, 1986: 57). Once they get into transfer courses, collegiate reformers believe students need more exposure to reading primary sources and writing papers based on analyzing texts rather than just relaying personal experience (Donovan et al., 1987: 30–31).

These efforts to tighten academic standards in the community college must be coupled with careful and energetic efforts to provide remedial education so that students are enabled to meet the standards (Brint and Karabel, 1989: 229). Otherwise, these tougher standards may result in a new form of inequality of educational opportunity. Accumulated experience with minimum competency testing provides ample warning that, without such a safety net, higher exit and entry standards fell many working-class and nonwhite students. Florida, a leader in introducing minimum competency testing (MCT), provides a striking example of its pitfalls. The imposition of MCT for high school graduation resulted in very large numbers of working-class and minority students being held back. And the recent proposal to raise minimum requirements on the College Level Academic Skills Test (CLAST) governing movement between the sophomore and junior years in public colleges threatens to have the same effect. According to Robert McCabe, president of Miami-Dade Community College, the proposed rise in passing levels for the CLAST would increase the failure rate for all students from 14 to 52%, for blacks from 36 to 79%, and for Hispanics from 29 to 70% (Blumenstyk, 1989).

Evaluation: These Reforms Are Necessary but Insufficient

The collegiate reformers have been heeded by many. The 24 community colleges participating in the Urban Community College Transfer Opportunity Program (UCCTOP) of the Ford Foundation have pioneered many elements of the collegiate reform program (Center for the Study of Community Colleges, 1988; Donovan et al., 1987; Pincus and Archer, 1989). Moreover, many states—most notably, California, Florida, New York, Illinois, and Texas—have implemented many of the recommendations made by the collegiate reformers (California Postsecondary Education Commission, 1989; Florida State Department of Education, 1988; Illinois Community College Board, 1989; Jaschik, 1988).

This pledge of faith in the collegiate reform program seems warranted. As we have seen, its recommendations directly address the perils faced by baccalaureate aspirants in their odyssey: attrition in the lower division, difficulty in transferring to the upper division, and mortality in the upper division. Moreover, there is evidence to back up the effectiveness of these proposals. For example, the transfer centers established at 20 California community colleges do seem to have significantly raised transfer rates. The transfer rate in 1989 was significantly higher for community colleges with transfer centers than for those without transfer centers, even after controlling for differences between these institutions in number of full-time students, student body composition, organizational characteristics, and attributes of the surrounding community (California Community Colleges, 1991: 12, 27–32).[4]

Nevertheless, I would argue that the collegiate reform program cannot fundamentally eliminate the institutional obstacles that hinder the baccalaureate attainment of community college entrants. However extensive the changes it proposes, the collegiate reform program has largely ignored the need to change the community college's very structure and position within the higher education system. The fact that it would leave the community college as a two-year, commuter institution that is structurally separate from the four-year colleges means that the community college's baccalaureate aspirants will continue to encounter major obstacles to their success.

As long as community colleges remain commuter institutions, they will never be able to integrate their students academically and socially to the same degree as four-year colleges, which are much more often residential. Devices such as arranging more events on campus and requiring faculty to interact more with students do enhance social cohesion, but they cannot begin to match college residential life in involving students in the life of a college (Astin, 1977; Tinto, 1987).

As long as community colleges remain two-year institutions, their baccalaureate aspirants will have to overcome the psychological difficulty that, to pursue their degree, they have to transfer to a new and foreign institution. Even if the university is in the same city, it remains a separate institution, with its own culture and organizational routines. After all, one has to apply to it and be accepted; it is not a matter of just moving from the sophomore to junior year simply by registering for new courses. As a result, many students will still choose not to brave the chasm between the institutions.

Finally, as long as community colleges remain institutionally separate from universities, transfer students will always run into difficulty in getting admitted, receiving financial aid, transferring their community college credits, and preparing themselves for upper-division courses. Because of their institutional separation from community colleges, four-year colleges will continue to prefer admitting new freshmen rather than older transfers and to give their own students priority in getting financial aid.

In addition, the curricular autonomy community colleges and universities enjoy from each other will continue to lead university officials and faculty to favor their courses over those offered by community colleges and thus to be reluctant to accept community college credits. Even when state law requires universities to accept community college general education courses or to give junior status to community college transfers with associate degrees of arts or of science, universities find many ways of avoiding this. A fairly common device is to require transfer students to "validate" their community college courses by passing a university entrance examination or by passing certain university courses (Bender, 1987: 19).

Thirdly, the institutional gulf between community colleges and universities will continue to make it hard for community colleges to adequately prepare their students to meet university standards. Because they are not members of the same institutions, university and community college faculty will continue to find it hard to keep up with each others' academic expectations. As a result, community college faculty often will not know if they are pitching their transfer courses at a level that university faculty find acceptable. This gulf can be partially bridged by the negotiations, visits, and exchanges proposed by the collegiate reformers. But these cannot substitute for the regular contact that occurs between teachers of upper-division and lower-division courses within a single institution, if for no other reasons than that in a four-year institution the two kinds of courses are usually taught by the same people. A few faculty acting as messengers between two different worlds cannot replace the experience of living within the same organizational milieu.

The failure of the collegiate reform program to attack the core of these fundamental features of the community college may explain why college transfer rates have not risen in recent years as much as one would hope. In fact, despite the efforts of the collegiate reform movement in many states and localities, transfer rates have actually dropped. Drawing on the National Survey of the High School Class of 1972 and the High School and Beyond survey of the 1980 high school senior class, one finds that the proportion transferring from a community college to a four-year college within four years of entering higher education dropped from 28.7% among 1972 community college entrants nationwide to 20.2% among 1980 community college entrants (Grubb, 1991: 202).[5] In fact, transfer numbers have dropped among the UCC/TOP community colleges, even as they have implemented many of the collegiate reform proposals. The number of students transferring from the north campus of Miami-Dade Community College to four-year colleges dropped from 2,121 in 1982–1983 to 1,192 in 1985–1986.[6] The Community College of Philadelphia saw its transfers decline in number from 402 in 1982–1983 to 338 in 1985–1986. And Cuyahoga (Cleveland) Community College experienced a drop from 1,337 to 1,063 over the same three-year period (Center for the Study of Community Colleges, 1988: 108, 110, 144, 146, 156, 160).

Structural Reform

The limitations of the nonstructural program of the collegiate reformers suggest the need for a new reform program, one that would change the very structure, and not just operations, of the community college. This structural reform would aim to overcome the institutional separation between community colleges and four-year colleges that lies at the root of so many of the obstacles encountered by baccalaureate aspirants entering the community college. One such structural reform has been mentioned now and again but has been conspicuously absent in the current debate over the future of the community college: transforming community colleges into four-year colleges. As I will show below, this reform has much to recommend it. But it also has liabilities. Hence, I would like to bring attention to another structural reform that also has great promise but has gone unmentioned: the conversion of community colleges into two-year university branches.

Transforming Community Colleges into Four-Year Colleges

This transformation has been raised now and again in debates over the community college, with the most notable recent proponent being L. Steven Zwerling (1976: 251–252), a leading critic of the community college. This is a highly controversial recommendation, one that has been denounced by commentators on the community college ranging from Burton Clark (1980: 23) to the Carnegie Commission on Higher Education (1970). Yet Zwerling's (1976) proposal deserves careful consideration, for its benefits would be great.

As four-year colleges, community colleges could make it much easier for students to move between the lower and upper divisions, without any of the difficulties and negative repercussions attendant today with transfer between community college and senior college. In moving from the lower to the upper division in a senior college, students would not be crossing a chasm between mutually suspicious colleges but traversing a barely discernible line within the same institution. They would take their financial aid and credit with them since the same student assistance and registration systems are involved. Their lower-division academic preparation would be much better attuned to the demands of upper-division courses because the faculty in the two divisions would usually be one and the same. And if they were to take any vocational courses, these would usually be creditable toward their baccalaureate degree, since capstone programs undoubtedly would multiply.

But many objections, some damaging, have been raised against this proposal. Some observers argue that converting the community college into a four-year college would not change its position in the higher education prestige hierarchy. Whether two-year or four-year, community colleges would still be at the bottom of the academic prestige hierarchy (Karabel, 1972: 557). This objection ignores, however, the fact that students are judged as much by the level of their degree as where it comes from. A baccalaureate degree from a very indifferent four-year college is almost always of higher repute than an associate's degree from a good community college. Moreover, once armed with the ability to confer baccalaureate degrees, many community colleges would pull ahead of the many mediocre four-year colleges that are less well known and have poorer resources. Although even the best community colleges—such as

Miami-Dade, the Community College of Philadelphia, or Los Angeles Community College—would be entirely unlikely to shoot to the top or even middle of the college prestige hierarchy, they would probably race past many four-year colleges.

A second objection that might be made is that converting even the larger community colleges into four-year colleges would be horrendously expensive, requiring major new expenditures to hire liberal arts faculty and stock libraries. But on examination, it is not clear that, especially in the case of the larger community colleges, this would be a major problem. Most have well-stocked libraries and, if anything, a surplus of liberal arts faculty eager to teach traditional four-year college courses.

A narrower criticism is that many community colleges are too small to be turned into efficient and effective four-year colleges. They would never have enough staff to offer effective four-year courses. However, this objection could be met by allowing only community colleges above a certain size, say 2,000 students, to become four-year colleges.

But, the question might be raised, would the newly minted four-year colleges be content to remain four-year colleges, or would they push to develop graduate programs, following the well-worn path of the academic revolution trod by the teachers colleges (Jencks and Riesman, 1968; Labaree, 1990)? The cost of such a wholesale academic revolution would be insupportable, but it is questionable whether this specter would materialize. State coordinating boards and commissions are much stronger today and thus much better able to contain any major push for institutional social mobility. Hence, the newly minted four-year colleges are unlikely to be successful in any push to become universities.

A fourth objection raised by observers is that the transformed community colleges would produce too many bachelor's degree holders, thus fueling educational inflation and overeducation (Clark, 1980; Karabel, 1972: 557). This may indeed happen. But it prompts the question whether it is indeed best to equilibrate the demand for and supply of the limited number of good, "college-level" jobs by diverting many baccalaureate aspirants into pursuing sub-baccalaureate degrees rather than by explicitly confronting the excess of demand over supply by changing the supply of good college-level jobs (Carnoy and Shearer, 1980; Carnoy and Levin, 1985; Levin, 1984; Zwerling, 1976: 252–255). And if in the short run many baccalaureates are unable to get college-level jobs, they have gained much in cultural and political sophistication from their college experience (Bowen, 1977).

But even if the previous objections can be set aside, there are two that are much less easily dismissed. A four-year community college may not adequately meet the needs of the 65 to 80% of community college entrants who are not baccalaureate aspirants but rather are looking for vocational education, remedial education, or adult recreational education (Clark, 1980: 23). To be sure, many four-year colleges have provided vocational, developmental, and adult education for many years, and many more are adding programs in these areas as they try to cope with declines in the number and ability of traditional college students. Moreover, as a matter of tradition, community colleges transformed into four-year colleges are likely to retain a good part of their nonbaccalaureate programs. Furthermore, some contraction in vocational education would be desirable, because there is evidence that community colleges produce more vocational-education graduates in various fields than the economy can absorb (Grubb, 1988; Mitchell, 1986). Still, in becoming four-year institutions, community colleges may retract their nonbaccalaureate programs too much, given the historically weaker commitment to vocational and adult education of four-year colleges.

In addition, the idea of transforming community colleges into four-year schools simply may be utterly impracticable politically (Richardson, 1989). It is likely to attract the obdurate, and perhaps fatal, opposition of many existing colleges. Numerous community colleges might be opposed because they are used to the present structure. Unprestigious four-year colleges might fight the change for fear that it would create a fearsome competitor for students, funds, and power. And many selective universities and four-year colleges might be opposed because they have historically seen the community college as protecting selective university admissions by diverting away less able college students, particularly into occupational education (see Chapters 7 and 12). Four-year community colleges might incite greater student appetite for traditional university education, leading many more to seek admittance to a university.

The concerns raised above do indicate that transforming community colleges into four-year institutions may be difficult. However, it may be worth pursuing, especially in the case of the larger urban community colleges, which have the faculty and facilities to offer four-year programs. As it is, some of them are beginning to take this path. Miami-Dade Community College has secured permission to offer baccalaureates in two fields and to build dormitories. And in California, faced with increasing fiscal stringency, the state is encouraging baccalaureate students to complete more of their education at the community college. They are now allowed to take up to 90 credits at the community college before transferring. From here it is but a short step to letting students complete their bachelor's degree at the community college.[7]

But what if it proves impossible to turn a large number of community colleges into four-year colleges, especially in the case of community colleges that are small and lack the necessary resources? In fact, there is another alternative that also addresses the need for a change in the community college's structure and relation to four-year colleges. It is converting community colleges into two-year branches of the state universities. It goes entirely unmentioned in current discussions of alternatives to the community college, but this policy seems to provide many of the same benefits of transforming community colleges into four-year colleges.

Converting Community Colleges into State University Branches

Although the community college has become the norm for two-year colleges, it is by no means the only way a rewarding comprehensive two-year education can be provided. An alternative very much worth considering is the two-year state university branches that are found in several states: Alaska, Connecticut, Hawaii, Kentucky, Louisiana, New Mexico, Ohio, Pennsylvania, and South Carolina (Cohen and Brawer, 1989: 103).

Converting community colleges into university branch systems seemingly would produce many of the same benefits as transforming community colleges into four-year colleges. Although usually housed separately from four-year campuses, university branches appear to make it much easier to transfer than do community colleges. Moreover, university branches would be less likely to catalyze the opposition of the state universities than would new independent four-year colleges.

Several features of the branch campuses appear to make them better conduits to the baccalaureate than community colleges. First, branch students are less likely to be seduced away from their baccalaureate aspirations by the allure of vocational education leading to immediate employment. University branches usually put less emphasis on vocational education than do community colleges and thus are less likely to entice or pressure students to enter these programs. This is not to say that university branches lack vocational education. Although some are entirely academic, as in the case of the regional campuses of the University of Connecticut (Katz, 1987), the branch systems in Alaska, Hawaii, Kentucky, and New Mexico maintain strong vocational programs.[8] This presence of vocational education is good. It addresses the argument that the community college must meet the needs of nonbaccalaureate aspirants as well as baccalaureate aspirants (Beckes, 1964; Medsker, 1960). At the same time, vocational education in the branches is not so strong as to become the obstacle to the pursuit of the baccalaureate that it is in the contemporary community college (see Chapter 4). Some may still criticize this lesser commitment of university branches to vocational education on the grounds that it would starve the labor market's demand for middle-level workers. However, as we saw in Chapter 3, the highly vocationalized community college is often *over*shooting labor market demand for middle-level workers (Grubb, 1988; Mitchell, 1986; Pincus, 1980).

The second way in which university branches improve on community colleges in facilitating pursuit of the baccalaureate is by making it easier to gain admission and transfer credits to the universities than is the case for community college students. Branches usually are treated by their parent universities as integral parts of one system. In its statement of the general principles and assumptions guiding the organization and operation of its Commonwealth system of two-year branches, Pennsylvania State University states: "The University functions as one institution and not as a collection of separate campuses or program delivery systems. . . . the concept [is] of one university, one academic program, and one faculty" (Pennsylvania State University, 1983: 3). Therefore, university branch students are treated not as foreigners, but as members of the university, with movement to the central campus being typically regarded more as a matter of changing campuses than of applying for admission. As the University of South Carolina at Columbia puts it, "movement between USC campuses [which include several two-year branches] is not considered transfer by the university" (South Carolina Commission on Higher Education, 1979: 54). Students are able to transfer their credits more easily because the parent universities are more committed to accepting them. Often this commitment is based on the fact that the parent university must approve the branch courses in advance (New Mexico State Governor's Task Force on Higher Education Reform, 1986: 31; Pennsylvania State University, 1983: 7; University of Connecticut, 1987: 81). In New Mexico, new programs and course offerings at the university branches "must be routed through the approval process of parent institutions. . . . A benefit of this lengthy process is that the course is generally transferable from a branch to the parent institution" (New Mexico State Governor's Task Force on Higher Education Reform, 1986: 31). In fact, branch courses often have the same content and numbers as central campus lower-division courses (University of Connecticut, 1987: 81).[9]

Finally, university branch students encounter fewer difficulties after transfer than do community college entrants. They are more likely to receive financial aid, because several university systems operate a unified student aid program that includes the branches (Katz, 1987). Moreover, branch students are more likely to be prepared for upper-division courses. Because of the course approval system mentioned above, branch lower-division courses are much closer to main campus lower-division courses than community college courses typically are (see above). As the University of Connecticut (1987: 81) puts it, "courses offered there [at the local branches] are identical to those offered at the main campus and occupy the same place in the university's curriculum as those offered at Storrs." Moreover, branch faculty are likely to be better apprised of the academic standards and concerns of main-campus faculty than are community college faculty because they usually are appointed by the central administration and often are members of universitywide departments (Pennsylvania State University, 1983: 3, 4, 8).

A number of studies of student attainment reinforce the impression that university branches better facilitate the attainment of baccalaureate degrees. Trent and Medsker (1968) found that a higher proportion of university extension center students than community college students eventually transferred to, and graduated from, four-year colleges. They followed 241 university branch students and 1,104 community college students in 16 different communities nationwide who entered college full time in fall 1959. By June 1963, 54% of the branch students had transferred to a four-year college, whereas only 42% of the community college entrants had done likewise. Moreover, 17% of the branch entrants, but only 11% of the community college entrants, had received a bachelor's degree.

More recent studies show a similar pattern of results. A study of 1,528 students entering the 4 two-year branches of Ohio University in fall 1966 found that by fall 1971 48% had transferred either to the main campus in Columbus or to another accredited four-year or two-year college (Vaughan, 1971: 111). This transfer percentage is far higher than the 15 to 20% typical for community colleges (see Chapter 4). Furthermore, university branches seem to have a better record of persistence in college than do community colleges. A study comparing 238 community college students transferring to the main campus of Kent State University in fall 1985 against 292 students transferring the same year from the university's seven regional two-year campuses found that the latter were much more likely to persist to graduation. By the summer of 1990, 64.1% of the regional branch transfers, but only 43.3% of the community college transfers, had graduated with a baccalaureate degree (Knight, 1990).

These studies are by no means conclusive. They do not control for the known differences between the two student populations on such things as average family background, high school record, and educational and occupational aspirations. Controlling for these differences undoubtedly would reduce the university-branch advantage, since university-branch students tend to have more advantaged families, higher test scores, and better grades than community college students (Knight, 1990; Vaughan, 1971: 81–85, 116). Nonetheless, these studies raise the real possibility that university branches may better facilitate baccalaureate attainment than do community colleges.

If approximating the benefits of transforming community colleges into four-year colleges in one area, facilitating baccalaureate success, conversion into two-year branches has a decided advantage in a second area. State universities, long the arbiters of state higher educational policy, are much more likely to favor the conversion of community colleges into university branches than their transformation into four-year colleges. As it is, while being opposed to the multiplication of four-year colleges, universities in many states have sponsored the formation of two-year branches. One only has to think of the branch systems established by the Universities of Alaska, Connecticut, Kentucky, Ohio, and South Carolina, Ohio State University, Kent State University, and Pennsylvania State University. To be sure, other universities might oppose taking on two-year branches out of fear that it would increase their administrative load and open their doors to many more students. In fact, the Universities of Illinois and Washington made this very decision in the 1940s and 1950s. But on the whole, universities would probably prefer to have community colleges converted into university branches rather than four-year colleges because the former would be under university control while the latter would most likely be independent and competing institutions.

Summary and Conclusions

The community college is in crisis. Strong empirical evidence backs up the claim that its many baccalaureate aspirants are significantly hindered in their pursuit of a bachelor's degree by the fact of entering a community college rather than a four-year college. But if the crisis of the community college is clear, the solutions are less obvious. The discovery that baccalaureate aspirants encounter many *institutional* obstacles on their way to success has prompted a wide variety of reform proposals, ranging from recasting the community college as an essentially noncollegiate institution to vigorously reviving its original commitment to collegiate education.

Both empirical evidence and our nation's political values argue against the noncollegiate program, which would virtually amputate transfer education in favor of organizing the community college around vocational and community education. A wholesale emphasis on noncollegiate education would leave homeless the perhaps one-third of community college students who aspire to a baccalaureate degree.

The program of the collegiate reformers should be given preference instead. Their recommendations directly acknowledge the needs of baccalaureate aspirants, targeting several of the key obstacles in their way. Still, though valuable and eminently worth implementing, the collegiate reforms do not address the fact that the obstacles baccalaureate aspirants encounter are rooted not just in the community college's policies but in its very *structure*. Even revamped in the way the collegiate reformers envision, its nature as a vocationally oriented, two-year, commuter institution that is separate from the four-year colleges will always leave substantial obstacles in the path of baccalaureate aspirants.

Hence, we should also consider structural reforms that try to span the institutional chasm between community colleges and four-year colleges. We have discussed two policies in particular: transforming community colleges into four-year colleges, a recommendation that has surfaced now and again in policy discussions on the future of the community college; and converting community colleges into branches of the state universities, a policy that has not been raised at all in those discussions. Though not without defects, each policy has strong benefits that recommend it for serious consideration. Our evidence on both these structural reforms is still tentative and not conclusive, but it is strong enough to indicate that we should vigorously explore both of these possible futures for the community college.

In the end, we may want to think of the reform of the community college as a flexibly extending project. At the very least, the nonstructural changes suggested by the collegiate reformers should be implemented, for they promise significant benefits, are fairly uncontroversial, and will not preclude further, more structural reforms. Next, if further research backs this and circumstances allow, community colleges should be brought under the aegis of the state universities in order to help overcome the structural barriers that will still remain after the nonstructural reforms are implemented. Finally, we should transform the larger community colleges into four-year colleges if circumstances are especially favorable.

Orfield and Paul (1992: 98–101) have recently made a proposal that is rather similar to mine, but it diverges in a key and I would argue fatal way. They would split the academic and transfer programs of the community college from the vocational and community education programs, assigning them to different two-year colleges. The academic and transfer colleges would then become branches of the state universities following the example of the Center System of the University of Wisconsin. I understand Orfield and Paul's logic: that this would create a much clearer organizational mission and avoid the incoherence that besets the comprehensive community college. Unfortunately, I think their proposal will create major problems of its own. Students who enter the vocational institutions and later decide to transfer—a group that has been rapidly multiplying in recent years—will have a hard time transferring since their institutions will be very much oriented in a nontransfer direction and will eschew any formal connections to the universities. Conversely, students who begin with transfer orientations but later change their mind will have difficulties "transferring" to vocational education. In any case, it is highly questionable whether Orfield and Paul's proposal will be politically practicable given that vocational institutions are increasingly sending their students to the university and are calling for formalizing this linkage. This broadening of vocational-technical schools, which in effect entails the creation of new community colleges, is already occurring in Indiana, Oregon, South Carolina, and even Wisconsin (Bender, 1990: 14).

However the community college is changed, it is important that its comprehensive nature be preserved. Too many students want, and would benefit from, vocational education for it to be eliminated. However, it would be beneficial if the community college were to become substantially less vocationally driven than it now is.

But while pursuing these reforms, it is important that we not seek in community college reform more than can be promised. As long as the rest of our society remains unchanged, even a transformed community college will be a contradictory institution, one that is a graveyard of hope even as it is a nurturer of ambition (Brint and Karabel, 1989; Clark, 1980). The community college sits at the fault line between two conflicting imperatives: the democratic demand for a college that promotes equality and democratic citizenship and the limitations of a capitalist economy that has only so many good jobs to give out and constantly must be fed with workers who have only those skills and ambitions to fill the mass of middle-level and even lower-level jobs that it does make available. The community college addresses the first imperative by opening its doors

272 THE CONTRADICTORY COLLEGE

wide to students who would otherwise be unable or unwilling to enter higher education. But the community college also succumbs to the second imperative by encouraging the bulk of its students to pursue a vocational program rather than "unrealistic" ambitions for a baccalaureate degree.[10]

This contradiction could be greatly attenuated with the advent of a very different kind of economy, one much less hierarchical and inegalitarian than our present capitalist economy. In a democratic socialist economy, the community college could play a much less contradictory role. With workers taking over many of the tasks and responsibilities now monopolized by managers and owners, many more jobs would require the advanced conceptual skills that are traditionally the province of baccalaureate training.[11] Consequently, the community college would not feel the need, and would not be pressed by others, to encourage the bulk of its students to give up their hopes for a baccalaureate education and instead pursue vocational studies.

From Research to Theory: Implications for Educational History and Politics and Political Sociology

The state relative autonomy approach developed in Sections III and IV is not of parochial significance. Far from being applicable only to the question of the rise and differentiation of the community college, it also carries important implications for the study of educational change generally, the politics of education, and political sociology. The fields of educational change and politics of education have begun to explore the role of the state in educational policymaking, but their concept of the state is still undeveloped and would benefit greatly from attention to the role of relatively autonomous government officials. For political sociology, on the other hand, the notion of the relative autonomy of the state is familiar. But even there the perspective developed in this book would be useful, for it recommends a broader concept of the state than is current in political sociology today.

Educational Change

The study of the dynamics of educational change—whether within history of education or sociology of education—has been rife with debate. The main antagonists have been the adherents of our long-standing companions: pluralist functionalist theory and instrumentalist Marxist theory. In many ways, the debate has taken the form of a dialectic in which one theory overthrows another, only to succumb in turn to its own logical and empirical flaws (as well as a changing intellectual and political climate). Pluralist functionalism—as represented by such scholars as Martin Trow (1961), Burton Clark (1962), and Lawrence Cremin (1977)—held sway for many years. But in the late 1960s and early 1970s, it was subjected to a sustained assault by Marxist instrumentalism, as championed by Samuel Bowles and Herbert Gintis (1976), Michael B. Katz (1968, 1987), and Clarence Karier, Paul Violas, and Joel Spring (1973).[1] In turn, Marxist instrumentalism has been criticized from a variety of vantage points, ranging from Marxist class struggle theory (Carnoy and Levin, 1985; Katznelson and Weir, 1985; Wrigley, 1982), institutionalist theory (Boli, Ramirez, and Meyer, 1985; Meyer and Hannan, 1979; Ramirez and Boli, 1987; Rubinson, 1986), and Weberianism (Archer, 1982; Collins, 1977, 1979).

This profusion of theories has greatly enriched our understanding of the dynamics of educational change, but it has also blinded us. The theoretical debate has tended to fall into theoretical sectarianism, where different theories engage in a zero-sum combat, heedless of the fact that each has a piece—but only a piece—of the truth. Each has partial insights that need to be synthesized in order to develop a theory adequate to the complexity of educational change.

In what follows, I examine the strengths and weaknesses of the dominant explanations of educational expansion, in light of my research on the community college. It provides an excellent ground to critique these theories because it constitutes a major educational institution, enrolling a third of all college students. It has developed over a long stretch of time in virtually all states, and all levels of our government have been involved in creating it. Furthermore, most theories of educational change have been shaped on the template of the history of elementary and secondary schooling, with little attention to the history of higher education and none to the history of the community college. Hence, the development of the community college provides a very illuminating case for spotlighting the strengths and weaknesses of these various theories of educational change. I will close this analysis with an argument for why state relative autonomy theory provides the best basis for synthesizing the insights of the various theories I will have critiqued.

Pluralist Functionalist Theory

Essentially, functionalists argue that educational expansion has been the product of economic change, with popular demand acting as the connecting link (Clark, 1962; Cremin, 1977; Trow, 1961). Educational expansion has been driven by the desire of parents to ensure greater economic opportunity for their children through education. Fueling this popular demand has been the evolution of the U.S. economy, as it has moved from an agrarian structure requiring only simple skills and little formal schooling to an industrial structure requiring complex skills and advanced educational training. As Martin Trow summarizes,

> The immediate force behind these trends [the growth in enrollments] in both secondary and higher education are changes in public sentiment—in people's

ideas of what they want and expect for their children in the way of formal education. . . . Behind these changes in sentiment are other social forces, not least among which is . . . change in our occupational structure. . . . between 1950 and 1960 the total labor force increased by only 8 per cent; but the number of professional, technical, and kindred workers grew by 68 per cent. (Trow, 1961 [1977]: 111)

This emphasis on parental demand, based on the changing require- ments of the economy, finds some resonance in the history of the commu- nity college. As we have seen, students and parents participated in the founding of one-quarter of the community colleges that I studied, and they were involved in vocationalizing efforts at one-third of the colleges.

But on the whole, pluralist functionalist theory fares poorly in ex- plaining the rise and transformation of the community college. At the local level, student and parental participation in the founding or vocationalization of community colleges, when it did occur, was almost always weak, taking not the active form of concerted and persistent involvement in local policymaking but rather the weaker forms of en- dorsement and simple expression of opinion. And at the state and national levels, student and parental participation was much weaker—in fact, virtually nonexistent. It could be argued that student enrollment in community colleges and their vocational programs constituted a form of student and parental demand for the community college and occupational education. But this flies in the face of the fact that this enrollment was itself the product of prior state and national decisions to encourage such enrollment. Through their early decisions to widely disperse community colleges and keep them cheap and to strongly tout vocational education, policymakers in fact created student interest in community colleges and occupational education.

Marxist Instrumentalist or Corporate Liberal Theory

Marxist theories of an instrumentalist or corporate liberal bent agree with pluralist functionalists that the demands of the economy have been the fundamental driving force behind educational change. But they forcefully challenge the pluralist emphasis on popular demand as the proximate agent mediating between the two. Instead, they point to the capitalist class as the main architect of elementary and secondary schooling in the 19th and early 20th centuries and of higher education in the post–World War II era. They argue that the capitalist class sought not only to expand the provision of schooling but also to ensure that such schooling offered vocational education, inculcated acceptance of capitalist imperatives, and transmitted the class hierarchy from one generation to another (Bowles and Gintis, 1976; Katz, 1968, 1987; Karier, Violas, and Spring, 1973). According to Samuel Bowles and Herbert Gintis,

> There can be little doubt that educational reform and expansion in the nineteenth century was associated with the growing ascendancy of the capitalist mode of production. Particularly striking is the recurring pattern of capital accumulation in the dynamic advanced sectors of the economy, the resulting integration of new workers into the wage-labor system, the expansion of the proletariat and the reserve army, social unrest and the emergence of political protest movements, and the development of movements for educational expansion and reform. . . . the leadership of the movements . . . was without exception in the hands of a coalition of professionals and capitalists from the leading sectors of the economy. (Bowles and Gintis, 1976: 178–179)

According to Bowles and Gintis, the capitalist class has controlled the political process both through direct intervention (getting the right candidates elected, etc.) and the manipulation of resources for educational research, innovation, and training.

The instrumentalist school's emphasis on the role of the capitalist class in fostering educational change has considerable validity. Business clearly played a powerful role in the development of the community college. Locally, businesspeople were involved in the founding of two-thirds of the community colleges that I studied and in the vocationalizing of all of the community colleges that were in my sample. And their role was typically strong. They usually provided a major part of the membership and often the leadership of local community college committees. Their motives certainly included—though they were not restricted to—securing publicly subsidized employee training and fostering local economic development.

However, although instrumentalist theory does capture many particulars of the history of the community college, it also fails in numerous ways. Business did not participate with the breadth and depth claimed by instrumentalist Marxist theory. Business absented itself from the politicking over federal community college and occupational education legislation. At the state level, business was involved to any significant degree only in Illinois, and this involvement was almost totally restricted to the Illinois Chamber of Commerce and did not include the other major Illinois business associations. Finally, at the local level, where business undoubtedly played a major role, it did not participate in the founding of several important community colleges, such as Chicago, Los Angeles, and New

York City. And even where it strongly participated, this involvement was usually catalyzed and organized by local educators. Furthermore, business's extensive participation in local efforts to vocationalize the community colleges of Illinois and Washington was largely restricted to the post-1960 period, yet that vocationalization had begun many years before.

The limitations of the instrumentalist theory suggest the need for other theories of educational change. Several different theories—ranging from Marxist class struggle theory to world system theory to Weberianism—have confronted the hegemony of functionalism and Marxist instrumentalism. Yet these challenging theories themselves have important limitations and need to be superseded in turn.

Marxist Class Struggle Theory

The corporate liberal school has been severely chastised by other Marxists of the "resistance" or "class conflict" approach for failing to realize that public schooling has been the product not just of capitalist commands but also of democratic demands on the part of the working class, nonwhites, and women (Carnoy and Levin, 1985; Hogan, 1985; Katznelson and Weir, 1985; Wrigley, 1982). Martin Carnoy and Henry Levin argue that

> Educational institutions are not just reproducers of dominant class conceptions of what and how much schooling should be provided; public schools also reflect social demands. Attempts by the capitalist State to reproduce the relations of production and the class division of labor confront social movements that demand more public resources for their needs and more say in how those resources are to be used. (Carnoy and Levin, 1985: 47)

The class struggle theory provides a welcome antidote to exaggerated claims for the political prescience and participation of the capitalist class. Unfortunately, it looks in the wrong direction for noncapitalist actors who have played a major role in educational change. As the history of the community college demonstrates, labor and other minority groups have simply not played that major a role in the development of American education. Active involvement of labor and minority groups in the founding and vocationalization of community colleges was quite infrequent and rarely went beyond endorsing policies framed by others. Only at the national level, and only occasionally at that, did labor actually lobby in favor of community college legislation.

Institutionalist or World Systems Theory[2]

Institutionalist theory has taken a different tack in criticizing its predecessors. It has focused its fire on the claim of both instrumentalist theory and pluralist functionalist theory that the changing demands of the economy provide the fundamental impetus for educational change. John Meyer and his colleagues provide strong evidence that educational expansion historically has not been tightly coupled to changes in skill demands, especially industrial skills. Instead, they point to a desire for cultural unification and nation building as the fundamental source of educational change (Boli, Ramirez, and Meyer, 1985; Meyer and Hannan, 1979; Ramirez and Boli, 1987; Rubinson, 1986). For example, Boli, Ramirez, and Meyer (1985: 156) state:

> [M]ass education is produced by the social construction of the main institutions of the rationalized, universalistic worldview that developed in the modern period— the citizen-based nation and state, the new religious outlook, and the economic system rooted in individual action. . . . Mass education arose primarily as a means of transforming individuals into members of these new institutional frames that emerged in Europe after the Middle Ages. . . . Because society was held to be essentially a collection of individuals, the success or failure of its effort to realize progress and justice was dependent on the nature of the socialization experiences encountered by the individual.

Institutionalist theory makes a useful contribution in criticizing economistic theories of educational change that ignore an interest in cultural unification and intergroup cultural emulation and competition. As we have seen in the case of the community college, various American localities and states were certainly motivated to establish and expand community colleges by a desire to keep up with other localities and states that they wished to emulate and compete with. Certainly, the California community college system was much on the mind of policymakers in Illinois and New York as they moved to build their own. Illinois government officials, for example, testified vividly that they envied California's pacesetter status and that they supported community college expansion out of a desire to stay in step. And we have seen that ideologies about how much education is proper and what are the characteristics of a "modern," "progressive" state certainly have played a role in this economic and cultural competition. This "bandwagon effect," as I have termed it, certainly goes a long way toward explaining the extraordinary similarity of community college development across the United States, despite its very decentralized origins.

At the same time, institutionalist theory is radically incomplete. Its proponents are critical of "differentiation" theories that focus on class and racial/ethnic differences and conflict. These theories, they charge, fail to explain the great homogeneity of American education, especially in comparative perspective (Boli et al., 1985: 147–149, 152–153). Yet we cannot understand the expansion and vocationalization of the community college unless we acknowledge the self-interests of business, educators of various stripes, and elected officials.

Besides ignoring group self-interest, institutionalist theory also neglects the role of the state. Though it argues that state officials have been the chief sponsors of formal education in most countries, it contends that the main architects in the United States of education have not been government officials but "movements motivated by religious, political, and economic visions of a progressive future" (Boli et al., 1985: 158. Also see Meyer et al., 1979: 596, 599; Rubinson, 1986: 535). But the history of the community college belies this claim. As we have seen, a wide variety of government officials—ranging from local educators and university officials to state governors and Congress members—have been crucial advocates of the founding and vocationalization of community colleges.[3]

Weberian Theory

Weberian theorists such as Randall Collins agree with institutionalist theorists that a desire for cultural unification has been a major factor in driving the expansion of schooling. But where the institutionalist theorists portray the values of these reformers in universalistic hues, Weberians emphasize their particularistic origins and their conflictual utilization:

> In the late nineteenth century, the conditions that had made middle class Protestantism a sealed cocoon of authority were breaking down. . . . The most significant effort to assert Anglo-Protestant culture was in the realm of education. Public schools, with their compulsory attendance laws, spread precisely in those states facing the greatest immigrant influx; the claims of educators to Americanize the immigrants was a major force in getting public support. (Collins, 1979: 98–99, 102)

Furthermore, Weberians break with institutionalist theorists by giving a prominent role to educators (Archer, 1982: 28–31, 44–45; Collins, 1979: 106–109, 122–127):

> The impetus for the foundation of public elementary schools came primarily from upper-class and upper-middle-class professionals, especially ministers, educators,

and lawyers. . . . Diverse coalitions were involved in establishing state-supported secondary schools, with one central element remaining constant: the educators themselves. (Collins, 1979: 106, 109)

And in the case of the development of higher education, Collins notes that the modern university system arose from the efforts of many colleges to escape the economic straits in which they found themselves in the late 19th century, with declining enrollments and a hazy social function. Colleges tried to become the gatekeepers to the rapidly expanding professions, thus assuring themselves a ready clientele of status-hungry students (Collins, 1979: 122–127).

The Weberian emphasis on the central role of educators is strongly backed up by the history of the community college. Although by no means the only important actors, educators clearly were at the very center of efforts to found and later vocationalize community colleges. Local educators often constructed and led the coalitions that secured approval for local community colleges. Local community college heads provided most of the initiative for the vocationalization of the community college. State educators—whether state university officials, state school superintendents, or heads of state education associations—strongly supported and often initiated state programs to encourage the founding and vocationalization of community colleges. Finally, at the national level, the American Association of Community Colleges strongly supported federal aid for community colleges and their vocational education programs.[4]

Despite this support for the Weberian claims in favor of educators, my community college analysis also points out the limits of this analysis. Weberians uses the term "educators" in a generic manner, which ignores the considerable differences of interest among them. Because of their differing institutional locations, local teachers and superintendents, state education departments, state universities, and community colleges often differ greatly in their interests. Furthermore, Weberian scholars have not sufficiently underscored and theorized on the fact that educators, especially in this century, are largely public officials. They share in the powers of the state and are subject to the constraints imposed on it by a democratic policy and a capitalist economy. Hence, educators' actions and motives need to be considered in light of theory and research on the role of the state in educational change.

State Relative Autonomy Theory

State relative autonomy theory puts government officials at the very center of any analysis of the genesis of educational change. As we have seen, educators have been among the most important of those government officials involved in the development of the community college. But a variety of other government officials have also played crucial roles. It is impossible to understand why community colleges arose and vocationalized so rapidly without also noting the strong support they have received from state governors and legislators and presidents and Congress members. In all cases, this governmental role was not simply a response to the demands of private interest groups. Government officials often supported the community college even in the absence of any strong demands from private interest groups. And in any case, they responded to autonomous interests and values of their own: whether prestige and professional advancement for local educators; protection for selective admissions in the case of university officials; institutional advancement for community college heads; and reduced higher education costs, greater economic growth, and an attractive political issue for state and federal elected officials.

But even as I range state relative autonomy theory against other theories of educational change, I also wish to argue that it can serve as a very fruitful ground on which these various theories can be synthesized. As we have seen above, each of the explanations of educational change that we have covered captures some valid aspect of the dynamics of community college expansion. What we need is a way to theoretically synthesize these various insights. State relative autonomy theory can do this. Its emphasis on the autonomous role of government officials respects the Weberian emphasis on the role of educators in educational change and, more generally, the nature of the state as a fundamental spring of power.

At the same time, state relative autonomy theory acknowledges the "society-centric" argument of functionalist, Marxist, and institutionalist theory that private interest groups rooted in civil society are also major sources of educational change. State relative autonomy theory makes clear that state officials are only *relatively* autonomous. They often defer to private interest groups because those groups control the votes, campaign contributions, and economic capital that allow government officials to be reelected. At the same time, state relative autonomy theory moves beyond society-centric theory by utilizing a more comprehensive theory of power. Most society-centric theories define power in a "decisionist" way, focusing on who takes part in political decisions. But as we have seen throughout this book, private interest groups can exercise power even when they do not participate (what Alford and Friedland, 1975, call "power without participation" or "systemic power"). This power has two facets, which I have called "resource dependence" and "ideological constraint" (see Chapter 2 for more). Because private groups control resources that government officials need to realize their own interests, those officials will often craft policies in the interest of those groups even without being asked to. In addition, government officials act in the interest of private groups because they simply subscribe to beliefs (such as equality of opportunity or the importance of a strong business sector) that happen to benefit nongovernmental groups such as students and business.

Because business controls much more material and ideological resources than do other groups, state relative autonomy theory views the capitalist class as exercising far more political power than other interest groups. At the same time, this point does not simply reiterate instrumentalist theory, for that theory has mistakenly focused on the power that the capitalist class exercises through direct political participation while ignoring its nonparticipative power of constraint.

The benefits of state relative autonomy theory are not restricted to the study of educational change. It can also enhance the study of educational politics.

Politics of Education

The politics of education literature is very aware that government officials play a key role in educational policymaking. A staple of this field is that school superintendents are powerful actors in their own right, often dominating their nominal superiors on boards of education (Campbell, Cunningham, Nystrand, and Usdan, 1985: 215–216; Kerr, 1964; Wirt and Kirst, 1982: 140–144; Zeigler, Jennings, and Peak, 1974: chaps. 8–13).

My research on the community college certainly supports an emphasis on the independent role of educational professionals. At the same time, this research also suggests two major defects in current scholarly analyses of the politics of education. As with studies in educational change, studies of politics of education give at best cursory attention to such important public officials as governors, legislative leaders, state education officials, and university administrators. This can be seen in two of the best-known textbooks on the politics of education. Although Campbell et al. (1985) have a chapter on state educational politics, only 9 to 10 pages directly deal with the role of state officials. Similarly, although Wirt and Kirst (1982) allocate two chapters to state educational politics, they spend only 3 to 4 pages on the actions of state officials.[5]

This inattention is unfortunate because the development of the community college indicates that these officials have played a very important role in educational policymaking. University administrators and state education department officials have been among the earliest and strongest supporters of the community college. And since World War II, governors and legislators have been great champions as well.

Secondly, and more importantly, when studies of the politics of education analyze the policymaking roles of public officials, they tend to restrict themselves to describing their roles—their powers, responsibilities, and actions—and the interest-group pressures acting on them. But they virtually never specify the individual and organizational *self-interests* and *values* that help animate public officials' actions.[6] Clearly, scholars in the field of politics of education are very aware of the political nature of education. They certainly draw a striking panorama of interest-group pressure, bureaucratic infighting, and community clashes. Furthermore, they have made much of the fact that educators such as school superintendents are by no means puppets, but in fact often shape the perceptions and even desires of their supposed masters. Nonetheless, the politics of education literature tends to explore the motives only of interest groups and citizens, leaving unexplored the precise motives that drive the actions of public officials.

The history of the community college indicates the costs of ignoring the values and self-interests of government officials. Motives as diverse as local educators' desire for prestige and college-level jobs, state governors' hope to keep down state higher education budgets, and community college heads' wish to strengthen business support for their colleges have powerfully motivated government officials to support the establishment and vocationalization of the community college. Without attending to these values and self-interests we simply cannot adequately explain the community college's development. Private interest group demand—whether from students, business, or the foundations—simply was not powerful enough to explain the sweep of the community college's expansion and vocationalization and the precise features the community college took on.

But if the politics of education literature needs to break its silence about the values and self-interests of government officials, where can it find guidance as to what topics and what language it should enunciate? Certain recent developments in political sociology provide a lodestar.

Political Sociology

My attention to the relatively autonomous role of government officials, in which they pursue their own interests and values within constraints set by business and other powerful actors, has drawn considerable inspiration from various strands in recent political sociology. These include above all the "state manager" theory of the state of Fred Block (1987), the "crisis management" perspective of Claus Offe (1984), Charles Lindblom's (1977) analysis of the "privileged position of business," the "state-centric" perspectives of Theda Skocpol (1979, 1980, 1985) and Stephen Krasner (1978), and Eric Nordlinger's (1981) analysis of the autonomy of democratic states. All these perspectives see government officials as pursuing values and interests of their own within a field of force set by the interests and power of private interest groups. In short, the state's actions are not reducible to the demands of civil society; in fact, it may oppose or even shape those demands. (For an exposition of the central claims of these state-centric positions, see Chapter 2.)

As must be evident, the state-centric perspective is strongly backed by my research. Even when interest-group pressure was absent, federal, state, and local officials actively promoted the community college.

But while buttressing the state-centric perspective, my research also indicates that it could be considerably improved in three areas. First, my research shows that the actors to which it applies should be expanded. Scholars using the state-centric perspective largely focus on chief national executive officials, such as presidents. But as the history of the community college's expansion and differentiation testifies, members of Congress and many state and local elected officials certainly fit state-manager theory's notion of self-interested government officials acting in relative autonomy from business demands. As we have seen, state governors and legislators are like presidents in that their desire for reelection drives them to ensure reasonable levels of state revenues and political support by pursuing economic growth.[8] Furthermore, we need to expand the category of relatively autonomous state managers still further to include nonelected as well as elected officials, for they too act independently on the basis of self-interests and values framed by their position within the state.

But in making this extension, we also have to broaden the range of self-interests considered germane to state manager theory. The self-interests motivating nonelected government officials who work in bureaucratized agencies—for example, community college heads—take a different form than is postulated by current state manager theory. If elected officials above all wish to be reelected and therefore are concerned with maintaining social order, national security, and adequate state revenues, nonelected officials instead are interested in protecting their position by increasing their agency's power, organizational status, and appropriations (Halperin, 1974; Rourke, 1969; Seidman, 1980). And their preferred tactic does not involve stimulating economic growth but rather pressuring their elected superiors by establishing alliances with private interest groups and other government officials. As we have seen, local community college heads intent on expanding their institutions and widening and stabilizing their revenue base moved energetically to foster strong links with influential groups in their community. For example, these community college heads have sought an alliance with business by, among other things, providing vocational education tailored to business needs. These allegiances have then been drawn on when the community college has needed to lobby the state legislature for more money or win citizen approval for a bond issue or tax increase (for more, see Chapter 10.)

Finally, my research argues for restraining the current tendency of state manager theory to emphasis how state managers' interests can lead them to break with the interests of business (Block, 1987: chap. 5; Skocpol, 1980). This is an important concern in an era when government has come to play a key role in steering the economy and will play an even more important role in years to come. Nonetheless, the expansion and differentiation of the community college suggests a reemphasis on one of the original themes of state manager theory: that government officials' interests, when coupled with business control over important resources, provide business with a powerful, and often unnoticed, lever over the state (Block, 1987: 59–62; Lindblom, 1977: 179; Offe, 1984: 120). As we have seen, business exerted great influence over the development of the community college, even when it was uninvolved in or even unaware of key decisions being made on the community college. What counted was that business controlled resources that government officials wanted to leverage: capital that presidents, Congress members, state governors, and state legislators wanted to have invested in order to secure politically popular economic growth; and jobs that community college heads wanted to offer their graduates.

Conclusion

State relative autonomy theory has significance beyond the community college alone, carrying important implications for the study of educational change, the politics of education, and political sociology. In the case of educational change, state relative autonomy theory provides both a critique of the dominant theories and a basis on which to reconcile their different and often competing claims. With regard to the politics of education, state theory addresses one of the most glaring omissions in the field: its failure to theoretically specify the independent values and interests that drive the actions of government officials. Finally, in the case of political sociology, the application of state relative autonomy theory to the case of the community college has illuminated the need for the theory of the state to widen its narrow focus on elected national officials to include subnational and nonelected government officials and nonelectoral motives such as increasing one's agency's power, organizational status, and appropriations.

Notes

Notes to Chapter 1

1. Community colleges—that is, public, two-year colleges operating under joint local and state control and offering programs in vocational education, liberal arts, adult and community education, and remedial education—make up most but not all of the category of public two-year colleges. Other public two-year colleges include two-year branches of state universities (such as the Commonwealth Centers of Pennsylvania State University) and public vocational-technical institutes and schools that offer almost exclusively occupational programs. I will usually use data on public two-year colleges in place of community colleges in particular because the federal government rarely breaks its data down below public two-year colleges to isolate community colleges. However, since community colleges make up the vast bulk of public two-year colleges, little distortion is introduced.

2. See note 2 of Chapter 10 for more on this.

3. My perspective draws on the work in education of Apple (1982) and Aronowitz and Giroux (1985) and in political sociology of Fred Block (1987), Charles Lindblom (1977), and Theda Skocpol (1979, 1980, 1985).

Notes to Chapter 2

1. The statement in this section are based on a content analysis of the writings of the following leading community college officials and scholars: Jesse Bogue (1950), Burton Clark (1960, 1980), Arthur Cohen and Florence Brawer (1982, 1987, 1989), Walter C. Eells (1931), Ralph Fields (1962), E. K. Fretwell (1954), Edmund Gleazer (1968, 1980), Norman Harris and John Grede (1977), Leland Medsker (1960; and Tillery, 1971), Charles Monroe (1972), and James Thornton (1972). Leonard Koos (1925) is not included because he did not try to assess the impact and origins of the community college and occupational education, which were then in their infancy, but instead polemicized in their favor.

2. The AACC has just recently taken this name. It was previously known as the American Association of Community and Junior Colleges (AACJC) and even earlier as the American Association of Junior Colleges (AAJC).

3. Burton Clark (1960, 1980) is, of course, a major exception. He is highly aware of and sophisticated in his use of functionalist theory.

4. The description in this section is based on a content analysis of works by the following leading scholarly critics of the community college: Samuel Bowles and Herbert Gintis (1976), Jerome Karabel (1972, 1974, 1986), David Nasaw (1979), Fred Pincus (1974, 1980, 1983, 1986, 1989), and L. Steven Zwerling (1976). Steven Brint and Jerome Karabel (1989) are not listed here because their perspective differs considerably from Karabel's earlier work. Hence, they are treated separately under their self-appellation, "institutional theory."

5. The Marxian influence is most evident and self-conscious in the work of Bowles and Gintis, Karabel, and Pincus. In Karabel's case, however, a strong undercurrent of Weberian theory is also present. For more on Marx and Weber, see Giddens (1971). Nasaw and Zwerling make very similar arguments as the above, but it is not clear to what degree they identify themselves as Marxists.

6. Brint and Karabel (1989) call their approach "institutionalist" because of the way it explains the vocationalization of the community college. This will be discussed below.

7. Sociological functionalists also often resort to pluralism when they explain the origins and development of social institutions rather than just describe their social purposes. See, for example, Trow (1961).

8. Well-known representatives of the instrumentalist position include Miliband (1969) and Domhoff (1983). Other varieties of Marxist theory, particularly those that are termed "structuralist," deemphasize the self-conscious political action of the capitalist class and look to other mechanisms, such as a relatively autonomous state, to explain how society comes to conform to capitalist interests. For more on the distinction between instrumentalist and structuralist Marxism, see Gold, Lo, and Wright (1975) and Skocpol (1980).

9. I follow Alford and Friedland (1975: 430) in defining political participation as "those present and past activities by private citizens and private or public organizations and groups that are more or less directly aimed at influencing the selection of governmental structures and personnel and the actions they take or do not take." Hence, it subsumes the first of Steven Lukes's (1974) three dimensions of power.

10. I use the term "resource dependence" to describe this form of constraint in order to connect my argument to resource dependence theory in the field of complex organizations (Aldrich and Pfeffer, 1976; Pfeffer and Salancik, 1978).

11. Oddly enough, several of the advocates agree. Though they say so quietly and unhappily, several acknowledge that many students were not thrilled by the prospect of occupational education and actively avoided it (Cohen and Brawer, 1982: 197, 206; Harris and Grede, 1977: 293; Monroe, 1972: 110; Thornton, 1972: 71).

12. Some of the critics also mention the role of the American Association of Community Colleges (Karabel, 1972: 546; Pincus, 1980: 337; Zwerling, 1976: 52–55). But only Karabel examines its role and motives in any detail. He argues that it sought in occupational education a new identity for the community college, one that did not involve being a "junior" college that largely devoted itself to preparing students for transfer to the four-year colleges. This point is elaborated in detail in Brint and Karabel (1989).

13. For extensive critiques of functionalism and especially instrumentalist Marxism, as well as efforts to develop the notion of the relative autonomy of education, see Apple (1982), Aronowitz and Giroux (1985), and Liston (1989).

14. Both are indebted to the theory of "hegemony" of the great Italian Marxist theorist, Antonio Gramsci (1971). Gramsci argues that the power of dominant groups usually and most stably rests not on force but on consent, on constructing a moral-political vision that is accepted by subordinate groups. For excellent elucidations and critiques of Gramsci's thought, see Boggs (1976), Forgacs (1988), and Sassoon (1987). At the same time, it should be noted that there are great resemblances between this notion of hegemony and the Weberian concept of legitimacy (Giddens, 1971; Weber, 1968).

15. Similar arguments can be found in Charles Lindblom's (1977) examination of the "privileged position of business," the "state-centric" perspective of Stephen Krasner (1978), the "crisis management" studies of Claus Offe (1984), and Eric Nordlinger's (1981) analysis of the autonomy of democratic states.

16. A wide variety of studies buttress Block's claim that the state of the economy powerfully influences the popularity and even stability of governments. For example, the state of the economy is one of the strongest determinants of presidential and congressional election results (Jacobson, 1983; Tufte, 1978).

Notes to Chapter 3

1. For a thorough description of the arguments made by the functionalist, Marxist instrumentalist, and instrumentalist schools, see Chapter 2.

2. The five labor market variables were the proportion of a state's 1980 labor force engaged in occupations related to the vocational field in question, the 1970–1980 change in that proportion, the state unemployment rate in 1980, the earnings differential between those with one to three years of college and those with a high

school degree only in 1980, and the average earnings of women 18 to 24 with a high school diploma in 1980 (the male variable apparently failed to prove significant in an earlier equation). The four demographic variables were the state population, the average education of adults, the proportion black of the state population, and the proportion Hispanic.

3. Grubb's (1988) findings must be taken with a degree of caution since they are based on a state-level analysis, which may fail to capture important features of the local labor markets that community colleges primarily address. I am indebted to David Crook for this observation.

4. Even if the output of community college occupational-education programs were precisely calibrated to labor market demand, there would still be reason to doubt the claim that community colleges have addressed a clear economic need for "middle-level" workers who need not high school training but distinctively *postsecondary* vocational training. Community college occupational programs are often not of distinctly postsecondary level. In fact, many have been traditionally offered by the high school. For example, 22% of all fall 1977 Illinois occupational-education enrollments were found just in the following traditionally *secondary* vocational programs: secretarial work; medical, dental, and legal office assistance; auto repair; welding; machining; tool and die making; heating and air-conditioning repair; ornamental horticulture; child care; home economics; and cosmetology (Illinois Community College Board, 1978a). The fact that the community college trains people who could also be trained by secondary schools puts in doubt any claim that the community college is simply responding to a clear labor market demand for *postsecondary* training.

5. See the statements by Clark Kerr and Robert Waldo in Chapter 7 on the role of university officials in the development of the community college.

6. The social composition variables are seven and in all but one case hold for 1970: the proportion Black of the state's population; the proportion Hispanic; the proportion rural; the average educational attainment of adults; the female labor force participation rate; the proportion of the population between the ages of 18 and 30; and the proportion of the 1980 population living in another state in 1975. The educational structure variables are three: community college enrollments as a percentage of the population aged 18 to 30 in 1969; four-year college enrollments as a fraction of the same population group; and the proportion of 1970–1971 associate's degrees awarded in vocational fields. Finally, the labor market variables are five and in all cases hold for 1970: the earnings ratio of those with 16 and more years of education compared with those with 13 to 15 years of education; the earnings ratio for those with 13 to 15 years of education compared with those with 12 years; the average earnings of 18- to 24-year-olds with 12 years of education; the unemployment rate; and the proportion of the labor force in professional jobs. The community college enrollment coefficient does not reach statistical significance, however, because of the small number of cases (the 50 states).

7. Brint and Karabel (1989: 216, n20) do note that their figures pertain to full-time students. And Pincus has recently lowered his estimate of the proportion wanting a baccalaureate degree, putting it at either 25 or 60% depending on the precise definition of aspirations used (Pincus and Archer, 1989: 10–11). See below for more.

8. There are important exceptions to this pattern, however. In a study of five states, Orfield and Paul (1992: 84, 88) found that two states with high community college enrollments (Florida and California) had lower college attendance rates in 1988 than two other states with lower community college shares (Illinois and Wisconsin): 55.0% and 57.1% versus 76.9% and 73.7%. However, it should also be noted that Indiana, which has only one community college (although numerous postsecondary vocational schools), had a very low proportion of high school graduates entering higher education: 44.5% (Orfield and Paul, 1992: 84, 87).

9. Tinto (1974) conducted a similar study that may contradict Medsker and Trent's (1964) findings. However, its research design precludes reaching any definitive judgment. He regressed college attendance rates of Illinois and North Carolina high school graduates in the 1966 SCOPE survey on type of college locally available, student ability, and family background (parents' education and occupation). He estimated 36 separate equations for various combinations of state, sex, and either father's education (five levels) or student ability (four levels). Students in towns with community colleges had higher college going rates than students in towns with other kinds of postsecondary institutions in only 6 of the 36 equations. Unfortunately, Tinto did not calculate the average effect of community college presence, aggregating across all cases. Moreover, he had to exclude Chicago from his analysis, a key omission given the fact that it contains over half of Illinois's population and community college enrollments.

10. These date are cited in Table 3–2. The data cited in the text for two-year colleges apply with little distortion to community colleges in particular, because community colleges enroll 90% of two-year college students. The remainder are enrolled by private two-year colleges and two-year branches of state universities.

11. Two studies provide the upper and lower boundaries for estimates of the distribution of aspirations among community college students. On the low side, the National Postsecondary Student Aid Survey of all college students in fall 1986 found that 18% of those enrolled in community colleges wanted to complete a baccalaureate degree (while 48% wanted an associate degree, 11% sought a vocational certificate, and 23% had other goals) (Grubb, 1991: 195). On the high side, a nationwide survey of community college students enrolled in *credit courses* found that 36% sought to transfer (while 50% sought job entry and job upgrading skills and 15% came out of personal interest) (Cohen and Brawer, 1989: 49, 52). The NPSAS study probably yields too low an estimate of baccalaureate ambitions among community college entrants, because it includes sophomores who have already been influenced by the community college's emphasis on

vocational and adult education. On the other hand, the Cohen and Brawer (1989) survey is biased upward by the fact that it is restricted to students in credit courses and therefore excludes many enrolled in adult and community education. Meanwhile, the average percentage pursuing a baccalaureate degree across three states in the late 1970s was 32%: 37% in California in 1978 (Sheldon, 1982: I 29–34, II 27); 32% in Maryland in fall 1978 (McConochie, 1983: 10); and 27% in Virginia in fall 1975 (Adams and Roesler, 1977: 15). The reason the instrumentalists and institutionalists are so far off the mark with their estimate that three-fourths of community college students aspire to a bachelor's degree is that they rely on the freshman national norms of the American Council on Education–Cooperative Institutional Research Project (ACE-CIRP). These norms ignore part-time students, who have lower aspirations than full-time entrants and make up about two-fifths of community colleges enrollments (Cohen and Brawer, 1987: 94; Sheldon, 1982; U.S. Bureau of the Census, 1988: 53).

12. The NLS-72 questioned over 20,000 high school seniors nationwide in spring 1972 and followed them up in the fall of 1973, 1974, 1976, 1979, and 1986.

13. This analysis may underestimate the real institutional effect because it controls for living arrangements, which constitute part of the college effect. As will be discussed in Chapter 4, one of the reasons that community college entrants attain fewer B.A.s is that they suffer a higher rate of attrition, which is traceable in part to the institution's lack of dormitories and thus weaker social integration of its students.

14. Such students should overlap fairly closely with those who are baccalaureate aspirants. Although many students in community college academic programs do not aspire to a baccalaureate degree (Cohen and Brawer, 1989: 304), this is less often the case for younger students entering community college right out of high school, as is the case with the studies discussed here.

15. Velez's estimates are undoubtedly conservative because he controls for living arrangements, which mediate the institutional impact of the community college on its entrants' educational attainment. See the discussion in Chapter 4 on the role of social integration in explaining why community college students less often secure bachelor's degrees.

16. Anderson (1984) compared community college entrants against entrants to five different kinds of institutions: private two-year colleges, public and private four-year colleges, and public and private universities. In all cases, community college entrants lagged behind. In Table 3–2, I use state four-year colleges as the comparison group because they enroll more students (22.5% of all college students) than do public universities (19.3%) and all private institutions put together (22.3%) (U.S. National Center for Education Statistics, 1985: 8).

17. Breneman and Nelson (1981: 90–92) obtained these figures by estimating separate regression equations for the educational attainment of four-year college

entrants and of public two-year college entrants. They then applied the coeffi-cients from each regression equation to the values for each student and determined which students would benefit more from the application of the regression weights for the community college equation than from the application of the weights for the four-year college equation.

18. I rely on Monk-Turner's (1983) article in preference to her 1990 article because in the latter she controls not only for educational attainment but also receipt of a baccalaureate degree, further attenuating the community college effect. In the 1990 study she finds that those entering a community college attain occupations 2.8 points lower on the Duncan index than entrants to four-year colleges with similar backgrounds, educational accomplishments, and work expe-riences (Monk-Turner, 1990).

19. There is reason to believe that Lavin and Hyllegard's (1991) estimate may be close to the true figure. Monk-Turner's estimate of a 3.5-point net difference appears to be unduly low because of a questionable decision she made in her analysis. In estimating the effects of college entered on occupational status, she controlled for educational attainment. But this resulted in wiping out one of the main paths by which college entered affects occupational status. Breneman and Nelson (1981: 84–86) find that much of the effect of college type on occupational attainment is mediated by years of education attained. This is also the conclusion of Pascarella and Terenzini (1991: 441) after reviewing a number of studies.

20. Kane and Rouse's study is not cited in Tables 3–5 and Appendix Table A3–5. However, their analysis is very similar to Grubb's (1993, 1994a, b) study in that they used the 1986 followup of the National Longitudinal Survey of the High School Class of 1972 and they control for the same variable as he does. It was their study that uncovered the errors that required Grubb to revise the economic return figures in his 1992a and 1993 articles.

Notes to Chapter 4

1. Factors other than student composition may actually explain considerably more than one-third of the baccalaureate gap. The reason is that the lower educational attainment of socially disadvantaged students is a product not just of the abilities and motivations that they bring to school but also of how schools react to such students (Dougherty and Hammack, 1990: chap. 6). For more on this, see below.

2. By "dropout," I mean that, at the time of a follow-up, a student was no longer enrolled in *any* postsecondary institution and had not earned a postsecondary degree. It is important to distinguish withdrawal *from the higher education system as a whole* from withdrawal *from a single institution* because there is evidence that the two differ sustantially in their causes (Tinto, 1987). Yet many studies persist

in studying withdrawal from a particular college and simply extrapolating their findings to systemic withdrawal.

3. Grubb (1991: 214) found that, among students from the high school class of 1980 who entered the community college, 18.3% dropped out with 12 or fewer credits. Meanwhile, a study of a large midwestern suburban community college found that, when followed up for four years, 37% of the students enrolling in nine large liberal arts and vocational curricula had stayed only one semester. The highest percentage leaving after one semester was for those enrolled in real estate (74%), a field in which the students needed only one course in order to be eligible to sit for the state licensing exam (Bers, 1988: 165–166, 170).

4. This finding must be taken only as suggestive, however, since Anderson counts as withdrawal not only dropping out of higher education but also moving out of the academic program into the vocational program.

5. It could be argued that community college students are not disadvantaged by receiving less financial aid because their tuitions are lower than those for four-year college students. That is true. In 1991–1992, the average in-state tuition and fees at public two-year colleges was $962 but $2,134 at public four-year colleges (U.S. National Center for Education Statistics, 1992a: 307–308). However, community college students more often have family obligations. Moreover, they are also more price sensitive in their enrollment decisions (Grubb and Tuma, 1991: 376–377).

6. Tinto first enunciated his theory of the determinants of college persistence and withdrawal in 1975. This initial conceptualization, which synthesized and extended the existing theoretical and empirical literature on college dropout, in turn provoked a great deal of research testing his central concepts. For the most part, this research has impressively validated his ideas, showing that they apply not just to four-year colleges, but with appropriate modifications, to two-year colleges as well (Anderson, 1984, 1988; Munro, 1981; Pascarella and Chapman, 1983a; Pascarella and Terenzini, 1991; Terenzini and Pascarella, 1980).

7. The finding that differences in social integration lead to differences in persistence between community colleges and four-year colleges does not contradict the repeated finding that social integration is of little importance in explaining differences in persistence *among* community college entrants alone (Pascarella and Chapman, 1983a: 98–99; idem, 1983b: 37, 43–44; Pascarella and Terenzini, 1991: 402; U.S. National Center for Education Statistics, 1977b: 178, 184). Social integration cannot have much impact on differences in persistence among community college students alone because there is little variation among community colleges in social integration and its causes such as campus residence. Since the independent variable varies little, it is by definition unable to explain differences in the dependent variable (Pascarella and Terenzini, 1991: 414). However, social integration can be significantly associated with differences in persistence *between*

community college and four-year college entrants because it varies greatly between the two types of institutions.

8. Anderson (1984: 14–15) found that, according to the NLS-72, community college students in academic programs fall between private four-year college students and public four-year bollege students in the proportion stating that they know a faculty member well enough to ask for a letter of recommendation. However, it is not clear if these figures would hold for all community college students since the NLS-72 sample is restricted to those just out of high school and enrolled in the academic program.

9. For applications of this point to elementary and secondary education, see Apple (1982), Fine (1991), Giroux (1983), Solomon (1992), and Willis (1981).

10. Arriving at the transfer rate for community colleges is difficult given the defects of all the major sources of data: national surveys of students entering college right out of high school; follow-up studies of community college entrants done by state coordinating boards; and surveys done by community colleges themselves. Each arrives at a different estimate because it focuses on a particular segment of the total transfer population. In the case of the national High School and Beyond survey, the proportion transferring to a four-year school within four years is 20.2% among students entering community college directly out of high school in 1980 (Grubb, 1991: 202). However, the seeming solidity of this estimate is somewhat deceptive: it is based on students entering college directly out of high school, thus ignoring the two-thirds of community college entrants who delay entry to college. These early entrants tend to have higher aspirations and thus are more likely to transfer (U.S. Bureau of the Census, 1988: 54). The studies done by states arrive at varying estimates, in part because they focus on different student groups and use follow-up periods of varying length. The Maryland State Board for Community Colleges has esti-mated that the transfer rate three and one-half years later (spring 1982) for its 1978 *degree credit* community college entrants was 24.3% (McConochie, 1983: 18–19). Similarly, the Texas Higher Education Coordinating Board has calcu-lated that 19.3% of first-time community college students enrolling in 1981 in *general academic courses* had transferred to Texas public universities within three and one-half years (by spring 1985) (Texas College and University System Coordinating Board, 1988: 2). However, a California study of *all* entrants to 15 California community colleges in 1978 found that the proportion who said they had transferred within *two and one-half* years (by spring 1981) was 9.5% (Sheldon, 1982). Finally, drawing on 114 community colleges nationwide, the Transfer Assembly Project of the Center for the Study of Community Colleges at UCLA has estimated that 11% of their entrants in 1985 transferred to four-year colleges within four years (Cohen, 1992: 35).

This welter of studies gives us a range of estimates. The national studies range between 11 and 20%, and the three state studies vary between 9.5 and 24.3%

(with an average of 17.7%). It seems prudent, therefore, to set the "true" transfer rate within four years of entrance for all community college entrants (irrespective of program and aspirations) at 15 to 20%. This transfer rate is lower than the baccalaureate completion rates reported in Appendix Table 3–2 because the transfer estimate pertains to all community college entrants, irrespective of aspirations and age. But the baccalaureate completion rates in most cases apply only to students who entered college directly out of high school and are, in the majority of cases, baccalaureate aspirants.

11. This figure is restricted to students entering college directly out of high school. However, this group makes up a much greater proportion of all college entrants in the case of four-year colleges than of community colleges.

12. Even if all of the 38.3% of two-year college entrants who aspired to a baccalaureate and were still enrolled in two-year colleges in fall 1974 did eventually transfer (which is quite unlikely), the community college transfer rate would total only 87.6%, still well below the continuation rate for comparable four-year college entrants (U.S. National Center for Education Statistics, 1977b: 191–192).

13. Rendon (1992) writes eloquently on the importance of the community college not writing off the transfer chances of its less advantaged students. For more on what can be done to improve their transfer rates, see Chapter 15.

14. Similar figures turn up in studies by state coordinating bodies. A longitudinal study of students entering nearly 20 California community colleges in fall 1978 found that three years later 16.1% of the "technical transfers" (those who were judged to have baccalaureate aspirations but largely took vocational courses) had transferred to a four-year school. This figure compared favorably with the 19.7% of academic transfer aspirants who also transferred within three years (Sheldon, 1982: 1–31, 3–29, 4–26, 4–28). Similarly, 14% of 1983–1985 occupational program graduates in Illinois and 27% in Maryland went on to four-year colleges (Illinois Community College Board, 1987; Maryland State Board for Community Colleges, 1988).

15. Besides the demoralizing impact of the community college's growing vocationalization, the liberal arts were also weakened by the decline in the academic aptitude and academic interest of entering students, the revolt against curricular restrictions in the late 1960s, and the desire of community colleges to hold on to students under the enrollment-driven funding system in place in the 1970s (Cohen and Brawer, 1989: 297–300, 308; Grubb, 1991: 207, 214–215; McCabe, 1981: 7–8; Palmer, 1986: 55–56).

16. This weakening of transfer encouragement even among liberal arts instructors may help explain Grubb's finding that the percentage of academic associate's degree holders transferring within four years of college entrance

dropped from 68.7% among 1972 college entrants to 48.9% among 1980 college entrants (Grubb, 1991: 200).

17. Several studies have found that four-year colleges recruit less actively from community colleges with high minority enrollments, in part because they send few transfer students (Richardson and Bender, 1987: 81; Turner, 1992: 31).

18. Willingham and Findikyan (1969: 26) also found a substantial gap between transfer students and four-year natives in the proportion receiving financial aid. The gap is probably smaller today, since transfer students are more numerous and many colleges compete vigorously for them. Yet there is still no federal program specifically for transfer students, and many states have taken little initiative in this area.

19. There is a great need for studies that determine how much of the gap between community college transfers and four-year natives in upper-division mortality rates is due to student-centered versus institutional factors. (See below for more.) Although I doubt it, student-centered factors may explain the entire gap. In their study of the City University of New York, Alba and Lavin (1981: 234) find no difference between community college transfers and four-year college natives in their likelihood of earning a baccalaureate once high school record is controlled.

20. Indirect evidence of the impact of credit loss is that Illinois community college students transferring to four-year colleges with 60 or more credits are considerably more likely to eventually receive a baccalaureate degree than those transferring 14 credit hours or less: 65% versus 41% (Illinois Community College Board, 1986b: 75). Clearly, this piece of evidence must be taken as only suggestive, since this pattern may reflect not the impact of transferring more credits but the fact that students who transfer more credits are perhaps simply older, more mature, and better motivated.

21. However, even having this guarantee stated in law does not ensure that general education credits will be accepted. If the general education programs of universities and community colleges deviate too much, university faculty will begin to question whether the community college courses should be transferred in their entirety (Illinois Community College Board, 1989: 3–5). As a result, universities will find various ways to deny credit to community college general education courses (Bender, 1987: 19).

22. This problem has eased in recent years as many four-year colleges have established "capstone" programs in technical fields. Under these programs, four-year colleges give credit for community college vocational courses and require students to cap them with liberal arts courses. However, the complaint has been made that such programs rarely operate effectively after a few years. Once established, their faculty give admissions preference to native freshmen rather than community college transfers (Richardson and Bender, 1987).

23. See the section on lower-division persistence for a discussion of the general research literature on the impact of social and academic integration on college persistence.

24. Pascarella and Terenzini (1991: 403–404) note that orientation activities have a significant positive impact on persistence in college, net of the effect of other independent variables.

25. Pascarella and Terenzini (1991: 384) find that college persistence to the degree is higher in colleges where students frequently participate in college-sponsored activities and where the peer environment is more cohesive (students have a high number of college peers whom they regard as close friends).

26. Summarizing the general literature on college dropout, Pascarella and Terenzini (1991: 388) find that college grades are a very major predictor of persistence in college.

Note to Chapter 5

1. Enrollments also grew rapidly, but at a smoother pace, multiplying by nearly a factor of 20 between 1930 and 1960. Unfortunately, reliable figures for community college enrollments in the years before 1930 are not available.

Notes to Chapter 6

1. This mode of initiative and governance is typical of elementary and secondary education but not of higher education. In the former, state governments delegate much of their operating authority to local school districts, even though they retain ultimate sovereignty over education. Moreover, citizens exert a voice over elementary and secondary education not only indirectly, by electing representatives to school boards, but often directly, by voting in referenda on tax increases and bond issues (Iannaccone and Cistone, 1974: 16, 27; Wirt and Kirst, 1982: 192–193).

2. My account relies on the histories by Fretwell (1954) and Smolich (1967) and the memoirs by Brown (1922) and Deam (1931).

3. My sources for this history are the histories by Dow (1967), Eells (1931), Gray (1915), Reid (1966), and Winchell (1933), and the memoir by the college's founder, C. L. McLane (1913).

4. This account relies on the dissertation by Jack Hill (1978) and my interviews with the following participants and observers: Williamson County school superintendents Leslie Stilley (1981) and Lee Booth (1981); Logan College officials, including Presidents Nathan Ivey (1981) and Robert Tarvin (1981);

and Logan College trustees James Walker (1982), Harold Rice (1981), Rannie Odum (1981), and Clifford Batteau (1981). Two of the trustees are businesspeople, one is a farmer, and one is a worker.

5. There are other interest groups to which the functionalist and instrumentalist theories give scant or even no attention: labor, farmers, minority groups, and the private colleges. An examination of the evidence indicates that, indeed, these groups had only minor impact on the development of the community college.

6. These and all subsequent statistics on the percentage of local community college foundings in which a given actor participated are averages of the percentage for each state. For example, the figure in the text is an average of the following figures: the 17% of community college foundings in which students participated in California; the 20% in Illinois; the 50% in New York; and the 14% in Washington. An average across the states is used in place of a simple proportion of all community college foundings, irrespective of state, in order to control for the fact that I studied differing numbers of community colleges in each state. The effect of averaging is the same as if I had studied the same number of community colleges in each state.

7. Brint and Karabel (1989: 147) found that business was actively involved in the founding of several community colleges in Massachusetts in the 1960s.

8. It could be argued that the percentage I give in the text somewhat understates business involvement because it pertains only to participation by business qua business. Many civic clubs—such as the Jaycees and the Lions—are dominated by businesspeople, so their participation could arguably be credited to business's account. Moreover, the participation of newspapers and radio and TV stations should perhaps be added as well to the business account, because they are businesses and are often intimately involved in the business-centered "growth coalitions" that dominate local politics (Molotch, 1976). (For more on the growth coalition, see below.)

9. Beginning with George S. Counts in 1929, researchers typically have found a substantial representation of businesspeople on school boards. For example, a nationwide survey of 4,072 school boards in 1958–1959, just before the community college boom of the 1960s, found that business owners and managers made up 34.5% of school board members (Campbell, Cunningham, Nystrand, and Usdan, 1985: 180).

10. Salwak (1953: 277) found that 59% of the administrators of all community colleges founded nationally in the period 1940–1951 stated that community pride and desire to keep pace with developments in neighboring towns played a role in the founding of their community college.

11. Although ignored by most students of the community college, this role of local educators should not be surprising. Students of educational politics have

long noted that local educators are key actors in educational policymaking, exercising considerable autonomy (Campbell et al., 1985: 215–220; Kerr, 1964; Wirt and Kirst, 1982: 140–144; Zeigler, Jennings, and Peak, 1974). At the same time, some of these scholars have reminded us that this autonomy is not unconstrained (Boyd, 1976). See below for more on this.

12. Walker's analysis is backed up by several accounts of the founding of John A. Logan College. See the sources cited in note 4.

13. This account relies on interviews with Shoreline school superintendent, Raymond Howard (1981); school board members, Francis Holman (1981) and Pinckney Rohrbach (1981); Shoreline Community College president, Richard White (1980) and dean of student services, Doane Blair (1980); area resident and labor leader, Jim Bender (1981); and Shoreline consultant and dean of the University of Washington School of Education, Frederick Giles (1981).

14. This motive was important at the local level across the nation. Littlefield (1941: 99) and Salwak (1953: 276–278) surveyed administrators of all community colleges founded nationwide in the periods 1930–1939 and 1940–1951 and found that 71% and 73%, respectively, stated that one reason their community college was founded was a desire for a geographically and economically accessible institution of higher education.

15. The chief state school officer goes by various titles, such as state superintendent of instruction, state school superintendent, state commissioner of education, and so forth. In many states, such as California, Illinois, and Washington, this is an elective position, whereas in others, such as New York, it is appointive, with the decision being made by the state board of education (if there is one) or the governor (Campbell et al., 1985; Wirt and Kirst, 1982).

Notes to Chapter 7

1. There is sizable variation around this national average. For example, California, Washington, and Delaware provide over 75% of community college revenues, Texas a little over one-half, and Illinois, Wisconsin, and Kansas one-third or less (Cohen and Brawer, 1989: 129). These figures are for current income revenues and do not include receipts for plant expansion, which are available only sporadically. Good figures for college revenues since 1978–1979 are not available, because the Reagan-Bush cutbacks in funding for the Department of Education forced it to reduce its reporting of data.

2. By 1980, 15 states had a state board specifically for community colleges, while another 10 provided for coordination or governance through a state higher education board, 14 through a state board for all education, and 5 through a

university system with community colleges (Cohen and Brawer, 1989: 102). New York is one of the states that provides for regulation through a state higher education board, namely, the State University of New York and the City University of New York.

3. Across the three studies, the price elasticity of community college tuition ranged between –0.44 and –0.69. That is, other conditions held equal, for every 1% decrease in community college tuition, community college enrollments rise by two-fifths to two-thirds of a percent. See Chapter 3 for more details on these findings. Many studies have accumulated showing the significant impact of tuition differences on college choice, even with other variables controlled. See, for example, Manski and Wise (1983: 19–20) and Rosenfeld and Hearn (1982: 140–141).

4. Brint and Karabel (1989: 15–17, 97, 209) find that business played little role in state-level decisions to establish and expand the community college in Massachusetts as well.

5. The Illinois State Chamber's unusual activism was due in good part to the fact that it had a staff member with the direct responsibility to monitor educational issues and help formulate the Chamber's position on them (Beckwith, 1981; Broman, 1981; and Scott, 1981). The other associations lacked such a staff member, choosing to focus on more narrowly defined business concerns.

6. The Carnegie Commission's positions were clearly consonant with those of its parent, the Carnegie Corporation. Alan Pifer, its president, stated that he was "confident that the truly vast endeavor of the Carnegie Commission on Higher Education . . . has already been of immense value to the nation and will continue to be for many years to come. Again, I do not pretend to be neutral witness, but . . . one who has followed the Commission's work in detail and participated in nearly all of its meetings. . . . " (Carnegie Corporation, 1973: 7).

7. The American Association of Community Colleges just recently took that name. Its previous name was the American Association of Community and Junior Colleges and, even earlier, the American Association of Junior Colleges. I will use the current name except when I cite publications issued by the earlier incarnations of the association.

8. See below for more on what the American Association of Community Colleges did with these funds and how much impact they had. In addition to the grants listed in the text, Kellogg and Carnegie, along with the now defunct General Education Board, provided large amounts of aid to various universities and community colleges to run workshops and graduate programs to train administrators for community colleges. The Kellogg Foundation offered a total of $4 million in grants between 1960–1961 and 1970–1971. And the Carnegie Corporation gave $139,000 in 1965 (American Association of Junior Colleges, 1967;

Brick, 1963: 173–175; Carnegie Corporation, 1965; General Education Board, 1939–1947; and Kellogg Foundation, 1960–1961, 1970–1971).

9. In this, the foundations may resemble the Chicago Progressive era educational reformers so well described by David Hogan (1985). Without intending to serve the interests of the capitalist class, these reformers, such as John Dewey and Jane Adams, worked to bring the schools into conjunction with the needs of an emerging corporate capitalism. Seeing the harms inflicted by the increasing incompatibility of the schools and the economy, but viewing the economy as essentially unalterable, they devoted their efforts to harmonizing its relationship to education by reforming the schools.

10. I do not include the State University of New York here because, although it strongly supported community college expansion, it is more of a state higher education board than a state university. Unlike the Universities of California, Illinois, and Washington, it is in charge of the community colleges and has considerable voice over private higher education. Moreover, SUNY did not have true university campuses until the 1960s, when university centers were established at Albany, Binghamton, and Stony Brook and the University of Buffalo became a public institution. Before that, SUNY was simply composed of the community colleges and several former teachers colleges.

11. Whereas the Universities of California, Illinois, and Washington very strongly supported the expansion of the community college, the less nonelite state colleges and universities played little role. Usually originating as teachers colleges, with ambitions of their own to grow, they had little to gain from community college expansion. But their leeriness of the community college did not translate into active opposition, because there were more than enough students to go around and they were too weak to be effective opponents.

12. To be sure, California and New York developed statewide university systems. However, these statewide systems were not established as alternatives to community college growth. In fact, the University of California explicitly stated that it would not establish a branch in a new area until it first had a community college (Liaison Committee, 1957). Moreover, the branches were far fewer than the number needed to substitute for community college expansion.

13. Even as late as 1964, the University of Illinois was still subject to ambivalent feelings about the community college. The university only tepidly and rather sullenly supported the 1965 Public Junior College Act. In fact, it actually floated a proposal in December 1964 to conduct a study of whether a system of four-year university branches was needed. The university's justification was that rapidly swelling enrollments demanded an immediate answer that the community colleges could not provide (University of Illinois, 1964: 339–346). The timing of this proposal was quite intriguing: right before the passage

of the 1965 Public Junior College Act. It suggests that the university had come to realize that the community colleges could become formidable competitors for funds and enrollments.

14. In fact, it has recurred in the 1990s. Hammered by declining state aid, the University of California has been trying to persuade students who are eligible to enter the university to begin at the community college and to later transfer (Mercer, 1992).

15. Apparently the University of Illinois did not keep company with the Universities of California and Washington on this. David D. Henry, president of the University of Illinois (1955–1970), and other observers state that the university's postwar support for community colleges was not motivated by a desire to make its student body more selective (Clabaugh, 1981; Henry, 1981). The university may have been deterred from pursuing greater selectivity by the fact that legislators and other political elites were cool to the idea (Orfield and Paul, 1992: 33–34). Another factor may have been the university's heated rivalry with Southern Illinois University, an institution that was bidding for parity of prestige and was emphatically committed to virtually open admissions.

16. Kerr's predecessor, Robert Sproul, made a very similar statement 20 years earlier (Sproul, 1958: 101). (See Chapter 3 for this statement.) In fact, this sentiment has deep roots, going back to the greatest figure in the California community college movement, Alexis Lange, the founding dean of the University of California School of Education, and past him to various late 19th-century university presidents who called for truncating the first two years of college and relegating them to the high school (Eells, 1931; Lange, 1916: 2, 4; idem, 1917: 473). Beyond protecting its gates, the University of California also valued community college expansion as a means of hindering the growth of its long-standing rival, the California State University system (Brenner, 1979: 250–251, 285–286; Cothran, 1979: 101; Post, 1986; Sproul, 1931b: 113–114). See below for more.

17. This influence rested on the lobby's high degree of unity and acknowledged expertise and the fact that education was not a highly controversial issue in state politics. However, with the onset of that turbulent decade, the 1960s, these conditions eroded, and so did the power of the educational lobby. Education became enmeshed in controversy, governors and legislators became more interested in educational policy, and the various components of the educational lobby turned on each other (Wirt and Kirst, 1982).

18. In the 1920s, the Department of Education occasionally did issue statements supportive of two-year colleges, especially if they were private. But this support never was strong, never eventuated in material support, and in the 1930s gave way to stern and explicit opposition to community colleges (Doran, 1961: 266, 276, 347; Graves, 1931: 107–108; New York State Department of Education, 1929: 78).

19. The New York State Education Department's receptivity to the interests of the private colleges stemmed from several sources. The large number, long lineage, and prestige of the private colleges in New York State and the absence of a state university until 1948 gave private higher education pride of place. In addition, the department had many social ties to private higher education. Most of the regents and top officials of the Education Department were private college graduates (Carmichael, 1955: 28–29, 38–39n; Tomkins, 1967: 94). Furthermore, several important departmental officials were recruited from the private colleges. J. Hillis Miller, the associate commissioner for higher education (1941–   ), was formerly president of Keuka College. Samuel Capen, the associate director of the famous Regents' Inquiry into the Character and Cost of Public Education in the State of New York (1938), was president of the then private University of Buffalo (Abott, 1958: 178, n25).

20. See note 10 for the reasons SUNY is best treated as a state higher education board than a state university.

21. It could be argued that California already had a higher education board, in the form of the Liaison Committee of the University of California and the State Department of Education. In reports in the 1950s and, of course, the master plan of 1960, it provided the functional equivalent of the master planning done by the State University of New York and the Illinois Board of Higher Education. However, the Liaison Committee was not an independent creature. It was staffed by the University of California and the State Department of Education, and its reports were largely advisory to them.

22. I use the word "seemingly" because in recent years the question has been raised whether, contrary to belief, community colleges really do save money for the states. Not only do they attract many students who would otherwise not enter higher education (see Chapter 3), but their per capita costs might not be lower. Cohen and Brawer (1989: 139–140) note that the median expenditure per full-time freshman in 1976–1977 was $1,959 at community colleges, barely lower than the $2,020 spent by public research universities. On the other hand, Grubb (1988) finds that, controlling for a variety of state social and economic characteristics, states with high community college enrollments have lower than average costs for educating students in community colleges (Grubb, 1988: 310).

23. Mazzoni (1989: 84) has noted a similar phenomenon in Minnesota, where state governors took on certain education issues in the 1970s and 1980s—such as school choice—because they were likely to produce votes.

24. This fear has a sensible basis. A quantitative study of 269 gubernatorial elections between 1949 and 1984 found that if state government revenue grew faster than the state personal income the share of the vote garnered by the incumbent's party was significantly reduced. The control variables were national per capital income growth, the inflation rate, and whether the person running was of the same party as the president (Peltzman, 1987: 295).

25. For evidence on the importance of economic conditions to state officials' reelection chances, see Chubb (1988: 148), Lockard (1969: 242), Stein
(1990: 48–49), and Osborne (1990). However, see Peltzman (1987) contra. In a
study of the determinants of people's votes in the 1982 gubernatorial elections,
Stein (1990: 48–49) found that voters who had economic difficulties (their
family economic situation had worsened in the past year or one of their family
members was unemployed) and who held the governor responsible—either
alone or with the president—for the state's economic condition were significantly less likely to vote for the incumbent governor. (One-third of the voters
held the governor, with or without the president, responsible for the state's
economy; the remainder held the president alone or neither the president nor the
governor mainly responsible.) The control variable was party identification. In
a study of 666 gubernatorial elections between 1940 and 1982, Chubb (1988:
148–149) found that the percentage of the vote going to the Democratic party
was significantly affected (p less than 0.10, two-tail test) by the degree of
growth in real per capita income in the state. The control variables were the
share of the vote going to the Democratic party in prior gubernatorial, presidential, and Senate elections, whether it was a presidential or senatorial election
year, the annual change in the national real per capital disposable income, and
changes in voter turnout. However, in a study of 269 gubernatorial races
between 1949 and 1984, Peltzman (1987: 295) found that changes in the state
economy (per capita income growth or change in the state unemployment rate)
had little impact on the share of the vote received by the incumbent party.
Assuming the weight of the evidence lies with Stein and Chubb, it is possible
that they actually understate the impact of economic conditions. Even when
voters do not think that governors are mainly responsible for the state's
economic condition, they do expect the governor to try to make the best of
national economic conditions (Stein, 1990: 33–34). Hence, bad economic
conditions may not sink a governor if she or he gives evidence of trying to
actively make the best of a bad situation. Because most governors do make this
attempt, this mediated relationship may weaken the statistical association, but
not the substantive relationship, between state economic conditions and people's
vote for governor.

26. The State University of New York declared in 1950, in one of its very first
statements about the community college, that New York State needed to have
97,000 more students enrolled in two-year colleges. This standard was justified on
the basis that it was "based upon the pre-war achievement in the California tuition-
free junior college system" (State University of New York, 1950b: 30). A similar
envious emulation of California was also present in the state of Washington
(Washington State Department of Education, 1960: 2–3).

27. The bandwagon effect that I am describing resembles DiMaggio and
Powell's (1983) "mimetic isomorphism," in which organizations cope with
uncertainty by copying models that seem legitimate.

306 THE CONTRADICTORY COLLEGE

28. This process of status seeking resembles the mechanism, identified by John Meyer and his colleagues (see, for example, Boli, Ramirez, and Meyer, 1985; Ramirez and Boli, 1987), in which mass education has spread worldwide, across quite different societies, because states have come to see it as a key element defining a properly modern nation-state.

29. The AACC's continual efforts to find ways of making the community college useful to powerful political actors exemplifies what James March and his colleagues term "garbage can" decision making: rather than having problems in search of solutions, one has would-be solutions in search of problems that they can claim to resolve (Cohen, March, and Olsen, 1972). Whenever a new concern develops in education, such as lifelong education or educational excellence, the AACC has always been quick to demonstrate the community college's utility in resolving that concern. (See Gleazer, 1968, 1980; Parnell, 1984, 1990).

30. The AACC's role in fostering common state policies toward the community college provides an excellent example of what DiMaggio and Powell (1983) call "normative isomorphism," in which professional groups lay the basis for interorganizational similarity by promulgating standards for organizational structure and behavior.

Notes to Chapter 8

1. This earmarking was repealed by the 1965 Higher Education Act, Title VII (Congressional Quarterly, 1965: 297).

2. In 1958, Congress passed the National Defense Education Act, whose Title VIII allowed community colleges to receive funding for their occupational education programs. However, the funding appears to have been primarily for the operation of postsecondary vocational programs rather than the construction of facilities (Congressional Quarterly, 1958: 217–220).

Notes to Chapter 9

1. The fact that, as Chapters 3 and 4 show, the community college hinders the success of baccalaureate aspirants does not mean that government officials were being disingenuous when they claimed to support the community college in the name of educational opportunity. This goal was sincere; the fact that the community college contradicted it in significant part was not known by most government officials until very recently.

2. Institutionalists also give great weight to the role of the foundations. While I agree that they played an important role, I find that the evidence reviewed above does not point to as decisive a role as claimed by instrumentalists and institutionalists.

3. Although the institutionalist school does note the role of federal officials in developing the community college, its emphasis is on their role in vocationalizing the institution. Moreover, the institutionalists focus on describing the actions of federal officials and give very little attention to their motives. In particular, they fail to examine how the actions of federal officials were shaped by their self-interests and values.

4. The clearest systematic variation was in the degree to which local drives were largely solo efforts by local educators or else were based on a significant degree of community mobilization. However, this was not associated in any evident way with the population size, political structure, or economic character-istics of localities.

Notes to Chapter 10

1. The terms "occupational education" and "vocational education" will be used interchangeably here to refer to community college programs preparing students for immediate employment, without requiring them to get a baccalaure-ate degree. However, an increasing number of vocational students are transferring to four-year colleges and getting baccalaureate degrees before entering the job market full time.

2. Cohen and Brawer (1989: 209) state the lower end of the range, citing a 1986 survey of community colleges nationwide that found that 38% of students were enrolled in career programs. Palmer (1990a: 22) gives a higher figure: of 7,558 randomly selected students in 95 community colleges nationwide, 4,064 (54%) were either in a vocational-education class when surveyed or stated they were enrolled in a vocational-education program leading to an associate degree. Finally, Grubb (1991: 203, n7) provides the highest estimate: among those participating in the High School and Beyond survey of the 1980 high school class, 62% of the community college entrants took more than one-half of their first-semester coursework in vocational courses. It is likely that the lower range figure for the 1980s is more correct. The average figure across five states—California, Florida, Illinois, Michigan, and Washington—is 40%. (See Table 10–1.) In any case, these different estimates could be reconciled if Cohen and Brawer are tapping those who are majoring in occupational education while Palmer and Grubb are reaching not just majors but all those who take any occupational education courses.

3. These figures are based on my analysis of the figures supplied in the exhibits for each of the Illinois and Washington community colleges in this quadrennial compilation.

4. See note 2 for more on the various estimates of vocational enrollments in the 1980s.

5. The American Association of Community Colleges was formerly known as the American Association of Community and Junior Colleges and, still earlier, as the American Association of Junior Colleges. I will use the current name except when citing publications issued under the older names.

6. To be sure, both the functionalists and instrumentalists note the role of the federal government and the American Association of Community Colleges. To this, functionalists add the role of local community college officials and state departments of education, and instrumentalists point out the role of the state universities. But these acknowledgements are typically brief and virtually never treat governmental actors as acting with initiative, pursuing interests and values of their own.

7. The institutionalist school does discuss the role of state governors, legislators, and boards of higher education in the case of Massachusetts (Brint and Karabel, 1989: 144–163, 185–186, 192–196, 199–200). However, Brint and Karabel do not mention these actors in their discussion of developments outside Massachusetts. Federal officials also get mentioned (Brint and Karabel, 1989: 68–71, 95–96, 108–111, 210). But along with state officials, they are not the central actors in the theory of the vocationalization of the community college that frames their analysis (chaps. 1, 8).

Notes to Chapter 11

1. The critics and defenders of the community college largely do not mention labor, farmers, and the private colleges. In large part this is correct. Except in isolated instances, they played little role according to my interviews with a wide range of interest groups and government officials.

2. Business has not been the only employer participating. Nonprofit entities such as hospitals and government agencies also have sought programs that would train employees for them. But profit-making firms have constituted the dominant fraction of the employer group.

3. To a great degree the latter part of this statement holds for Belleville and Moline as well. Though beginning in the late 1940s, business involvement with the expansion of occupational education at these community colleges was quite weak until the late 1960s (Badgley, 1981; Brune, 1981; Haberacker, 1981).

4. It bears mentioning, however, that the average for all trustees was just as high: 89%. Furthermore, another survey of Illinois Community College trustees around the same time found that the business trustees might have been, if anything, somewhat *less* vocationally minded than the other trustees. When asked if vocational education was always a purpose of community colleges, the percentage saying yes was 87% for the businesspeople but 92% for the wage earners and

farmers and 96% for the local community college administrators (Brandt, 1968). I will expand at length below on the implications of this very interesting finding that community college administrators were even more vocationally oriented than business.

5. The six cases with weak business involvement included Chicago. According both to staffers of the community college and to area businesspeople, the links between the community college and the business community in Chicago have long been weak, with business having little to do with the development of vocational education (Grede, 1981; Monroe, 1981; Springer, 1982; Wellbank, 1981).

6. This influence through shared sense of identity or mutual interest comes close to the concept of power through constraint that I develop below.

7. Although minority students, especially blacks, have been the most opposed, many nonminority students have shared this sentiment (Steward, 1982). Moreover, not all minority students and groups have rejected vocational education. In Chicago, some prominent Latino leaders supported occupational education (Aranda, 1981).

8. The evidence points to the opposite conclusion, however. See Chapter 3.

9. There are some statistical analyses that address the question of student demand, but their meaning is ambiguous. Corman and Davidson (1984) found, in a study using states as the unit of analysis, that enrollments in community colleges and postsecondary vocational schools in 1976 were significantly and positively correlated with a measure of vocational-technical labor-market demand: the ratio of unemployment for professionals and managers to that for craft and clerical workers. However, using a similar methodology, Grubb (1988) found little impact of labor market conditions on occupational education. He found that the following labor market variables are *not* significant predictors of state-by-state differences in the numbers graduating with associate degrees in six different occupational programs in 1980–1982: proportion of state labor force in the occupations related to the program; 1970–1980 growth rate of the occupations; overall state unemployment rate; and average earnings of women 18 to 24 with 12 years of education (Grubb, 1988: 312). Aside from this conflict in findings, there is another reason to question these findings: do these labor market variables measure student demand or employer demand for vocational-technical education?

10. This commitment to meeting the needs of the "community" has provided business with a very powerful influence over vocational education without requiring it to participate in, or even be aware of, vocational policymaking. I examine below this power of ideological constraint over the actions of government officials.

11. The AACC received its first major foundation grant in 1939–1940, when the General Education Board, one of the many Rockefeller philanthropies, granted

310 THE CONTRADICTORY COLLEGE

it $70,000 to conduct a study of the present state of and needed developments in terminal education, focusing on vocational education (Brick, 1963: 123–124; Brint and Karabel, 1989: 62; Eells, 1941; General Education Board, 1939: 94; idem, 1940: 45). But it was in the late 1950s that the AACC really struck gold. The Kellogg Foundation made the first of many gifts, which would total $3.8 million by 1978, with the bulk of these going to further vocational education. See above for more.

Notes to Chapter 12

1. Though their exhortations catch our attention, we should also note that the state universities also spurred vocationalization unwittingly. As the institutionalists stress, by monopolizing training for the most prestigious occupations, the universities left community colleges with no direct occupational market for their graduates. This gave community colleges a strong incentive to establish a niche of their own: supplying occupational education for the so-called middle-level occupations (Brint and Karabel, 1989: 16–17, 135, 201–202, 208–209; Labaree, 1990).

2. This differential in operating aid no doubt reflected real differences in costs. But in Illinois the premium for vocational courses was extended not just to expensive technical courses but also to much cheaper clerical training. Moreover, this differential aid was often enacted without any clear knowledge of what indeed were the real costs of offering one or another kind of course.

3. In New York, the State University of New York also supported vocationalization. But it is best regarded as a state higher education board than a university, for it not only governs the four university centers in Albany, Binghamton, Buffalo, and Stony Brook, but also runs the former state teachers colleges and supervises the community colleges. The university centers, meanwhile, did not consciously encourage vocationalization, although they may have exercised the unwitting influence I discuss above in note 1.

4. The Illinois state department of education is a partial exception. In 1961, the department proposed a state system of vocationally oriented community colleges (McLure et al., 1960), a recommendation that provided considerable impetus for the establishment in 1965 of a state community college system committed to providing vocational education. After 1965, the department acted in concert with the Illinois Community College Board and Board of Higher Education to promote occupational education in the community colleges (Glenny, 1981; Illinois Community College Board, 1967: 14; Smith, 1980: 245). Yet, prior to the 1960s, the department was silent on the issue of occupational education. And soon after it issued the McLure report in 1960, it floated the idea of a system of area vocational education schools under the aegis of the K–12

system. It is unclear if this was the intent, but such a system would have severely hampered efforts to establish a system of vocationalized community colleges (Broman, 1981; Browne, 1981).

5. See Chapter 7 for more. The views of the Universities of California, Illinois, and Washington are conveyed by the president of the University of California (Sproul, 1931a: 111–112), the dean of the University of California School of Education (Lange, 1916: 3–5), the provost of the University of Illinois (Griffith, 1945: 162–163, 244), and the University of Washington (1960: 6). I gleaned the views of the state governors and legislators from the published remarks of New York Governor Nelson Rockefeller (1970: 452–453) and California Governor Ronald Reagan (Trombley, 1970: 7), and my interviews with the legislative analyst of the California legislature in the 1960s (Post, 1986), the speaker of the New York General Assembly in the 1960s (Duryea, 1985), the governor of Washington in the 1960s and 1970s (Evans, 1980) and a top aide of his (Dolliver, 1981). For the views of state education departments and boards of higher education, see the following: California State Department of Education (1933: 19); Illinois Board of Higher Education (1966: 40); Smith (1980, 1981); Browne (1981); New York State Department of Education (1964); Washington State Board for Community College Education (1968: 4); Washington State Department of Education (1960: 1).

6. For the views of the state universities in California and Illinois, see Griffith (1945: 162–165) and Lange (1918: 213–214). For the views of governors and legislators in Illinois, Massachusetts, and New York, see the following: for Illinois, Illinois Community College Board (1966: 38), Jepson (1980), Wellman (1981); for Massachusetts, Brint and Karabel (1989: 131, 144–145, 191); and for New York, LaValle (1981: 85) and Rockefeller (1970: 452). For the views of the state departments of education and higher education boards, see Brint and Karabel (1989: 148, 151); Brossman and Roberts (1973: 44); Illinois Board of Higher Education (1964: 39–40); Illinois Community College Board (1979: 19); New York State Department of Education (1957: 37–40); State University of New York (1964: 16); Washington State Board for Community College Education (1968: 4); Washington State Department of Education (1960: 2).

7. See note 25 in Chapter 7 for more. State officials' interest in occupational education has risen especially fast in the last 20 years (Osborne, 1990). Going into the early 1970s, economic growth became more problematic as the American economy weakened and increasingly produced plant shutdowns and persistent youth and minority unemployment. For example, 30% of manufacturing plants with more than 100 employees operating in 1969 had closed by 1976. And even as the average state gained 505,626 jobs during the 1969–1976 period, it also lost another 446,046 jobs through plant closures and relocations (Bluestone and Harrison, 1982: 30–32). As a result, governors and legislators have been acutely

aware of how much the economic growth of their states depends on corporate decisions regarding job location.

8. For discussions of the bandwagon effect in economic and social policymaking more generally, see Goodman (1979) and Walker (1969).

9. The University of Washington supported the community college as a means of protecting its selectivity (Waldo, 1981). However, I have found no evidence that its support of occupational education was impelled by this desire. And I have found no evidence of a similar pursuit of selectivity on the part of the University of Illinois or the university centers of the State University of New York. (See Chapter 7 for more.)

Note to Chapter 13

1. Depending on the state, community colleges had been able to receive federal funds for their occupational programs under earlier legislation. In California, because they were considered part of the secondary school system until the 1960s, the community colleges had been able to get funds under the 1917 Smith-Hughes Act, which restricted federal aid to programs of "less than college grade" (Reid, 1966: 284). However, the legislation of the 1960s enlarged the flow of federal vocational education aid from a trickle to a torrent.

Notes to Chapter 14

1. The fact that community college officials have supported occupational education in the name of meeting students' needs does not mean necessarily that it indeed meets them effectively. In fact, as Chapter 3 shows, occupational education graduates do not make as much money as baccalaureate graduates, even controlling for their different background and other prematriculation characteristics. But what is important here is that government officials sincerely believe in the efficacy of occupational education and that this belief has motivated their action.

2. Institutionalists also give great weight to the role of the foundations. I agree that they played an important role, but I also find that the evidence reviewed above does not point to as decisive a role as institutionalists claim.

3. In addition, Brint and Karabel's (1989) analysis is hindered by the fact that their main source of data on the role of state governors and legislators is Massachusetts. Hence, they largely restrict their analysis of these state officials to their actions in this state. Unfortunately, not only is this only one state, but its community college system has developed in an unusual way, starting much later than most states and involving a much greater amount of state regulation that has been typical across the United States.

Notes to Chapter 15

1. See the thoughtful review by McCartan (1983) of these "college for community" and "community college as college" positions.

2. The personal factors have been well addressed in the burgeoning literature on developmental and remedial education (Cohen and Brawer, 1989: chap. 9).

3. However, these capstone programs must be protected against their tendency, once established, to favor four-year college freshmen rather than community college transfers (Richardson and Bender, 1987: 173–174).

4. The transfer rate is measured as the number of transfers per 100 full-time community college students two years previous. The student characteristics controlled are the age, sex, and race composition of the student body. The institutional attributes of the community college controlled are proximity to University of California and California State University campuses, age of college, expenditures per student, and amount of instruction delivered off campus. And the characteristics of the surrounding community controlled are the population density, racial composition, and college-going rate.

5. Grubb estimates that at best one-quarter to one-third of this drop of 8.5% in transfer rates is due to changes in the composition of students entering the community college (Grubb, 1991: 207).

6. In fact, among new, full-time "degree-seeking" students—a fairly exclusive and academically ambitious group—entering Miami-Dade's doors between 1980 to 1982, only 25% transferred to a state university and only 8% received a bachelor's degree by January 1988. Even among students who entered the community college already eligible to attend a state university immediately, the percentages were not much better: 41% and 17%, respectively (Belcher, 1989: 9, 38).

7. I am indebted to L. Steven Zwerling for bringing these developments to my attention.

8. The proportion vocational of their enrollments is 39% in Alaska (fall 1986 FTEs), 39% in New Mexico (1979–1980 FTEs), 40% in Kentucky (fall 1986 FTEs), and 47% in Hawaii (fall 1983 head count) (Hauselman and Tudor, 1987: 1–2, 29; New Mexico State Board of Education Finance, 1980: 3, 26; Polk, 1984: 8, 31; University of Alaska, 1987: 18–31; University of Hawaii, 1986).

9. This is not to say that transferring from a branch to the main campus is frictionless. Transfers from the University of Alaska's community colleges to its four-year campuses have found that, while their community college credits are fully accepted toward the total needed for a baccalaureate, they often do not receive full credit for courses in their *major* (Alaska State Commission on

Postsecondary Education, 1985: 107). Meanwhile, in New Mexico, students at the branch campus of one state university have had difficulty moving to another state university (New Mexico State Governor's Task Force on Higher Education Reform, 1986: 31; Richardson, 1989).

10. For more on this contradictory position of education in a society both democratic and capitalist, see Carnoy and Levin (1985) and Brint and Karabel (1989).

11. For outlines of the nature of a democratic socialist economy, see Carnoy and Shearer (1980) and Zwerdling (1980).

Notes to Chapter 16

1. These scholars largely do not self-consciously name themselves pluralist functionalists or instrumentalist Marxists. My labeling of their positions rests on the consonance between these positions and the recognized tenets of functionalism and instrumentalist Marxism.

2. The general institutionalist theory of educational change is not the same as—though it overlaps on some particulars with—Brint and Karabel's (1989) institutionalist theory of the community college.

3. Government officials have also played a key independent role in the expansion and differentiation of elementary and secondary schooling and of the universities (Kaestle, 1983; Tyack, 1974; Tyack and Hansot, 1982).

4. Educators have also been major actors in the rise and differentiation of elementary and secondary schooling (Archer, 1982; Collins, 1979; Kaestle, 1983; Labaree, 1988; Tyack, 1974; Tyack and Hansot, 1982).

5. This is not to say that monographic studies of the role of state officials in educational policymaking are unavailable. One can quickly point to, for example, Campbell and Mazzoni (1976), Eulau and Quinley (1970), Marshall, Mitchell, and Wirt (1989), Masters, Salisbury, and Eliot (1964), Mazzoni (1989), Milstein (1973), and Usdan, Hurwitz, and Minar (1969). However, as we can see in Campbell et al. (1985) and Wirt and Kirst (1989), these studies have not been strongly integrated into the general literature on politics of education. Moreover, these studies are still subject to the other criticisms I make of the research literature on politics of education.

6. The one exception is in the case of teachers, whose interests are explored in some detail in the politics of education literature. See, for example, Campbell et al. (1985: 253–273) and Wirt and Kirst (1989: 212–216).

7. But it is not just the area of community college policymaking that gives evidence of the importance of attending to government officials' values and self-

interests. The educational excellence reform movement sparked in 1983 by the National Commission on Excellence in Education also cannot be adequately explained without recourse to the independent, self-interested action of government officials, including educators. Their desire for reinvigorated public attention to education and a renewed flow of resources has led educators to play a key role in shaping, and even sparking, the "excellence" movement (Dougherty, 1992; Dougherty and Sostre, 1992).

8. Empirical studies in political science back up this argument. On Congress, see Fiorina (1977: 50–55) and Jacobson (1983: 106–110). On state governors, see Lockard (1969: 242), Osborne (1990), and Goodman (1979). In fact, this perspective also applies to city mayors: see Friedland (1983: 20, 42–43) and Peterson (1981: 29, 144–145).

References

Abbott, Frank. 1958. *Government Policy and Higher Education: A Study of the Regents of the University of the State of New York, 1784–1949*. Ithaca, NY: Cornell University Press.

Abell, Harry. 1974. "Selected Characteristics of Elected Members of Boards of Trustees in Public Community and Junior Colleges in the State of Illinois." Ed.D, Southern Illinois University. (DAI 35/12-A, 7668)

Adams, June J., and Elmo Roesler. 1977. *A Profile of First Time Students at Virginia Community Colleges, 1975–76*. Richmond: Virginia Community College System. (ERIC ED 153 694)

Adelman, Clifford. 1992. *The Community College as American Thermometer*. Washington, DC: Government Printing Office.

Alaska State Commission on Postsecondary Education. 1985. *Alaska Postsecondary Education, 1986–1990: A Statewide Plan*. Juneau: Author. (ERIC ED 265 898)

Alba, Richard, and David Lavin. 1981. "Community Colleges and Tracking in Higher Education." *Sociology of Education* 54: 223–247.

Aldrich, Howard, and Jeffrey Pfeffer. 1976. "Environments of Organizations." *Annual Review of Sociology* 2: 79–105.

Alford, Robert, and Roger Friedland. 1975. "Political Participation and Public Policy." *Annual Review of Sociology* 1: 429–479.

———. 1985. *Powers of Theory*. New York: Cambridge University Press.

Allen, James E., Jr. 1959. *Addresses and Papers of James E. Allen, Jr.* Albany, NY: New York State Department of Education.

American Association of Community and Junior Colleges [earlier name of the American Association of Community Colleges]. 1971. *1971 Community and Junior College Directory*. Washington, DC: Author.

———. 1982. *1981 Community and Junior College Directory*. Washington, DC: Author.

———. 1989. "Mission Statement." *Community, Technical, and Junior College Journal* 59 (February–March): 20–26.

American Association of Community Colleges. 1992. *Community, Technical, and Junior Colleges Statistical Yearbook: 1992 Edition.* Washington, DC: Author.

American Association of Junior Colleges [earliest name of the American Association of Community Colleges]. 1931. "Directory of the Junior College, 1931." *Junior College Journal* 1 (January): 223–235.

———. 1941. "Junior College Directory, 1941." *Junior College Journal* 11 (January): 281–300.

———. 1950. "Junior College Directory, 1951." *Junior College Journal* 21 (November): 172–175.

———. 1961. "Junior College Directory, 1961." *Junior College Journal* 31 (January): 270–302.

———. 1962. *Principles for Community College Legislation.* Washington, DC: Author.

———. 1964. *A National Resource for Occupational Education.* Washington, DC: Author.

———. 1967. *American Association of Junior Colleges: The 1960s to the Decade Ahead.* Washington, DC: Author.

American Council of Education. 1940. *American Junior Colleges.* 1st ed. Washington, DC: Author.

American Vocational Association. 1960. "AVA Seeks Views of Presidential Nominees on Vo-Ed." *American Vocational Journal* 35 (October): 22.

Anderson, Kristine. 1981. "Post-High School Experiences and College Attrition." *Sociology of Education* 54: 1–15.

———. 1984. *Institutional Differences in College Effects.* Unpublished paper, Florida International University. (ERIC ED 256 204)

———. 1988. "The Impact of Colleges and the Involvement of Male and Female Students." *Sociology of Education* 61 (July): 160–178.

Anton, Thomas. 1966. *The Politics of State Expenditures in Illinois.* Champaign-Urbana: University of Illinois Press.

Apple, Michael. 1982. *Education and Power.* London: Routledge.

———. 1988. *Teachers and Texts.* London: Routledge.

Aranda, Mario. 1982. Personal interview with the executive director, Latino Institute. Chicago, Illinois.

Archer, Margaret S. 1982. "Introduction: Theorizing about the Expansion of Educational Systems." Pp. 3–64 in Archer (ed.), *The Sociology of Educational Expansion.* Beverly Hills, CA: Sage.

Arnove, Robert F. (ed.). 1980. *Philanthropy and Cultural Imperialism.* Bloomington, IN: Indiana University Press.

Aronowitz, Stanley, and Henry Giroux. 1985. *Education under Siege.* South Hadley, MA: Bergin and Garvey.

Astin, Alexander W. 1972. *College Dropouts: A National Study.* Washington, DC: American Council on Education. (ACE Research Reports 7(1).)

———. 1975. *Preventing Students from Dropping Out.* San Francisco: Jossey-Bass.

———. 1977. *Four Critical Years.* San Francisco: Jossey-Bass.

———. 1983. "Strengthening Transfer Programs." Pp. 122–138 in George Vaughan (ed.), *Issues for Community College Leaders in a New Era.* San Francisco: Jossey-Bass.

Astin, Alexander W., Helen S. Astin, Kenneth C. Green, Laura Kent, Patricia McNamara, and Melanie Reeves Williams. 1982. *Minorities in American Higher Education.* San Francisco: Jossey-Bass.

Aulston, M. D. 1974. "Black Transfer Students in White Colleges." *NASPA Journal* 12: 116–123.

Badgley, William. 1981. Personal interview with the president, First National Bank of Belleville. Belleville, Illinois.

Baratta, Frank, and Ed Apodaca. 1984. *A Profile of California Community College Transfer Students at the University of California.* Berkeley, CA: University of California. (ERIC ED 260 754)

Baron, Robert F. 1982. "The Change from Transfer to Career Education: A Case Study of Genesee Community College." Ph.D., State University of New York at Buffalo. (DAI 43/05-A, 1401)

Batteau, Clifford. 1981. Personal interview with member of the Board of Trustees, John A. Logan College. DuQuoin, Illinois.

Bauman, M. Garret. 1990. "Every Student Is a Story." *New York Times,* January 7, 1990. Section 4A (Education Life), p. 70.

Bayer, Alan E., Jeannie T. Royer, and Richard M. Webb. 1973. *Four Years after College Entry.* Washington, DC: American Council on Education. (ACE Research Reports 8(1).) (ERIC ED 077329)

Becker, Howard S. 1952. "Social Class Variations in the Teacher-Pupil Relationship." *Journal of Educational Sociology* 25 (April): 451–465.

Beckes, Isaac. 1964. "The Case for Community Junior Colleges." *Junior College Journal* 34 (April): 24, 26–28.

Beckwith, Robert. 1981. Personal interview with the manager, Education Department, Illinois State Chamber of Commerce. Chicago.

Belcher, Marcia. 1989. *Institutional Effectiveness of Miami-Dade Community College.* Miami: Miami-Dade Community College. (ERIC ED 311 962)

Bender, James. 1981. Personal interview with the secretary-treasurer of King County Labor Council. Seattle.

Bender, Louis W. 1987. *Transfer and Articulation among the Public Institutions of Higher Education in New Jersey: A Report to the Chancellor.* Trenton, NJ: State Board of Higher Education. (ERIC ED 283 586)

———. 1990. "State Articulation Policies: Myths and Realities." Pp. 3–22 in Bender (ed.), *Spotlight on the Transfer Function.* Washington, DC: American Association of Community and Junior Colleges.

Benson, J. Kenneth. 1975. "The Interorganizational Network as a Political Economy." *Administrative Science Quarterly* 20: 229–249.

Berg, Rodney. 1982. Telephone interview with the president of Everett Junior College (1960–1966) and College of DuPage (1966–1978). Plano, Texas.

Bernstein, Alison. 1986. "The Devaluation of Transfer: Current Explanations and Possible Causes." Pp. 31–40 in L. Steven Zwerling (ed.), *The Community College and Its Critics.* (New Directions for Community Colleges No. 54). San Francisco: Jossey-Bass. (ERIC ED 271 169)

Bers, Trudy. 1988. "Student Major Choices and Community College Persistence." *Research in Higher Education* 29: 161–173.

Beyle, Thad, and Lynn Muchmore (eds.). 1983. *Being Governor.* Durham, NC: Duke University Press.

Blair, Clarence. 1981. Telephone interview with the superintendent of schools, St. Clair County, Illinois, 1939–1971. Belleville, Illinois.

Blair, Doane. 1980. Personal interview with the dean of student services, Shoreline Community College. Seattle.

Block, Fred. 1987. *Revising State Theory.* Philadelphia, PA: Temple University Press.

Blood, Milton. 1987. "Transferring Credit from Four-Year Colleges: Business School Official Replies." *Chronicle of Higher Education* 33 (April 8): 45.

Bluestone, Barry, and Bennett Harrison. 1982. *The Deindustrialization of America.* New York: Basic Books.

Blumenstyk, Goldie. 1989. "Raising Standards on Florida's Competency Test for College Students Stirs Controversy." *Chronicle of Higher Education* 35 (July 12): A22.

Boggs, Carl. 1976. *Gramsci's Marxism*. London: Pluto Press.

Bogue, Jesse P. 1950. *The Community College*. New York: McGraw-Hill.

Boli, John, Francisco O. Ramirez, and John W. Meyer. 1985. "Exploring the Origins and Expansion of Mass Education." *Comparative Education Review* 29: 145–170.

Bolton, Frederick. 1926. "The Establishment of Junior Colleges." *Washington Education Journal* 5 (May): 270–274, 293–294.

―――. 1933. "Status of the Junior Colleges in Washington." *Junior College Journal* 4 (November): 57–65.

―――. 1940. "Junior College Legislation." *Washington Education Journal* 20 (December): 60.

Booth, Lee. 1981. Telephone interview with the superintendent, Herrin High School District. Herrin, Illinois.

Bowen, Howard. 1977. *Investment in Learning*. San Francisco: Jossey-Bass.

Bowles, Dymphna. 1988. "Transferability in the Liberal Arts and Sciences." Pp. 27–38 in Carolyn Prager (ed.), *Enhancing Articulation and Transfer*. (New Directions for Community Colleges #61). San Francisco: Jossey-Bass.

Bowles, Samuel, and Herbert Gintis. 1976. *Schooling in Capitalist America*. New York: Basic Books.

Boyd, William L. 1976. "The Public, the Professionals, and Educational Policymaking: Who Governs?" *Teachers College Record* 77: 539–572.

Boyd, William L., and Charles T. Kerchner (eds.). 1988. *The Politics of Excellence and Choice in Education*. Bristol, PA: Falmer Press.

Boylan, Francis. 1940. "The Program of Placement at Wright." *Junior College Journal* 10: 426–428.

Brademas, John. 1963. [Remarks on the Higher Education Facilities Act]. *Congressional Record,* 88th Congress, First Session, Part 11. Washington, DC: Government Printing Office.

―――. 1967. "View from Capitol Hill." *Grade Teacher* 85 (November): 12, 14, 16.

Bradley, Cecil. 1981. Personal interview with the dean of vocational education, South Seattle Community College. Seattle.

Brandt, Gene. 1968. "Perceptions of Junior College Purposes Held by Various Illinois Junior College Authorities." Ed.D., Illinois State University. (DAI 29/05-A, 1385)

Brawer, Florence, and J. Friedlander. 1979. *Science and Social Science in the Two-Year College*. (Topical Paper #69). Los Angeles: ERIC Clearinghouse for Junior Colleges. (ERIC ED 172 854)

Breneman, David W., and Susan C. Nelson. 1981. *Financing Community Colleges*. Washington, DC: Brookings Institution.

Brenner, Johanna. 1979. "Public Higher Education in 'Postindustrial Society.' " Ph.D., University of California, Los Angeles. (DAI 40/04, 2286)

Brick, Michael. 1963. *Forum and Focus for the Junior College Movement*. New York: Columbia University, Teachers College Press.

Brint, Steven, and Jerome Karabel. 1989. *The Diverted Dream: Community Colleges and the Promise of Educational Opportunity in America, 1900–1985*. New York: Oxford University Press.

Broman, James. 1981. Personal interview with the manager, Education Department, Illinois State Chamber of Commerce, 1964–1967. Chicago.

Brossman, Sidney. 1986. Telephone interview with the executive director, California Community Colleges, 1968–1977. San Diego.

Brossman, Sidney, and Myron Roberts. 1973. *The California Community Colleges*. Palo Alto, CA: Field Education Publications.

Brouillet, Frank. 1980. Personal interview with the state superintendent of public instruction. Olympia, Washington.

Brown, Edwin G., Sr. 1961. "Message to the Legislature, January 3, 1961." *Assembly Journal, 1961*. Sacramento: State of California.

———. 1965. "Public Higher Education in California." Pp. 104–109 in Logan Wilson (ed.), *Emerging Patterns in American Higher Education*. Washington, DC: American Council on Education.

Brown, J. Stanley. 1922. "The Growth and Development of Junior Colleges in the United States." Pp. 27–29 in George Zook (ed.), *National Conference on Junior Colleges, 1920, and the First Annual Meeting of the American Association of Junior Colleges, 1921*. (U.S. Office of Education Bulletin, 1922, #19). Washington, DC: Government Printing Office.

Brown, Robert. 1986. Telephone interview with the vice president, California Taxpayers Association, 1966–1974. Washington, DC.

Browne, Robert. 1981. Personal interview with the executive director, Illinois Board of Higher Education, 1961–1965. Springfield, Illinois.

Bruce, Terry. 1980. Personal interview with the assistant majority leader of the Illinois Senate. Springfield, Illinois.

Brune, Rey. 1981. Telephone interview with the director of public relations, John Deere Co.; member, Board of Trustees, Blackhawk Community College, 1962–1970; and member, Illinois Community College Board, 1970–1976. Moline, Illinois.

Bruno, Louis. 1981. Personal interview with the state superintendent of public instruction, 1961–1973. Olympia, Washington.

Business Week. 1972. "The Job Gap for College Graduates in the '70's." September 23, pp. 48–58.

California Community Colleges. 1984. *Transfer Education.* Sacramento, CA: Office of the Chancellor. (ERIC ED 250025)

———. 1986. *Study of Contractual Education Programs in the California Community Colleges.* Sacramento: Author. (ERIC ED 275390)

———. 1989. *Transfer and Articulation with Four-Year Colleges and Universities.* Sacramento: Author. (ERIC ED 303 224)

———. 1991. *Trends in Transfer from California Community Colleges.* Sacramento: Author. (ERIC ED 341 443)

California Postsecondary Education Commission. 1985. *Reaffirming California's Commitment To Transfer.* Sacramento: Author.

———. 1986. *Update of Community College Transfer Student Statistics, University of California and California State University, Fall 1985.* Sacramento: Author. (ERIC ED 271 186)

———. 1987. *Strengthening Transfer and Articulation Policies and Practices in California's Colleges and Universities.* Sacramento: Author. (ERIC ED 293 602)

———. 1989. *Update of Community College Transfer Statistics, 1988–89.* Sacramento: Author. (ERIC ED 313 073)

California State Department of Education. 1920. *Twenty-Ninth Biennial Report of the Superintendent of Public Instruction.* Sacramento, CA: Author.

———. 1922. *Minutes of the State Board of Education for June 26 through July 3, 1922.* Sacramento: Author.

———. 1928. *The Need for Terminal Courses in the Junior College.* (Bulletin C–6). Sacramento: Author.

———. 1933. *Thirty-Fifth Biennial Report of the Superintendent of Public Instruction.* Sacramento: Author.

Campbell, Roald F., and Tim L. Mazzoni, Jr. 1976. *State Policy Making for the Public Schools.* San Francisco: McCutchan.

Campbell, Roald F., Luvern L. Cunningham, Raphael O. Nystrand, and Michael D. Usdan. 1985. *The Organization and Control of American Schools*. 5th ed. Columbus, OH: Merrill.

Carlson, Donald. 1982. Telephone interview with the president of the Elmhurst National Bank; and member, Board of Trustees, College of DuPage, 1966–1970. Elmhurst, Illinois.

Carmichael, O. C., Jr. 1955. *New York Establishes a University*. Nashville, TN: Vanderbilt University Press.

Carnegie Commission on Higher Education. 1970. *The Open Door Colleges*. New York: McGraw-Hill.

———. 1973. *Priorities for Action*. New York: McGraw-Hill.

Carnegie Corporation. 1956–1978. *Annual Report*. New York: Author.

Carnegie Council on Policy Studies in Higher Education. 1979. *Giving Youth a Better Chance*. San Francisco: Jossey-Bass.

Carnegie Foundation for the Advancement of Teaching. 1990. *The Condition of the Professoriate: Attitudes and Trends, 1989*. New York: Author.

Carnoy, Martin, and Derek Shearer. 1980. *Economic Democracy*. White Plains, NY: M. E. Sharpe.

Carnoy, Martin, and Henry M. Levin. 1985. *School and Work in the Democratic State*. Stanford, CA: Stanford University Press.

Center for the Study of Community Colleges. 1988. *An Assessment of the Urban Transfer Opportunity Program. The Ford Foundation's Second Stage Transfer Opportunity Awards. Final Report*. Los Angeles: Author. (ERIC ED 293 573)

Chapman, David W., and Ernest T. Pascarella. 1983. "Predictors of Academic and Social Integration of College Students." *Research in Higher Education* 19: 295–322.

Chase, William G. 1969. "Implications of Federal Legislation from 1958 through 1969 for Expansion and Improvement of Public Junior Colleges in Illinois." Ed.D., Illinois State University. (DAI 30/07-A, 2744)

Chavez, Jose. 1975. "Presidential Influence on the Politics of Higher Education: The Higher Education Act of 1965." Ph.D., University of Texas at Austin.

Chestnut, Edith. 1973. "The Involvement and Influence of Voluntary Community Organizations in the Development of a Community College: The Schenectady Community College." Ph.D., State University of New York at Albany. (DAI, 34/04-A, 163)

Chicago School District. 1956. *Report on the Chicago City Junior College*. Chicago: Author.

Choy, Susan P., and Antoinette G. Gifford. 1990. *Profile of Undergraduates in American Postsecondary Institutions.* (NCES 90-353). Washington, DC: Government Printing Office. (ASI 1990 4846-3.9)

Chubb, John E. 1988. "Institutions, the Economy, and the Dynamics of State Elections." *American Political Science Review* 82 (March): 133–154.

Clabaugh, Charles. 1981. Personal interview with the state senator for Champaign-Urbana, 1939–1975. Champaign-Urbana, Illinois.

Clark, Burton R. 1960. *The Open Door College.* New York: McGraw-Hill.

———. 1962. *Educating the Expert Society.* San Francisco: Chandler.

———. 1980. "The 'Cooling Out' Function Revisited." Pp. 15–32 in George Vaughan (ed.), *Questioning the Community College Role.* (New Directions in Community Colleges no. 32). San Francisco: Jossey-Bass.

Cloud, A. J. 1941. "The Present Progress of Terminal Education." *California Journal of Secondary Education* 16 (March): 153–156.

Clowes, Darrel A., and Bernard H. Levin. 1989. "Community, Technical, and Junior Colleges: Are They Leaving Higher Education?" *Journal of Higher Education* 60 (May–June): 349–355.

Clune, William, and John Witte (eds.). 1990. *Choice and Control in American Education.* 2 vols. Bristol, PA: Falmer.

Cohen, Arthur M. 1988. "Degree Achievement by Minorities in Community Colleges." *The Review of Higher Education* 11 (4): 383–402.

———. 1990. "The Case for the Community College." *American Journal of Education* 98 (August): 426–442.

———. 1992. "Calculating Transfer Rates Efficiently." *Community, Technical, and Junior College Journal* 62 (February–March): 32–35.

Cohen, Arthur M., and Florence B. Brawer. 1977. *The Two-Year College Instructor Today.* New York: Praeger.

———. 1982. *The American Community College.* 1st ed. San Francisco: Jossey-Bass.

———. 1987. *The Collegiate Function of the Community College.* San Francisco: Jossey-Bass.

———. 1989. *The American Community College.* 2d ed. San Francisco: Jossey-Bass.

Cohen, Arthur M., Florence B. Brawer, and Estela Bensimon. 1985. *Transfer Education in American Community Colleges.* Los Angeles: Center for the Study of Community Colleges. (ERIC ED 255 250)

Cohen, Michael D., James G. March, and Johan Olsen. 1972. "A Garbage Can Model of Organizational Choice." *Administrative Science Quarterly* 17 (March): 1–25.

Cole, Norwood. N.d. *The Founding Year of Skagit Valley College.* Mt. Vernon, WA: Skagit Valley College.

Collins, Randall. 1977. "Some Comparative Principles of Educational Stratification." *Harvard Educational Review* 47: 1–27.

———. 1979. *The Credential Society.* New York: Academic.

Congressional Quarterly. 1958, 1963, 1965. *Congressional Quarterly Almanac* (yearly). Washington, DC: Congressional Quarterly, Inc.

Cooperative Institutional Research Program. 1992. *The American Freshman: National Norms for Fall 1992.* Los Angeles: University of California at Los Angeles, Higher Education Research Institute. (ERIC ED 352 891)

Corman, Hope, and Patricia Davidson. 1984. "Economic Aspects of Post-Secondary Schooling Decisions." *Economics of Education Review* 3: 131–139.

Corrick, Delmar. 1975. "Perceptions of the Missions of the Community Colleges in the State of Washington by Faculty, Administrators, Trustees, Legislators, and Students." Ph.D., Washington State University. (DAI 36/02-A, 729)

Cothran, Dan Allen. 1979. "The California Community Colleges and the Limits to Growth." Ph.D., Cornell University. (DAI 40/09A, 5178)

Cox, James N. 1971. "The Urban Community College: A Case Study of the Los Angeles City College from 1929 to 1970." Ed.D., University of California at Los Angeles. (DAI 32/07-A, 3716)

Crawfurd, Allan P. 1959. "The Junior College Movement in Washington State from 1915 to 1955, with Proposals for Further Development." Ed.D., University of Denver.

Cremin, Lawrence. 1977. *Traditions of American Education.* New York: Basic Books.

Crook, David, and David Lavin. 1989. "The Community College Effect Revisited: The Long Term Impact of Community College Entry on Baccalaureate Attainment." Paper presented to the 1989 annual meeting of the American Educational Research Association, San Francisco.

Cross, K. Patricia. 1985. "Determining Missions and Priorities for the Fifth Generation." In William Deegan and Dale Tillery (eds.), *Renewing the American Community College.* San Francisco: Jossey-Bass.

Dahl, Robert A. 1961. *Who Governs?* New Haven: Yale University Press.

Darknell, Frank. 1980. "The Carnegie Philanthropy and Private Corporate Influence on Higher Education." In Robert F. Arnove (ed.), *Philanthropy and Cultural Imperialism.* Boston: G. K. Hall.

Deam, Thomas. 1931. "Evolution of the Joliet Junior College." *Junior College Journal* 1 (April): 2.

Deegan, William L., and Ronald Drisko. 1985. "Contract Training: Progress and Policy Issues." *Community, Technical, and Junior College Journal* 55 (March): 14–17.

DiMaggio, Paul J., and Walter W. Powell. 1983. "The Iron Cage Revisited: Institutional Isomorphism and Collective Rationality in Organizational Fields." *American Sociological Review* 48: 147–160.

Dolliver, James. 1981. Personal interview with former assistant to Governor Daniel Evans, 1965–1976; later justice of the state Supreme Court. Olympia, Washington.

Domhoff, G. William. 1983. *Who Rules America Now?* New York: Simon and Schuster.

Donovan, Joseph D. 1952. "Certain Factors Affecting the Inauguration of the Program of Institutes for Applied Arts and Sciences in New York State." Ph.D., State University of New York at Buffalo.

Donovan, Richard A., Barbara Schaier-Peleg, and Bruce Forer (eds.). 1987. *Transfer: Making It Work.* Washington, DC: American Association of Community Colleges.

Doran, Kenneth. 1961. "New York, New Yorkers, and the Two-Year College Movement." Ph.D., Syracuse University. (DAI 23/01, 143)

Dougherty, Kevin J. 1987. "The Effects of Community Colleges: Aid or Hindrance to Socioeconomic Attainment?" *Sociology of Education* 60 (May): 86–103.

———. 1988a. "The Politics of Community College Expansion." *American Journal of Education* 96 (May): 351–393.

———. 1988b. "Educational Policymaking and the Relative Autonomy of the State: The Case of Occupational Education in the Community College." *Sociological Forum* 3 (Summer): 400–432.

———. 1992. *Schools to the Rescue: The Political Origins of the Educational Excellence Movement.* Report to the Spencer Foundation. New York: Manhattan College.

Dougherty, Kevin J., and Floyd M. Hammack (eds.). 1990. *Education and Society.* San Diego, CA: Harcourt Brace Jovanovich.

Dougherty, Kevin J., and Lizabeth Sostre. 1992. "Minerva and the Market: The Sources of the Movement for School Choice." *Educational Policy* 6 (June): 160–179. Reprinted in Peter W. Cookson, Jr. (ed.), *The Choice Controversy.* Newbury Park, CA: Corwin Press.

Dow, John A. 1967. "History of Public School Organization and Administration in Fresno County, California." Ph.D., University of Southern California. (DAI 28/05-A, 1684)

Drake, Sandra. 1977. *Research Report: A Study of Community and Junior College Boards of Trustees.* Washington, DC: American Association of Community and Junior Colleges.

Dreeben, Robert. 1967. *On What Is Learned in School*. Boston: Allyn and Bacon.

Duryea, Perry. 1985. Telephone interview with the speaker of the New York House of Representatives, 1961–1978. Montauk, New York.

Eaton, Judith S. 1984. "Community College Culture." *Community, Technical, and Junior College Journal* 55 (August–September): 52–55.

———. (ed.). 1988. *Colleges of Choice: The Enabling Impact of the Community College*. New York: American Council on Education and Macmillan Publishing.

———. 1990. "Three Myths of Transfer Education." *Community, Technical, and Junior College Journal* 59 (June–July): 18–20.

Eaton, Judith S., Thomas R. Hawk, Samuel Hirsch, and Aram L. Terzian. 1988. "An Academic Model for Urban Community College Education." *Community, Technical, and Junior College Journal* 58 (April–May): 40–43.

Ebbesen, James A. 1969. "Junior College Board Members: Their Personal Characteristics and Attitudes toward Junior College Functions, State of Illinois, 1968–1969." Ed.D., Northern Illinois University. (DAI 30/06-A, 2285)

Education Commission of the States. 1970. "Task Force IV: Vocational Education in Higher Education." *Higher Education in the States* 1 (November): whole issue.

Eells, Walter C. 1931. *The Junior College*. Boston: Houghton Mifflin.

———. 1941. *The Present Status of Terminal Education*. Boston: Houghton Mifflin.

Elazar, Daniel J. 1984. *American Federalism: A View from the States*. 3d ed. New York: Harper and Row.

Ensign, Gary C. 1972. "New York State Community Colleges and their Environment: Administrators' Perceptions." Ph.D., University of Michigan. (DAI 33/ 11-A, 6113)

Ernst, Charles, and Rand Johnson. 1991. "Planning and Developing an ATC." *Community, Technical, and Junior College Journal* 61 (October–November): 22–25.

Eulau, Heinz, and Harold Quinley. 1970. *State Officials and Higher Education*. New York: McGraw-Hill.

Eurich, Alvin. 1985. Personal interview with the chancellor of the State University of New York, 1949–1951. New York.

Evans, Daniel. 1980. Personal interview with the governor of Washington, 1965–1977. Olympia, Washington.

Fahey, Laurence. 1966. "The California Legislature and Educational Decisionmaking." Ph.D., Claremont Graduate Center, California. (DAI 28/02-A, 388)

Fields, Cheryl. 1987a. "Many Aggressive Community Colleges Focusing on Training Workers for Fast Growing Fields." *Chronicle of Higher Education* 33 (February 25, 1987): 21.

———. 1987b. "Education 'Brokers' Are Helping Two Year Colleges Train Workers to Fill Needs of Local Business." *Chronicle of Higher Education* 33 (March 11, 1987): 30.

Fields, Ralph R. 1962. *The Community College Movement.* New York: McGraw-Hill.

Fine, Michelle. 1991. *Framing Dropouts.* Albany: State University of New York Press.

Fiorina, Morris. 1977. *Congress: Keystone of the Washington Establishment.* New Haven, CT: Yale University Press.

Florida State Department of Education. 1983. *A Longitudinal Study Comparing University Native and Community College Transfer Students in the State University System of Florida.* Tallahassee: Author. (ERIC ED 256 405)

———. 1985. *Report for Florida Community Colleges, 1983–1984. Part 1: Statistical Tables.* Tallahassee, FL: Author. (ERIC ED 256 403)

———. 1988. *The Role of Florida's Community Colleges in Articulation.* Tallahassee, FL: Author. (ERIC ED 300 042)

Florida State University System. 1983. *Fact Book, 1981–82.* Tallahassee, FL: Author. (ERIC ED 312 936)

———. 1986. *Fact Book, 1984–1985.* Tallahassee, FL: Author. (ERIC ED 312 937)

———. 1989. *Fact Book, 1987–88.* Tallahassee, FL: Author. (ERIC ED 312 939)

Forgacs, David (ed.). 1988. *A Gramsci Reader.* New York: Schocken.

Fretwell, Elbert K. 1954. *Founding Public Junior Colleges.* New York: Teachers College Press.

Friedland, Roger. 1983. *Power and Crisis in the City.* New York: Schocken.

Friedrich, Carl. 1963. *Man and His Government.* New York: McGraw-Hill.

Gaventa, John. 1980. *Power and Powerlessness.* Urbana-Champaign, IL: University of Illinois Press.

General Education Board. 1939–1947. *Annual Report.* New York: Author.

Giddens, Anthony. 1971. *Capitalism and Modern Social Theory.* Cambridge, England: Cambridge University Press.

Giles, Frederick. 1981. Personal interview with the president of Everett Junior College (1949–1961). Seattle, Washington.

Giroux, Henry. 1983. *Theory and Resistance in Education*. South Hadley, MA: Bergin and Garvey.

Given, John. 1957. "The Attitudes of Selected Community Groups toward Junior College Education in Los Angeles." Ph.D., University of California at Los Angeles.

Gladieux, Laurence and Thomas Wolanin. 1976. *Congress and the Colleges*. Lexington, MA: Lexington Books.

Glazer, Judith. 1989. "Nelson Rockefeller and the Politics of Higher Education in New York State." *History of Higher Education Annual* 9: 87–114.

Gleazer, Edmund, Jr. 1968. *This Is the Community College*. Boston: Houghton Mifflin.

———. 1980. *Values, Vision, and Vitality*. Washington, DC: American Association of Community and Junior Colleges.

Glenny, Lyman. 1981. Telephone interview with the executive director of the Illinois Board of Higher Education, 1965–1968. Berkeley, California.

Godfrey, Eleanor P., and Engin L. Holmstrom. 1970. *Study of Community Colleges and Vocational Technical Centers*. Washington, DC: Bureau of Social Science Research. (ERIC ED 053 718)

Gold, David, Clarence Lo, and Erik Olin Wright. 1975. "Recent Developments in Marxist Theories of the Capitalist State." *Monthly Review* 27 (October): 29–43.

Gooch, William. 1980. Personal interview with the dean for occupational-vocational education, College of DuPage. Glen Ellyn, Illinois.

Goodman, Robert. 1979. *The Last Entrepreneurs*. Boston: South End Press.

Goodwin, David. 1989. *Postsecondary Vocational Education. Final Report*. (Vol. IV of the National Assessment of Vocational Education.) Washington, DC: Government Printing Office. (ASI 1989 4806–3.5)

Gordon, David. 1982. Telephone interview with the executive director, Association of Washington Business, 1955–1979. Seattle, Washington.

Gordon, Sheila. 1975. "The Transformation of the City University of New York, 1945–1970." Ph.D., Teachers College, Columbia University. (DAI 38/07-A, 4325)

Goslin, David. 1965. *The School in Contemporary Society*. Atlanta: Rand McNally.

Gouldner, Alvin. 1979. *The Future of Intellectuals and the Rise of the New Class*. New York: Oxford.

Gramsci, Antonio. 1971. *Selections from the Prison Notebooks of Antonio Gramsci*. Quintin Hoare and Geoffrey Nowell-Smith (eds.). New York: International Publishers.

Graves, Frank. 1931. *Addresses and Papers, 1926–1931.* Albany: New York State Department of Education.

Gray, Asa. 1915. "The Junior College in California." *School Review* 23: 465–473.

Grede, John. 1981. Personal interview with the vice-chancellor for vocational-technical education, City Colleges of Chicago, 1970–1980. Palos Hills, Ill.

Grede, John, and Andrew Korim. 1969. *Master Plan—Occupational Education in Chicago City College.* Chicago: Chicago City College.

Green, Rep. Edith. 1970. "People, Jobs, and Federal Priorities." *Compact* 4 (August): 4.

Greenwood, Noel. 1971. " 'Painful' Study of State Higher Education Due." *Los Angeles Times* (April 4): 4.

Griffith, Coleman, with Hortense Blackstone. 1945. *The Junior College in Illinois.* Urbana: University of Illinois Press.

Grubb, W. Norton. 1984. "The Bandwagon Once More: Vocational Preparation for High Technology Occupations." *Harvard Educational Review* 54: 429–451.

———. 1988. "Vocationalizing Higher Education: The Causes of Enrollment and Completion in Public Two-Year Colleges, 1970–1980." *Economics of Education Review* 7: 301–319.

———. 1989. "The Effects of Differentiation on Educational Attainment: The Case of Community Colleges." *Review of Higher Education* 12 (Summer): 349–374.

———. 1991. "The Decline of Community College Transfer Rates: Evidence from National Longitudinal Surveys." *Journal of Higher Education* 62 (2): 194–217.

———. 1992a. "Postsecondary Vocational Education and the Sub-Baccalaureate Labor Market: New Evidence on Economic Returns." *Economics of Education Review* 11: 225–248.

———. 1992b. "Finding an Equilibrium: Enhancing Transfer Rates while Strengthening the Comprehensive Community College." *National Center for Academic Achievement and Transfer Working Papers* 3 (6). Washington, DC: American Council on Education.

———. 1993. "The Long-Run Effects of Proprietary Schools on Wages and Earnings: Implications for Federal Policy." *Educational Evaluation and Policy Analysis* 15 (Spring): 17–33.

———. 1994a. "The Economic Effects of Sub-Baccalaureate Education: Corrections and Extensions." Unpublished paper, University of California, Berkeley.

———. 1994b. Personal communication.

Grubb, W. Norton, and John Tuma. 1991. "Who Gets Student Aid? Variations in Access to Aid." *Review of Higher Education* 14 (Spring): 359–382.

Gulick, Lester. 1938. *Education for American Life: The Regents' Inquiry into the Character and Cost of Public Education in the State of New York.* New York: McGraw-Hill.

Haberacker, H. J. 1981. Personal interview with the president of Belleville Area Community College, 1967–1974. Belleville, Illinois.

Hall, Hal. 1982. Telephone interview with the superintendent, Belleville Township High School District, 1946–1957. Washington, DC.

Halperin, Morton. 1974. *Bureaucratic Politics and Foreign Policy.* Washington, DC: The Brookings Institution.

Halperin, Samuel. 1985. Telephone interview with the Office of Education legislative specialist, 1961–1965; assistant commissioner of education for legislation, 1965–1967; and deputy assistant secretary of health, education, and welfare, 1967–1970. Washington, DC.

Hardin, Thomas L. 1975. "A History of the Community Junior College in Illinois: 1901–1972." Ph.D., University of Illinois. (DAI 36/09-A, 5800)

Harris, Norman C. 1964. *Technical Education in the Junior College.* Washington, DC: American Association of Junior Colleges.

Harris, Norman C., and John Grede.1977. *Career Education in College.* San Francisco: Jossey-Bass.

Hauselman, A. J., and Dan Tudor. 1987. *Compendium of Selected Characteristics: University of Kentucky Community College System, 1986–1987.* Lexington, KY: University of Kentucky. (ERIC ED 289 543)

Henry, David D. 1956. "The Junior College and the Load Ahead." Address at the Ten Year Junior College Celebration, Belleville Junior College, March 7, 1956. Unpublished manuscript, University of Illinois.

———. 1981. Personal interview with the president of the University of Illinois, 1955–1970. Champaign-Urbana, Illinois.

Hill, Jack D. 1978. "Critical Decisions in the Origin and Development of John A. Logan College." Ph.D., Southern Illinois University. (DAI 39/04-A, 2100)

Hill, Merton. 1938. *The Functioning of the California Public Junior Colleges.* Berkeley: University of California Press.

Hills, J. R. 1965. "Transfer Shock: The Academic Performance of the Junior College Transfer." *Journal of Experimental Education* 33: 201–215.

Himes, Catherine. 1936. "Composition in Chicago Junior Colleges." *Junior College Journal* 7 (November): 86.

Hoffland, Ginger, and William Evans. 1986. *Parallels: A History of the Los Angeles Community College District.* Los Angeles: Los Angeles Community College District.

Hogan, David J. 1985. *Class and Reform: Schools and Society in Chicago, 1880–1930.* Philadelphia: University of Pennsylvania Press.

Holderman, Kenneth. 1964. "The Case for University Branch Campuses." *Junior College Journal* 34 (April): 25, 28–30.

Holman, Francis. 1981. Personal interview with member, Board of Education, Shoreline Public Schools. Seattle, Washington.

Holmstedt, Raleigh. 1967. "Indiana Conference of Higher Education, 1945–1967." *Bulletin of the Indiana University School of Education* 43 (January): whole issue.

Holmstrom, Eleanor, and Ann Bisconti. 1974. *Transfers from Junior to Senior Colleges.* Washington, DC: American Council for Education.

Howard, Barbara L. 1990. "The Articulation/Transfer Activities of the Los Rios Community College District." Pp. 49–59 in Louis W. Bender (ed.), *Spotlight on the Transfer Function.* Washington, DC: American Association of Community Colleges.

Howard, Raymond. 1981. Personal interview with the superintendent of schools, Shoreline Public Schools, 1944–1965. Seattle, Washington.

Iannaccone, Laurence, and Peter Cistone. 1974. *Politics of Education.* Eugene, OR: University of Oregon, ERIC Clearinghouse on Education Management.

Idisi, C. Onokata. 1979. "Shawnee College: An Analysis of the Organization and Establishment of a Postsecondary Institution." Ed.D., Southern Illinois University. (DAI 40/08-A, 4326)

Illinois Board of Higher Education. 1963. *Master Plan Committee H: Vocational, Technical, and Adult Education.* Springfield: Author.

———. 1964. *A Master Plan for Higher Education in Illinois.* Springfield: Author.

———. 1966. *A Master Plan for Higher Education in Illinois: Phase II.* Springfield: Author.

Illinois Community College Board. 1966. *Proceedings of First Statewide Junior College Conference.* Springfield: Author.

———. 1967. *First Biennial Report, 1965–1967.* Springfield: Author.

————. 1970. *Proceedings of Fifth Statewide Junior College Conference*. Springfield: Author.

————. 1978. *Curriculum Enrollment Summary in the Public Community Colleges of Illinois: 1977–1978*. Springfield: Author. (ERIC ED 160 143)

————. 1979. *Seventh Biennial Report, 1977–78*. Springfield: Author.

————. 1984. *Fall 1979 Transfer Study, Report 4: Third and Fourth Year Persistence and Achievement*. Springfield: Author. (ERIC ED 254 275)

————. 1986a. *Economic Development Grant Report, Fiscal Year 1986*. Springfield: Author. (ERIC ED 275 361)

————. 1986b. *Illinois Community College Board Transfer Study: A Five Year Study of Students Transferring from Illinois Two Year Colleges to Illinois Senior Colleges in the Fall of 1979*. Springfield: Author. (ERIC ED 270 148)

————. 1986c. *Student Enrollment Data and Trends in the Public Junior Colleges of Illinois: Fall 1985*. Springfield: Author. (ERIC ED 270 146)

————. 1987. *Follow-Up Study of Students Who Completed Community College Occupational Programs during Fiscal Years 1983–1985*. Springfield: Author. (ERIC ED 282 614)

————. 1989. *Current Issues in Transfer Articulation between Community Colleges and Four Year Colleges in Illinois*. Springfield: Author. (ERIC ED 304 168)

Illinois Higher Education Commission. 1957. *Illinois Looks to the Future in Higher Education*. Springfield: Author.

Illinois State Chamber of Commerce. 1966. *The Illinois Junior College System*. Springfield: Author.

Illinois Taxpayers Federation. 1955. *Legislative Manual and Fiscal Facts for the 69th General Assembly, 1955*. Springfield: Author.

Ingalls, Roscoe. 1939. "Vocational Education in the Junior College." *Junior College Journal* 9: 449–455.

Ivey, Nathan. 1981. Personal interview with the president, John A. Logan College, 1968–1973, and president, Thornton Community College, 1973–1980. South Holland, Illinois.

Jacobs, David. 1974. "Dependency and Vulnerability: An Exchange Approach to the Control of Organizations." *Administrative Science Quarterly* 19: 45–59.

Jacobson, Gary. 1983. *The Politics of Congressional Elections*. Boston: Little, Brown.

Jaschik, Scott. 1986. "Community Colleges Are Changing their Roles to Meet Demands for New Types of Job Training." *Chronicle of Higher Education* 32 (April 12): 13–16.

————. 1988. "California Legislature Passes a 'Historic' Measure to Reorganize the State's Two Year College System." *Chronicle of Higher Education* 35 (September 7): A17, 24.

Jencks, Christopher S., and David Riesman. 1968. *The Academic Revolution.* Chicago: University of Chicago Press.

Jepson, James. 1980. Personal Interview with member, Illinois Senate Democratic Staff, 1977–1980, and associate director for fiscal affairs, Illinois Board of Higher Education, 1980– . Springfield, Illinois.

Johns, Arthur. 1948. "A Study of Procedures in the Development of Terminal Courses in a Selected Group of California Public Junior Colleges." Ed.D., University of California, Berkeley.

Johnson, Naomi. 1987. "Academic Factors that Affect Transfer Student Persistence." *Journal of College Student Personnel* 28 (July): 323–329.

Kaestle, Carl F. 1976. "Conflict and Consensus Revisited." *Harvard Educational Review* 46: 390–396.

————. 1983. *Pillars of the Republic.* New York: Hill and Wang.

Kane, Thomas J., and Cecilia Elena Rouse. 1993. "Comment on W. Norton Glubb, 'The Varied Economic Returns to Postsecondary Education.' " Unpublished paper, Harvard University and Princeton University.

Karabel, Jerome. 1972. "Community Colleges and Social Stratification." *Harvard Educational Review* 42: 521–562.

————. 1974. "Protecting the Portals: Class and the Community College." *Social Policy* 5 (May–June): 12–18.

————. 1986. "Community Colleges and Social Stratification in the 1980s." Pp. 13–30 in L. Steven Zwerling (ed.), *The Community College and Its Critics.* (New Directions in Community Colleges, no. 54). San Francisco: Jossey-Bass. (ERIC ED 271 169)

Karier, Clarence, Paul Violas, and Joel Spring. 1973. *Roots of Crisis: American Education in the Twentieth Century.* Chicago: Rand McNally.

Katz, Louis. 1987. Telephone interview with the associate vice president for academic affairs, University of Connecticut. Storrs, Connecticut.

Katz, Michael B. 1968. *The Irony of Early School Reform.* Cambridge, MA: Harvard University Press.

————. 1987. *Reconstructing American Education.* Cambridge, MA: Harvard University Press.

Katznelson, Ira, and Margaret Weir. 1985. *Schooling for All.* New York: Basic Books.

Kelley, F. William, Jr. 1981. Personal interview with the associate director for community college programs, Illinois Board of Higher Education. Springfield.

W. K. Kellogg Foundation, 1959–1980. *Annual Report.* Battle Creek, MI: Author.

Kennedy, John F. 1963. "January 29, 1963 Message to Congress on Education." Pp. 975–979 in *Congressional Quarterly Almanac, 1963.* Washington, DC: Congressional Quarterly, Inc.

Kerr, Clark. 1978. "Higher Education: Paradise Lost?" *Higher Education* 7: 261–278.

————. 1980. "Changes and Challenges Ahead for Community Colleges." *Community and Junior College Journal* 50 (May): 4–10.

Kerr, Norman D. 1964. "The School Board as an Agency of Legitimation." *Sociology of Education* 38 (Fall): 34–59.

Kintzer, Frederick. 1989. *Articulation and Transfer: A Review of Current Literature on Statewide and Interinstitutional Program Models and Trends.* Trenton, NJ: New Jersey State Department of Higher Education. (ERIC ED 311 946)

Kintzer, Frederick, and James L. Wattenbarger. 1985. *The Articulation/ Transfer Phenomenon.* Washington, DC: American Association of Community and Junior Colleges. (ERIC ED 257 539)

Kissler, Gerald, Juan Lara, and Judith Cardinal. 1981. "Factors Contributing to the Academic Difficulties Encountered by Students Who Transfer from Community Colleges to Four-Year Institutions." Unpublished paper, University of California at Los Angeles. (ERIC ED 203 920)

Knight, William. 1990. "GPA and Attrition Information for Students Relocating to the Kent Campus of Kent State University from Four Two-Year Colleges and from the KSU Regional Campuses." Unpublished paper, Kent State University, Kent, Ohio.

Knoell, Dorothy. 1987. *Transfer, Articulation, and Collaboration Twenty-Five Years Later: A Restudy of Relationships between Two- and Four-Year Colleges.* Washington, DC: American Association of Community and Junior Colleges and California Postsecondary Education Commission.

Knoell, Dorothy, and Leland L. Medsker. 1965. *From Junior College to Senior College.* Washington, DC: American Council on Education.

Kohen, Andrew, Gilbert Nestel, and Constantine Karmas. 1978. "Factors Affecting Individual Persistence Rates in Undergraduate College Programs." *American Educational Research Journal* 15: 233–252.

Koltai, Leslie, and David Wolf. 1984. "A Reasonable Consensus." *Community, Technical, and Junior College Journal* 55 (August–September): 42–45.

Koos, Leonard V. 1924. *The Junior College*. Minneapolis: University of Minnesota Press.

———. 1925. *The Junior College Movement*. Boston: Ginn.

Krasner, Stephen. 1978. *Defending the National Interest*. New York: Princeton University Press.

Labaree, David. 1988. *The Making of an American High School*. New Haven, CT: Yale University Press.

———. 1990. "From Comprehensive High School to Community College." Pp. 203–240 in Ronald Corwin (ed.), *Research in the Sociology of Education and Socialization*, vol. 9. Greenwich, CT: JAI Press.

Lagemann, Ellen C. 1983. *Private Power for the Public Good*. Middletown, CT: Wesleyan University Press.

Laney, Arthur. 1981. Telephone interview with the assistant superintendent for vocational and adult education, Chicago Board of Education. Chicago.

Lange, Alexis. 1916. "The Junior College, with Special Reference to California." *Educational Administration and Supervision* 2: 1–8.

———. 1917. "The Junior College as an Integral Part of the Public School System." *School Review* 25: 465–479.

———. 1918. "The Community College—What Manner of Child Shall This Be?" *School and Society* 7 (February 23): 211–216.

Lape, Keith. 1980. Personal interview with the associate director for education program services, Illinois Community College Board. Springfield.

Lara, Juan. 1981. "Differences in Quality of Academic Effort between Successful and Unsuccessful Community College Transfer Students." Paper delivered at the 1981 annual meeting of the American Educational Research Association. Los Angeles: University of California, Los Angeles. (ERIC ED 201 359)

LaValle, Kenneth. 1981. (Untitled legislative memorandum on Chapter 113, 1981 Laws). In *New York State Legislative Annual, 1981*. New York: New York State Legislative Annual, Inc.

Lavin, David E., and David B. Crook. 1990. "Open Admissions and Its Outcomes: Ethnic Differences in Long-Term Educational Attainment." *American Journal of Education* 98 (August): 389–425.

Lavin, David E., and David Hyllegard. 1991. "Income and Occupational Status: The Value of Credentials, the Effects of Ethnicity and Gender." Forthcoming in Lavin and Hyllegard, *The Value of College*. New Haven, CT: Yale University Press.

Lee, Charles. 1985. Telephone interview with the majority staff director, Senate Subcommittee on Education, 1963–1972. Seaview, Oregon.

Lee, Valerie, and Kenneth Frank. 1990. "Student Characteristics that Facilitate the Transfer from Two-Year to Four-Year Colleges." *Sociology of Education* 63 (July): 178–193.

Lehner, Robert. 1972. "Public Views of State Governors." Pp. 258–269 in Thad Beyle and Oliver Williams (eds.), *The American Governor in Behavioral Perspective*. New York: Harper and Row.

Leister, Terry. 1975. "An Analysis of the Centralization of Community College Authority in Washington State from 1917–1973 Using Easton's Political Systems Framework." Ph.D., University of Washington. (DAI 37/02-A, 834)

Levin, Henry. 1984. "Jobs: A Changing Workforce, A Changing Education?" *Change Magazine* (Oct.): 32–37.

Levine, David. 1986. *The American College and the Culture of Aspiration, 1915–1940.* Ithaca, NY: Cornell University Press.

Liaison Committee of the State Board of Education and the Regents of the University of California. 1957. *A Study of the Need for Additional Centers of Public Higher Education in California.* Sacramento: California State Department of Education.

———. 1960. *A Master Plan for Higher Education in California, 1960–1975.* Sacramento: California State Department of Education.

Lindblom, Charles. 1977. *Politics and Markets.* New York: Basic Books.

Lindsay, Frank. 1939. "Enrollments in the Various Curriculums of California Public Junior Colleges." *California Schools* 10 (December): 303–308.

Liston, Daniel P. 1989. *Capitalist Schools?* Boston: Routledge.

Little, A. D., Inc. 1966. *A Policy Plan for Community College Education in the State of Washington: Report to the Superintendent of Public Instruction.* Olympia: Washington State Department of Education.

Littlefield, Henry W. 1940. "Factors Influencing the Growth of Junior Colleges." Ph.D., Yale University.

Lockard, Duane. 1969. *The Politics of State and Local Government.* 2d ed. New York: Macmillan.

London, Howard. 1978. *The Culture of a Community College.* New York: Praeger.

Lukes, Steven. 1974. *Power: A Radical View.* London: Macmillan.

Lyke, Robert, Thomas Gabe, and Steven R. Aleman. 1991. *Early Labor Market Experiences of Proprietary School Students.* Washington, DC: Congressional Research Service, Library of Congress. (ERIC ED 332 003)

Mallan, John. 1985. Telephone interview with the legislative director of the American Association of Junior Colleges, 1963–1966. Washington, DC.

Manski, Charles F., and David Wise. 1983. *College Choice in America.* Cambridge, MA: Harvard University Press.

Marshall, Catherine, Douglas Mitchell, and Frederick Wirt. 1989. *Culture and Educational Policy in the American States.* Bristol, PA: Falmer Press.

Martinko, Agnes. 1978. *Success of Transfer Students in Pennsylvania.* Harrisburg: Pennsylvania State Department of Education. (ERIC ED 156 849)

Martorana, S. V. 1963. "The Legal Status of American Public Junior Colleges." In Edmund Gleazer (ed.), *American Junior Colleges.* Washington, DC: American Council on Education.

Maryland State Board for Community Colleges. 1983. *The Role of Community Colleges in Preparing Students for Transfer to Four-Year Colleges and Universities.* Annapolis: Author. (ERIC ED 230 255)

———. 1988. *Maryland Community Colleges: 1987 Program Evaluations.* Annapolis: Author. (ERIC ED 295 699)

———. 1990. *Databook and Annual Report.* Annapolis: Author. (ERIC ED 315 136)

Masters, Nicholas, Robert H. Salisbury, and Thomas E. Eliot. 1964. *State Politics and the Public Schools.* New York: Knopf.

Mazzoni, Tim L. 1989. "Governors as Policy Leaders for Education: A Minnesota Comparison." *Educational Policy* 3: 79–90.

McCabe, Robert. 1981. "Now Is the Time to Reform the American Community College." *Community and Junior College Journal* 51 (May): 6–10.

———. 1988. "The Educational Program of the American Community College." Pp. 93–115 in Judith Eaton (ed.), *Colleges of Choice.* New York: Macmillan.

McCartan, Ann-Marie. 1983. "The Community College Vision: Present Challenges and Future Visions." *Journal of Higher Education* 54: 679–692.

McConnell, T. R. 1962. *A General Plan for Higher Education.* New York: McGraw-Hill.

McConochie, Daniel. 1983. *Four Years Later: Followup of 1978 Entrants, Maryland Community Colleges.* Annapolis: Maryland State Board for Community Colleges. (ERIC ED 234 850)

McDowell, F. M. 1919. *The Junior College.* (U.S. Bureau of Education Bulletin, 1919, #35). Washington, DC: Government Printing Office.

McGrath, Dennis, and Martin B. Spear. 1991. *The Academic Crisis of the Community College.* Albany: State University of New York Press.

McKinney, Robert Q. 1967. "An Analysis of Factors Affecting the Legal Status of the Community and Junior College in the Pacific Northwest, 1935 to 1965." Ph.D., Washington State University. (DAI 29/05-A, 1435)

McKinney, Samuel. 1981. Personal interview with the pastor, Mt. Zion Baptist Church, and member, Washington Council for Postsecondary Education. Seattle, Washington.

McLane, C. L. 1913. "The Junior College, Or Upward Extension of the High School." *School Review* 21 (March): 161–170.

McLure, William P., George C. Mann, Herbert H. Hamlin, M. Ray Karnes, and P. Van Miller. 1960. *Vocational and Technical Education in Illinois*. Urbana, IL: University of Illinois.

Medsker, Leland L. 1938. "Chicago Faces the Issue of Terminal Courses." *Junior College Journal* 9: 109–111.

———. 1960. *The Junior College*. New York: McGraw-Hill.

Medsker, Leland L., and James W. Trent. 1964. *The Influence of Different Types of Public Higher Institutions on College Attendance from Varying Socioeconomic and Ability Levels*. Berkeley, CA: Center for Study of Higher Education, University of California. (ERIC ED 002 875)

Medsker, Leland L., and Dale Tillery. 1971. *Breaking the Access Barriers: A Profile of Two-Year Colleges*. New York: McGraw-Hill.

Mehan, John. 1987. Telephone interview with the vice president for corporate relations for the U.S. Chamber of Commerce. Washington, DC.

Meisterheim, Matthew J. 1974. "A History of the Public Junior College in Illinois, 1900–1965." Ed.D., Northern Illinois University. (DAI 35/01-A, 233)

Melville, John G., and Thomas J. Chmura. 1991. "Strategic Alignment of Community Colleges and State Economic Policy." *New Directions for Community Colleges* #75. San Francisco: Jossey-Bass.

Mercer, Joyce. 1992. "States Turn to Community Colleges as Route to Bachelor's Degree as 4-Year Campuses Face Tight Budgets and Overcrowding." *Chronicle of Higher Education* 38 (May 6): 1, 28.

Merton, Robert K. 1968. *Social Theory and Social Structure*. 3d ed. New York: Free Press.

Meyer, John W., and Michael Hannan (eds.). 1979. *National Development and the Modern World System*. Chicago: University of Chicago Press.

Meyer, John W., David Tyack, Joane Nagel, and Audrey Gordon. 1979. "Public Education as Nation-Building in America." *American Journal of Sociology* 85: 591–613.

Michigan State Department of Education. 1985. *Michigan Community Colleges Fiscal Year 1983–1984 Activities Classification Structure (ACS) Databook.* Lansing: Author. (ERIC ED 254 295)

Middleton, Donald. 1980. Personal interview with the director, Student Personnel Services, John A. Logan College. Carterville, Illinois.

Miliband, Ralph. 1969. *The State in Contemporary Capitalism.* New York: Basic Books.

Miller, J. Hillis. 1937. "More State Scholarships or Junior Colleges—Which?" *School Review* 45: 331–332.

Milstein, Mike. 1973. *Educational Policymaking and the State Legislature: The New York Experience.* New York: Praeger.

Mitchell, Myrtle et al. 1986. *Change and the Future of Vocational Education.* Olympia, WA: Washington State Vocational Directors Council. (ERIC ED 268 284)

Moe, Richard. 1980. Personal interview with the assistant director for occupational education, Washington State Board for Community College Education. Olympia, Washington.

Molotch, Harvey. 1976. "The City as a Growth Machine." *American Journal of Sociology* 82: 309–332.

Monk-Turner, Elizabeth. 1983. "Sex, Educational Differentiation, and Occupational Status." *Sociological Quarterly* 24: 393–404.

———. 1990. "The Occupational Achievements of Community and Four-Year College Entrants." *American Sociological Review* 55 (October): 719–725.

Monroe, Charles R. 1972. *A Profile of the Community College.* San Francisco: Jossey-Bass.

———. 1981. Telephone interview with the president of Wilson (later Kennedy-King) College of the Chicago City Colleges. Arbata, Colorado.

Monroe, Kristen. 1984. *Presidential Popularity and the Economy.* New York: Praeger.

Monzhimer, Jim. 1980. Personal interview with the assistant to the president for vocational education, Shoreline Community College. Seattle.

Morrison, D. G., and S. V. Martorana. 1962. *State Formulas for the Support of Public Two Year Colleges.* (U.S. Office of Education Bulletin, 1962, #14). Washington, DC: Government Printing Office.

Morrison, D. G., and Clinette F. Witherspoon. 1966. *Procedures for the Establishment of Public 2-Year Colleges.* (U.S. Office of Education Bulletin, 1966, #14). Washington, DC: Government Printing Office.

Mueller, Van, and Mary McKeown (eds.). 1986. *The Fiscal, Legal, and Political Aspects of State Reform of Elementary and Secondary Education.* Cambridge, MA: Ballinger.

Mundt, John. 1973. *Long-Range Planning for Community College Education.* Tallahassee, FL: Florida State University, Department of Education.

Munro, Barbara. 1981. "Dropouts from Higher Education." *American Eductional Research Journal* 18: 133–141.

Murphy, Joseph (ed.). 1988. *The Educational Reform Movement of the 1980s.* Berkeley, CA: McCutchan.

Murphy, Raymond. 1982. "Power and Authority in the Sociology of Education." *Theory and Society* 11: 179–203.

Mussatti, James. 1986. Telephone interview with the general manager, California State Chamber of Commerce, 1939–1961. San Francisco.

Nasaw, David. 1979. *Schooled to Order.* New York: Oxford University Press.

Nespoli, Lawrence A. 1991. "Investing in Human Capital: State Strategies for Economic Development." *New Directions for Community Colleges* #75. San Francisco: Jossey-Bass.

Netsch, Dawn Clark. 1980. Personal interview with member of the Illinois Senate. Springfield.

Neumann, William, and David Riesman. 1980. "The Community College Elite." Pp. 53–71 in George Vaughan (ed.), *Questioning the Community College Role.* (New Directions in Community Colleges #32). San Francisco: Jossey-Bass.

New Mexico State Board of Educational Finance. 1980. *Factbook on New Mexico Public Two-Year Community Colleges and Vocational Schools, 1979–1980.* (ERIC ED 198 886)

New Mexico State Governor's Task Force on Higher Education Reform. 1986. *Excellence and Accountability.* Santa Fe: New Mexico Commission on Postsecondary Education. (ERIC 272 079)

New York City Board of Higher Education. 1962. *Long Range Plan for the City University of New York.* New York: Author.

New York State Department of Education. 1929. *25th Annual Report for the Year Ending July 31, 1928.* Albany: Author.

———. 1935. *Minutes of the Board of Regents for January 25, 1935.* Albany: Author.

———. 1944. *Regents Plan for Postwar Education.* Albany: Author.

———. 1947. *A Guide to the Development of Programs for the Institutes for Applied Arts and Sciences.* (Bulletin #1332). Albany: Author.

————. 1957. *Needs and Facilities in Higher Education in New York State*. Albany: Author.

————. 1964. *The Comprehensive Community College*. Albany: Author.

Nielsen, Dorothy. 1981. Personal interview with the registrar, Everett Junior College. Everett, Washington.

Nixon, Richard M. 1970. "March 19 Message to Congress on Higher Education." Pp. 37A–39A in *Congressional Quarterly Almanac, 1970*. Washington, DC: Congressional Quarterly, Inc.

Nora, Amaury, and Laura Rendon. 1990. "Determinants of Predisposition to Transfer among Community College Students: A Structural Model." *Research in Higher Education* 31 (3): 235–255.

Nordlinger, Eric. 1981. *On the Autonomy of the Democratic State*. Cambridge, MA: Harvard.

Nunley, Charlene R., and David W. Breneman. 1988. "Defining and Measuring Quality in Community College Education." Pp. 62–92 in Judith S. Eaton (ed.), *Colleges of Choice*. New York: American Council on Education and Macmillan Publishing.

O'Connor, James. 1973. *The Fiscal Crisis of the State*. New York: St. Martin's.

Odegaard, Charles. 1980. Personal interview with the president of the University of Washington, 1958–1973. Seattle.

Odum, Rannie. 1981. Personal interview with member of Board of Trustees, John A. Logan Community College. West Frankfort, Illinois.

Offe, Claus. 1984. *Contradictions of the Welfare State*. Cambridge, MA: MIT Press.

Olsen, Keith W. 1974. *The G.I. Bill, the Veterans, and the Colleges*. Lexington, KY: the University Press of Kentucky.

Orfield, Gary, et al. 1984. *The Chicago Study of Access and Choice in Higher Education*. Chicago: University of Chicago, Committee on Public Policy. (ERIC ED 248 929)

Orfield, Gary, and Faith G. Paul. 1992. *State Higher Education Systems and College Completion: Final Report to the Ford Foundation*. Chicago: University of Chicago.

Orme, Reginald. 1950. "William H. Snyder." Ph.D., University of California at Los Angeles.

Osborne, David. 1990. *Laboratories of Democracy*. Boston: Harvard Business School Press.

Page, Ray. 1981. Personal interview with the state superintendent of public instruction, 1963–1971. Springfield, Illinois.

Palmer, Jim. 1986. "Bolstering the Community College Transfer Function: An ERIC Review." *Community College Review* 14: 53–63.

———. 1990. "Is Vocationalism to Blame?" *Community, Technical, and Junior College Journal* 60 (June–July): 21–25.

Pantages, T. J., and C. F. Creedon. 1978. "Studies of College Attrition: 1950–1975." *Review of Education Research* 48: 49–101.

Parnell, Dale. 1984. *The Neglected Majority*. Washington, DC: American Association of Community and Junior Colleges.

———. 1990. "A New Economic Development Paradigm." *Community, Technical, and Junior College Journal* 60 (February March): 9.

Parsons, Talcott. 1959. "The School Class as a Social System." *Harvard Educational Review* 29: 297–318.

Pascarella, Ernest, and David W. Chapman. 1983a. "A Multi-institutional, Path Analytic Validation of Tinto's Model of College Withdrawal." *American Educational Research Journal* 20: 87–102.

———. 1983b. "Validation of a Theoretical Model of College Withdrawal." *Research in Higher Education* 19: 25–48.

Pascarella, Ernest, and Patrick T. Terenzini. 1991. *How College Affects Students*. San Francisco: Jossey-Bass.

Pedtke, Dorothy. 1979. "A History of Kaskasia College." Ph.D., Southern Illinois University. (DAI 40/08-A, 4444)

Peltzman, Sam. 1987. "Economic Conditions and Gubernatorial Elections." *American Economic Review* 77 (May): 293–297.

Pennsylvania State University. 1983. *Statement of Policies, Procedures, and Guidelines for the Commonwealth Educational System*. University Park, PA: Author.

Perfumo, Paula. 1981. "The Impact of Diverse Economic, Educational, and Political Constituencies on Vocational Education Programs in California." Ph.D., University of California at Los Angeles. (DAI 42/10-A, 4428)

Persell, Caroline Hodges. 1977. *Education and Inequality*. New York: Free Press.

Peters, Donald. 1969. "The Founding of Genesee Community College." Ph.D., State University of New York at Buffalo. (DAI 30/06-A, 2267)

Peterson, Basil. 1962. "The Vocational and Technical Education Function of California Junior Colleges." *Junior College Journal* 33 (December): 198–203.

Peterson, Paul. 1981. *City Limits*. Chicago: University of Chicago Press.

Pfeffer, Jeffrey, and Gerald R. Salancik. 1978. *The External Control of Organizations.* New York: Harper and Row.

Pincus, Fred L. 1974. "Tracking in Community Colleges." *Insurgent Sociologist* 4 (Spring): 17–35.

————. 1980. "The False Promises of Community Colleges: Class Conflict and Vocational Education." *Harvard Educational Review* 50: 332–361.

————. 1983. "Class Conflict and Community Colleges: Vocational Education during the Reagan Years." *The Review and Proceedings of the Community Colleges Humanities Association* 4: 3–18.

————. 1986. "Vocational Education: More False Promises." Pp. 41–52 in L. Steven Zwerling (ed.), *The Community College and Its Critics.* (New Directions in Community Colleges, no. 54). San Francisco: Jossey-Bass. (ERIC ED 271 169)

————. 1989. "Contradictory Effects of Customized Contract Training in Community Colleges." *Critical Sociology* 16 (Spring): 77–93.

Pincus, Fred L., and Elayne Archer. 1989. *Bridges to Opportunity? Are Community Colleges Meeting the Transfer Needs of Minority Students?* New York: College Board.

Pincus, Fred L., and Suzanne DeCamp. 1989. "Minority College Students who Transfer to Four-Year Colleges: A Study of a Matched Sample of B.A. Recipients and Non-Recipients." *Community and Junior College Quarterly of Research and Practice* 13 (3–4): 191–219.

Piven, Francis Fox, and Richard Cloward. 1977. *Poor People's Movements.* New York: Pantheon.

Polis, Henry. 1980. Personal interview with deputy director, Washington State Commission for Vocational Education. Olympia.

Polk, Barbara. 1984. *Hawaii's Community Colleges: New Directions for the 80s.* Honolulu: University of Hawaii. (ERIC ED 266 820)

Polsby, Nelson. 1981. *Community Power and Political Theory.* 2d ed. New Haven, CT: Yale University Press.

Ponitz, David. 1989. "Community Colleges Can Help American Manufacturing Be More Competitive." *Community, Technical, and Junior College Journal* 59 (February–March): 59.

Post, A. Alan. 1960. "A Review of State School Building Aid, Pay As You Go Financing, and State Support for Junior College Outlays." *California Taxpayers Association Tax Digest* 38 (March): 56, 68–70.

————. 1986. Telephone interview with the legislative analyst, California Legislature, 1949–1977. Sacramento.

Price, Hugh Douglas. 1964. "Schools, Scholarships, and Congressmen." Pp. 53–105 in *Alan Westin* (ed.), *The Centers of Power*. New York: Harcourt, Brace, and World.

Radcliffe, Charles. 1985. Telephone interview with chief minority counsel, House Education Subcommittee, 1963–1982. Annapolis, Maryland.

Ramirez, Francisco, and John Boli. 1987. "The Political Construction of Mass Schooling: European Origins and Worldwide Institutionalization." *Sociology of Education* 60: 2–18.

Reid, Alban. 1966. "A History of the California Public Junior College Movement." Ph.D., University of Southern California. (DAI 27/02-A, 375)

Rendon, Laura I. 1992. "Eyes on the Prize: Students of Color and the Bachelor's Degree." *National Center for Academic Achievement and Transfer Working Papers* 3 (2). Washington, DC: American Council on Education.

Rendon, Laura I., and Mark Thomas Taylor. 1989–1990. "Hispanic Students: Action for Access." *Community, Technical, and Junior College Journal* 60 (December–January): 18–23.

Rhine, Shirley. 1972. *Technician Education—Who Chooses It?* New York: National Industrial Conference Board.

Ricciardi, Nicholas, and John Harbeson. 1941. "Principles of the Junior College Curriculum Study." *California Journal of Secondary Education* 16.

Rice, Harold. 1981. Personal interview with member, Board of Trustees, John A. Logan Community College. DuQuoin, Illinois.

Richardson, Richard C. 1989. Personal communication. Tempe, Arizona.

Richardson, Richard C., and Louis Bender. 1987. *Fostering Minority Access and Achievement in Higher Education*. San Francisco: Jossey-Bass.

Riesman, David. 1980. *On Higher Education*. San Francisco: Jossey-Bass.

Riles, Wilson. 1986. Telephone interview with the state superintendent of public instruction, 1971–1983. Sacramento, California.

Rist, Ray. 1973. *The Urban School: A Factory for Failure*. Cambridge, MA: MIT Press.

Rockefeller, Nelson. 1961. "Annual Message to the Legislature, Jan. 7, 1961." *New York State Legislative Annual, 1961*. New York: New York State Legislative Annual, Inc.

———. 1963. "Annual Message to the Legislature, January 9, 1963." In *Public Papers of Gov. Nelson A. Rockefeller*. Albany, NY: State of New York.

———. 1966. "Speech at Broome Community College." In *Public Papers of Gov. Nelson A. Rockefeller*. Albany, NY: State of New York.

————. 1970. "Message to the Legislature on the Full Opportunity Program, March 9, 1970." *New York State Legislative Annual, 1970.* New York: New York State Legislative Annual, Inc.

Rohrbach, Pinckney. 1981. Personal Interview with member, Board of Education, Shoreline Public Schools. Seattle, Washington.

Rolph, Gov. James. 1931. "Inaugural Address." Pp. 177–190 in *California Assembly Journal,* 49th session.

Rosellini, Albert. 1961. "Message of Governor Albert D. Rosellini to the Legislature." *Washington House of Representatives Journal, 37th Legislature.* Olympia, Washington: State of Washington.

Rosenbaum, James. 1976. *Making Inequality.* New York: Wiley.

Rosenfeld, Rachel, and James Hearn. 1982. "Sex Differences in the Significance of Economic Resources for Choosing and Attending a College." Pp. 127–157 in Pamela Perun (ed.), *The Undergraduate Woman.* Lexington, MA: Lexington Books.

Ross, Hugh. 1963. "University Genesis in the Growth of Junior Colleges in California." *Higher Education Quarterly* 3: 143–152.

Rourke, Francis E. 1969. *Bureaucracy, Politics, and Public Policy.* Boston: Little, Brown.

Rubinson, Richard. 1986. "Class Formation, Politics, and Institutions: Schooling in the United States." *American Journal of Sociology* 92: 519–548.

Rubinson, Richard, and John Ralph. 1984. "Technical Change and the Expansion of Schooling in the United States, 1890–1970." *Sociology of Education* 57: 134–152.

Sabato, Larry. 1983. *Goodbye to Good Time Charlie.* 2d ed. Washington, DC: Congressional Quarterly Press.

Saling, Gerals. 1970. "Identification of Major Groups from Which Selected Washington State Legislators Obtain Advice Regarding Educational Legislation." Ed.D., Washington State University. (DAI 31/03-A, 984)

Salwak, Stanley. 1953. "Some Factors Significant in the Establishment of Public Junior Colleges in the United States (1940–1951), with Special Reference to Massachusetts." Ph.D., Pennsylvania State University.

Sandeen, Arthur, and Thomas Goodale. 1976. *The Transfer Student.* Gainesville, FL: University of Florida. (ERIC ED 154 750)

Sassoon, Anne Showstack. 1987. *Gramsci's Politics.* Rev. ed. London: Hutchinson.

Savage, Daniel. 1987. "It's Time to Stop Thwarting Students Who Try to Transfer Business Credits to Four-Year Colleges." *Chronicle of Higher Education* 33 (April 18): 56–57.

Sax, Roland. 1981. Personal interview with the editor, *Belleville News Democrat*. Belleville, Illinois.

Schmidt, William. 1988. "Community Colleges Emerge as Centers for Job Training." *New York Times* (June 20): A1, B8.

Schuilling, Walter. 1978. *From Jantzen to Jensen: San Bernardino Valley College's First Fifty Years.* San Bernardino, CA: San Bernardino Valley Community College District.

Scott, Barbara Ann. 1983. *Crisis Management in American Higher Education.* New York: Praeger.

Scott, Maurice. 1981. Personal interview with the executive director of the Illinois Taxpayers' Federation, 1955–1977. Springfield, Illinois.

Seattle Community College District. 1970. *Occupational Advisory Committees Communications Systems Handbook.* Seattle: Author.

Seattle Schools. 1964. *Application for a Community College in Seattle.* Seattle: Author.

Seidman, Earl. 1985. *In the Words of the Faculty.* San Francisco: Jossey-Bass.

Seidman, Harold. 1980. *Politics, Position, and Power.* 3d ed. New York: Oxford University Press.

Sheldon, M. Stephen. 1982. *Statewide Longitudinal Study: Report on Academic Year 1978–1981, Part 5: Final Report.* Los Angeles: Pierce College. (ERIC ED 217 917)

Simms, Charles. 1948. *The Present Legal Status of the Public Community College.* (George Peabody College for Teachers Contributions to Education #403). Nashville, TN: George Peabody College for Teachers.

Simonsen, Edward. 1950. "An Evaluation of the Laws Governing Public Junior Colleges in California." Ed.D., University of California, Berkeley.

Skocpol, Theda. 1979. *States and Social Revolutions.* New York: Cambridge University Press.

———. 1980. "Political Responses to Capitalist Crisis: Neo-Marxist Theories of the State and the Case of the New Deal." *Politics and Society* 10: 155–200.

———. 1984. "Emerging Agendas and Recurrent Strategies in Historical Sociology." Pp. 356–391 in Theda Skocpol (ed.), *Vision and Method in Historical Sociology.* New York: Cambridge University Press.

———. 1985. "Bringing the State Back In." Pp. 3–25 in Peter Evans, Dietrich Rueschemeyer, and Theda Skocpol (eds.), *Bringing the State Back In.* New York: Cambridge University Press.

Slutsky, Bette. 1978. "What Is a College For?" *New Directions for Community Colleges* 24: 9–14. San Francisco: Jossey-Bass.

Smith, Elizabeth Brient. 1991. "Responding to Industry Demands: Advanced Technology Centers." *Community, Technical, and Junior College Journal* 61 (October–November): 18–21.

Smith, Gerals. 1980. *Illinois Junior College Development: 1946–1980.* Springfield, IL: Illinois Community College Board.

———. 1981. Personal interview with the executive director of the Illinois Community College Board, 1965–1970. Springfield, Illinois.

Smolich, Robert. 1967. "An Analysis of Influences Affecting the Origin and Early Development of Three Mid-Western Public Junior Colleges—Joliet, Goshen, and Crane." Ed.D., University of Texas at Austin. (DAI 28/10-A, 3951)

Snyder, William H. 1930. "The Real Functions of the Junior College." *Junior College Journal* 1 (November): 76–78.

———. 1933. "Curriculum Development." *National Educational Association Journal* 22 (March): 87–88.

Solomon, R. Patrick. 1992. *Black Resistance in High School.* Albany: State University of New York Press.

Somers, Gerald, Laure Sharpe, and Thelma Myint. 1971. *The Effectiveness of Vocational and Technical Programs.* Madison, WI: University of Wisconsin, Center for Studies in Vocational and Technical Education. (ERIC ED 055 190)

South Carolina Commission on Higher Education. 1979. *Policies of South Carolina Senior Colleges and Universities Concerning Transfer from Two-Year Colleges.* Columbia: Author. (ERIC ED 177 994)

Spady, William. 1970. "Dropouts from Higher Education: An Interdisciplinary Review and Synthesis." *Interchange* 1: 64–85.

———. 1971. "Dropouts from Higher Education: Toward an Empirical Model." *Interchange* 2: 38–62.

Spilley, Arnold. 1986. Telephone interview with the president of the Indiana State Teachers Association, 1972–1975. Indianapolis.

Springer, Ralph. 1982. Telephone interview with the director of urban affairs, Chicago Association of Commerce and Industry, 1971–1981. Chicago.

Sproul, Robert G. 1931a. "Certain Aspects of the Junior College." *Junior College Journal* 1 (February): 274–280.

———. 1931b. "Inaugural Address." *Educational Record* 12 (April): 104–124.

———. 1958. "Many Millions More." *Educational Record* 39: 97–103.

Starr, James. 1982. Telephone interview with the president of Wenatchee Valley College, 1953–1963. Yuba, California.

State University of New York. 1950a. *Master Plan*. Albany: Author.

———. 1950b. *Second Annual Report, 1949*. Albany, NY: Author.

———. 1961. *Annual Report, 1960*. Albany: Author.

———. 1964. *Stature and Excellence, the Master Plan Revised, 1964*. Albany: Author.

———. 1968. *Creation of the Future*. Albany: Author.

———. 1969. *Report of the Chancellor for 1967–68*. Albany: Author.

———. 1976, 1989. *Application and Enrollment Patterns of Transfer Students*. Albany: Author. (ERIC ED 131880, 310702)

Stein, Robert M. 1990. "Economic Voting for Governor and U.S. Senator: The Electoral Consequences of Federalism." *Journal of Politics* 52 (February): 29–53.

Stemmer, Roland. 1981. Personal interview with vocational education instructor, Everett Junior College. Everett, Washington.

Steward, William. 1982. Telephone interview with the president of Wenatchee Valley College, 1963–1977. Wenatchee, Washington.

Stewart, Charles. 1922. "Junior Colleges as Completion Schools." Pp. 42–44 in George Zook (ed.), *National Conference on Junior Colleges, 1920, and the First Annual Meeting of the American Association of Junior Colleges, 1921*. (U.S. Office of Education Bulletin, 1922, #19). Washington, DC: Government Printing Office.

Stilley, Leslie. 1981. Personal interview with the county superintendent of schools for Marion County, Illinois 1961–1967. Marion, Illinois.

Stoddard, George. 1944a. "New York's Plan for New Institutions." *Junior College Journal* 15 (October): 60–64.

———. 1944b. *Tertiary Education*. Cambridge, MA: Harvard University Press.

Stoker, Robert. 1971. "Contra Costa Junior College District's Historical and Administrative Development." M.S. in Ed., California State University at Hayward.

Stratton, William. 1981. Personal interview with the governor of Illinois, 1953–1961. Chicago.

References 351

Sulock, Joseph. 1982. "The Demand for Community College Education." *Economics of Education Review* 2: 351–361.

Sundquist, James. 1968. *Politics and Policy.* Washington, DC: Brookings Institution.

Swain, Philip. 1982. Telephone interview with the director of educational relations, training, and manpower development, Boeing Corporation, 1971–1981. Seattle, Washington.

Szymczak, Donald R. 1977. "Origin and Development of Southeastern Illinois College, 1960–1976." Ed.D., Southern Illinois University. (DAI 38/05-A, 2604)

Tarvin, Robert. 1980. Personal interview with the president of John A. Logan Community College. Carterville, Illinois.

Terenzini, Patrick, and Ernest Pascarella. 1980. "Toward the Validation of Tinto's Model of College Student Attrition: A Review of Recent Studies." *Research in Higher Education* 12: 271–282.

Terrey, John. 1980. Personal interview with the executive director of the Washington State Board for Community College Education. Olympia.

Terry, Robert. 1981. Personal interview with the president of Seattle Central Community College, 1976–1981. Seattle, Washington.

Texas College and University System Coordinating Board. 1988. *Analysis of Student Transfer and Persistence.* Austin: Author. (ERIC ED 294 630)

Thornton, James W., Jr. 1972. *The Community-Junior College.* 3d ed. New York: Wiley.

Tilton, Theodore. 1980. Personal interview with the provost, College of DuPage. Glen Ellyn, Illinois.

Tinto, Vincent. 1974. "Public Junior Colleges and the Substitution Effect in Higher Education." Paper presented to the 1974 Annual Meeting of the American Educational Research Association. (ERIC ED 089 808)

———. 1975. "Dropout from Higher Education: A Theoretical Synthesis of Recent Research." *Review of Educational Research* 45: 89–125.

———. 1987. *Leaving College.* Chicago: University of Chicago Press.

Tomkins, Calvin. 1967. "Profiles: A Certain Attitude toward Change." *New Yorker* (November 18): 67–128.

Trent, James, and Leland L. Medsker. 1968. *Beyond High School.* San Francisco: Jossey-Bass.

Trombley, William. 1970. "Reagan Task Force to Review Plan for Education." *Los Angeles Times* (September 6): B1, 7.

Trow, Martin. 1961 [1977]. "The Second Transformation of American Secondary Education." *International Journal of Comparative Sociology* 2: 144–166. Reprinted in Jerome Karabel and A. H. Halsey (eds.), *Power and Ideology in Education.* New York: Oxford University Press.

Tufte, Edward. 1978. *Political Control of the Economy.* Princeton, NJ: Princeton University Press.

Turner, Caroline Sotelo Viernes. 1992. "It Takes Two to Transfer: Relational Networks and Educational Outcomes." *Community College Review* 19 (Spring): 27–33.

Tyack, David. 1974. *The One Best System.* Cambridge, MA: Harvard University Press.

Tyack, David, and Elizabeth Hansot. 1982. *Managers of Virtue.* New York: Basic Books.

Tyler, Henry. 1965. "Full Partners in California's Higher Education." *Junior College Journal* 35 (March): 4–7.

U.S. Advisory Council on Vocational Education. 1968. *Vocational Education: The Bridge between Man and His Work.* Washington, DC: Government Printing Office.

U.S. Bureau of the Census. 1923. *Fourteenth Census of the United States Taken in the Year 1920. Population. Volume III: Composition and Characteristics of the Population by States.* Washington, DC: Government Printing Office.

———. 1943. *Sixteenth Census of the United States: 1940. Population. Volume II: Characteristics of Population.* Washington, DC: Government Printing Office.

———. 1983. *1980 Census of Population. General Social and Economic Characteristics.* PC80-1-C. Washington, DC: Government Printing Office.

———. 1988. *School Enrollment—Social and Economic Characteristics of Students: October 1986.* (Current Population Reports, Series P-20, No. 429). Washington, DC: Government Printing Office.

———. 1993. *School Enrollment—Social and Economic Characteristics of Students: October 1991.* (Current Population Reports, Series P-20, No. 469). Washington, DC: Government Printing Office.

U.S. House of Representatives. Committee on Education and Labor. 1962. *Congressional Action for Higher Education: Report of the Advisory Group on Higher Education,* 87th Cong., 2d sess. Washington, DC: Government Printing Office.

———. 1968a. *Hearings on HR 15066, Partnership in Earning and Learning Act. 90th Congress, 2d sess.* Washington, DC: Government Printing Office.

———. 1968b. *Hearings on H.R. 16460, 90th Congress, 2d sess.* Washington, DC: Government Printing Office.

————. 1971a. *Hearings on the Higher Education Amendments of 1971.* Washington, DC: Government Printing Office.

————. 1971b. *Higher Education Act of 1971: Report to Accompany HR 7248.* (H. Rept. 92-554). Washington, DC: Government Printing Office.

U.S. National Center for Education Statistics. 1969. *Opening Fall Enrollment in Higher Education, 1968. Pt. A: Summary Data.* Washington, DC: Government Printing Office.

————. 1971. *Fall Enrollment in Higher Education, 1970: Supplementary Information. Summary Data.* Washington, DC: Government Printing Office. (HE 5.254.54052-70)

————. 1973a. *Financial Statistics of Institution of Higher Education: Current Fund Revenues and Expenditures, 1969–1970.* Washington, DC: Government Printing Office.

————. 1973b. *Associate Degrees and Other Formal Awards below the Baccalaureate, 1970–71.* Washington, DC: Government Printing Office. (ASI 1973 4604-2)

————. 1977a. *Transfer Students in Institutions of Higher Education.* Washington, DC: Government Printing Office. (ASI 1977 4586-1.19)

————. 1977b. *Withdrawal from Institutions of Higher Education.* Washington, DC: Government Printing Office. (ASI 1978 4586-1.26)

————. 1981a. *The Condition of Education.* Washington, DC: Government Printing Office. (ASI 1981 4868-4)

————. 1981b. *Associate Degrees and Other Formal Awards below the Baccalaureate, 1978–79.* Washington, DC: Government Printing Office.

————. 1982. *Fall Enrollment in Higher Education, 1980.* Washington, DC: Government Printing Office.

————. 1983a. *Postsecondary Schools with Occupational Programs, 1982.* Washington, DC: Government Printing Office. (ASI 1983 4864-3)

————. 1983b. *Expenditures for Vocational Education.* Washington, DC: Government Printing Office.

————. 1984a. *Fall Enrollment in Colleges and Universities, 1982.* Washington, DC: Government Printing Office.

————. 1984b. *Education Directory, Colleges and Universities, 1983–84.* Washington, DC: Government Printing Office.

————. 1985. *Fall Enrollment in Higher Education, 1983.* Washington, DC: Government Printing Office.

————. 1987. *Digest of Educational Statistics, 1987.* Washington, DC: Government Printing Office.

————. 1989a. *Digest of Educational Statistics, 1989.* Washington, DC: Government Printing Office.

————. 1989b. *Enrollment, Completion, Attrition, and Vocational Course Taking Patterns in Postsecondary Education: A Comparison of 1972 and 1980 High School Graduates Entering Two-Year Institutions.* Washington, DC: Author. (ASI 1989 4848-33)

————. 1990. *Patterns and Trends of Stopping Out from Postsecondary Education: 1972, 1980, 1982 High School Graduates.* Washington, DC: Government Printing Office. (ASI 1990 4842-41)

————. 1991a. *Digest of Education Statistics, 1991.* NCES 91-697. Washington, DC: Government Printing Office.

————. 1991b. *Enrollment in Higher Education, Fall 1989.* NCES 91-217. Washington, DC: Government Printing Office. (ASI 1991 4844-2; ERIC ED 334945)

————. 1992a. *Digest of Education Statistics, 1992.* Washington, DC: Government Printing Office. (ASI 1992 4824-2)

————. 1992b. *Current Fund Revenues and Expenditures of Institutions of Higher Education, Fiscal Years 1982–1990.* Washington, DC: Government Printing Office. (ASI 1992 4844-6)

U.S. Office of Education. 1901. *Report of the Commissioner of Education for the Year 1899–1900.* Washington, DC: Government Printing Office.

————. 1923. *Biennial Survey of Education, 1918–1920.* (Bulletin, 1923, #29). Washington, DC: Government Printing Office.

————. 1932. *Biennial Survey of Education, 1928–1930.* Washington, DC: Government Printing Office.

————. 1937. *Biennial Survey of Education, 1932–1934.* Washington, DC: Government Printing Office.

————. 1947. *Biennial Surveys of Education in the United States, 1938–1940, 1940–1942.* Washington, DC: Government Printing Office.

————. 1954. *Biennial Survey of Education in the United States, 1948–1950.* Washington, DC: Government Printing Office.

————. 1962. *Biennial Survey of Education in the United States, 1956–1958, chap. 4, sec. 2 (Statistics of Higher Education: Receipts, Expenditures and Property).* Washington, DC: Government Printing Office.

———. 1964a. "The Vocational Education Act of 1963." *School Life* 46 (March–April): 3–12.

———. 1964b. *Comprehensive Report on Enrollment in Higher Education, First Term 1961–1962*. (Circular #743). Washington, DC: Government Printing Office.

———. 1968. *Vocational and Technical Education: Annual Report/ Fiscal Year 1968*. Washington, DC: Government Printing Office.

U.S. Panel of Consultants on Vocational Education. 1963. *Education for a Changing World of Work*. Washington, DC: Government Printing Office.

U.S. President's Commission on Higher Education. 1947. *Higher Education for American Democracy*. 6 vols. Washington, DC: Government Printing Office.

U.S. President's Committee on Education Beyond the High School. 1957. *Second Report*. Washington, DC: Government Printing Office.

U.S. Senate, Committee on Labor and Public Welfare. Subcommittee on Education. 1965. *Hearings on the Higher Education Act of 1965 (S. 600)*. Washington, DC: Government Printing Office. (CIS (89) S1695)

University of Alaska. 1987. *Statistical Abstract, 1987*. Fairbanks: Author. (ERIC ED 292 437)

University of Connecticut. 1987. *Bulletin, 1986–87*. Storrs, CT: Author.

University of Hawaii. 1986. *Factbook, 1985. University of Hawaii Community Colleges*. Honolulu: Author. (ERIC ED 266 819)

University of Illinois. 1947. *The Role of the Public Junior Colleges in Illinois*. Urbana: University of Illinois Press.

———. 1964. *Transactions of the Board of Trustees*. Urbana: University of Illinois Press.

University of Washington. 1960. *A Statement on the Role of the University in Higher Education in Washington*. Seattle, WA: Author.

Usdan, Michael, Emanuel Hurwitz, and David Minar. 1969. *Education and State Politics*. New York: Teachers College Press.

Vahaplus, Christopher. 1982. Telephone interview with press secretary for Illinois Governor Otto Kerner, 1962–1968. Columbia, South Carolina.

Van Alstyne, Carol, Cathy Henderson, Charles Fletcher, and Yi Sien. 1973. *Comparison of the Characteristics of Transfer and Nontransfer College Students*. Washington, DC: American Council on Education. (ERIC ED 084 028)

Van Tassell, Helen. 1982. Telephone interview with the dean, Wenatchee Valley College, 1943–1954. Wenatchee, Washington.

Vaughan, James. 1971. "A Longitudinal Study of the Retention, Attrition, and Transfer of Students at the Regional Campuses of the Ohio State University." Master's thesis, Ohio State University. (Thesis MA1971V367)

Velez, William. 1985. "Finishing College: The Effects of College Type." *Sociology of Education* 58: 191–200.

Velez, William, and Rajshekhar G. Javalgi. 1987. "Two-Year College to Four-Year College: The Likelihood of Transfer." *American Journal of Education* 96 (November): 81–94.

Waddell, Geneva. 1990. "Tips for Training a World-Class Work Force." *Community, Technical, and Junior College Journal* 60 (February–March): 22–27.

Waldo, Robert. 1981. Personal interview with the vice president for governmental relations, University of Washington. Seattle.

Walker, Jack. 1969. "The Diffusion of Innovations among American States." *American Political Science Review* 63: 880–899.

Walker, James. 1982. Telephone interview with the chair of the Board of Trustees, John A. Logan Community College, 1967–1970. Herrin, Illinois.

Walmsley, Gary, and Mayer Zald. 1973. *The Political Economy of Public Organizations.* Lexington, MA: Heath.

Walters, Pamela B. 1984. "Occupational and Labor Market Effects on Secondary and Postsecondary Educational Expansion in the United States, 1922–1979." *American Sociological Review* 49 (October): 659–671.

Walton, Karen. 1984. "Transfer of Undergraduate Credit." *College and University* 58: 217–228.

Washington Educational Association. 1929. "Report of the Committee on Legislation." *Washington Education Journal* 9 (November): 86–87.

———. 1939. "School Needs in the 1939 Legislature." *Washington Education Journal* 18 (January): 91–93.

Washington State Board for Community College Education. 1968. *1968 Report to the Governor.* Olympia: Author.

———. 1969. *1969 Report to the Governor.* Olympia: Author.

———. 1970. *Washington's Open Door Colleges: Comparing the State's Community Colleges with Recommendations by the Carnegie Commission on Higher Education.* Olympia: Author.

———. 1987. *Washington Community Colleges Academic Year Report, 1985–1986.* Olympia: Author. (ERIC ED 276491)

Washington State Department of Education. 1960. *Report on Community and Junior Colleges: 1959–1960.* Olympia: Author.

———. 1961a. *Report on Community and Junior Colleges: 1960–1961.* Olympia: Author.

———. 1961b. *Report of Junior College Education to the 1961 Legislature.* Olympia: Author.

Washington State Governor's Office for Program Planning and Fiscal Management. 1976. *Alternative on the Pathway to 1985. Vol. 2: The Costs and the Hard Choices.* Olympia: Author.

Washington State Legislature. Joint Committee on Higher Education. 1971a. *An Open Door Study at Community Colleges.* Olympia: Author.

———. 1971b. *Laws of 1971.* Olympia, WA: Author.

Weber, Max. 1968. *Economy and Society.* 2 vols. Berkeley: University of California Press.

Weir, Margaret, Ann S. Orloff, and Theda Skocpol (eds.). 1988. *The Politics of Social Policy in the United States.* Princeton, NJ: Princeton University Press.

Weis, Lois. 1985. *Between Two Worlds: Black Students in an Urban Community College.* Boston: Routledge and Kegan Paul.

Wellbank, Harry. 1981. Personal interview with the director of human resources of Sears, Roebuck, and member, Education Committee, Illinois State Chamber of Commerce. Chicago.

Wellman, Fred. 1981. Telephone interview with the executive director of the Illinois Community College Board, 1970–1980. Inverness, Florida.

Wells, Herman B. 1956. "The Outlook for Higher Education." Pp. 1–9 in National Association of State Colleges and Land Grant Universities, *Proceedings.* Washington, DC: the Association.

White, Richard. 1980. Personal interview with the president of Shoreline Community College. Seattle, Washington.

Wilber, F. Parker. 1969. "Occupational Education and Administration." Pp. 18–37 in American Association of Community and Junior Colleges (ed.), *Occupational Education in the Two-Year College.* Washington, DC: American Association of Community and Junior Colleges.

Wiley, Deane. 1966. "Political Interaction of Education and the California Legislature, 1849–1963." Ph.D., Claremont Graduate Center.

Williams, Carolyn. 1989–1990. "Broadening Access for Black Students." *Community, Technical, and Junior College Journal* 60 (December–January): 14–17.

Willingham, Warren, and Nurhan Findikyan. 1969. *Patterns of Admission for Transfer Students*. New York: College Entrance Examination Board.

Willis, Paul. 1981. *Learning to Labour*. New York: Columbia University Press.

Willits, Victor W. 1968. "A Comparative Analysis of State Implementation of the Higher Education Facilities Act of 1963 with Respect to Public Community Colleges and Technical Institutes." Ph.D., University of California, Berkeley. (DAI 30/03-A, 939)

Wilms, Wellford. 1980. *Vocational Education and Social Mobility*. Los Angeles: UCLA. (ERIC ED 183 966)

Winandy, Donald, and Robert McGrath. 1970. "A Study of Admissions Policies and Practices for Transfer Students in Illinois." *College and University* 45: 186–192.

Winchell, Lillbourne A. 1933. *History of Fresno County and the San Joaquin Valley*. Fresno, CA: A. H. Cawston.

Wirt, Frederick, and Michael Kirst. 1982. *Schools in Conflict*. San Francisco: McCutchan.

Wrigley, Julia. 1982. *Class Politics and Public Schools: Chicago, 1900–1950*. New Brunswick, NJ: Rutgers University Press.

Young, Kenneth. 1985. Telephone interview with a legislative representative of the American Federation of Labor–Congress of Industrial Organizations, 1965–1977. Washington, DC.

Zeigler, L. Harmon, M. Kent Jennings, and G. Wayne Peak. 1974. *Governing American Schools*. North Scituate, MA: Duxbury Press.

Zook, George (ed.). 1922. *National Conference on Junior Colleges, 1920, and the First Annual Meeting of the American Association of Junior Colleges, 1921*. (U.S. Office of Education Bulletin, 1922, #19). Washington, DC: Government Printing Office.

Zwerdling, Daniel. 1980. *Workplace Democracy*. New York: Harper and Row.

Zwerling, L. Steven. 1976. *Second Best: The Crisis of the Junior College*. New York: McGraw-Hill.

Index

Where numerous pages are cited, the most important are highlighted in bold print.

359

26, 33–34, 124–125, **129–130, 141–142, 148, 156–160,** 184, 186; in California, 142, 156, 157, 157n12, 158n14, 160; in Illinois, 142, 156, 157–158, 159, 160n15; in Indiana, 157; in New York, 156n10, 163, 170n26; in Washington, 139, 142, 156, 157, 159, 160
role in vocationalizing community colleges: in general, 219, **222,** 225, **227–228,** 240; in California, 219, 227–228; in Illinois, 219; in New York, 225n3; in Washington, 219, 228n9
Students: characteristics of community college entrants, 3–5; percentage of community college entrants with baccalaureate aspirations, 53; role in establishing community colleges, 30–32, 34, 124–125, **129, 131–133, 147–149, 176–177,** 183–184; role in vocationalizing them, 199, 204–209, 221–222, 236, 239, 241

Taxpayer groups, role in establishing community colleges, 129
Thornton, James W., Jr., 17n1
Tinto, Vincent, 51n9, 88–89, 88n6
Transfer to four-year colleges, rates, 5–6, 57, 92; obstacles, 92–105
Trow, Martin, 23n7, 273, 274–275
Two-year university branches, 119, 266–269

U.S. Congress: role in establishing community colleges, 34, 125, **176, 179–181,** 186; role in vocationalizing them, 232–236
U.S. President: role in establishing community colleges, 34, 125, **176, 179–181,** 186; role in vocationalizing them, 232–236

Urban Community College Transfer Opportunity Program (UCC/TOP), 251, 260

Velez, William, 55
Vocationalization of community colleges: debate over, 29–35; empirical analysis, 191–242; enrollments in occupational education, 5, 191–194

Washington State, community college establishment
general features, 116, 120, 122, 145–146, 150, 155–156, 165, 188
establishment of specific colleges: Centralia, 123; Clark (Vancouver), 123; Columbia Basin (Pasco), 123; Everett, 123, 140–141; Grays Harbor (Aberdeen), 123; Lower Columbia (Longview), 123; Mount Vernon (see Skagit Valley); Olympic (Bremerton), 123; Seattle, 123, 131; Shoreline (Seattle), 123, **137–139,** 140; Skagit Valley (Mt. Vernon), 123, 139, 140; Wenatchee, 123, 131; Yakima, 123
Washington State, vocationalization of community colleges
general features, 194, 204–205
vocationalization of specific colleges: Edmonds, 200; Everett, 196, 199, 209–210; Seattle, 196, 206, 216; Shoreline (Seattle), 196, 207, 210–211, 220; Wenatchee, 192, 196, 205, 207, 213
Washington State interest groups, state university, state agencies, and state officials. *See* Washington State subentry under appropriate categories

Weberian theory, assessment of views on dynamics of educational change, 279–280

Willis, Paul, 89n9

Wirt, Frederick, and Michael Kirst, 136n11, 282, 284n6

World systems or institutional theory, assessment of views on dynam-ics of educational change, 278–279

Zeigler, L. Harmon, M. Kent Jennings, and G. Wayne Peak, 136n11

Zwerling, L. Steven, 18n4, 19, 20n5, 263, 265n7t